Leopoldville:

A Tragedy Too Long Secret

Leopoldville:

A Tragedy Too Long Secret

ALLAN ANDRADE

Library of Congress Control Number: 2008908680
ISBN: Hardcover   978-1-4363-7320-3
                Softcover   978-1-4363-7319-7

Andrade, Allan, 1937-
Leopoldville: A Tragedy Too Long Secret

Includes bibliographical references and index.
ISBN

1. Leopoldville (Ship)
2. World War, 1939-1945—Naval operations, America.
3. World War, 1939-1945—Naval operations, German.
4. World War, 1939-1945—Naval operations—Submarine.
5. World War,1939-1945—Personal narratives, American.
6. Survival after airplane accidents, shipwrecks, etc.
7. Shipwrecks—English Channel. I. Title.

Cover illustration by Richard Rockwell

This book was printed in the United States of America.

To order additional copies of this book, contact:
Xlibris Corporation
1-888-795-4274
www.Xlibris.com
Orders@Xlibris.com
50401

CONTENTS

In memory of

Staff Sergeant Benjamin Joseph Blaskowski

In January 1993, I decided to write a book concerning the contribution that advertisements in periodicals such as *Life* and the *Saturday Evening Post* made toward the home-front morale and the victory effort of World War II. While conducting the necessary research I learned of the unique ad campaign, "Back Home For Keeps" Community Silverplate Oneida Ltd., New York, from a small article that appeared in the May 14, 1945, issue of Life magazine. As a result I focused all of my efforts on Oneida Ltd.

From the beginning I received tremendous cooperation from the management at Oneida Ltd., which made available thirty-two issues of *The Community Commando,* the firm's World War II employee newspaper. Reviewing these papers I learned that more than 700 former Oneida Ltd. employees served in the various branches of the Armed Forces and, tragically, 32 of them were killed. I decided to investigate the circumstances of the deaths of those 32 former employees as a special tribute to their memory and sacrifice.

One of those former Oneida Ltd. employees was an orphan who celebrated his twentieth birthday on December 1, 1944. He was reported killed on December 25, 1944, in a troopship sinking somewhere in European waters. It was this orphan, a former Onieda Ltd. maintainance department worker, who eventually led me to the Leopoldville disaster, and it is to him that I dedicate this book.

Acknowledgments

A special thanks to artist Richard Rockwell, nephew of America's beloved illustrator, Norman Rockwell for his drawings depicting the Leopoldville disaster. They were contributed by Richard Rockwell in memory of his best friend and college roommate, Wilbur Sloan, of New Castle, Pennsylvania, who died in the S.S. Leopoldville disaster.

I am especially indebted to New York City Congressman Gary L. Ackerman for his assistance in obtaining the many Leopoldville documents from the National Archives, College Park, Maryland. Thanks to U.S. Senator Bob Dole, New York City Councilman Andrew S. Eristoff, New York City Mayor Rudolph Giuliani, Waterbury, Connecticut, Mayor Philip A. Giordano, Brooklyn Borough President Howard Golden, New York State Senator Serphin Maltese, Manhattan Borough President Ruth Messinger, Staten Island Borough President Guy V. Molinari, New York State Governor George Pataki, Queens Borough President Claire Shulman, and New York City Council Speaker Peter Vallone, who were among the first politicians to respond to my appeal to remember and honor the young men lost in the S.S. Leopoldville disaster.

This book could never have been written without the assistance of the more than 100 individuals from over thirty states with direct connections to the S.S. Leopoldville disaster. It is the voices of the young soldiers killed, preserved through their letters home and on 78-rpm. Your Man in the Service. Pepsi Cola courtesy records, the accounts of the survivors, and the cherished memories of the Leopoldville widows and sons and daughters, whom fate decreed would never know their fathers, that is the foundation and strength of this history of the disaster. It is their words, not mine, that will endure as a permanent chronicle of this horrific catastrophe. Therefore, this book is truly their story and not mine.

My gratitude to those Leopoldville survivors who made contributions to this narrative knows no bounds. It was Donna Hesse, widow of survivor Robert Hesse, the guiding light in the forming of the Panther Veterans Organization (PVO), who first helped me get started with my research into the tragedy. I am especially grateful for the friendship of Vincent Codianni and his wife Rosalia and to Jack C. Randles, who invited me to be the guest speaker at the Company I, 262nd Infantry, 66th Division reunion dinner held in Baltimore, Maryland in 1996. I will also always treasure the 1996 Memorial Day weekend spent in New York City and Waterbury, Connecticut, with California Leopoldville survivor George Chun Fat and his nephew, Michael.

The many other Leopoldville survivors who made contributions to my research and this work are listed in alphabetical order: Raymond J. Avery, Robert K. Banks, George Bigelow, Walter Beran, Walter Blunt, William E. Boggs, Fred R. Brent, Walter T. Brown, Irwin Buckner, Norman Bullett, Bill Cline, Alfred Corti, Gerald Crean, Arnold Dahlke, Karen Dermody (daughter of Joe Cycon), E.P. Bill Everhard, Gus Ferrare, Ira Frye, Donald E. Gengler, Bernard Groont, Nancy Gunn (daughter of Joe Cycon), Frank C. Haugh, Corlis L. Holt, Hank Koetje, Jack B. Landovitz, Vernon Lindahl, Gen. Donald G. MacWilliams, Ret., Vincent Matrese, Joseph Matusiak, George E. Miller, Romeo Mitri, Rev. Arnold Olson, Frederick J. Perkins, Guy Petty, Virginia Pisano (widow of Fred Pisano), Paul A. Plotkin, Jerry Pospisil, George Stanley Rehder, Frank A. Sample, Clark Guy Sawyer, Keith Simons, David Troyka, Albert Via, Sterling Viets, George Watson, Melvin F. Whaley, Morton Pete Wood, Robert M. Wurdeman, and Alex Yarmosh. I thank them all. Special thanks to Irwin Uran for his longstanding support in my efforts to promote public awareness of the catastrophe.

I am also indebted to the following members of the 66th Division for their various contributions: Joseph F. Anzenberger, Sr., Jack Chvat, William B. Clements, Edward Haas, Joseph Jordon, Donald H. Rivkin, Ray Roberts, James Simmons, Tom Tumbarello, and Miguel Velez.

It is the intimate cherished memories shared with me by the Leopoldville widows, brothers, sisters, and other family members and friends who lost their loved ones that constitute the heart of this book and all of their names are gratefully acknowledged: Charles Anderson, Danielle Appleby, Helen Appleby, Preston Appleby,

Roger Baker, James Blazek, Pete Borovich, Don Brisbin, Dr. Loretta Graves Brown, JoAnn Browning, Sam Busic, Anthony Cacace, Sandra J. Cardens, Jerry Catalano, Gene Christensen, Virginia Claybrook, Celine Cobb, Kenneth R. Cobb, Richard O. Cobb, Tom Cordle, Mable Cross, Marie DiGiambattista, Donna DiMaio, Velma Acri DiMartile, Frank DiMola, William Lee Frost, Dan Hathaway, Margaret Loftis Gallman, Bertha Grogan, Evelyn C. Harzinski, Vicki Hines, Eleanor Hixenbaugh, Alison Hoffman, Louise Babb Horn, Sherry Jones, Joseph elly, Grace Kiskodden, Louise Knight, Kathy Kurhanewicz, Joseph Loiacano, Gertrude Leck, Bill and Carol Lorenzo, Melissa Miller, Mary Morris, Mary Mueller, Sharon J. Mulvaney, Nancy T. Nash, Frances M. O'Neil, George M. Paden, Tobias Polgreen, Joseph T. Reichert, Susan Scharneck, Barbara Shaw, James Sgroi, Fran Shields, Debra Budge Smith, Mary Steranko, Percy Tripp, Bonnie Truelock Taylor, Geneva Thompson, Euleta Turner, Charles Vogel, Pete Walz, Arthur Weaver, Dan Wellen, Margaret Wellen, Michael Wilson, and Helen Zundel.

Those who participated in the Leopoldville rescue effort or had some direct connection to the catastrophe and made contributions to my research are James Ash, Robert Blank, Debbie Brogdon, P.J. Casadonte, Judge John V. Corrigan, Ret., Kathryn Dallas, Nancy T. Evans, Richard Freeburg, Sally Garner, Mary Gwen (Washburn) Heflin, Wes Johnson, Will D. Keister, Robert Langavin, Betty Letts, Helen M. Livesey, Wesley J. McEntarfer, Dominick Scala, William T. Stauffer, John Tellers, Don and Marilyn Williams, and Richard A. Young.

I received invaluable assistance in my research and in promoting public awareness of the catastrophe from the following American Legion leaders: Reggie Allen, Al Carpenter, Frank L. Giordano, Bill McClintock, Vito H. Meliti, Boyd Nelson, and Terry Nolan. Other veteran group leaders who helped were Robert Allyn, Tri-County Council Vietnam War Era Veterans; John Behan, Director, New York State Division of Veterans Affairs; John P. Fievet, Rohna Survivors Memorial Association; Vincent McGowan, President, United War Veterans Council of New York County; Col. John G. Chiarella, Sr. Ret., Veterans Memorial Commmittee of Waterbury, Connecticut; Joanne Danna, President, Gold Star Wives of America, Inc.; Michael Handy, New York City Mayors Veterans Affairs Officer; Frank Hanner, Director, National Infantry Museum, Fort Benning, Georgia; and Jo Pace and Don Sacco, Veterans Memorial Committee of Waterbury, Connecticut.

Others who assisted in my research are also gratefully acknowledged: Lawrence Bond, Reuters News Agency; Norman Brouwer, South Street Seaport Museum, New York City; Fran Feher, Guidance Department, Belle Vernon Area High School; Dr. Steve Grove, historian, United States Army Military Academy; David Gymburch, Public Relations, Oneida Ltd.; Father William Karg, St. Joseph R.C. Church, Sharon, Pennsylvania; Rolland E. Kidder, researcher/author; Mason Logie, diver/researcher; William D. Matthews, president/chairman, Oneida Ltd.; Willie E. Moore, Jr., Recreation Supervisor, County of Union New Jersey Department of Parks and Recreation; Elizabeth Safly, Truman Library, Independence, Missouri; Harris Sarney, principal, Bayside High School, Queens, New York; Bertrand Sciboz, French research/diver, Karen B. Sinniger, diver/researcher; Frank Skala, Bayside High School Alumni Association historian; John Tellers, brother of Father Tellers; Lucia Teresi, reference librarian, James Prendergast Library Association, Jamestown, New York; and Gayle Grunwald and Dietrich Werner, Century House Historical Society, Rosendale, New York.

Special thanks to Wayne Abbott, Producer/Director, Northern Sky Entertainment, Ltd. Toronto, Canada for making it possible for me to retrace the steps of the 66th Division from England to France and for permission to use a few of his photographs from that trip.

The following leaders of the Grand Lodge Masonic Fraternity, State of New York, have consistently supported my efforts to promote public awareness of the tragedy: Richard W. Bateman, assistant grand secretary; Dick Fletcher, director, Masonic Service Association of the United States (MSA); Stewart C. McCloud, deputy grand master; Al McConnach, Brooklyn District deputy; and Elizabeth L. Pounder, grand secretary, Fraternal Order of the Eastern Star, State of New York (OES).

Various members of the news media greatly helped in establishing my credibility by publishling articles using my research materials in their newspapers: Wayne M. Berry, *Poughkeepsie Journal,* Poughkeepsie, New York; Chris Buckley, *The Valley Independent,* Monessen, Pennsylvania, William Gordon, *Newark Star-Ledger,* Newark, New Jersey; Phyllis Harris, *The Oneida Daily Dispatch,* Oneida, New York; Cristie Herbst, *The Post-Journal,* Jamestown, New York; Dennis Hevesi, *The New York Times,* New York City, New York; Mike Hurewitz, *Times-Union,* Albany, New York; Paul Kirby, *Daily Freeman,* Kingston,

New York; Bob Moore, *El Paso Times*, El Paso, Texas; Joe Napsha, *Greensburg Tribune Review*, Greensburg, Pennsylvania; Mark Peterson, *Stars & Stripes*, Washington, D.C.; Katie Racette, *Observer*, Rio Rancho, New Mexico; Jeff Salyers, *Sullivan Daily Times*, Sullivan, Indiana; Dave Tobin, *Post-Standard*, Syracuse, New York; Jason Togyer, *Washington Observer Reporter*, Washington, Pennsylvania; and Sara Tykol, *The Gazette*, Croton-On-The-Hudson, New York.

A simple thank you to my wife Barbara seems totally inadequate. There should be some special medal that could be awarded to her for tolerating this seemingly never-ending research and the costs associated with postage, long distance telephone calls, and travel. This book is as much hers as it is mine since without her patience, encouragement, and support, the project would not have come to fruition. There is no question that whatever good I have accomplished in our thirty-nine years of marriage is due to the simple fact that Barbara has always been there for me. Thank you, sweetheart!

Allan Andrade

Frank S. Vogel—Class of 1944

Foreword

On December 7, 1941, the fire storm of World War II that the United States had evaded for 2 years fell from the skies over Pearl Harbor, and the youth of America lost their innocence. Three years had passed since that terrible day, and most seniors of Bayside High School, located in the New York City borough of Queens, no doubt had read in their Triangle Yearbook the following poem, written by senior classmate Joan Gordon Bair.

Class of January 1944

Our hearts are filled with pride; our heads held high.
    We've striven long and hard to reach this goal.
Against the background of a war-torn sky,
    We forge ahead to our appointed role.
Amidst the smoke of cannon, now unfolds
    The path we take. Our faith burns brightly still;
Although we know not what the future holds,
    The world is ours, to do with what we will!

On January 27, 1944, the Principal of Bayside High School, Dr. George J. Crane, stepped up to the podium, cleared his throat, and began his address to the January graduating class.

"Fully aware of the obstacles in the attainment of a diploma under present circumstances, I congratulate you and your parents today in the realization of your ambition.

Notwithstanding the siren call of the world enticing you from your studies to the temporary, inflation-blown clink of war-won dollars, never for one moment have you allowed your vision to be blurred or to be diverted from its original objective – the satisfaction of graduation from the Bayside High School.

It has been said that the future belongs to those who prepare for it–not to those who merely intend to prepare for it. Surely this future belongs to you, for each day of your 4-year stay here you have actually been preparing for it by hard work and constancy of purpose.

That this future may hold for you everything that you most desire and cherish is my sincere wish."

Frank S. Vogel, a graduating senior from Whitestone, Queens, listened intently to Principal Crane's address and, at the conclusion, rose from his seat with his classmates. The auditorium resounded with the applause of young men facing the prospect of going off to war and of the young girls who those boys would soon leave behind. An outstanding athlete who had been a member of both the school basketball and swim teams, Frank S. Vogel, known as Stretch to his friends, was aware that he "knew not what the future held". He certainly had no idea however, that his path would lead him to Company F, 262nd Regiment, of the ill-fated 66th Division.

Frank Vogel, who turned 19 on November 12, 1944, Oneida, New York, youth Benjamin Joseph Blaskowski, who turned 20 on December 1, 1944, and Brooklyn youth Angelo Catalano, who turned 21 on December 24, 1944, along with more than 2,000 American boys from all across America "forged ahead to their appointed role" aboard the Belgian troopship *Leopoldville* in the English Channel on Christmas Eve 1944.

On that eve of December 24, 29-year-old Lieutenant Gerhard Meyer, Commander of the German U-boat 486, waited off the coast of Cherbourg, France, for the arrival of the *Leopoldville* to fulfill his destiny in what would become the worst disaster to ever befall an American Infantry Division as the result of an enemy submarine attack.

Imagine, if you can, the screams of hundreds of American boys crying out to God and their mothers before they succumbed to the frigid 48-degree waters of the English Channel! By Christmas morning, 1944, nearly 800 American boys aboard the *Leopoldville* had died, 493 bodies of the recently graduated high school youths from across the nation were never recovered, and 650 of the survivors were injured. The death toll from New York State alone was 80, including 39 from New York City. So traumatic were the events of that Christmas Eve that the lives of those who lost their loved ones, those who survived the ordeal, and those who participated in the rescue were never to be the same.

The S.S. *Leopoldville* disaster was a true national calamity. There were boys killed from forty-six of the then forty-eight states in the Union. Only the states of Delaware and Wyoming were not represented in the roll call of death. This book details the most cherished memories of *Leopoldville* survivors, participants in the rescue effort, and the widows, brothers, sisters, and other relatives and friends of the young men killed in the tragedy. I could not have written this book without the generous cooperation and support received from the more than one hundred people from nearly forty states with direct connections to the catastrophe who freely shared those recollections with me. At the end of this volume is a list of the more than 1,400 who survived and an In Memoriam list of those killed; such is the magnitude of this disaster.

On December 17, 1996, Queens Borough President Claire Shulman issued a Commemoration in honor and memory of the six youths from the Borough of Queens, New York, who were killed in the S.S. *Leopoldville* disaster. Unable to attend the ceremony, William Lee Frost, a former classmate of Frank S. Vogel, sent the following eulogy. It was my honor to read his tribute in accepting the framed Commemoration on behalf of the Leopoldville Memorial Association.

Frank S. Vogel was a cherished member of the winter 1944 graduating class of Bayside High School. Looking at his youthful, smiling, confident photo in our yearbook, we recall our happy days in Queens before his untimely death in defense of our country. May his memory be blessed!

Frank Vogel symbolizes the hundreds of young men fresh out of high school from across the country who died aboard the S.S. Leopoldville. May all their memories be blessed.

Jack or Glenn Lowry (one of the identical twins). Many of the young soldiers of the 66th division who were originally selected for the Army Air Corps Cadet and the Army Specialized Training Program (ASTP). They were the brightest youths with the highest moral character that America had to offer at that time. As the war progressed the Army needed more infantrymen than pilots or specialists, so both of these programs were disbanded. As a result, many of these men were transferred to the 66th Division.

Introduction

It is, of course, impossible to recount all of the several thousand stories of the *Leopoldville* survivors—those who died, those who mourned the loss of their loved ones, and those who participated in the rescue effort. The alphabetized list of brief biographies of individuals my research uncovered exemplifies the stories of all who were touched by the catastrophe. My selection was dictated by researching old newspaper and magazine articles and developing leads that brought me to people who had direct connections to the calamity. I am especially indebted to the many individual members of the Panther Veterans Organization (PVO), who shared their personal stories with me. They, in turn, referred me to still others affected by the tragedy. Well over 200 letters were written to people all over the country, and my choice of characters depended on those who responded to my request for information. A network of "contact people" slowly began to grow during 1994 and continues to grow even as this book is published. I wish to thank everyone who contributed to this work, and their names can be found in the Acknowledgments. In the course of the narrative, other characters will appear without introduction.

At the time of the S.S. *Leopoldville* disaster, American religious life was dominated by the Christian and Jewish faiths. In their narratives, several individuals movingly express how their faith sustained them in that hour of crisis and remained a source of strength for the rest of their lives.

Peter L. Acri

Peter L. Acri was born on October 6, 1923, in Harrisburg, Pennsylvania. He was very active in the Boy Scouts and became an Assistant Scoutmaster. In the eight grade of junior high school, Pete met Velma and it was love at first sight. At William Penn High School in Harrisburg, he played alto saxophone in the school band and orchestra. After graduating high school in 1941, Pete went to work as an electrician for the H.P. Foley Company.

Once the United States entered the war, however, Pete and a couple of his closest friends decided to enlist in the Army. Although his friends were accepted, Pete faced disappointment when he was rejected because of a temporary medical condition; an examination had detected albumin in his urine.

Undaunted, Pete returned to his local induction center every day for a week determined to enlist along with his buddies. He so impressed the presiding officials that special papers were drawn up enabling him to be inducted and called to active duty. On that winter's day of February 15, 1943, Peter L. Acri reported to the New Cumberland, Pennsylvania, Reception Center. He completed basic training at the Army Air Force 713 Training Group in Atlantic City, New Jersey, and then proceeded to Camp Crowder, Missouri, as a member of a Signal Corps unit.

Many months passed and Pete's Army training kept him and Velma apart, but the long separation only intensified their longing for each other. The young lovers decided to marry. Velma had never traveled anywhere by herself, but she now found the courage to make the long trip to Neosho, Missouri, where she and Pete were married on August 21, 1943. Looking back, Velma later wrote, "I only had a week off work, and it was quite difficult leaving him after being together such a short time." Velma continued, "In October I learned that we were going to have a little one, and we were so happy! In the meantime Pete was accepted in the Army Specialized Training Program (ASTP) at the University of Missouri. He believed that furthering his education would be a good advantage for the future. However, the war in Europe was intensifying, and he, along with many others, was put into the infantry and sent to Camp Rucker, Alabama, where he trained for combat."

Peter L. Acri became a member of the 66th Panther Infantry Division. Velma gave birth to an 8-pound baby boy, James Douglas Peter Acri, in May 1944. Pete was extremely proud to have a son. In his many letters to Velma, Pete expressed his hope for their future, after he was discharged from the Army. Recalling those days, Velma wrote, "He expressed hope to purchase a small home, and he discussed the type and color decor I would like." August 1944 was a happy time for the Acri family. Pete was home on leave and the couple was able to spend their first wedding anniversary together. James Douglas was 3 months old. The day that Pete had to leave came all too quickly. Pete's older brother Bob, his wife (who was Velma's sister), his mother, and, of course, Velma, and the baby all went to see him off at the train station.

Pete kissed everyone goodbye, then turned to his brother and asked him to take care of his son. "Don't let him be a sissy," said Pete, and he walked away and never looked back.

Peter Acri and his comrades spent October at Camp Shanks, New York. Equipment was checked, and the men were given physical examinations and shots as final preparations for going overseas were completed. The men received passes, and there was time to visit New York City. Some fondly remembered seeing Army defeat Navy in a football game at Yankee stadium while others tasted the culinary delights offered at the city's various restaurants. Many took in the nightclub acts of such entertainers as Ella Fitzgerald.

Preston B. Appleby

Helen Appleby, the sister-in-law of Preston Appleby, wrote, "In 1943 and 1944 our country was at war and resembled a huge anthill, alive night and day with military preparations."

At that time her husband Walter was a chemical engineer for Shell Oil Company. He was exempt from the Army because he was doing research on jet fuel for planes. Preston and Helen's brother, however, were both serving in the armed forces. Helen first met Preston at Rice University in Houston, Texas. Along with other friends, Helen and Walter often joined Preston for Saturday night dances at the University. Preston was an attractive young man with a slender athletic build. He had blond hair, blue eyes, and a winning smile. They enjoyed many good times together and frequently dined at Mexican restaurants after the dances.

Preston was an accomplished golfer, who learned the game as a caddie. Many famous golfers traveled to Houston for various competitions and as Preston's game improved, he had the opportunity to play with them. But the war interrupted private pleasures and pursuits, and Preston was soon inducted in the Army. During his training he was stationed at El Paso, Texas, where he met and fell in love with Margie Cass. After training at Camp Rucker,

Alabama, he became yet another member of the 66th Panther Infantry Division.

In 1944, Preston received his orders for overseas duty. Helen remembered the day when Preston came to her apartment, dressed in full uniform, to say goodbye. Autumn leaves were falling, and the war was raging in Europe. Preston arrived about mid-morning and Helen had just put her baby in his crib for a nap. Helen later wrote of their parting, "Preston was trying to keep a 'stiff upper lip,' and made jokes as he bade us farewell." Suddenly Preston turned to her and asked if he could see "baby David" before he left. Helen did not want to wake the sleeping infant but felt that Preston's wish was too important to refuse. Preston smiled as he looked down at the sleeping child in the crib. He took Davy in his arms, cuddling and talking to him. When he saw that Davy was in a playful mood, Preston swung him up to the ceiling, catching him on the way down. "Then" reminisced Helen, "he patted the baby gently, tucked him back in the crib, and left hurriedly, waving from the front sidewalk."

Elmer August Baker

Another ASTP member, Sergeant Elmer August Baker, attended the University of Nebraska in Lincoln. The eldest of six children, he was born on November 12, 1922, in Cedar City, Missouri, a tiny town across the Missouri River, just north of Jefferson City. His birth was premature and since in those days there were no neonatal units, Elmer was kept in a shoebox near the woodstove to keep him warm. He remained small in stature for some time, which delayed his entering school. Most of Elmer's boyhood years were spent on a small farm near New Bloomfield, Missouri, and according to family lore, he was a competent swimmer, diver, and an avid hunter—a crack shot with a rifle. Finally, attaining a height of almost 6 feet as a high school athlete, the lanky youth lettered in both basketball and track. Elmer graduated from New Bloomfield High School in 1942 as the class valedictorian.

After graduation, he married his high school sweetheart, Geneva Parris. The newlyweds moved onto a small farm and worked the land. The Missouri River flooded regularly, and Elmer's daughter, Sandra Joyce, was born on June 28, 1942, during a flood that covered the area. It was necessary for Elmer's mother-in-law to cross the swollen river in a rowboat to see her newborn granddaughter.

Elmer was inducted into the service on January 25, 1943. After basic training at Fort Leonard Wood, Missouri, he was sent to Fort Crook, Nebraska, to the Ordnance Motor Transport School. During his stay at Fort Crook, Elmer was chosen to enter the ASTP program at the University of Nebraska. When the program was disbanded, he was sent to Camp Robertson, Arkansas, for reassignment. On April 10, 1944, Elmer Baker joined Company K of the 262nd Regiment at Camp Rucker, Alabama.

Walter F. Beran

Like Peter Acri and Elmer Baker, Walter F. Beran came from the disbanded ASTP program. He grew up in The Grove, a close knit farming community in Central Texas. As a boy, Walter performed various chores at the general store and soon discovered he preferred business over picking cotton. At the time, cotton-pickers were paid 25 cents per 100 pounds.

After high school, Walter attended Temple Junior College, in Temple, Texas. One day, to avoid a Spanish exam, Walter took an entry test to get into the Army ASTP program. The next thing he knew, he was in the Army Reserve at Baylor University in Waco, Texas. But, after only 3 months the program was disbanded and Beran found himself in the Infantry.

Robert Blank

Robert Blank graduated from the Army Transportation Corps Officer Candidate School (OCS) as a second lieutenant in late November 1944. After a short leave to Prairie du Chien, Wisconsin, to visit his wife and infant daughter, who was born on November 9, 1944, he reported to the New York port of embarkation and was assigned to the liberty ship *Jonas Lie* as a cargo security officer. The ship was named for an artist of some repute.

Blank's assignment was to convey the manifest of the ship's cargo, as well as other classified papers and material, to the Army Port Commander at their destination, which was unknown at the time of their departure. Another function that Blank performed was to secure the deck cargo, which on this voyage were Sherman tanks.

The ship's Army personnel soon laughed him out of that exercise. They would not have thought it so funny, if they knew as the Navy personnel did, that tanks had to be secured and checked more carefully than other cargo.

Berthed at Staten Island, on December 9, 1944, the Jonas Lie sailed out of New York Harbor and joined a very large convoy that was escorted by destroyers and frigates. By that point in the war, the U-boat threat was believed to be over. It was, therefore, a light-hearted Merchant and Navy gun crew that crossed the Atlantic. The convoy moved very slowly because it had to accommodate the capacity of the slowest vessels, which could only average 8 knots. As a result, the convoy was only about halfway across the Atlantic when the Battle of the Bulge erupted.

Benjamin Joseph Blaskowski

Staff Sergeant Benjamin Joseph Blaskowski, of the 66th Panther Infantry Division was born on December 1, 1924. Benjamin's parents died when he was a small boy, and he was raised by his aunt, Mrs. Catherine Witusik, who lived in Oneida. His brother Sylvester served in the U.S. Coast Guard; he survived the war but passed away in 1993. Benjamin was formerly employed in Oneida Ltd.'s Maintenance Department before he entered the Army in April 1943. A member of Company L., 262nd Regiment, he trained at Camp Blanding, Florida, from April to July of 1943.

On April 15, 1943, at Camp Blanding, the brown-haired, blue-eyed, Blaskowski, along with 15,000 other recruits, stood at rigid attention on the drill field in front of Major General H. F. Kramer. There, along the shores of Lake Kingsley, they witnessed the Activation Ceremony of the 66th Division.

Walter Blunt

Raised on his parents' farm in western Illinois, Walter attended a one-room rural school that taught grades 1 through 8. In high school, the 6-foot-tall youth succeeded in making the basketball team. He continued his education at Western Illinois Teachers College located in Macomb. At about that time he started dating a high school girl, who would later become his wife.

Blunt was inducted in June 1943 at Camp Grant, Illinois. After basic training at Camp Hood near Waco, Texas, he was one of those selected for Special Engineer training at Aberdeen, South Dakota, as part of the ASTP program. The incentive for soldiers with above average intelligence recruited by the Army to participate in the program was the promise of a free college education and a commission upon graduation. As only Privates were accepted in the program, many of the ASTP recruits, believing the Army's assurances, passed up immediate opportunities for OCS or gave up their noncommissioned ranks. But the impending invasion of Europe caused the ASTP to be disbanded in March 1944, and Walter Blunt, along with most of his classmates, was sent to Camp Robinson, Arkansas, where he joined the 66th Division.

Dan and Sam Borovich
Brothers Dan and Sam Borovich were coal miners from McDonald, Pennsylvania, when they entered the Army in April 1942. Following their basic training at Fort Riley, Kansas, they were assigned to New York as Military Police (MPs). In September of 1943, they were both discharged honorably to better serve their country working in the Montana copper mines.

The brothers soon returned to the coal mines of McDonald. Dan was employed by Pittsburgh Coal Company at the Montour no. 9 mine while Sam worked for the Utah Construction Company at Pittsburgh Coal Company's Russell Stripping Operations. But fate intervened, and in May of 1944, the brothers were inducted again and were en route to England with the 66th Division by the Fall of 1944.

Walter T. Brown
On the same day that the 66th Division was activated, Walter T. Brown, from Lynn, Massachusetts, reported for duty at Camp Devens in Massachusetts. About a week later he joined the 66thDivision at Camp Blanding. Florida. Brown was therefore one of the original men of the Division. The new rookie would later write, "I never fired a rifle before entering the service." Of his rigorous training at Camp Blanding, Brown recalled, "One day a southern Colonel told us that we were not here to die for our country. Kill the enemy and let him die for his."

Norman Bullett
Norman Bullett was born in Cicero, New York, on February 1, 1926. Having grown up in a small town, Bullet would later say, "Being

brought up in a close loving family helps you develop moral qualities that stay with you. When I was old enough, I helped take care of 600 chickens; that responsibility made me realize that I could do things on my own." Bullett attended high school in North Syracuse, where he played on the varsity basketball team. In his junior year he turned 18 and was drafted into the Army. He joined the 66th Division at Camp Rucker in September 1944. Staff Sergeant Benjamin Blaskowski was Bullett's squad leader. Bullett would write of Blaskowski, "I met some real nice non-coms, but Ben stood out by himself. He was always there when I or anyone else in the squad had a problem; that meant a great deal to us replacements."

Carl and Clarence Carlson

Carl and Clarence Carlson, from Jamestown, New York, were twins. They entered the Army on the same day, May 5, 1944, and received their basic training at Camp Blanding, Florida. Both young men were described by their mother as ". . . just ordinary boys. Some people thought that they looked alike and even confused them at times, but they weren't at all identical in their appearance or their interests."

The Carlson family lived near the Jamestown Baseball Park, and Carl who was keenly interested in sports spent his evenings rooting for his favorite local team, the Falcons. Both brothers attended Jamestown High School, and Carl majored in art, where he enjoyed design and illustration classes.

In contrast, Clarence's love was music. During his summer vacations he earned sufficient money as a newspaper carrier to purchase an accordion and pay for music lessons. Clarence became an accomplished accordion player and was in great demand to perform at Jamestown High School dances. It was his intention to continue studying music after the war. While at Jamestown High School, Clarence also studied woodshop and furniture construction, two of his favorite subjects.

The biggest venture shared by the brothers was the scheming and planning necessary to buy a car. Neither brother knew how to drive, but they decided that was unimportant; they would learn to drive after they had purchased the prized vehicle. The desire for the car never waned, but the money they earned always was spent elsewhere—new clothes, music lessons, or whatever. As members of the 66th Division, from their earliest basic training they were tagged as, "those blonde twins."

Angelo Catalano

Twenty-year-old Angelo Catalano of Brooklyn, New York, also a Sergeant in company L, knew Benjamin Blaskowski well. Angelo was one of eight children, five brothers and three sisters. During 1944, an excited Catalano arrived home on leave with his southern sweetheart Beverly Wilson, from Maryville, Tennessee.

Beverly was to live with Angelo's family until the war was over, at which time the young lovers were to be married. Angelo's 14-year-old brother Jerry thought that Beverly was the most beautiful girl he had ever seen. She was blonde and blue eyed and everyone in the family took to her immediately.

George Chun Fat

Sergeant George Chun Fat was born on January 6, 1910, in Kalapana, Puna, Hawaii, and was the fourth child of eight children. George's father was Chinese and at the tender age of 12 had been shanghaied by a Hawaiian ship crew. At that time, Chinese laborers were contracted for 3 years at $3 a month to work on Hawaiian sugar plantations.

In 1930, at the age of 20, George joined the Hawaiian National Guard. The Guard was activated by President Roosevelt in 1940. Following the bombing of Pearl Harbor, George spent the daylight hours stringing barbed wire along the beaches, and at night was on guard duty. Sergeant George Chun Fat joined Company I, 262nd Regiment, 66th Division, at Camp Blanding, Florida, in 1943.

Bill Cline

Sergeant Bill Cline, Company B, of the 263rd Regiment, would remain unknown to Sergeant Walter T. Brown until the incredible events of Christmas Eve 1944 would bind them together for the rest of their lives. Bill Cline was born in Medford-Medford Lakes, New Jersey, on April 6, 1924, to German parents. He attended Mount Holly Regional High School, where he joined the ROTC. Cline was drafted in 1943 and joined the 66th Division at Camp Blanding. His first sergeant was prejudiced toward young men who had been in the ROTC program and immediately called them together and read them the riot act. "You ROTC people can expect promotions to come—VERY DAMN SLOWLY," he bellowed.

Francis X. Coakley

Lieutenant Francis X. Coakley was born in Elizabeth, New Jersey. His school days were spent at Sacred Heart Grammar School and Battin High School. Coakley worked for a Wall Street firm, but the 1929 stock market crash convinced him that golf offered a much more secure future. Coakley learned golf as a caddy and became a teaching pro at Galloping Hill Golf Club, in Union, New Jersey. He was described as "an ebullient man, with an outgoing nature and an engaging wit, which made him a much sought after dinner speaker." A man of many talents, he also was a good baseball player and showed some prowess in the boxing ring. But it was golf at which he excelled.

In 1940 Coakley qualified for the National Open in Cleveland, Ohio, and the PGA championship in Denver, Colorado. His demeanor earned him the nickname "gentleman golfer." Coakley's golfing career, however, was interrupted by World War II. He spent a year in Special Services touring for bond sales but wanted action, so he asked to be transferred to line duty. By 1944, Coakley was a Lieutenant in Company C, 264th Regiment of the 66th Division.

Thomas A. Cobb

Ridgewood resident Thomas A. Cobb graduated from St. Luke's High School, Ho-Ho-Kus, New Jersey, in 1941. He then worked for the Wright Corporation in Paterson until he entered the Army in the ASTP at the University of Nebraska. He came to the 66th Division when the program was disbanded. From his letters home, it is clear that Cobb, like many other young men from the ASTP, was extremely unhappy to find himself in the infantry. On June 5, 1944, Cobb wrote his mother, "This company commander of ours grows worse every day. Saturday afternoon is supposed to be a 'make-up' period for important things you missed during the week. Well, all of us in the ASTP & Air Corps were made to go to work all day yesterday, even though most of us hadn't missed any necessary duties. We were the only company out there drilling. He is really hated . . . It's bad enough being in the Infantry without the officers making it worse. The first sergeant is mean too . . . The old men in the company expect to be shipped overseas next week sometime. I dream of the time I can sit at home and not worry about what's going to happen next . . . "

He wrote these words in a letter dated July 3, 1944. "Sometimes I wish I had something wrong with me so I wouldn't have to be in the Army or at least in the Infantry . . . It's good you were able to get all those cherries. I certainly would enjoy one of those nice cold cherry pies with milk. I haven't had anything like that since I was home last."

Thomas Cobb's disenchantment with the infantry was again reflected in his letter of August 7, 1944.

"Dear Mother, To show you how fast they use those Infantry replacements overseas, while I was on furlough they shipped a lieutenant from this company. Since that time he has been in action, returned to England, and is now in France again. Remember that boy I told you about, who was trying for the Coast Guard Academy. Well, he was discharged from the Army while I was on furlough. He didn't think he had a chance to get into the Coast Guard, but he must have done all right on the test. He starts school in the fall, so he'll spend a lot of time at home before he goes to New London. I wish I had tried at least. To get out of this life and go there must certainly make one feel good."

Just 4 days later, in his next letter home, Cobb would again paint a vivid description of life in the infantry.

"Now we spend most of our time in the woods. We were supposed to be outside for 3 days, but they took us in last night to clean Ordnance equipment today. It certainly was terrible out there . . . It's almost 100 degrees and very humid. The worst thing is heat rash and prickly heat, which I have. My back never did dry out all day . . . "

Another frequent subject of Thomas Cobb's letters was his dog, Tannie, a mixed breed that included English Setter. Wrote Cobb on October 4, 1944, "I hope the Little One is behaving herself and not going after too many postmen. She reminds me of Dagwood's dog [a reference to Daisy, Dagwood Bumstead's dog from the comic strip, 'Blondie'], always after the postmen."

His mother also wrote letters telling of Tannie's latest adventures. On November 21, 1944, she wrote, "You should see your Little One in her cozy little box under the sideboard. She likes it under there better than next to the stove . . . She is behaving better at night, too, if you know what I mean! Celine (Cobb's sister) scolds her for any infractions, and it seems to work. We also put her outdoors just before we turn in for the night . . . "

Cobb knew that soon his turn would come to cross the Atlantic. ". . . I don't know whether I'll be in this country or not at Christmas," he wrote in a letter of October 4, 1944.

The Cobb family lived in an old, somewhat narrow two story frame house that was taller then the other houses in the area. The dwelling quickly became known as "the lighthouse." The old house had no central heating, and warmth was provided by an old coal stove, a Dauntless, located in the home's large kitchen. It was Thomas Cobb's job to keep the coal fire burning and to remove the burned ashes. As the day for shipping out and facing the enemy in battle drew nearer, Cobb yearned for those days at the lighthouse tending to the Dauntless, and 1 month before being shipped overseas, he wrote home on October 15, 1944, "Things don't look so bright . . . we probably won't stay here much longer. When it was quite far off I didn't mind it too much but now that it is closer I'm beginning to get worried. I wish I was back in the old Lighthouse with nothing to worry about but tending to the Dauntless and taking Tannie for romps.

"I wasn't supposed to tell you about shipping and all that, but I have already and I suppose everyone else has too."

With each letter, Cobbs mood grew more melancholy.

"October 18, 1944 . . . Dear Mother, Well my days in this country are very limited indeed. They are working 24 hours a day packing. It all seems so unbelievable . . . I wouldn't mind going over so much if I wasn't in the Infantry. There are many things I feel like telling you, but I can't write them very well."

"I certainly won't spend Christmas here if I pass my birthday here. I'll try to call you up on Sunday. I get so sad and worried over here in a safe and fairly comfortable camp. I don't know what I'll do over there."

"October 27, 1944 . . . Dear Mother, Nobody seems to know when we are to leave. We are all packed. They really cart along a lot of truck. We have a box of sporting equipment for the company, as well as a box of games, bingo, checkers, chess, cribbage, etc. I don't know when we'll use them."

"November 4, 1944 . . . Dear Mother, I hope you haven't been worrying about me too much. From now on my mail will be censored.

I'm not in Camp Rucker anymore, but I'm not allowed to tell you where I am. I'm still in the U.S., though. Perhaps you can guess where from the address. I can't write much without saying anything that is not allowed."

Hal Fitzgerald Crain

West Point Graduate Captain Hal Fitzgerald Crain looked forward to his overseas duty with eager anticipation. Hal Crain was born in New York City on September 12, 1918. At the age of 7 his parents moved to Los Angeles, California, and it was there that he received his grammar and high school education. He was a good student, and history was one of his favorite subjects. Multitalented, he was a gifted illustrator and a piano player. From his study of the piano, which he began at the age of 5, he developed a love for classical music.

As a sophomore at Hollywood High School, Crain enrolled in the "Pershing Rifles," an ROTC course. He graduated in February 1936, and spent a few months on his uncle's ranch in Oregon before entering UCLA in the autumn of the same year. At UCLA, Crain distinguished himself in history subjects and was admitted to the History Club. He was one of only two underclassmen so honored. While at UCLA he became determined to enter West Point. Hal Crain received a congressional appointment, but at the last minute a complication developed. The minimum weight requirement at the Academy was 136 pounds. Although he was 6 feet tall, Crain was an angular boy, underweight all his life. Bent on meeting the weight requirement, Hal Crain stayed in bed for 3 weeks before the day of his examination, so he wouldn't lose any weight. He passed and entered the Military Academy in July 1939.

At West Point "determination" was recognized as one of the dominant traits of his character. He would never admit the possibility of defeat in anything he decided to do. He tackled every challenge with great enthusiasm. Although Crain's tall, slender physique was a disadvantage in lacrosse and soccer, his persistence and determination earned him winning numerals, monograms, and major and minor A's in the two contact sports.

Crain graduated on January 19, 1943, and was sent to the 66th Division where he was assigned as a platoon leader in a rifle company. His company commander at the time said he was a good officer with troops, was honest, and possessed good leadership qualities. As a

West Point graduate, Crain received promotions much quicker than other officers in the division. In a year, he was promoted to captain and took command of Company F, 262nd Regiment.

Hal Crain's reputation as a leader grew. He loved his work and took his responsibilities seriously. He was respected for his concern for his men, and he always did his best to ensure that they were thoroughly trained. Wrote Crain, "The outfit is really shaping up. I feel so confident of our being able to do our job. We are tops! There is none better anywhere! My officers and noncoms are the finest bunch I ever hope to have. They are superb. The Captain wants a job done, and lo, it is done to perfection."

After one regimental inspection that took place during the summer of 1944, Captain Crain wrote, "When the Colonel came, I was so proud to report, 'Sir, Captain Crain commanding Company F, 262nd Regiment reports!' The colonel was very pleased, but I was thrilled at the wonderful job that had been done by those non-coms and men. Wait till we face the enemy! Any enemy! They just won't be able to lick us."

Sergeant Walter T. Brown would say of Captain Crain, "We of Company F had a great deal of respect for this man; maybe it was because he was so militaristic and a disciplinarian and yet so fair in all his dealings with us. As far as I can remember, he never rode in the company jeep as other company commanders did when we had 25-mile hikes. He would walk with the rest of us; and the last 2 or 3 miles, we would double time past any company that was in front of us, until we arrived at our company area. However, any man that did not finish or had fallen out during the hike received no weekend pass and, quite often, was confined to his bunk for the weekend, with the Charge of Quarters checking on him by order of the Captain."

Still recalling memories of Captain Crain, Sergeant Brown concluded, "I think those three hallowed words of West Point—Duty, Honor, and Country—were engraved within him." Captain Crain himself would write home to his father, "I plan to stay in the Army; I know my stuff; I know I can take my men any place they have to be taken and bring them back. During the early morning hours, in the Forward Assembly area, I have walked alone with my thoughts, getting things straight in my mind; regardless of what happens to me, the Army comes first, along with those straightforward things called ideals."

Married less than two years, Captain Crain was the father of a baby son he had hardly seen. As the 66th Division crossed the Atlantic,

Crain eagerly awaited the troopship's arrival in the England he had previously only read about.

Jerry Crean

Jerry Crean was drafted into the Army in October 1942, but it wasn't until May of 1944 that he joined the 66th Division. Crean grew up in Butler, New Jersey, and graduated from Butler High School where he played on the basketball, baseball, and football teams. Jerry Crean excelled at football and at the tender age of 18 was probably the school's youngest football coach. During his school years, Jerry, his best buddy, and their two girlfriends made up a foursome that shared many good times together. But adulthood and the war would change things and turn their simple world upside down.

After being drafted, Jerry served as a medic in four or five different outfits. Then, as the invasion of Europe drew closer, volunteers were requested for the Infantry. They would be needed to care for the anticipated casualties in the assault. Jerry Crean volunteered and was packed off to Camp Rucker. Said Crean of his training there, "We were a well-oiled machine when we debarked."

Joe Cycon

Born to Polish immigrant parents in Buffalo, New York, on March 19, 1921, Joe Cycon was one of thirteen children. He was the youngest son and was raised primarily by his mother because his father died when he was only 5 years old. His daughter Karen wrote of her father, "To say that they were poor is an understatement. His experience was not unique at that time. He left school after completing the eighth grade."

Joe Cycon moved to the southern tier of New York State, where he joined the Civilian Conservation Corps (CCC) and worked on a reforesting project in the Margaretville area of the Catskill Mountains. The camp was located in Masonville, New York, just a few miles from the town of Sidney. He elected to remain there after leaving the CCC and worked at several jobs before obtaining employment at the Scintilla Division of Bendix Aviation, which was then and, to a certain extent, continues to be a mainstay of the community.

During his CCC days, Joe Cycon met and dated a local girl for two years before he left for the Army in April of 1943. He began to ask her to marry him almost as soon as he left. She accepted, and they were married on a furlough in August of 1943. Sergeant Joe

Cycon, Company F of the 262nd Infantry, became good friends with two other sergeants from that company, Walter T. Brown and Bill Donnelly.

Sydney E. Garner

Born in 1915, Sydney E. Garner was a native of England, but he came to the United States in 1921 and grew up in Gary, Indiana. Sydney always wanted to be a doctor and, following pre-medical school, attended Indiana University but had to drop out for financial reasons. Syd and Sally Garner were married on October 29, 1940, but after the United States entered the war, like millions of other young couples, their hopes and dreams were put on hold for the duration of the conflict.

Syd enlisted in the Navy during 1942. Their first daughter, Susan, was born in 1944. At the time, Syd was in New Orleans on maneuvers. In April, he was transferred to Miami, Florida, and Sally and the baby moved there to be with him. As with most things in military life, matters do not always work out as planned. Sally and baby Susan were reunited with Syd for only 1 week when Lieutenant Sydney Garner was shipped to an undisclosed location overseas. A very disheartened Sally Garner returned with her baby to Gary, Indiana. A participant in the S.S. *Leopoldville* disaster rescue effort, Syd Garner's path was destined to cross that of the young men of the 66th Division.

Donald Earl Gengler

Staff Sergeant Donald Earl Gengler, the youngest of four children, was born and raised in St. Louis, Missouri. He was on the basketball and baseball teams of Normandy High School and played the trombone in the school band. He graduated from high school in 1941 and continued his studies at a technical school, but Gengler's life changed drastically when his mother died in 1942 and he was drafted in February 1943.

Obstacle courses, long marches, sweltering Florida days on the firing ranges, and endless lectures on subjects varying from military law to the care of a wounded buddy on the battlefield were all a part of the tough exercises. Gengler wrote of their training at Camp Blanding, "We walked everywhere. Even if convoy trucks would come by we still walked. We got some free time but I was too tired to go to town. I would go to the PX for a beer and then back to the barracks and sleep. Once or twice my good friend Clancy Rachow, who was also from St. Louis, and I would go to Jacksonville or St. Augustine."

During July 1943, a long train trip brought the 66th Division to its next destination, Camp Robinson, Arkansas. Training at Camp Robinson became increasingly more difficult as the division was forged into a tough combat team. Maneuvers lasted two or three days, and live mortars were fired at locations in front of the men. On one of those maneuvers, a piece of shrapnel struck Donald Gengler in the face. At the group hospital he received several stitches to close the wound.

Recalling the training at Camp Robinson, Donald Gengler later wrote, "The hardest time we had was a 10-day, 50-mile maneuver to Conway, Arkansas. Simulated battles with other regiments were conducted during the maneuver. We were dirty, hot, and exhausted but becoming better trained for what was to come."

The Division was transferred to Camp Rucker, Alabama, on April 10, 1944. At Rucker, hard training continued, including house-fighting tactics, jungle combat, and assaulting fortified positions. Personal physical stamina, through strenuous calisthenics and exhausting road marches with full field packs, was also stressed. Said Staff Sergeant Gengler of those marches, "The weather was so hot that we started at midnight for the cooler temperature. As Squad Leader I felt an obligation to complete all of the 25-mile hikes. Everyone who completed the hikes was given a weekend pass. Fatigue and sore feet kept me from taking advantage of many of the passes."

Frank Haugh

Private Frank Haugh, Company D of the 264th Regiment, was without a doubt the luckiest man in his company if not the entire 66th Division. He was born and raised in Millvale, Pennsylvania, a suburb of Pittsburgh. In 1924, when he was less than 6 months old, he contracted pneumonia. The family doctor who delivered him sadly informed his parents that he probably would not survive the night. At this critical juncture in his young life, there was one slight chance he could be saved. That tiny ray of hope took the form of a new doctor in town who had recently graduated from medical school. His name was Dr. Koenig, and he agreed to come to the house to see what he could do. Dr. Koenig stayed with the baby the entire night and was as amazed as everyone else when the baby survived and later recovered from the deadly pneumonia. The grateful Haugh family was convinced that their son had been saved by a higher power beyond the skills of medical science for some future purpose, as yet unknown.

During 1940, Frank Haugh experienced yet another brush with death. Frank had just passed his driver's examination, and as his reward his father let him use the family car. With two of his best friends, he drove off, eager to enjoy his new found freedom. Around dusk that evening, he and his friends decided that Frank should push the speed of the vehicle to its limit. The road on which they intended to test the car's top speed was four lanes, with the two inside lanes used by trolley cars. The section of road where they decided to race the car consisted of an open stretch for several miles. Since there were no passenger stops, the trollies that traveled those tracks normally reached their top speed along that same stretch of road.

Haugh and his friends zipped along at between 60 and 70 mph in the opposite direction of the trolley tracks. When they neared a car in front of them, Frank elected to pass it. It had started to rain, and as Frank swung wide to pass, the car skidded on the wet tracks. Horrified, as he began to lose control of the car, all Frank Haugh could see coming straight toward him from the opposite direction was a speeding trolley!

His friend in the front passenger seat grabbed his arm in panic and it appeared that a head-on collision was a certainty. With disaster less than 100 yards away, the car veered wildly off the wet trolley tracks into the outside lane as the trolley passed safely on the right. Grateful that no car was in the outside lane, Frank Haugh finally was able to stop the automobile but not before the two front wheels bounced over a curb. The curb had stopped the car from plummeting some 20 feet onto railroad tracks below. A shaken Haugh exited the car to inspect any damage done to the vehicle, but the frightened youth's legs went outfrom under him and he collapsed on the road. Once again, the life of Frank Haugh had been spared, along with those of his friends.

By early 1943, one could no longer enlist in the army, but one could volunteer to be drafted early. Frank knew that he would have a problem passing the physical exam because he had an amblyopic astigmatism in his right eye, which meant that he had only 20/200 vision in that eye. He prepared for the eye exam by memorizing the standard eye chart used in those days. Frank passed the exam and was sworn into the Marine Corps.

When Frank arrived at Parris Island in South Carolina, he learned that another physical exam would be necessary. This time it was impossible to fake the eye exam. The doctor would push a button and immediately a new combination of five letters would appear. Frank's poor vision in his right eye was detected quickly and he failed the exam. The Corps realized his desire to serve in the Marines and offered to operate on his right eye to correct his vision. However, there was a risk that if the procedure failed, he could wind up with double vision. Frank decided that the risk was too great, and after first being threatened with a court martial for fraudulent enlistment he was eventually granted a Medical Discharge.

Back home, Frank contacted the Adjutant General of the Army, who issued a special waiver of his Medical Discharge, which permitted him to serve. However, he was excluded from overseas duty, particularly if it involved combat duty. Accepted into the Army, Haugh qualified for the ASTP. He was sent to the University of Nebraska, where he consistently ranked in the top 10% of the class. Then, as previously noted, the ASTP was shut down. Along with several hundred others from his group, Haugh ended up in the 66th Division.

Frank's first assignment was in Company A as a rifleman. Despite his eye problem, he managed to qualify with all weapons, from pistol to bazooka. His superiors recognized that he had just barely qualified on the use of weapons and transferred him to Company D, a Heavy Weapons Company. He was assigned to the second platoon, which was a machine gun platoon. General eyesight was sufficient for using the machine gun. He was also given a crack at driving a jeep, but his poor night vision thwarted such an assignment. Although Frank Haugh should have been excluded from overseas duty, the realities of war by the Fall of 1944 had superseded that provision of his armed forces commitment.

Gregory C. Jurlina

Company F, 262nd Regiment Staff Sergeant Gregory G. Jurlina was born in Yugoslavia on October 11, 1921, and came to America in July 1929. The family settled in Donora, Pennsylvania, where Greg attended Donora public schools. As a pupil in the ninth grade, he won the Legion Award for outstanding student. Greg loved working with his hands and at the age of 16 helped his father to remodel the house. He graduated from high school in 1941.

A member of the ASTP, Greg studied engineering at the Colorado School of Mines before being transferred to the 66thDivision. He always sent his mother a pillow cover from each Army camp at which he was stationed. The last pillow cover his mother received before Greg was shipped overseas was from Camp Rucker, Alabama.

General Herman Frederick Kramer

General Herman Frederick Kramer was born in Lincoln, Nebraska, on November 2, 1892. At the age of 18 he enlisted in the Nebraska National Guard. He saw service on the Mexican border in 1916 and in February 1917 entered the regular Army as a second lieutenant. Kramer's advancements continued, and during those early years he attended and graduated from the University of Nebraska.

General Kramer, a husky man with a thick neck and powerful shoulders, greeted the men and promised a stiff training program in the Infantry, ensuring that no man would be lost in combat because of poor knowledge or preparation. He believed that the Infantry, was the backbone of the Army and that this Division must destroy the enemy before any battle could be brought to a successful close.

General Kramer was well prepared to lead his men. He was one of the few American officers who attended and graduated from the German War College in Berlin, which was the equivalent of our West Point Military Academy. When the Nazi troops rolled into Poland, he had served as an American observer. He was therefore well acquainted with the "German war machine" and knew his men would be up against a formidable adversary. General Kramer commanded the 66th Infantry Division until August 8, 1945. He then went to Japan. In late 1945 and early 1946, he commanded the 97th Trident Division on the Island of Honshu. His last assignment was Commander of the 87th Division in the Philippines in late 1946 and early 1947. In 1947 he retired from the Army. Ironically, his first Division was known as the Black Panthers and his last as the Black Hawks.

Helen M. Livesey

Army nurse Helen M. Livesey of the 199th General Hospital, crossed the English Channel aboard the troopship *Leopoldville* during December 1944. One week later, it was the 66th Division's turn to board the *Leopoldville*. The trip for her was completed without incident, but because of later events, she has always felt tied to the men of the 66th Division and their fate. There were 96 women in her unit.

Helen Livesey's link to the 66th Division began on Halloween night of 1944 when she sailed for England aboard the troopship *West Point*. Helen Livesey remembers that departure well. "There was a full moon over the harbor. All of us, both men and women, stood at the back of the ship and watched Boston recede into the horizon, and everyone sang 'God Bless America.' Till the day I die I will never forget that night."

Helen Livesey has written of her World War II service, "We were all people of the Depression; most were trained in hospital programs that were cheap or free, but included much hard work and rigid discipline . . . All of the programs had strict curfews, so there was not much social life, even though most of us were young. You can imagine the contrast—travel, higher pay, easier work, and the officer's commission, of course. So despite the hardships, this was a broadening experience that we would not have had otherwise . . . We had a lot of freedom; off hand I can think of eight or nine nurses, including myself, who became engaged to or married one of the young enlisted men in the detachment or to patients."

Glenn and Jack Lowry

The Lowry twins, Glenn Elvin and Jack Nevin, were born on April 15, 1924, in Belle Vernon, Pennsylvania. After graduating from Rostravette High School on May 29, 1942, the boys both worked as loaders in the Automatic Finishing Department at the Allenport Works of the Pittsburgh Steel Company. Jack Lowry, who was mechanically inclined, along with his brother Glenn, joined the Army Air Corps on February 18, 1943. The two brothers trained at Birmingham Southern College, in Alabama, with the 17th Army Air Force College Training Detachment and later at Camp Wolters, Texas.

The time came when the aircrew training program was disbanded and Glenn and Jack Lowry were reassigned to the 66thDivision. In October 1944, home on leave before being shipped overseas, the twins received a postcard containing the following message from a Company I buddy from Sullivan, Indiana, who was home himself, on furlough. "Hello fellows, hope you're home by now. I'm being lazy and eating lots. It looks as if the baby might be Ralph Jr., after all. You know these women. You can't win. Ha! I'll see you soon. Your pal, Ralph Truelock"

Wesley McEntarfer

Like Syd Garner, Wesley McEntarfer participated in the S.S. *Leopoldville* disaster rescue effort. He grew up in Fredonia, New York. McEntarfer's father was a Methodist minister and while attending Taylor University in Upland, Indiana, the younger McEntarfer grappled with the decision whether to follow in his father's footsteps. Then war broke out, and he opted to enlist in the Navy rather than wait to be drafted. Probably because of his college background and typing skills, McEntarfer was made a Yeoman. In January 1944 he boarded the *Queen Mary* from Bayonne, New Jersey, bound for "somewhere." That somewhere turned out to be the Firth of Clyde and a small Navy base near Helensborough, Scotland.

Following the Normandy Invasion, McEntarfer was transferred to Cherbourg, France. The Navy's job was to control the allied shipping coming into the harbor and ensure that cargo and ammunition were unloaded as quickly as possible and transported to the front. Said McEntarfer, "It was hectic but not a very exciting place to be."

Romeo Mitri

Born into a very musical Italian family in the upstate New York town of Cohoes on November 2, 1924, Romeo Mitri started clarinet lessons at the age of eight. He joined the Musicians' Union at the age of 15 and at 17 tried to join the Navy School of Music but was rejected because of his teeth. He had an overbite which could cause a concussion from the deafening noise of the ship's guns firing. After graduating from Cohoes High School in 1942, he was drafted into the Army. When the 66th Division was activated, he was sent to Camp Blanding and was assigned to Company I of the 264th Regiment.

Arnold T. Olson

Chaplain Arnold Olson was born on February 23, 1910, in Minneapolis, Minnesota. His ministry led him to the Salem Evangelical Free Church, Staten Island, New York, from 1933 to 1948. However, his service as the church's pastor was interrupted by World War II. Almost every Sunday his church said farewell to another young man or woman entering the armed forces. On April 11, 1943, a service flag was dedicated, on which eventually more than fifty stars were sewn as the ranks of the church's youth dwindled.

Pastor Olson meanwhile grappled with the decision to volunteer for the service. He would later recall, "The hearts of parents and grandparents were getting heavier. Sweethearts became more lonely as each week passed. The service flag hang-ing on the wall near the pulpit was a constant reminder, as if one were needed."

It was just before Christmas of 1943 that he arrived at Camp Robinson and announced to the Chief of Chaplins for the Division, "Chaplain Olson reporting for duty as ordered, sir!"

On March 16, 1944, during an amphibious training exercise, two assault boats tied together were proceeding across a lake when one of them capsized, dragging the other down with it. Chaplain Olson arrived at the scene within a few minutes of the accident and before all eleven of the drowned soldiers' bodies had been recovered. Memorial services were held on March20 with three regimental chaplains and a rabbi participating in the ceremony. It was Chaplain Arnold T. Olson, however, who was asked to deliver the eulogy. Little did he know then that in less than a year, the tragic drowning of those eleven soldiers would be overshadowed by a disaster of such magnitude that even today the consequences of it are difficult to comprehend.

Frederick J. Perkins

Frederick J. Perkins was born in Littleton, New Hampshire, on August 29, 1917. Later, the Perkins family moved to East Concord, Vermont, and it was there that Fred Perkins attended grammar school and high school. Unfortunately, he had to quit high school after only 6 months. Fred's brother paid for his train transportation to school, and work at his brother's mill job had slacked off.

Fred went to work at a mill where onion bags were made. He worked his way up from laborer to web pressman printing onion bags for which he was paid 20 cents an hour. Sometime later he moved to Canajoharie, New York, where he worked at a mill that produced paper bags for Gold Medal and Sunnyfield. Then war came, and Frederick Perkins found himself a member of Company I, 262nd Regiment.

Fred G. Pisano

Fred G. Pisano was from Brooklyn, New York. He entered the Army on January 23, 1942, and graduated from the Officers candidate course on April 1, 1943. A lieutenant assigned to Company K, 262nd

Regiment of the 66th Division, he was born on November 6, 1919. His mother abandoned him on May 26, 1921, and he was committed by the Department of Public Welfare to the Angel Guardian Home, a branch of the Convent of the Sisters of Mercy in Brooklyn. Fred was adopted on September 29, 1921, by Francis and Louisa Pisano. The little child provided the Pisano family with a wonderful Christmas present, as the final papers were signed on December 24, 1923.

Waldron Mosher Polgreen

At age 35, Waldron Mosher Polgreen was older than most of the men in Company K of the 262nd Regiment. He was born on June 22, 1909, and grew up in Albany, New York. He attended Albany Academy and then continued his education at Hamilton College for 1 year before transferring to Northeastern University in Boston, Massachusetts. After graduating, he worked in his father's real estate and insurance office. Waldron Polgreen was proud of his Dutch heritage, and his mother, Grace Edith Mosher Polgreen, traced family Dutch descendants back to the seventeenth century who settled in the Albany area. His mother, in fact, helped organize the Dutch Settlers Society of Albany, which was founded in 1924. Waldron became chairman of the Society's committee to survey Dutch colonial buildings in the Albany area, and between the years of 1936 and 1942, using a box camera, he photographed many of the homes that he located in Albany, Rensselaer, and Greene county.

Waldron Polgreen and his wife Frances, along with their two sons, Richard and Henry, continued to live in Albany. Then World War II came and he was drafted. A third son, Tobias, was born during 1944.

Gerald Raymond

The spring of 1944 saw thirty year-old Gerald Raymond of Des Moines, Iowa, busily engaged in his business of selling livestock minerals and feed to nearby farmers. He was married and the father of two children, and military service was far from his thoughts until the notification that he was drafted arrived in the mail. The war would now dramatically change Gerald Raymond's life through an experience that he could not have imagined as he said goodbye to his wife Fern, his eight year-old daughter Colleen, and his seven year-old son Bill.

Gerald was introduced to Army life at nearby Camp Dodge, Iowa, and then went to Texas for basic training. After more training at a base in Georgia, Gerald arrived in New York in November 1944 with the 66th Division. As his Division crossed the Atlantic, Gerald felt depressed. Looking out over the ship's rail at the heavy seas, images of his children's happy faces from past Christmases flashed through his mind. Gerald Raymond thought to himself, "Daddy won't be home for Christmas this year." The spray from the waves slapped his face as Gerald's eyes surveyed the seemingly boundless ocean. "Lord, watch over my family and keep us all safe till we are back together again," he prayed.

George Stanley Rehder

Lieutenant George Stanley Rehder from Wilmington, North Carolina, looked forward to arrival in England. He had heard that good bourbon whiskey could not be had in England or on the Continent. He therefore made certain that three beautiful fifths of "Golden Wedding" bourbon found their way from the States into his footlocker. Armed with his American bourbon, once overseas he eagerly anticipated exchanging the booze for whatever his heart desired. However, there was one flaw in his plan—his by-the-book commanding officer, Captain George E. Plott.

Ira Chris Rumburg

After graduating from West Valley High School in Spokane, Washington, Ira Chris Rumburg continued his education entering Washington State College in 1934. The 6-foot-3, 190 pound Rumburg in his senior year was elected both Captain of the football team and president of the student body. Besides football, he was a heavyweight wrestler and earned three letters and captured the Northern Division wrestling title in his weight class. A member of the ROTC program, he achieved the rank of cadet lieutenant colonel. After graduating from WSC he was commissioned a second lieutenant in the Army. His initial assignment was at Hunter Liggett Military Reservation in California. Later he was assigned to command training in England until he returned to the states as an infantry instructor, training soldiers in preparation for the invasion of Europe. In the Fall of 1944, Lt. Colonel Ira C. Rumburg returned to England this time with the 66th Infantry Division.

Guy Clark Sawyer

One of the men in Sergeant Chun Fat's platoon was Guy Clark Sawyer, who was raised on a farm in Winchester, Tennessee. Sawyer attended a one-room country schoolhouse and had never been outside of his home state until he was drafted in 1943. Sawyer would say, "The lessons I learned on the farm served me well in the military—hard work, dedication, and accepting responsibilities."

Ralph A. Truelock

Ralph A. Truelock, a student at Sullivan High School, Sullivan, Indiana, was an all-around athlete who played baseball and basketball. He met school cheerleader Bonnie McCombs during the 1941 class year, and they were soon going steady. They were married on April 28, 1943, just before Ralph was inducted into the Army. Also a member of the ASTP, Ralph Truelock was sent to Camp Wolters, Texas, and later Maryville College in Maryville, Tennessee. At Fort Benning, Georgia, he received his navigator's license but as the ground fighting in Europe intensified, he was transferred back into the Infantry. Ralph joined Company I, 262nd Regiment, at Camp Rucker in June 1944.

Albert Via

Albert J. Via came from the western Maryland coal mining town of Frostburg. Born on September 28, 1916, he was part of a large family that consisted of six boys and one girl. Al reached the eighth grade at St. Michael's Elementary School, but as the Depression worsened, he left school and went to work stocking shelves in his father's grocery store.

As a boy, Al Via's mother taught him to cook, and in the Army he was soon picked for that assignment. It wasn't long before he was placed in charge of the kitchen. While on a weekend pass in Wilmington, North Carolina, Al Via sat in a restaurant and looked up from his menu at the waitress ready to take his order. "Why you're gorgeous!" he blurted out. "I'm going to marry you!" The pretty waitress, Melva, beat a hasty retreat and another girl waited on him.

Sometime later, he won $300 in a crap game and returned to the same restaurant seeking a date with the pretty waitress. He was eager to impress her with the large sum that was burning a hole in his pocket, but Melva wasn't hungry. Their first date consisted of sharing two cokes and then returning to Melva's home, where they sat on the front porch swing and talked.

The following Saturday, Al Via found himself broke. With only two dimes to his name he thought, "I'll call on Melva; she's a cheap date." As Melva finished her shift, she said, "I'm starved; let's eat."

The two sat down in a booth at the restaurant where Melva worked. "I'm not hungry, I'll just have a coke," the broke Al Via responded to the question, "What'll you have?" Meanwhile, Melva ate two pork chops, mashed potatoes, and gravy with gusto. Al nervously played with the two dimes in his pocket as Melva ordered dessert. Al was on the verge of sheer panic. As Melva finished her meal, he reached into his pocket for the money he knew wasn't there! Waving him off, Melva picked up the check. "You didn't eat anything; I'll pay my own way," she said firmly. She even paid for his coke. Protesting lamely, Al was greatly relieved.

Al Via and Melva continued to date, and their romance blossomed. As he had predicted when their eyes first met, Al and Melva were married in 1943. During 1944, he was transferred into the 66th Division. His moment of unbelievable personal crisis was then just months away.

Morton "Pete" Wood

Childhood was tough for Morton "Pete" Wood, Jr., a short, skinny youth who grew up with the added hardship of dealing with a persistent stutter that caused him to be very shy. He had three years of Cadet Corps training in high school in Washington, D.C., which he would later say did more than anything to give him a feeling of self-worth. One of his proudest moments was when he attained the rank of Captain in the Corps.

This was followed by three years at Virginia Military Institute in which hazing gave all of his class a tough time. Said Wood, "It was a real confidence-builder for those who stuck it out." What was supposed to be the Class of 1944 was called into the Army in the Spring of 1943, and Wood went through basic training in anti-aircraft artillery. In early 1944, he was accepted into OCS, where he continued to be plagued by chronic stuttering but worked hard and succeeded in making second lieutenant. Afterward, Pete Wood would write, "This, I consider my toughest accomplishment (other than getting the girl I loved desperately, but secretly, to marry me, some years later)."

Upon graduating from OCS, Lieutenant Wood and the rest of his class were immediately transferred to the Infantry. In August of 1944, Lieutenant Wood was transferred to the 66thDivision at Camp Rucker as a Rifle Platoon Leader of the 3rd Platoon, Company I, 264th Regiment.

Chapter 1

Christmas 1944
Approaches

"Dear Son, Today is Christmas Eve, and I hope you are planning to have a nice time and a drink for me."
. . . Louise Cacace

During the Fall of 1944, it appeared that Sergeant Joe Cycon's Company F, 262nd Regiment buddy Sergeant William Donnelly would be transferred to a different outfit and might even receive a Medical Discharge. Cycon wrote his wife Margie on October 20, from Camp Rucker, "I hate to see him go . . . We are very good friends and he's a likeable guy . . . he's a true friend if there ever was one, but a lot of other guys left that I was good friends with so that's the way it is in the Army—they come and go."

This letter was followed by another dated October 26 in which Cycon told her his division probably would soon leave the United States. "Darling, Whatever happens now try not to worry too much, as everything will turn out all right in a short time. Things are pretty dark now. I mean it's pretty certain that our outfit is going overseas, but I expect we won't see actual combat and I'll be back soon."

o o o

The expected transfer and Medical Discharge of Bill Donnelly did not occur, but as Joe Cycon had surmised, on November 15, 1944, as part of a 150-ship convoy, the 66th Division was shipped overseas aboard a ship built in northern Germany, named the *George Washington*.1 A unit of the North German Lloyd Line, she made her maiden voyage to New York on July 12, 1909. When war broke out in Europe, the ship was forced to remain in port at New York, where it was seized by U.S. officials on April 6, 1917. The troopship's overall length was 699 feet with a beam of 78 feet, and drew 32 feet of water. She had a 37,000-ton displacement and was driven by twin propellers and quadruple expansion reciprocating engines rated at 21,000 hp and 21 knots top speed. The transport ship had a crew of 40 officers and 907 men. Records from World War I state that she could accommodate 485 commissioned officers and 6,551 men. During World War I, the *George Washington* performed with distinction, carrying a total of 48,373 fighting men to Europe. Only the U.S.S. *Leviathan* surpassed that figure.

After World War I, the vessel was reconverted for commercial sailing and in June of 1920 went over to the American Line. Then she was sold to the United States Line, where she performed trans-Atlantic voyages. With the outbreak of World War II in Europe, the *George Washington* was readied for service as the *Catlin* and scheduled to be turned over as a lend-lease to the British. But this never occurred and the ship remained the *George Washington*. At Baltimore harbor from 1942 to 1943, she was converted from a coal burner to an oil-burning ship.

o o o

Sergeant Miguel Velez, Company I, 262nd Regiment, stood by the ship's rail and watched as his native New York City faded in the distance. Later he noted in his diary, "We were drifting farther and farther away from the Statue of Liberty and home sweet home. Most of us bowed our heads in sadness, wishing we were returning home instead of going away. We watched the skyscrapers until we couldn't see even the sight of land but only water all around. Then, there wasn't anything to watch but the destroyers and ships in this tremendously large convoy."

o o o

One of those who bowed his head as the Statue of Liberty faded in the distance was Mess Sergeant Albert Via, of Frostburg, Maryland.

Tears welled up in his eyes as he thought of Melva, his new bride, and he wondered if he would ever see her again.

Sgt. Elmer Baker (2nd from left) with Panther buddies in a New York City night club just prior to shipping overseas.

o o o

Sergeant Elmer Baker, the former farm boy from Missouri, celebrated his nineteenth birthday on November 12 in New York City with his Company K, 262nd Regiment buddies. Three days later, on that first day aboard the troopship as the *George Washington* headed out to sea, he wrote a V-mail letter to his aunt, Mrs. Virgil Hughes, of Cedar City, Missouri.

"Hello All, How is the big City of Cedar making out? . . . Boy O boy, New York City is sure a big place . . . always something interesting going on. I sure enjoyed my stay there. Thanks for the birthday card. Wish I could have been there to thank you for it in person. I'm somewhere at sea now, God only knows where. I haven't been sick yet but am expecting it anytime. Ha! Tell everyone hello for me. Bye, Your nephew Elmer"

o o o

Aboard ship, during this autumn voyage of 1944, Lieutenant Morton "Pete" Wood, Jr., pondered what the future held in store for him. Also crossing the Atlantic aboard the *George Washington*, was

Lieutenant Preston Appleby, whose thoughts were not of the fighting that awaited him in Europe but of the day when he could step into a bright and warless world. He longed to return to peace and the girl he had left back home. His thoughts were of Margie Cass, the light of his life, and he prayed for the day when the war would be over and he could once again hold her in his arms. On that "great day," the lumps in their throats would melt away and all of their hopes and dreams would spring alive. It would be time to take a holiday from heartache, when their kisses would be real, and not paper, and they could plan their future life together with confidence.

Lieutenant Appleby was confident that the war would soon be over. Had he not seen the September 11, 1944 cover of *Life* magazine with Nazi prisoners walking along a road in France with their hands on their heads? *Life* had described them as apart of the multitude of some 200,000 German prisoners that the Americans had captured in France. Why, just 2 days before the 66th Division sailed, Lieutenant Appleby read of General MacArthur's return to the Philippines. Maybe, just maybe, it would be all over by Christmas!

Lieutenant Preston Appleby   Margie Cass

With these thoughts racing through his mind, Lieutenant Appleby stood by the rail of the *George Washington,* surveyed the vastness of the Atlantic Ocean, and read and reread the most recent letters he had received from Margie. "My Dearest, . . .Gosh Darling, I miss you something awful! I feel as if I'm only half here. I really am because the other half is with you. I was so glad you decided to come to El Paso on your furlough,

Butch; it was wonderful being with you again. I just wish you could be here all the time. It was with a heavy heart that I left the station Friday night. I felt that I couldn't stand to leave you behind. To top it off, I caught the same taxi that had taken us home the night before, and that didn't help.

Darling, please don't forget that you promised me you would have your picture taken. I hope you will not delay in having it done. Have one made for your mother, too, and if you like you can send her picture with mine and I will see that she gets it for Christmas. Hon, I'd like a small one too because I plan on buying myself a billfold—then I could have a picture of you with me every minute of the day. I'd be so proud of it, darling!

Mother said to tell you she thought your roommate missed you . . . Did you have a nice trip back? Hope you didn't meet too many pretty blondes! Well, Butch, guess I'll say goodnight. It's 10 o'clock and my bedtime . . . Until I'm with you again, 'I'll Walk Alone.'2 All my love, Margie . . . P.S. I love you terribly!"

Lieutenant Appleby, paused for a moment as he looked out over the waves that were carrying him far from the girl he treasured. Then he carefully unfolded Margie's letter of October 20 and resumed reading her expressions of love, which meant so much to him. "Dearest darling, Needless to say how delighted I was to receive your sweet letter . . . For awhile I had begun to think you had forgotten me. The first letter I received from you after you left was October 9, and the next day I received one that had no postmark of any type on it. To look at the envelope one would think it had never gone through the post office. I do wish you would date your letters, Butch, so I can have some idea how long it has taken for me to receive them.

". . . Say, Hon, I really like the picture and I would love to have a large one like it. Be sure and sign it, too, darling . . . I started writing you at work, but as you can see, I didn't get to finish. I mailed you a little Christmas remembrance—I was afraid to wait any longer to mail it. I do hope you get it before you leave! Speaking of leaving, darling, gosh I do wish you didn't have to go. Please take good care of yourself. Always remember, sweetheart, that there is one ole gal in Texas (El Paso to be exact) who thinks you are the most wonderful guy of them all and is looking forward to seeing you again soon.

"Please write me soon and often, darling. I miss and love you terribly and your letters do wonders for me . . . Be sweet and think of me often, Butch. All my love, Margie . . . P.S. Remember I love you always!"

For a long while, Lieutenant Appleby stood by the ship's rail and stared out at the rolling sea, lost in his private thoughts. Then, after returning his prized letters to a safe pocket inside his jacket, he slowly walked to the steep stairway that led below deck.

o o o

During the ocean voyage, Private First Class Edward Haas found himself having dinner in the same dining room in which President Wilson ate on his several trips to Europe during 1918 to confer on the League of Nations. The League of Nations had failed, and now the flames of war engulfed Europe. Not knowing what the future held in store for him, Haas thought back to his childhood when he grew up in Jamaica, Queens, New York, during the "Great Depression."

His father had been a longshoreman much of his life, but there were few vessels being loaded or unloaded on the Hudson River during those years. Edward's father was constantly out of work, and Edward, along with his brother John, became the family breadwinners through their high school years by working as newsboys and grocery clerks. Edward graduated from John Adams High School in 1938 and went to work at the Brewster Aeronautical Corporation, which made a plane for the Navy called the Brewster Buffalo. Working in a defense plant kept Haas from being drafted, but he would say of the Buffalo, "it's a good thing we never had to call upon it to protect our shores—it was a lousy plane."

During mid-1943, Haas passed the test to become an Army Air Corps Cadet. He was assigned at Cochran Field, Macon, Georgia, for Primary Flight Training. But after only a month or so of training, the program was canceled. Said Haas, "I, along with all my gung-ho fly-boy-heroes-to-be, was informed that the Army needed guys to carry M-1's more than to fly planes." Haas, assigned to Company K, 264th Regiment, with the 66th Infantry Division, at Camp Rucker, Alabama, would write, "We were washed out of our nice, neat bedrooms and into the barracks again."

o o o

Thomas A. Cobb, born on November 20, 1922, observed his twenty-second birthday at sea. On that day, he began a letter to his mother, which he completed on November 24. "Dear Mother, Well, I am writing this now but it will be a while before I can mail it. Right now I'm on the ship sitting on my bunk. There is hardly anything you are permitted to say. I am suffering at the moment with that old malady of sea travelers, seasickness. It certainly makes you feel rotten. Our company has been assigned to working in the galley. My particular job is to bring the day's supplies from the hold up to the galley. It's hard work but it only lasts 1 to 2 hours. We get plenty to eat. They really have a tremendous amount of food on board . . . After we finish our job the baker gives us pie and ice cream. No matter how bad I feel, I always have room for that. I have a pretty good idea of where we are going but naturally I'm not permitted to say. . . This is a few days later than when I wrote the first part of the letter. I've gotten over my seasickness so now the rocking of the ship doesn't bother me. We have movies aboard. Yesterday I was halfway through 'Destry Rides Again' when the film had to be stopped because of the blackout. I spent my birthday at sea and now I'm waiting to eat Thanksgiving dinner—my second one away from home."

o o o

That Thanksgiving Day at sea, Glenn Lowry also took time out from his duties to pen a letter home, which read in part, "Jack and I went to church service this afternoon. We have been attending church service every evening . . . I enjoyed my stay in New York. I only hope it's not too long before I see New York again. My Thanksgiving dinner was very good—turkey and all the trimmings."

o o o

In his letter home to Velma, dated December 12, Private First Class Peter Acri wrote of the crossing and about an encounter with a submarine . . . "We have been told that we can go into more detail about our trip now so please pardon the delay in my response to your questions. We left New York at about 7 AM [on November 15; actual date censored]. I was asleep at the time so I didn't get to see the Statue of Liberty. The boat's name I don't think I can say yet, but I can say it was one of the biggest. The trip itself wasn't too interesting since all we did was roll from side to side and stern to stern. I didn't get seasick at all, but I came close once or twice. The food wasn't bad, what we could get of it. They only served two meals a day to all except the crew and the men who did guard duty. Luckily, I was one of the guards, so I didn't starve too much. Also my post happened to be near the crew's quarters and I managed to swindle extra food out of them daily. Tell Bob to forget the Merchant Seaman's job; they don't pay what he thinks they do. He's better off where he is and a lot safer. During the trip we had a sub scare. A few depth charges were dropped and we lost the sub in a cloud of waves. Our escort vessels stayed behind a little and hunted for it but I don't think they got it; anyway it didn't do us any harm. As a matter of fact it took some of the dryness away from the trip."

o o o

The crossing was a slow process, but all the ships reached Southampton, England, safely. Sergeant Miguel Velez noted their arrival in his diary.

"In ten days we started seeing land and finally the beautiful countryside of England. When we docked at Southampton, we noticed how misty it was and the darkness that was England. Nevertheless, it was a relief to stand on solid soil again, after almost two weeks on the ocean, rocking and bouncing up and down on the ship through the raging sea."

A train took the men to Camp Piddlehinton near Dorchester, England, and the soldiers settled into their new quarters. In a letter to his parents dated November 29, Jack Lowry wrote, "We are stationed somewhere in southern England. I know you are glad to hear that. Since we arrived the weather has been misty and it has rained a couple of times . . . We are living in small one-story barracks. The beds are only 5 feet, 10 inches long, which is too short for me. We sleep on straw ticks. They are a lot more comfortable than the cots we had on board ship . . . Please do not worry about us, at least not at the present."

Sergeant Benjamin Blaskowski celebrated his twentieth birthday on December 1. In his thoughts of Blaskowski, Pfc. Norman Bullett would later say, "Ben was checking on all of us to see that everything was okay; he sure was a great guy." Pfc. Walter Blunt, also of Company L, recalled Sergeant Blaskowski as "very clean cut, rather handsome, friendly, and always with an attitude that showed respect and concern for the men under his leadership."

While December 1 was a red-letter day for Sergeant Blaskowski, it was the day that Sergeant Miguel Velez nearly died! When he was well enough, the New York City youth noted in his diary,

"On December 1, I was still sick and it seemed I was getting worse, when the ambulance came for me; I was shivering to beat hell and I didn't want to go until Lieutenant Bell made me and I'm very thankful. I don't know how I made it, after hearing that I had double pneumonia and the difference of a few hours would have meant my death. I was a bed patient for two weeks, after which I reported to the hospital after meals, but a week later I was back in bed with the shakes again. By Christmas I was feeling much better and walking around. I asked the Ward Officer if he had heard anything about my division. He hadn't, but said he would let me know as soon as he heard anything."

o o o

Staff Sergeant Donald Gengler used his time in England to sample fish, chips, and warm beer. Here too, he was introduced to the buzz bomb, which would send people running for bomb shelters until the sirens stopped.

o o o

Meanwhile, Velma Acri had begun to receive Pete's letters. "November 30, 1944 . . . England . . . Dearest, I've already written a V-mail letter and sent a cablegram to you. I hope both arrived okay. We've been having a bit of trouble with our mail system but I think it's about cleared [up] by now. I received three letters from you yesterday, one dated November 13 and also one each for November 16 and 17. I'm sorry you were all rattled about me not calling you from the big city. I got in once but I didn't call for two reasons. First, we were instructed that for security reasons no member of this outfit would, unless under emergency, call out of New York. There were to be no visitors to meet anyone. The Army asked us to do that to protect the security of the unit. The second reason, and more important of the two, was because I couldn't bring myself to say that last goodbye. If you remember correctly while I was home Ose₃ called from California to give his last adieus. It's pretty hard for me to forget the looks on Mom's, Pop's and even your own face, after the call was over. I decided it was better under the circumstances not to call at all rather than repeat that scene. Believe me darling, I wanted nothing more than to talk to you, to have you come and see me and for us to be together for as long a time as we could, but it just couldn't be. If you think for one minute that I didn't want to have you with me so I could love you up, even if it would have been for an hour or two, you're losing trust in our love. Don't ever doubt me hon, because without your trust and companionship I have nothing to come back to. I must close now as this is all the paper I have. I borrowed this from one of my barracks buddies. All my love and kisses, your ever faithful hubby, Pete"

As Christmas approached, Velma had a portrait taken of her and baby Jim, which she mailed to Pete as a special gift.

o o o

Upon arriving in England, Lieutenant Preston Appleby was equally quick to pen a letter to his parents.

"Somewhere in England . . . Dear Mom and Dad, As you can see, I finally got over. I am sorry, I couldn't write before, but it was impossible. This is really a beautiful country. Every part of it seems to be well taken care of. I enjoyed my boat ride and as usual I didn't get seasick, although quite a few of the boys did. I am glad I got to call you from New York. I enjoyed my one trip there. As usual I can't write much about anything due to censorship. I can sympathize with the other censors though as I have to censor the mail in my company and it is quite a job. As for the Christmas present you can send it airmail, I believe. Write Mrs. Cass and Margie and tell them you heard from me. How is Davy? I imagine he is quite a rascal by now. Tell everyone hello and that I hope I get to see them soon.

Lots of love, Bub [nickname]"

o o o

The Lowry twins had been promoted to Private First Class, and Jack proudly wrote home on December 3, "I took Glenn's and my shirts and jackets to the tailors to have PFC stripes sewed on this afternoon. The weather is the same day after day. The weatherman doesn't have much of a job predicting scattered showers and low ceiling."

Glenn Lowry wrote his parents the same day as Jack. "Received your letter of November 24 today. Jack and I went to town last night. We sent cablegrams to our girls and went to church this morning.

Our chow is getting a little better. I only hope it continues. Jack wrote a V-mail [letter] so I am sending this airmail. Tell me which is faster? . . . Please, see if you can send the *Post Gazette* to me. We don't get any news over here. Send it for three months if you can."

Jack's next letter was December 6, which said in part, "It is now 1:50 AM. I have to stay up all night and take care of the two stoves in my barracks. The job is easy but staying awake is not quite that simple. I have to watch them fairly close because the wind is blowing and the small stoves will soon burn out."

o o o

Margie Cycon was pregnant and Sergeant Joe Cycon's December 6th letter home expressed concern for her well-being.

"How is Junior coming along; I hope you are not having any trouble—it worries me alot. I wish I could be with you when you go to the hospital; be sure to keep me informed of all the details. I don't want to miss out on anything."

o o o

On December 8, Company I, 262nd Regiment held a "Hello England" party. The notice read, The boys of Company I are at it again.

They're reeling and rocking and filled with vim.

They're giving a party to celebrate, and would like to have you for a date.

So put on your party clothes, and come on down.

And we'll show you how to go to town.

The notice also included the following greetings. "As Commander of Company I, and on behalf of my command, I cordially welcome all of you to our 'Hello England' party and dance.

May our traditional friendship be strengthened and lengthened by the greater understanding and mutual regard fostered by this meeting. Here's to a good time for all. Cordially, Jack F. Gangwere, Captain"

o o o

Glenn Lowry mentioned the party in his letter home dated December 10.

"I didn't feel well Friday and Saturday but I feel a lot better today. Our company had a party Friday. Jack and I went, but I couldn't enjoy myself because I didn't feel well. Jack and I went to town yesterday afternoon; we went shopping. Everything is rationed, even handkerchiefs. Everything is so high priced. We bought some Christmas cards, which I'll have to send today.4 I doubt if they will get there in time. Jack and I went to church this morning; I wanted to go to church in town, but it was raining."

Glenn wrote to his parents again the next day, "Received two airmail letters from you today. They were written on November 22 and 24. We had an inspection today. Tonight and tomorrow Jack and I are on guard duty. I am glad you got Zelda and Norma Jean something . . . I haven't gotten that Christmas package you sent to Camp Rucker yet."

o o o

When Joe Cycon wrote to his wife on December 10, his thoughts were of their past Christmas holidays together. "Everytime I think of Christmas it makes me feel lonesome and homesick for the good old days. Remember how nice it used to be . . . I'd like to see all that snow at home now, that's what I like, a white Christmas." (Just 2 days later, Cycon wrote Margie again.) "I'll still have my stocking up Christmas Eve. Who knows, maybe they have a Santa Claus here too."

o o o

Glenn Lowry's next letter written on December 17 also mentioned the approaching holiday. "How are you? I feel fine and hope you are the same. Jack and I went into town last night, to the Red Cross and to the YMCA. We came back to camp early because it was raining. We planned to go to church today, but we both slept in. For chow today we had chicken, peas, potatoes, bread pudding, and pineapple. I sure hope we get some mail soon . . . Just think, 1 week from tomorrow is Christmas."

o o o

Christmas Eve was just 1 week away, but Thomas Cobb was still struggling with his feelings of gloom. His letter to his mother, dated December 14, read in part, "Right at the moment I'm feeling quite low.

The training in prospect is none too pleasant. It's comforting to think of home and the things there. I suppose as the time lengthens I'll get more homesick for the USA. I found that I can buy a flashlight here in the PX; it's a good one so you needn't send me one. A wristwatch would be very useful, so if you happen to see one that you think is good, I would like it. I don't like to ask for things, but they are very hard to get here and must be imported from the US anyway. Perhaps you will get this about Christmas time. I hope you have the usual gala time."

o o o

Many people had expected the war to be over by Christmas and the mood on the home front was upbeat. As the holiday rapidly approached, Thomas Cobb's despondency was not shared by Mrs. Louise Cacace of Brooklyn, New York. She was sure that the New Year would soon see her son's return home. Her cheerful V-mail letters to her son, Staff Sergeant Anthony Cacace, Company E of the 262nd Regiment, were typical of the confidence in the future shared by millions of other mothers across the country. "December 15, 1944 . . . Dear Son, I hope this letter finds you well and happy. We are all well at home. How do you like it in England now that you've been there awhile. I bet it's nice seeing a lot of new things. Dad is fine; he will be coming home from the hospital soon. He sends you his love and a very Merry Christmas and a Happy New Year. He said not to drink too much but to have a drink for him and you can have one for me too. Grandma and all of your aunts send their love. They wrote to you and also sent you cards, but if you write to us and ask for something, we will send you a package . . . so please ask each one of us for something, like razor blades or toothpaste. Anything, just so you get a package. . . . Brother [nickname], if you have time, write to Sonny; he wants to hear from you. I sent you his address and I also sent him yours. Let me know if you get this letter sooner than the other ones. I love and miss you very much. Write often. Here is a kiss X."

The following day, December 16, 1944, Louise Cacace wrote still another cheerful letter to her son Anthony. She had no way of knowing that even as she penned her message, her dream that her son would soon be home was being shattered. That same day, December 16, 1944, German forces broke through the Ardennes as they had in 1940 and the monumental conflict known as The

Battle of the Bulge had begun. "December 16, 1944 . . . Dearest Son, Another day and no mail. I hope you are in the very best of health. Brother, I got a Christmas card from John's girlfriend and a letter from Chubby; he said he wrote to you but got no answer. I'll write to him and tell him why . . . Son, did you get any mail from Vin? If you did let me know. Dad is fine; I'm going to visit him tonight. Brother, I still didn't get the E allotment. [This was a deduction from the soldier's monthly paycheck that was sent back home to his family.] Maybe I'll get it next month, but it would have been handy for the holiday. As long as you are okay though I don't care . . . While I'm writing I'm waiting for Sally. I think she is here now. Yep, that's her. She says hello and sends you her love. I'll end now with love and kisses."

Anthony's mother was a prolific letter writer and yet another letter was sent on December 18. ". . . Dear Son, I love and miss you very much. I got your letter and was happy to hear that you are getting my mail. You should get plenty; I write every day. Thanks a lot son for the money you sent me. I'll let you know as soon as I get it. Dad is fine and he will be home soon. He sends you his love . . . The other night you were almost an uncle, but it was a false alarm . . . I guess you will be an uncle before you get this letter. I'll let you know right away. Son, I'll send you a package and as many cigarettes as I can get because it's very tough getting them at home. Boy did I get a lot of Christmas cards. I hope you get mine in time, and your aunts sent cards to you too. When I finish this letter, I have to get dressed and go to see your dad . . . I go everyday. So son, thanks again, and God bless you and watch over you and all the boys always.

Love and kisses, I love you, Mom"

o o o

With Christmas just 5 days away, Thomas Cobb also penned another letter to his mother. The Christmas spirit, however, still eluded him. "December 20, 1944 . . . Dear Mother, Well, guess where I am? In London. I'm on a pass. I don't have too much time; I wish I had more. I'm writing this in one of the numerous Red Cross Clubs. If it wasn't for these clubs it would certainly be hard to do things . . . Today I wanted to go to Trafalgar Square, so I got on the bus but got off too soon. I walked around awhile and then asked a bobby the way . . . I'm back in camp now. I couldn't mail this in London. You can only send mail through the company. I walked down Whitehall Street past the Admiralty, War

Office, Downing Street, and other buildings around that district. The fog was very bad as I said before and I couldn't see too well. I also went into Westminster Abbey. There are plenty of tombs there. I got a letter from you and one from Celine, both postmarked November 29. I also got one from Jane and a Christmas card from Bernd. I can't think of much more to say . . . I hope you get this in a short time. Yours, Tom"

o o o

The men of the 66th Division were not looking forward to their own Christmas away from home, which for many of them was their first separation from family and loved ones back in the States. Company F, 262nd Regiment, Sergeant Joe Cycon's last letter home to Margie before Christmas was dated December 21, 1944. "I hope you have a nice Christmas or as good as can be expected; we won't have a white Christmas here or probably none at all, but we are thankful to be alive, healthy, and safe. All that chow you had for Thanksgiving sure must have tasted good; when I read your letter it made my mouth water for a good home-cooked meal. Our food isn't bad if you like powered eggs and milk, I don't, but I have to eat; it's an injustice to my stomach and I'll appreciate anything you can do to help. Bill got the Christmas card you sent, and he really liked ita lot; he said to thank you for it. He also teased me, because that card said he was a man and he said you know a good Irishman . . . we have our arguments about the Irish and the Polacks, I'm glad we are together; he's a true friend. Honey, when you talk about all the snow at home and about having a Christmas tree it really makes me homesick. We used to have some fun every Christmas. I'd give anything to be home now with you darling. I love you more than words can say, and I'll always be waiting for the day we can be together again."

o o o

That Christmas Eve, Louise Cacace, Staff Sergeant Anthony Cacace's mother hadn't the slightest clue of the horrific tragedy that was unfolding even as she wrote her son his Christmas greeting.

"December 24,1944 . . . Dear Son, Today is Christmas Eve and I hope you are planning to have a nice time and a drink for me. I'm having one for you. Son, did you get the Christmas and birthday cards? I got a lot of cards; more this year than ever before. Sonny sent Ginny $25. Well, Brother, tonight is the night the doctor said Ginny would have her baby . . . I told her to wait until after Christmas—to hold out for your birthday. She said she will try . . . Well son, I've reached the end so I'll say Merry Christmas and a very Happy New Year. Lots of luck and God bless you son. I love and miss you very much. I'll mail you the package as soon as I get the cigarettes. Love from all at home. I love you. Here is a kiss X . . . Mom"

o o o

Like Louise Cacace, Rose Cobb's thoughts were of the joyous Christmas season, not of disaster and death. Her letter to her son Tom two days after Christmas was lengthy and uplifting. "December 27, 1944 . . . Dearest Tom, I hope you will receive the double V-mail letter we sent you on Christmas Day. We all wrote you little messages at Aunt Jane's. We just sat around all afternoon, had a late dinner, and then Dick and I left for home.

Celine Cobb and Tannie

Aunt Sue was there from Brooklyn and she rode down on the subway train. Celine stayed in Mt. Vernon and is coming home today . . .

Last night Dick accompanied me to the Novena. It was a nice clear night, but quite cold. We were glad Marie and Regina were there and brought us home. Marie had my Christmas gift with her. It was a set of 12 nice glasses, with yellow and red flowers on them. I gave her a string of beads, bought in Ridgewood, where I did all my Christmas shopping this year. Jennie B. is quite thrilled over joining the Waves. She leaves tomorrow . . . Did I tell you about the lovely Mexican basket that we received from Texas, filled with grapefruit, the pink kind? Bea Pursell had it sent to us and the grapefruit is quite sweet, so sweet that you don't need to put sugar on it. That is a help as sugar is getting to be very scarce and we are trying to save on it as much as we can. We bought a box of 'Dyno,' I think it's called. It is only about one-third as sweet as granulated sugar, though. . . . Ray came over on Christmas about 6 o'clock and fed Tannie. Dick wrote him a note just how to prepare the Grow-Pup dinner, which was to be mixed with some cooked beef heart . . . Whatever do you suppose??? Our Nid has a GIRLFRIEND—Marion!!! And he gave her a Christmas present—a Miraculous Medal! It must have been a beauty from all descriptions. And she gave him a pair of lovely pigskin gloves and something else, which I can't remember. Marion came over and went to midnight Mass with all of the Benzings and came back to the house for refreshments afterwards . . . I'll be writing again tomorrow, so I'll get this on its way. God bless and take care of my own 'Sweet Dud.' I am thinking of you constantly and praying for you, so have courage and faith that all will be well. Bye for now and lots of love, Mother"

o o o

The English Channel is 350 miles long and 150 miles broad at its widest point. That Christmas Eve, the 501-foot, 11,500-ton Belgian steamer *Leopoldville* had the task of ferrying troops of the 66th Division U.S. Army from Southampton, England, to Cherbourg, France (a trip of about nine hours), as reinforcements in the Battle of the Bulge, which was to decide the fate of Germany and so many millions of European people.

Named after the capital city of the Belgian Congo, the *Leopoldville* was built at Hoboken, Belgium in 1929. She was originally a liner whose three weather decks were covered in teakwood. Before the war, she cruised between Antwerp and Africa. But since the early stages of the war, the *Leopoldville* had been under charter to the Admiralty and converted into a troopship.

Her first three trips were made to St. John, New Brunswick, each time carrying 1,000 Royal Air Force recruits scheduled for training there. The *Leopoldville,* however, was not built to withstand the fierce weather of the North Atlantic, and the ship was damaged by the continued pounding from the ocean's violent storms. The vessel was therefore reassigned to the sunnier region of the Middle East. Toward the end of 1942, the ship carried on average, 2,000 men per voyage to ports in western and eastern Africa. Then, in November 1942, it returned to Glasgow, Scotland, where Captain Biebuyck was replaced by Captain Charles Limbor.

Limbor had a reputation as a calm, competent, extremely capable seaman. Limbor's wife and 15-year-old son fled to France when the war began. His wife hoped to join her husband but did not anticipate the speed of the German advance and was forced back to Nazi-occupied Ostend, Belgium.5 The Germans knew her location and that her husband commanded an Allied ship. The stress on Limbor was enormous, and he preferred the privacy of his own cabin where he confined his concerns for his family's safety to himself. He usually dined alone, escaping the war's brutality by listening to his large collection of classical records.

With her new captain, the *Leopoldville* transferred troops from Glasgow to Algiers by way of Gibraltar. At the end of January 1943, voyages between ports in Africa and the Suez commenced. In July 1943, the ship returned to the Mediterranean and landed troops in Sicily. The *Leopoldville* remained in the Mediterranean until April 1944 ferrying troops between Gibraltar, Algiers, Bone, Augusta, Port Said, and Suez.

At the end of April 1944, the *Leopoldville* returned to Glasgow where the vessel was completely refitted in preparation for its role in the coming invasion of the continent. On June 3, 1944, 2,154 British soldiers departed from Tilbury aboard the ship. The *Leopoldville* quickly joined the rest of the convoy and traversed the Straits of Dover under the protection of a smoke curtain. On June 8, the ship arrived off the invasion beaches and set anchor at the Pointe de Vair. Troops were immediately transferred from the vessel to landing craft, which brought them the remaining distance to shore.

By Christmas Eve 1944, the tired old steamer had made 24 Channel crossings and carried a total of 53,217 soldiers. Since being pressed into duty, the *Leopoldville* had transported a total of 124,220 troops. Unlike her sister ship, the *Albertville,* which on June 11, 1940 was sunk off Le Havre by German aircraft, the *Leopoldville* by all accounts was one of the luckiest vessels in the allied transport service. While other transport ships had been strafed, shelled, bombed, mined, and torpedoed, the *Leopoldville* had not even been scratched after almost four years of continuous service.

In fact, just the week before, the troopship had transported across the Channel—without incident—personnel of the 199th General Hospital Unit, which included Army nurse Helen M. Livesey. Nurse Livesey never forgot the beautiful china and silver service in the officer's dining room. "It was so incongruous on a troopship, with people in pants, boots, helmets, etc." The *Leopoldville* arrived in Le Havre on December 18, and the nurses looking out over the ship's rail could see the ruins of buildings destroyed by shells.

From Le Havre, the 199th Unit was transported to the French coastal town of Etretat.[6] There they remained for two or three weeks, delayed by the Battle of the Bulge. A few days before Christmas, the nurses were marched to the town auditorium to hear a lecture on avoiding land mines that were in the area. When they arrived, they found several French women rehearsing four and five year-old children for their Christmas program. The Army officer scheduled to give the lecture ordered the women to leave, but one of them refused and became embroiled in a shouting match with him. Finally, he backed down and the nurses were treated to the children's Christmas program.

Remembered Helen Livesey fondly, "I can still see those freezing, poorly dressed little kids singing and performing—talk about the resiliency of the human spirit! When it was over we stood up, applauded, cheered, stamped, and yelled—an ovation an opera star would welcome. Then, and only then, did we learn about the mines."

o o o

The countdown to Christmas 1944 was now only four days away. Glenn Lowry wrote his parents the last letter he would mail before the holiday. However, the letter had to first pass the censor and was therefore not actually postmarked until December 30, 1944, 6 days after the S.S. *Leopoldville disaster.*

A
Merry Christmas
and a Happy
New Year

Jack and Glenn Lowry

"December 21, 1944 . . . Somewhere in Southern England . . . Dear Mother and Dad, How are you? I feel fine and hope you are the same. Today I am on barracks guard. Jack is out with the Company. On our last pass Jack and I visited London. Four of us hired a taxi and went sightseeing around London. I'll tell you a few places we saw and visited. We went through St. Paul's Cathedral and Westminster Abbey. We saw Kensington Palace, Buckingham Palace, Scotland Yard, the Tower of London, the Bank of England, County Hall, and the Houses of Parliament. We drove down Bond Street and the Victoria Embankment. We drove through Hyde Park, the Marble Arch, and over the Tower Bridge. I sure hope I get some mail one of these days. I close for now and will write you again soon. Love, Glenn"

o o o

It was December 22, and the Christmas countdown was reduced by yet another day. The fate of the *Leopoldville*, which would forever change so many lives, drew nearer. Lieutenant Preston B. Appleby, sat peacefully on his bunk and read the most recent letter from his future mother-in-law Stella Cass. "November 24, 1944 . . . My Dear Dopted [pet name], Hope our letters have caught up with you by now. Thanksgiving was celebrated here yesterday. Seemed like Sunday, nothing more. Margorie just had to work one half day until noon. By the way, she was overcome by the lovely gifts you sent to her from New York. We all thought they were beautiful, and you are the young man whom I've so often heard say he didn't know how to buy gifts for girls! Shame on you! Your taste is super. Had a nice, long letter from your mother. She seems fine. A couple of weeks ago, one Sunday night about 1 o'clock, the phone rang and some man said, 'Mrs. Cass, how about some bacon, eggs, toast, and coffee?' It was none other than Major Frank. He had flown in from Anchorage, Alaska, was on his way to the Valley to see his wife, whose mother had died. He called us again last Sunday night, as they had stopped to refuel the plane on his way back to Alaska. Called at 1:30.

"Preston, I feel sure you are in England. You know I've always told you that was where you'd be sent. Son has been moved again—he even has a new A.P.O. I think this is the ninth A.P.O. he's had since being in the Army. He was in Signal Corps Warehouse in this new location, if he hasn't been moved again. A letter is long overdue—I'm pretty jittery . . .

"Sunday, November 27, 1944 . . . Hello, Here I am again. Had fried chicken and 'mustard greens' for dinner today, naturally. I thought of you and we wished you were here to share your favorite dish, and incidentally, mainly the joy of your presence. We are not planning any Christmas celebration; we are postponing that until you and brother (son) return . . . Margorie is also writing you. I told her I bet you'll get my letter first. Well, Preston dear, I'll say good night. We love and miss you so much.
Best love, 'Little Mosey'"

o o o

Many small parties had been arranged for the night of December 23, to which local girls had been invited. The merriment was to include an ample supply of beer and dance music. Lieutenant George Rehder would never forget how someone had gone into the woods at the camp and cut the top off of a fir tree, brought it into the mess hall, and nailed it to the floor. Some ropes were tied to the top of the tree to ensure its stability. Everyone helped decorate the tree.

Strips of silver were peeled from gum wrappers and bent into loops. Rings of silver foil were joined together, and a garland of silver gum wrappers circled the tree. A tin can was flattened and cut into a gleaming star, which was attached with wire to the top of the tree. Postcards from home became colorful ornaments, and red and green tissue paper were crumpled tightly into Christmas balls. Empty cigarette packs were hung from every branch. Dangling ornaments of Camel, Pall Mall, and Lucky Strikes transformed the tree into a beautiful sight and filled the mess hall with the Christmas spirit. Soldiers gathered around their tree, drank coffee, talked, laughed, and sang carols.[17]

The weather was cold and rain had been falling for several days. It was about mid-afternoon on December 23, and Corlis Holt was working in the Company Supply Room when an officer opened the door and shouted, "Pack up everything and get ready to move at 1900 [7 PM]!"

o o o

Private First Class Keith Simons, a 60mm mortar gunner in the Heavy Weapons Platoon of Company I, 3rd Battalion, 262nd Regiment, vividly recalled the day the order was given.

"We had been in England for about 5 weeks and were tired of the cold, humid, clammy, drizzly weather so the shipping orders were mighty welcome. We also were spoiling for a crack at the Germans."

Simon's company and others billeted in their area dumped the straw from their mattress covers into huge piles, which were then set on fire. Simons wondered if the "Jerries" in France could see the huge blazes and know that another outfit would soon be leaving England eager for a fight.

o o o

Mess Sergeant Al Via and his fellow cooks began roasting the Christmas turkeys at 3 AM on Saturday, December 23, so that they would all be ready in time for the holiday. Then, they received emergency orders that they were moving out. When the men were finally allowed to correspond home about what occurred that Christmas Eve, Private William E. Boggs wrote to his parents on June 22, 1945. "We were going to stay at Piddlehinton in England the 22nd of December and up to 10 o'clock on the 23rd. They had a big dinner on for Christmas Eve. They moved it up to 1 PM on the 23rd. The meal was prepared and ready to be served, but they pulled us out just like that and threw the food away."[7]

o o o

Company Executive Officer Second Lieutenant Donald MacWilliams was in the process of paying the troops when he was alerted to prepare the men for assignment on designated ships and sail that night from Southampton. The men were told to remove their divisional patches and any other forms of identification. Sergeant Walter T. Brown knew that the order to move out on such short notice, coupled with the tight security, could mean only one thing. They were heading for combat.

o o o

Lieutenant Preston B. Appleby, packed his gear as quickly as possible, determined to answer his future mother-in-law's recent letter before he left. Preston did his best to write her a cheery letter.

"England—December 23, 1944 . . . Dear Little Mosey, I received your swell letter yesterday and thanks a lot for writing. I wish I could call on the phone and say, 'How about some scrambled eggs and bacon.' Ours are of the powdered variety and not too palatable. Gosh, I sure miss you all. England is a beautiful country but rather too damp to suit me. By the way, tell Margie I am going to spank her if she doesn't write me at least one note while I am over here. I haven't heard from her since I left the southeast part of the States. I guess she is a worse letter writer than even me. [Preston knew that he was about to participate in a battle from which he might not return. It was difficult for him to hide his deep perception of impending danger and finality.] I can't say when I will get to the front lines, as that is taboo. In case you don't hear from me for some time I am sure you can find out from Mother, as she is the one they will notify. I have about become reconciled to at least being hit, as most reports from the wounded say it isn't a question of whether you get hit or not but how long before you do. Anyway, a plate of your eggs and bacon would put me right back on my feet. Write me soon. Lots of love to you all . . . Preston"

o o o

Walter Blunt and the other soldiers of the 66th Infantry Division marched double time through the streets of Dorchester to a waiting train that was to transport them to the port of Southampton. Although the soldiers arrived at the train two hours after their march began, they were forced to wait an additional four hours before boarding. Finally, the locomotive jerked forward, and a sweaty and shivering Walter Blunt, like so many others, was grateful that at last they were on the move.

The train carrying the 66th Panther Division soldiers rolled to a stop at the dock in Southampton. Far from the farm country of western Illinois, Walter Blunt stepped off the train in full battle gear. Ordered to remain in the immediate area while they waited to board their ship at Pier 38, Blunt and Private First Class William Kalinowski, another soldier from Company L, were grateful for the coffee and doughnuts provided by the Red Cross.

Clarinet player, Private First Class Romeo Mitri, Company I, 264th Regiment, from Cohoes, New York, carried his duffel bag for miles along the march route to the docks. Finally, the bags became so heavy for Mitri and the other men in the line of march that they started to drag them.

Company I, 262nd Regiment's duffel bags, however, were loaded onto trucks separate from those that carried the GIs. Private First Class Keith Simons, along with five other men, pulled baggage detail for the trip to Southampton. Their job was to load the 100-pound duffel bags on the trucks when they left camp, reload them from the trucks to a train, and remove them from the train onto more trucks for the ride to dockside. During the baggage transfer from the train to trucks in Southampton, two of the assigned men goofed off while Simons and the others worked. The loafers enjoyed watching the others work for about fifteen minutes before a sergeant put them to work. The resulting delay in getting the job done meant that while the men were at the pier ready to board the ship, their duffel bags had not yet arrived. Company F therefore took Company I's place in the boarding order.

Ira Frye, Company I, 262nd Regiment, was famished! They had begun their march to the dock without breakfast. Frye's company was next in line to board the ship that would have placed them in a compartment below the ship's waterline. Was it fate that reshuffled their berth assignment? Whatever, it would mean life for the twenty-seven year-old Englewood, Ohio, man instead of death. The arrival of the duffel bags had been delayed. Now, as they prepared to board the troopship the Company Commander spotted the Red Cross station nearby. He insisted that none of the men were to board the vessel until they had something to eat. Other companies therefore boarded ahead of them and took their compartment while Frye and his comrades ate.

A third member of Company I, 262nd Regiment, was Staff Sargeant Frederick Perkins, the young man who had made onion bags before the war. He learned that when their Company Captain, Jack Gangwere, heard that Company F had taken over their assigned compartment, both captains met and decided that since the Channel crossing would be less than 10 hours there was no point in disrupting the troops further. The companies would remain in place where they were. While Keith Simons, Ira Frye, and Frederick Perkins would cross the Channel in a compartment just below the waterline, the compartment where the men of Company F were quartered was beneath them.

It seemed to Edward Haas that utter confusion reigned on the pier. Catching his first glimpse of the two boats that were to carry them across the English Channel, Haas would say of them, . . ."two ugly looking tubs if ever I saw one."

"What lousy luck", thought Lieutenant George Rehder to himself. "Heading into battle on Christmas Eve." Things had not gone well for Lieutenant Rehder since arriving in England. A few days after they landed, he made the mistake of telling some friends about his secret stash of bourbon. It wasn't long before he was directed to report to a Colonel who informed him he had two choices. He could offer the bourbon to the colonel, who would pay him the full price the booze had cost him or it could be confiscated and turned over to the MP's. Reluctantly, Rehder sold the prized bourbon to the Colonel. Shortly thereafter, matters turned from bad to worse. Captain "by-the-book" Plott learned of the episode and believing that Lieutenant Rehder was attempting to "polish the Colonel's apple," decided to reprimand and restrict him to camp until such time as they sailed for the mainland.

Not yet aware of his punishment, Lieutenant Rehder left camp for a day of sightseeing in Dorchester, a short distance away. His lunch in a local restaurant was served by a very attractive English waitress, whom he arranged to meet that evening at 8 PM when she finished work. Rehder anticipated an evening of romance.

Before returning to Dorchester, Rehder checked into camp only to learn of Captain Plott's restriction. He pretended not to know of the order confining him to the base. He had no intention of missing his date. He made his way to the Dorchester library, located across the street from the restaurant. As the library clock struck 8, he dashed out the door into the foggy wet night ready to greet the pretty young girl. But as he bolted from the library, he ran smack into someone, knocking the surprised person head over heels into the gutter. Rehder looked down in horror at the American officer sprawled out in front of him. On the officer's shoulder patch was the Black Panther insignia and on his uniform, unmistakable captain's bars. It was Captain George E. Plott![8]

There was no date nor any further trips to town for Lieutenant Rehder, and the young waitress no doubt went home angry, believing that she had been stood up. Rehder was a firm believer of the old adage, "never two without three!" Standing on Pier 38 waiting for orders, Rehder thought to himself anxiously, "I lost my booze, I lost my date, God, what am I going to lose next?"

It was past midnight when Corlis Holt, Staff Sergeant Benjamin J. Blaskowski, and the rest of the 2,235 infantrymen of the 66th Panther Division, struggled up the gangplanks of the *Leopoldville,* with their duffel bags slung over their shoulders.

From the beginning, a series of errors was set in motion that resulted in tragic consequences. The Panthers learned, to their surprise, that they were not expected. During the afternoon, 2,000 paratroopers had boarded the vessel only to be told that they were on the wrong ship.

It wasn't until about 2:30 AM on December 24 that the men finally began boarding the ship, and that task wasn't completed until about 8 AM. Because of the delay in loading, many units were split up, separating men from their original squads and companies. Edward Haas, Company K, 264th Regiment, stood in one of a number of single lines of soldiers waiting to board the *Leopoldville* or the *Cheshire.* Remembered Haas, "Some person with authority stood at the head of the line with his hand down like a gate, then lifted it and directed the next batch to one boat or the other. As I recall, I was about the tenth on line to be directed to the *Cheshire.* I don't know how many were behind me before the next batch was directed to the *Leopoldville.*"

Thus, Company K was indiscriminately separated and destined to be on two different ships. Through a simple hand signal, fate had determined that Edward Haas would not sail aboard the *Leopoldville* and that hand signal probably saved his life. The same hand movement determined that nineteen of Edward Haas' comrades from Company K who did sail aboard the *Leopoldville* would be dead before Christmas morning.

Private First Class Norman Bullett, Company L, 262nd Regiment, would later say, "When we boarded the *Leopoldville* for the trip over, I never saw Blaskowski again." Corlis Holt's company was one of the lucky ones assigned close to the bow on the starboard side, which was well above the waterline. Lieutenant Rehder, Company H, 262nd Regiment, on the other hand, led his eighty-seven men down into the bowels of the rear cargo hold on the fourth level, which was the lowest deck.

Jack Chvat was assigned to a deep compartment far below the waterline. Chvat tried his best to adjust to the crowded, smelly conditions of his compartment but, like the rest of the men, was revolted by the accommodations. He had been aboard the vessel perhaps an hour when a sergeant made his way down to where they were quartered. "You, you, and you," said the sergeant motioning to Chvat, "We're short of drivers. Come with me." The wheel of fortune had spun and selected Jack Chvat to be lifted from the bowels of the doomed ship to transport jeeps, trucks, artillery, and command cars across the Channel aboard a Landing Ship Tank (LST). At the time Jack Chvat muttered curses under his breath for having been chosen to cross the Channel and brave the freezing weather in an open jeep. Only much later would he realize that he had mercifully been plucked from almost certain death.

Sergeant Bill Cline boarded the troopship as the result of a mix-up. Along with five or six others, he was in Dorchester waiting to go to London when his company, stationed in Charmouth Court, moved out without them. They boarded the ship at about 2:30 AM and reported to a British officer. Remembered Bill Cline, "He sent us inside and we stayed on the upper deck. No assignment, no nothing. As far as I know, we were never accounted for. It was cold, rainy, and miserable on the outside of the deck, so we stayed inside."

Lieutenant Robert M. Wurdeman was a member of Headquarters Company, 3rd Battalion, 262nd Regiment, which consisted of sixty-two men and two officers. After boarding the ship, they all proceeded immediately to their assigned quarters and went to bed. At 9 AM, Wurdeman was awakened by the ship moving out from the pier. During the morning, Troop Commander Lieutenant Colonel Martindale, of the 3rd Battalion, 262nd Regiment, had a meeting of all his unit commanders on board. Lieutenant Wurdeman was given a copy of the ship's "Standing Orders," and instructions for the boat drill, which was scheduled soon afterward.

All officers then reported to the quarters of the men below the decks and read them the Standing Orders. Lieutenant Wurdeman inspected his men to see that they had life preservers and informed them of their assigned stations for the coming boat drill. The general alarm sounded, and the troops proceeded in an orderly manner to their assigned stations. Company F had the position closest to the bow. After a brief inspection by the Troop Commander, all personnel were released to their quarters. Such was the boat drill. The troops knew where to report in the event of an emergency but did not have the slightest idea what they were supposed to do once they got there—a prime example of lack of instructions, which would later hasten the men and the ship's crew to their doom.

The convoy crossing the Channel with the transport ships *Leopoldville* and *Cheshire* carried some 4,000 troops from the 66thInfantry Division. The former luxury liner *Leopoldville* was built to carry only 360 passengers, but with cargo space converted to troop compartments, she now packed in more than 2,000 soldiers. The hatches, some 40 feet square, which normally were used to load the holds, were covered over at each deck level with wood flooring. Steep wooden stairs built through those floors were used by the troops to obtain access to each level through to the bottom deck. The ceilings were low, and bunks and hammocks were stacked four high. Crossing the Atlantic from the United States, the men had thought that bunks three high were tight. Surveying the crammed stacks of hammocks, one soldier referred to them as "poor men's shrouds," a remark that did not sit well with the soldiers who heard it.21 The aisles between the tiers were narrow and cluttered with packs, rifles, duffel bags, and steel helmets. Walking through this jumble was extremely difficult, and ventilation was practically nonexistent.

William T. Stauffer was a member of the 1652nd Engineer Utility Detachment. On October 16, 1944, he boarded the *Leopoldville* at Southampton and arrived at Omaha Beachhead on October 18. He and his fellow engineers went ashore via Landing Craft Tanks (LCT). Stauffer has never forgotten the deplorable conditions aboard the ship. "To say that there was mutual animosity among the four nationalities (Belgian ship's officers, Belgian Congo crew, British gun crew, and American troops) would be an understatement. The ship was extremely dirty and overcrowded. There were two men assigned to each bunk. The only food provided was some concoction they called 'mutton stew.' We were very glad we had K-rations to eat!"

As the 66th Infantry headed for combat, Lieutenant "Pete" Wood quickly discovered for himself the dismal troop accommodations that existed aboard the *Leopoldville*. The compartment for his company was several decks below the loading deck, down a vertical ladder that passed through holes about a yard in diameter at each level. Lieutenant Wood had first duty with the company in the hold and didn't get to his own bunk until he was relieved a couple of hours later. Although the officers' cabins were not fancy, "but," said Lieutenant Wood, "they were quite comfortable."

Private First Class Walter Blunt climbed down the steep staircase to his assigned compartment. He looked around and observed that there were several hammocks and picnic-type tables made of wood, with attached bench seats to sit on. They were scattered randomly about the compartment. Other than the few tables and hammocks, there was no place to sit or lie down except on the floor.

His eyes surveying the dirty, crowded condition of the ship, Private First Class Leo Zarnosky, was moved to say, "What a helluva boat. I don't think we'll make it across; let's swim."

Zarnosky was not alone in his view of the ship. His remarks prompted another soldier to declare he had, "caught catfish from better boats than this." Still another soldier leaned over the gangway railing and yelled, "I can see the oars of the galley slaves who are going to row us across the Channel!" Soon everyone was chiming in. "We'll never git whar we're goin'," a soldier called out. From one group of men a puzzled voice inquired, "But where are we going?" The answer proved to be all too prophetic when a chorus of shouts responded, "To the bottom!"

First Lieutenant John Masters, 262nd Medical Detachment, was one of those with good reason to be apprehensive about the way the crossing had begun. His medical unit was quartered at the lowest deck aft. Shortly before sailing he discovered that all of their drugs and bandages mistakenly were loaded aboard the *Cheshire*. Only by Masters' quick response in correcting the error did the Medical Detachment manage to have a portion of the vital supplies returned to the *Leopoldville*.

Bill Everhard, a 21-year-old Second Lieutenant in Company B, 264th Regiment, was a Platoon Leader responsible for the lives of thirty-seven men. He was assigned to a small cabin that he shared with three fellow officers, who were also his friends. The cabin was located amidships at the end of a very long passageway. Lieutenant Everhard was certain the cabin was situated below the waterline as it was necessary to climb down numerous flights of stairs to reach it. Lieutenant Rehder shared his "stateroom" and its two bunk beds with five other officers. The room could only hold four men at a time, and Lieutenant Rehder found it necessary to sleep on the floor.

Private First Class Vincent Codianni, a Brownie automatic rifleman, checked his gear as the *Leopoldville* departed from Southampton at 9:15 AM, December 24, for the 95-mile, 9-hour Channel crossing. The troopship quickly joined a small convoy escorted by the destroyer H.M.S. *Brilliant* and three other vessels.

About this time, Lieutenant Wood recalled, a "meal" was served. "Infantry soldiers don't expect first-class service, but this was last-class. A bucket of green, smelly sort of stew was lowered on a rope down through the ladder openings. It paused at each deck long enough for each man, if he had the stomach, to scoop out some stew with his mess kit. Most of it ended up clogging the latrines."

Months later, Private William Boggs wrote to his parents of the "meal." "We had no breakfast on December 24, but for dinner some very greasy food was served in our compartment on dirty plates. It was so bad that just thinking about it makes me feel like regurgitating, even now. That [meal] made me begin to feel sick. Supper was more of the same and I didn't eat any. However, I drew the detail of washing dishes. When I went to do the job, I took one look at the water, which looked like it hadn't been changed since the boat was built, and headed for the rail."

Private First Class Alfred Corti also found the meal totally disgusting. "We had egg omelet, and most of us got diarrhea and vomited. The crew had to put garbage cans on the decks. Boy, we were sick as hell. I don't get seasick because I worked on a private yacht for 6 years. Even crossing the Atlantic, I didn't get sick. But this was different. From time to time, I'd go up on deck, and then below. I couldn't lie in my hammock because the swaying made me sicker."

Lieutenant Wood didn't have to eat the "stew" because he knew that Officers' Mess was scheduled later in the ship's dining room. Like

199th Army nurse Helen Livesey had observed before him, the food and service brought about a revelation as to the differences in the treatment of enlisted men and officers in European maritime. Said Lieutenant Wood, "We had tablecloths, jacketed waiters, good food, and if I remember correctly, a glass of wine . . . I remember hoping that the guys in the platoon never found out about it. That memory is one of the strongest in my military service and helped to turn around any good opinions I may have had about rank and its privileges."

Christmas Eve on the Channel was clear, cold, and rough. The severe weather forced most of the men to their quarters below deck. Private First Class George Miller, a 60mm mortar gunner in the Weapons Platoon of Company E, 262nd Regiment, preferred the cold but fresh air of the open deck to the crowded conditions and stifling odor of the compartments below, which had made him nauseous. Miller convinced several of his buddies to go with him. Once on deck, they joined one of the rifle platoons and sat against a bulkhead singing Christmas carols. The water was very rough, and several of the men became sick and hung their heads over the railing. After about 45 minutes, some of them decided to go below to get out of the cold. Miller tried to convince them to stay a little longer and sing a few more carols. Only one soldier, Private First Class Richard Mathews, of Los Molinos, California, insisted on returning below. That decision would shortly cost him his life.

Private Earl Jacobs was only eighteen years old. The *Leopoldville* was carrying him farther from his York, Pennsylvania, home than he had ever been before. While his friends slept far below deck, Jacobs, excited to be on such a big ship, awoke from his sleep and decided to go topside and gaze at the approaching French coast. Two soldiers had made simple, seemingly insignificant judgments. Yet, for one of those soldiers, the path chosen was life, and for the other—death.

Private First Class Frank Haugh, the youth with poor vision in his right eye, whose Medical Discharge had been waived so that he could serve in the Army, but excluded from overseas duty and combat zones, nevertheless found himself on Christmas Eve of 1944 crossing the English Channel aboard the *Leopoldville*. Even as a child, he was never fond of the water and therefore never learned to swim. "I get seasick riding a merrygo-round," he would say, "so you can imagine how I am on a boat." As the troopship crossed the Channel, Haugh, to avoid seasickness, lay on his back with his eyes closed and fell into a deep sleep.

The *Leopoldville* had fourteen lifeboats that were supposed to be capable of holding 799 passengers. Floats lashed by cables to the open decks were designed to carry an additional 2,635 men.

Having crossed the Atlantic with the U.S. Navy, Lieutenant Bill Everhard and the rest of the troops and crew participated in daily boat drills, with lifeboats were turned out and ready to lower. But as the *Leopoldville* crossed the Channel, Lieutenant Everhard wondered why the lifeboats were inboard and why no lifeboat, fire, or abandon ship drills were held. Despite the fact that the ship had upwards of 6 hours after completing loading and before reaching the Channel waters. He was further concerned because the soldiers were not instructed how to lower the lifeboats or free the rafts. They were told that was the job of the crew. The 2,625 life jackets carried aboard the ship were issued haphazardly if at all. At about 3:30 PM three sonar contacts were made that resulted in depth charge attacks by the escorting vessels, yet no instruction was given the soldiers on how to fasten life jackets.

When the depth charges were dropped, Lieutenant Rehder, along with other officers, was eating his dinner in a small square room directly beneath the pilot house. The room had glass windows on both sides providing a partial view of the Channel waters. When the depth charges exploded Lieutenant George Rehder would say, "It was as if the floor was moving under us, and almost immediately there was a low rumble that surrounded the ship. It seemed to come through the walls and the floors and entered our ears as if it came up our spines. It was a very low-toned boom. It seemed to come from outside the ship, like a thunderstorm that was gathering in the distance."

Looking out of the windows, Lieutenant Rehder could see in the distance the British destroyers plowing through the waves at full speed, as large fountains of water billowed up behind them. The force of the exploding depth charges rattled the dishes on the table as everything in the room shook. The officers watched the destroyers lay their pattern of charges, but without success, and eventually the explosions ceased. After dinner, Lieutenant Rehder went below deck to the fourth level, where his men were quartered. He checked their condition and found most of them sprawled out asleep on the wooden deck floor. A few men who were unable to rest talked nervously while seven or eight were deeply engrossed in a poker game on an Army blanket that they had spread out. Satisfied that all was in order, Lieutenant Rehder worked his way through the dimly lit compartment and up the steep stairway to his cabin. Finding that two of the officers who shared the room with him had gone out on deck, he removed his helmet and shoes and lay down on an available bunk. Shortly, Lieutenant Rehder lapsed into a deep sleep.

Private Alfred Corti of Harrison, New York, was married and the father of two children—Marilyn, five, and Richard, three. At thirty-three years of age he was one of the oldest soldiers with the 66thDivision. Still suffering from seasickness, Corti found a stack of life jackets and laid them on the floor trying to make as comfortable a bed as possible. Meanwhile, Lieutenant Rehder enjoyed the luxury of his own cabin and bunk. The one comfort that the Private and the Lieutenant shared was that both were slumbering soundly before long.

Unknown to the sleeping Private Alfred Corti and Lieutenant George Rehder, just the day before, the coastal vessel *Shemish* was torpedoed and sunk as it approached Cherbourg harbor.

The German U-boat 486 was a VIIC, the most common type. A new submarine from the shipyards of Kiel, Germany, it had been launched on time in mid-February 1944, despite an air raid a week before its completion when a force of Halifax bombers laid mines in Kiel Bay. First Lieutenant Gerhard Meyer, of the class of 1935, became the U-boat commander. After training trials, the *U-486* left Kiel on its initial cruise on November 6. The submarine arrived at Oslo Fjord, Norway, and the base at Horten on November 9. The next 8 days were used to test the snorkel equipment. Then the submarine proceeded around the coast to Bergen, stopping at Kristiansand, Norway, along the way.

Finally, the U-boat set out on its first war patrol—its destination, the English Channel. The submarine was routed down the west coast of Ireland because a mine field had been laid from the south of Ireland to the Cornish coast. On this last Christmas Eve of the war, the *Leopoldville* neared the completion of yet another transport assignment without incident. The troopship was 5 miles from the entrance to Cherbourg harbor, as the *U-486* sliced through the water, periscope up, stalking the approaching *Leopoldville*. At the command of Lieutenant Gerhard Meyer, a salvo of torpedoes was fired from the *U-486*.

Chapter 2

To Live or Die

"Let there be enough room for me to get through."
. . . William Kalinowski

At Cherbourg, the allies had control of the air and there was
no fear of enemy bombing. Troops on the deck of the *Leopoldville*
watched as the first lights of the Normandy coast appeared. Soon
the friendly lights spread their warm glow up and down the rapidly
approaching shoreline. Soldiers accustomed to blackouts sang out
with enthusiastic shouts of joy, and rumors swept like a crashing
wave over the troops that the war's end must have been declared.

Aboard the *Cheshire*, Edward Haas found it to be "overcrowded,
dirty, and smelly." Haas therefore spent as much time as possible on
the open decks in the fresh air. He had no reason to think that life
aboard the *Leopoldville* was any better. He could see the *Leopoldville*
and the other ships in the convoy all around the *Cheshire* and felt
secure and in good hands. As darkness approached, he occasionally
heard what he believed were precautionary depth charges being
detonated. Recalling that night, Haas would say, "We were glad that
somebody was looking after us."9

Perhaps Haas would not have felt so assured if he had been
aware that a coastal ship was sunk outside the harbor just the day
before. Although the visibility was good, there was no antisubmarine
reconnaissance in conjunction with the convoy. Even more distressing,
Convoy Commander John Pringle did not know the exact number
of men he was escorting across the Channel.

Later, during the British Board of Inquiry into the sinking of
the *Leopoldville,* Pringle was asked if his sailing orders contained

information as to the number of troops aboard the *Cheshire* and the
Leopoldville. He replied he did not know because the sailing orders
were given in the form of signals. The Board pressed him, "Did it
occur to you on forming the convoy to ask the two transports what
they were carrying?" "No sir," was Pringle's reply, "but that has been
done ever since, sir."

Lieutenant Robert M. Wurdeman, who then resided in
Minneapolis, walked along the starboard rail of the *Leopoldville*'s
outer deck. He had just completed his watch in the hold. The skies
were darkening, but he could still see the other ships in the convoy.
He was almost midship when he was alarmed by a cry from the
crow's nest. "Torpedo to starboard!", shouted the sailor high above.
"Torpedo to starboard!"

Lieutenant Wurdeman leaned over the rail and gasped at the
sight of the slender, silver-colored missile some 50 feet away streaking
toward the boat. Behind the torpedo a long white wake extended
about 200 yards. Wurdeman clutched the rail and braced himself
for the shock. When it hit, the ship shook from stem to stern and
Wurdeman looked on in disbelief at the debris and bodies that were
hurled high into the air. Quickly regaining his composure, Lieutenant
Wurdeman raced toward his compartment from which could be
heard the cries of his men.

Staff Sergeant Donald Gengler, of St. Louis, Missouri, was
quartered in a crammed compartment below deck. It was so crowded
that the young soldiers straddled benches in order to rest. After
spending most of the day in the compartment, Gengler went topside
for some fresh air. It was windy and chilly but better than being down
in the compartment. Suddenly, there was a huge explosion, and
Gengler was thrown into the air. At first he thought the boiler had
blown up. He watched the debris flying up over the ship, ran down
to his squad, and guided his men out.

Eighteen-year-old Private Ralph Drew, from Midlothian, Maryland,
was playing penny ante with several fellows when Private Robert E.
Hawkins, Company I, 262nd Regiment, approached him and asked
him to join in a Christmas prayer. Bob Hawkins, also eighteen years
old, of Frostburg, Maryland, was known as a religious young man,
who planned to enter the ministry at the end of the war. Drew told
him he intended to play cards a little while longer, and Hawkins
returned to his quarters on the deck below toward the back of the

ship. Approximately 15 minutes later, the torpedo struck the ship in the area where Private Robert E. Hawkins was housed.[10] Said Ralph Drew later, "I doubt if anyone in that part of the ship knew what hit him."

Sergeant Bill Cline, who ended up on the troopship because his company moved out without him, had just gone outside on the starboard side of the ship because, as he recalled, "I was sick as hell." The explosion threw him against the bulkhead, causing a gash in his head and knocking him unconscious. When he came to, he discovered that someone had placed a coat over him. Said Cline, "I was still throwing up, but finally was able to stand."

Shortly after the *Leopoldville* left port, Private First Class Keith Simons met Private William D. Donaldson, of Grand Junction, Colorado. The two youths, both from Colorado, quickly discovered they had much in common and the conversation turned to fishing, hunting, camping, and how much they wanted to return home when the war was over. Quartered below decks, the two soldiers gathered up life preservers, which they used as mattresses under one of the tables and fell asleep.

The thunderous explosion slammed them upward, awakening them with a jolt. Said Simons, "My first impulse was to look around and see if any water was coming in. When it wasn't, I was extremely relieved." Simons and Donaldson handed out the life preservers that had served as their mattresses and then walked to the bow of the ship with several of their buddies to escape the crush of soldiers who mobbed emergency stations on the troopship's side.[11]One of those in the group with Simons, Sergeant Carl H. Miller of Los Angeles, California, who Simons described as a, "small but salty sergeant," was another soldier who made doubly sure that everyone had a life preserver.[12]

One of Simons' buddies in the group was Fred Schlerf, of Newark, New Jersey. Said Simons of him, "Fred, an ammunition bearer for my mortar, one of the best soldiers I ever knew, was quite hunchbacked. How he ever got into the Infantry I will never know. Yet, he never failed to do his job, and much more cheerfully than many of us."

As the ship listed precariously, Schlerf anxiously said to Simons, "You think we're going to make it, Sy?" "You're damn right we're going to make it; you know we are!," Keith Simons fired back as he slapped him good-naturedly on the shoulder. With this reassurance,

Fred Schlerf grinned silently at his friend Keith Simons and turned back to his spot at the rail.

Another young soldier in the group, Jack Randles, a redheaded, clean-living lad from Tennessee, blurted out to Simons, "I don't even know how to swim, Sy." Standing by the rail, using arm motions, Simons taught Jack Randles the basic dog paddle and reassured him that his life preserver would keep him afloat.

Sergeant Jerry Crean, the young football coach from New Jersey, heard a loud bang. He then felt the whole ship rumble. From that moment, all of his actions were dictated by his Army training. He had one thought—"Take care of your men." Crean gathered his platoon together and got them up on deck only to discover that about half of them had no life jackets. Without any hesitation, Crean went back below to search for the vests. The water in the compartment was already hip deep, but Crean searched until he found enough life jackets for all of his men.

Colonel Rumburg heard a soldier pleading for help from the deck below him. He called for ropes while he flashed his light down into the churning water approximately four to eight feet below. The water rose rapidly as it washed through the hole made by the torpedo. Rumberg tied a rope about his waist and was lowered through the jagged edges of the hole and dropped through the debris into the water. He swam as best as he could in search of the trapped soldier. While probing through the sharp pieces of debris a timber fell across his hand cutting off two of his fingers. Disregarding his own injury, he continued looking until he located the frightened soldier. He dragged the injured man to a position below their escape hole. The rushing water however, washed him and the soldier up to within a foot of the opening, causing the soldier to strike his head against a ragged piece of bulkhead, knocking him unconscious. Exhausted, Col. Rumburg could no longer hold the soldier's dead weight and the man slipped from his grip and was washed away. Rumburg again tried to find him but was too numb to sustain himself, let alone try to assist anyone else. After six to eight attempts, the soldiers above him finally lifted Rumburg from the water. The colonel was quickly taken to the infirmary to receive medical attention. Despite the loss of blood and his two fingers, Col. Rumberg was later observed several times carrying different soldiers to safety.

o o o

Sergeant George Chun Fat had sacked out under a mess table in his compartment, which was situated just below the main deck. Most of his men were asleep, but he found it difficult to rest with the loud humming noise of the troopship's engines. Suddenly, he was deafened by the exploding blast of the torpedo as it struck the ship. The boat shook violently and then appeared to stop. The table under which Sergeant Chun Fat had attempted to rest faced the entrance to the compartment and the stairway leading to the main deck. Debris blew in through the compartment's entranceway and covered the table under which Sergeant Chun Fat lay.

Unhurt, Sergeant Chun Fat could hear the moans and cries of soldiers from the compartments beneath him. He cleared away the debris and climbed atop the mess table shouting as loudly as he could for everyone to remain calm. Years afterward, Guy Sawyer would write of his Company Commander Captain Jack Gangwere, and Platoon leader Sergeant George Chun Fat, "With heartfelt thanks to these capable leaders, we were able to stay calm and not panic during this terrible time."

Sergeant Chun Fat looked up and saw a hole in the deck above him through which could be seen the sky. He gave the order for his men to climb up through the hole. One soldier held a flashlight, and Sergeant Chun Fat ordered the man to turn the light on him so he could better direct the escape of the men from the compartment.

A few of the men followed Sergeant Chun Fat to the compartment's doorway. There, by the entrance, a soldier's body lay facedown in the water. The stairs were blown away, but ropes were hanging down from the deck above. Sergeant Chun Fat jumped on a ledge, about 1 foot wide, that ran around the entranceway wall. He turned to help others climb on the ledge, but everyone had escaped through the ceiling hole in the compartment. When he reached the deck above, about a dozen of his men were waiting for him.

The men proceeded to their assigned distress area, but no one was there, as that was the location where the torpedo had hit. The group therefore made its way to midship and stood there waiting for further orders. After a period of time, an officer told Sergeant Chun Fat to follow him to the upper deck where all the lifeboats were secured.

The officer ordered him into a lifeboat, and the boat was lowered as men pushed the oars against the ship's hull. When the boat hit the water, one end stuck fast. A soldier removed his trenching shovel from his cartridge belt and hacked at the rope that prevented the boat from moving, until it finally broke loose.

Following the explosion, Private First Class Romeo Mitri, Company I, 264th Regiment, ran along silently with the other men in his company up the stairs, where they lined up on deck at their assigned location. He heard no orders about what to do and received no information regarding what was happening. The men with him never thought the Leopoldville might be sinking, and when someone started singing Christmas carols they all joined in. However, they did become alarmed when they saw the lifeboats filled with crewmen being lowered into the water.

When the torpedo struck, Mess Sergeant Al Via was knocked from his hammock and slammed against a mess hall table anchored to the floor, cracking several of his ribs. The intense pain made breathing difficult, but Via, along with his second cook Charley, made his way to the top deck. Once there, the two soldiers helped carry wounded men to the station where first aid was administered.

Unlike Al Via, who was thrown from his hammock, Frank Haugh was in such a deep sleep that not even the thunderous explosion woke him. Finally, someone roused him from his coma-like slumber and shouted, "Get with it. We've been hit!"

Haugh had been sleeping in his hammock with his shoes on, but with the exception of his overcoat, he left the rest of his equipment behind and headed topside. Once on deck, he discarded his overcoat. He preferred the cold to being weighted down, should he have to go into the water. Although he was very frightened, Frank Haugh was a deeply religious man and was certain that his faith would see him through the crisis. "I already had an intimate knowledge of God, and his Son, Jesus. I thought how strange it was that when I was facing the greatest test of my life, it should occur on the eve of the celebration of His birth. This led me to silently pray that He would provide the thought process and the way out of this situation. From then on I had no question in my mind that I was going to get through this situation safely, even if I did not know how at the moment."

Second Lieutenant William B. "Bernie" Clements, assigned to an Engineering Unit, was one of the 66th Division members that fate smiled upon. Just before boarding the *Leopoldville*, it was decided that he, like Jack Chvat, would make the Channel crossing aboard an LST with the trucks and other equipment. Clements, of Dover, Delaware, remembered years later, "I was sitting in my truck, taking a bit of rest when . . . Ka-Boom!" The LST's position in the convoy was about one-quarter of a mile from the *Leopoldville*, and as Clements looked toward the direction of the explosion it was obvious that the troopship had been hit.

Aboard the *Cheshire*, it seemed to Edward Haas that the *Leopoldville* had slowed down. Black smoke could be seen coming from its stack, but that did not seem unusual to him. Eventually, the *Cheshire* passed the *Leopoldville* at a distance of about1 mile. Remembered Haas, "At no time was I, or anyone else I know of, aware of any foul play; we just assumed that someone who knew what he was doing had decided that the *Cheshire* should enter the port first."

From his position on the *Cheshire*, Ernest Schnaible heard the torpedo explosion. "At the time we really didn't know what was going on." Reflecting on the tragedy many years later, Schnaible noted sadly, "Now I think about it often. I lost a lot of friends."

As George Miller and his comrades continued to sing Christmas carols, Richard Mathews headed for warmth below deck. He was halfway down the hatchway stairs when there was a loud explosion and the hatch cover was blown into the air. Said Miller, "The torpedo that shook the entire ship had hit just below the water line in the compartment where my Weapons Platoon was billeted. The explosion killed most of my buddies immediately. I was one of the lucky few from the entire platoon to survive, and the only survivor of my squad."

Captain John C. Van Sickle, Company K, 262nd Regiment, was in his quarters when he heard and felt a thud. He did not hear an explosion, but upon investigating, learned that the troopship had been torpedoed. He assembled and accounted for all of the men in his company, some of whom were drenched. Captain Van Sickle made sure that his men were issued life jackets and obtained blankets for the men who were wet. Because the boat was listing to port and having received no orders or information, he moved his company to the starboard side of the ship on his own initiative.

Second Lieutenant Henry Lawrence Balboni, Company E, 264th Regiment, was resting in his assigned stateroom with several others when the ship shuddered and became quiet. Immediately, the three rifle platoons of Company E went to their preassigned emergency stations. Said Lieutenant Balboni, "There was no sign of panic or even trepidation. The order banning smoking on deck was enforced because night had fallen. This caused some sarcastic comments because the emergency deck lights had been lit and shone down brightly on the troops on deck."

At about 5 PM, wearing only his regular uniform and a field jacket, Private William E. Boggs walked around the deck several times before starting back to his compartment for some warmer clothing. He got halfway to his quarters when the stench hit him. Boggs bolted for the rail. After a few more attempts to reach his compartment, Boggs gave up. He preferred being cold than confronting the stench from below! Boggs went back as far as he could on the starboard side of D deck, which was the lowest open deck. He stood behind a steel bulkhead, talking to some other GIs and saw the torpedo hit. Said Boggs, "We just stood there and watched the explosion. It seemed very slow. It was about 50 feet aft of our position . . . First, a bubble of black force came out. This turned to smoke, and through it erupted large pieces of debris." Continued Boggs, "Next, the rivets started sailing around making noises like rifle bullets. Only then did we move! We all turned and ran . . . to our abandon ship stations."

Although the men had been assigned abandon ship stations when the voyage began, Boggs did not remember any additional instructions regarding fire or lifeboat procedures.

Tom Schottelkotte, of Springfield Township, Ohio, was below deck lying on a bench. His compartment was below the waterline near the middle of the ship. He heard a "huge metallic bang" that rocked the ship and knocked him off of his bench.

The lights went out. He had no idea what happened, only that it was serious. Said Schottelkotte 50 years later, "We knew it wasn't good. Everything was so scrambled. Some of the guys were saying, 'We've had it.'"

Schottelkotte and the others rushed to the stairs and climbed up on deck. Once there, they fanned out in the pitch blackness. In the distance they could see a string of white lights stretching for a mile or two along the French shore. The lights were from Cherbourg, a safe haven that many would never reach that night.

Private First Class Allen T. Parker, Company C, 264th Regiment, was asleep when the violent explosion threw him from his hammock to the table below. Said Parker, "I was sleeping next to our Platoon Leader, Sergeant Homer T. Glanton.[13] He called to all the men to be sure to get their life jackets. The men showed no signs of panic and started leaving the compartment in an orderly fashion even before the alarm was sounded to go on deck." Continued Parker, "About a minute after we were hit, the lights went out, but the blue lights marking the gangway continued to burn."

When Parker reached the open deck, an officer told him to keep moving so that other men still below would have room to get out. He climbed over some life rafts and proceeded to the bow of the ship. There he met Privates Chace, Malczyk, Coffee, and Babiel, all men from his platoon. None of them seemed concerned, and the ship did not appear to be in any serious trouble as far as they could determine.

Private First Class Alfred Corti was jolted from his deep slumber by a loud explosion that appeared to come from just beneath him. Said Corti, "I must have been blown off the floor because of all the life preservers I had underneath me I could see only one and that was about seven feet away from me."

Corti quickly donned that one preserver and waded through the water, amid the floating bodies of young men who had been blown in all directions. He could hear some men screaming while others shouted orders. Corti made it up the stairs and found himself on the open deck. He would later say, "We prayed that the sub didn't have any more torpedoes because it would have been like taking candy from a baby [to finish us off] with the rest of her shots."[14]

As they waited to be rescued, Robert Banks and Don T. Rose, both from Company I, 262nd Regiment, and both from Chicago, Illinois, stood at the ship's rail and made small talk while cheering each other up. Finally, the ship listed so precariously that they lost their grip on the rail and were separated.

Annette Banks, awakened from her sleep that night because she heard her son crying out to her, prayed, and her prayers were answered. Robert Banks was saved, but Don Rose was not.

Staff Sergeant Frederick Perkins, also of Company I, 262nd Regiment, recalled the strong smell of gunpowder. "We thought that they had gassed us," he said. Perkins was knocked from his hammock, which was near the ceiling, to the floor. The water washed over his combat boots, and after putting on his life preserver, Perkins was one of the soldiers from his company who made it to the deck by climbing the metal stairs.

Once on deck, Perkins reported to his lifeboat station and climbed aboard a lifeboat filled with soldiers. Then unexpectedly, a Belgian officer ordered all of those soldiers not seriously injured out of the boat and proceeded to replace them with Belgian crew members and their belongings.

Private First Class Charles Reynolds spent the crossing, "lying on the floor, sick as a dog." During the afternoon he had managed to briefly stagger topside. Reynolds slept through the explosion. He was in no mood for jokes when his buddy ran up to him hollering, "We're hit! We're hit!" Said Reynolds, "I was so sick, I couldn't care if I went down with the ship." I told him, "Oh, it's just another dry run, but when I tried to stand up, I noticed the ship was listing really badly."

Reynolds followed a line of soldiers to the upper decks where he saw that the British destroyer *Brilliant* had pulled alongside to rescue survivors. Later Commander Pringle would state, "The first man to try and jump fell between the ships and that obviously deterred the remainder, so there was some delay before the stream of men began to come."

Reynolds watched a soldier paralyzed with fear, clutch the railing. Without success, he tried to break the young man's grip. Finally, unable to help the soldier who remained frozen to the rail, Reynolds leaped to the safety of the destroyer's deck. Recalled Reynolds, "Alarms were going off all over. The other destroyer escort was circling us, going Whoop! Whoop! Whoop!, trying to pick up the sub." From aboard the *Brilliant*, Reynolds turned back to a revolting sight, ". . . the gaping hole where the torpedo hit and the bodies sliding into the sea."

Frederick Perkins watched as crewmen aboard the *Brilliant* threw a large rope to the *Leopoldville* and saw it tied fast. But the motion of the rough sea snapped the rope like a piece of twine. The *Brilliant* then pulled alongside the front of the troopship, drifting in and out, as men jumped from the stricken vessel to her deck. When Perkins made his jump, he lost his helmet, which landed on the destroyer's deck and then bounced into the water.

Safely aboard the *Brilliant*, Perkins stood by the ship's rail and told soldiers still aboard the *Leopoldville* when to jump. Recalled Perkins,

"Soldiers' hands were freezing to the bars and the ropes and they couldn't let go. Water was washing over the *Brilliant*'s deck because there were so many people on board. They told us to get down below and then buttoned up the hatches."

Below deck, Perkins and the other survivors were offered hot tea. Later, an announcement was made that the constant bumping of the two vessels had cracked a seam in the *Brilliant*'s forward compartment and they were taking in water. The compartment was closed off, but a second announcement told them, "Don't be alarmed, but we have drifted into one of our mine fields." Recalled Perkins much later, "All we could do was sit there with our hands folded."[15]

Captain Hal Crain met Sergeant Walter T. Brown, of Lynn, Massachusetts, on deck. Sergeant Brown was a 60mm mortar section leader with Company F, 262nd Regiment. Captain Crain ordered him to go below to the compartment where Company F was quartered and check that every man had a life jacket. It was the last time that Brown would see Captain Crain.

After carrying out Captain Crain's order, Sergeant Brown returned to his hammock to catch up on his sleep. He awoke seasick. Ironically, Brown had crossed the Atlantic Ocean without ever being seasick, but on this day he jumped from his hammock and removed the liner from the steel outer shell of his helmet as he raced for the head. He held his helmet in his hands in case he couldn't get to the latrine or the ship's rail in time. In his hurry, Brown left his life jacket in the hammock. He ran as fast as he could up to the next deck where the "head" was located. Brown had exited the compartment where his unit, Company F, was quartered just before the torpedo hit at that exact location! The number 4 hold flooded almost immediately. The after parts of F deck collapsed instantly on top of G deck, and E deck collapsed partially onto F deck, killing and trapping more than 100 troops, including those from Company F, in the compartments below.

When Brown regained consciousness, the helmet liner and the helmet he had held in his hands were both gone. He found himself standing in the latrine with water spraying on him from pipes ruptured by the force of the torpedo. The lights had gone out and he was in complete darkness. Brown felt his way out of the latrine and along a corridor for some distance until he reached the area where the stairway had been.

Brown could see light . . . it was light from the sky. The stairway was gone, but there was sufficient debris hanging down that he was able to climb up onto the deck. Seeing that Brown was soaked, a soldier from Company C gave him his overcoat.

Remembered Brown, "This may seem a little funny, but I told him I would give it back to him when we were ashore." At that time, Walter Brown had no idea of the seriousness of their plight or that he would be one of only five survivors from his platoon.

Staff Sergeant Joseph J. Cycon was a Squad Leader in Company F. He was climbing the staircase and, like Brown, was also on his way to the latrine when the explosion occurred. Cycon was just above C deck midway on the steps when the blast blew out the entire staircase from under him. He fell to the second landing, and when he looked down he could see the water gushing in. The stairs fell over the opening to the hold, and as Cycon attempted to pull away the boards, only about five or six men in the compartment below managed to climb through. At the top of where the staircase had been were three officers. As the water rose rapidly, Cycon threw some ropes up to them and three men were able to climb up using the ropes. Cycon could see his Captain in the compartment below helping his men. He heard screaming and yelling from the compartment until the rising water quelled the desperate cries. Suddenly it was quiet, except for the sound of the inrushing water. Cycon worked his way up to B deck near a lifeboat.

Captain Hal Crain knelt at the top of a ladder, pulling soldiers up onto the deck. As he did so, he asked each man if he had seen anyone from Company F. When no more soldiers emerged, Crain headed down the ladder, without any hesitation, to the compartments below in search of his men. Helped by Sergeant Albert Montagna, of Company L, the two men probed Compartment E-4 without success. Later, Crain was again observed on a ladder, but this time the water was up to his chest and waves were breaking over his head. One soldier who was there as Crain pulled and pushed men to safety would later say, "He was using muscles he absolutely didn't have."

The shock of the terrific blast in the vicinity of the explosion smashed men against the walls of the hold. Steel beams and girders supporting the hull snapped like matchsticks. The lives of those buried under debris were snuffed out as the seawater poured in. Demolished staircases doomed those not already trapped under the rubble, and the cries of the wounded were quickly stilled as the inrushing waters filled the compartments.

One soldier determined not to die was William Kalinowski. Tired after supper, he had decided to nap on the floor near the stairwell in Compartment F-4. His head was propped against a post, and his feet were pointing toward the stairwell. He awoke to find himself immersed in ice-cold water. He was lying on the floor face up in pitch blackness. When he tried to pull himself up and he could not, he realized that something was pinning him down. He pushed with all his might, but he could not free himself. The obstruction that threatened to entomb him was just above his head and shoulders.

Kalinowski inched his way to the left as far as he could, but debris blocked him in. Likewise, exit to the right was blocked. He held his breath as the frigid water swept over him. The water receded just long enough for him to exhale and inhale quickly; he held his breath again. Before him flashed a picture of his family receiving the news of his death, and he expressed sorrow for his sins and resigned himself to the inevitable.

In a last-ditch effort, he stirred from his passive acceptance of death with the realization that he had not attempted to move in the direction in which his feet were pointing. Although it seemed an unlikely escape route, he felt that he had to try.

Kalinowski wiggled himself downward on his back, tighter and tighter, until he could go no further. His body was totally submerged, but as he moved to his left, he reached out with his hand to find open space. He snaked his way through the opening until his shoulder was halfway out. "God," Kalinowski prayed, "let there be enough room for me to get through!"

Kalinowski struggled and finally dragged himself out from under the collapsed wall that had held him fast. He still could not stand, and everything was pitch black. Then he saw a faint light and crawled toward it. The light was coming from where the stairwell had been, but a pile of rubble blocked his escape. Kalinowski squirmed over debris and dead bodies. The head of a dead soldier pressed against him, the matted hair reminding him of a lifeless doll. As he searched desperately for an opening through the rubble, Kalinowski heard moaning, praying, and some cries for help but no yelling or outcries of panic. "Did I get myself out of the last trap only to be caught in this one?" he thought. But the debris that blocked his path was wood, not steel, and he managed to toss a few pieces aside and free himself.

Once in the stairwell, Kalinowski felt a great sense of relief . . . only to be followed by despair. The stairs were gone, and he could not understand how he had escaped, but suddenly there he was on deck facing Sergeant Marman.[16] Shaking like a leaf, Kalinowski got down on his knees and offered a prayer of thanks.

Unable to stop shaking no matter how hard he tried, Kalinowski vowed that he would never sin again—a vow that caused him a great deal of conflict in later life because he took it very seriously.

Bleeding from head wounds, Kalinowski was brought to a medic by Sergeant Marman. The medic took him to the hospital deck and put him to bed. From his bed, Kalinowski looked at the soldier lying next to him. A clamp held the young man's tongue in place so that he would not swallow it, and Kalinowski grimaced in horror when he saw that the soldier had no face.

A short while later the word was given that all of the wounded who were able to walk were to report to the lifeboat station. Kalinowski grabbed his pants and shoes, as someone threw a blanket over his shoulders, and headed toward the lifeboats. Kalinowski would later recall his escape from the dying vessel. "One minute we were dangling 50 feet in the air; the next minute the bottom of the lifeboat was being whacked by a solid wall of water." His mind continued to flash back to the terrorizing incident. "As the wall of water lifted us, we were being clobbered by the heavy block and tackle. Then we got swamped. We finally broke away from the ship, but we had lost our oars and were adrift. I was freezing!"

A rescue boat spotted them and came to their aid. Crewmen threw them a line and took them in tow. The lifeboat, however, kept crashing into the rescue boat's propeller, and the soldiers in the front of the lifeboat were being cut up and were forced to let go of the tow line. The injured survivors from the *Leopoldville* had to make the dangerous jump from the lifeboat to the rescue vessel.

Kalinowski jumped and just managed to grab the boat's rail. A sailor snatched him from death's cold embrace and pulled him aboard. Safely aboard the craft, Kalinowski once again grimaced in horror, this time at the sight of a young man next to him whose pants and scrotum were torn open. He tried to reassure the panic-stricken soldier that his "private parts" were still intact, knowing that the youth would not be able to walk if he thought otherwise. Then Kalinowski was escorted below, and someone covered him with a sheepskin jacket. For the first time since his ordeal began, he felt warm and secure.

Chapter 3

Leap for Life

"Jump, lads, jump! Ye may never have another chance like this!"
. . . An officer aboard the H.M.S. Brilliant

Captain Jack F. Gangwere, Company I, 262nd Regiment, stepped out of his cabin to check the area, when suddenly he felt the *Leopoldville* become very quiet and still. Instinct told him that the ship had been hit. Immediately he thought of his men and went off in search of them. He stopped three soldiers and asked, "What's happened?" but no one knew. Still trying to locate his men, Captain Gangwere walked to the starboard side of the ship only to discover literally hundreds of soldiers crowding the open deck. Fearing that panic might set in because no one was in charge, Gangwere immediately assumed command. Gangwere would later recall, "I passed three officers; all of them were dazed with a starry look in their eyes, gazing out over the water."

When Lieutenant Wurdeman reached the entrance to the hold where his men were quartered, he saw the men streaming from the doorway. He therefore proceeded to his assigned boat station and directed his men to their positions. When it appeared that all of the men were on deck, he had First Sergeant Lutz take roll call. All men were reported present. Braced against the cold North Atlantic wind, a long but calm wait began. From time to time Lieutenant Wurdeman permitted a soldier to return to the hold with a flashlight to hunt for his belongings. The Troop Commander appeared occasionally to reassure the men that ships were coming from Cherbourg to tow them into port. At that time the *Leopoldville* was listing slightly and the majority of the men believed that they were out of danger.

Lieutenant Everhard lay stripped down on his bunk, trying to sleep, when the horrific explosion threw him off the bed. In seconds, an alarm bell began ringing, and he grabbed for his clothes and tried to lace his boots. Two of his cabin mates, already dressed, left the room immediately and headed topside; another soldier fumbled to put his clothes on. Just as Lieutenant Everhard was about to leave the cabin, a loud rumbling roar came from within the ship. The floor of the room pitched and Everhard was thrown onto the deck of the passageway. Behind him the cabin door slammed shut, with his friend still inside!

Water quickly covered the floor and rose rapidly. The trapped officer hollered and struggled vainly to pull the door open. Outside in the hall, Everhard pushed and pounded on the jammed door. He desperately searched for something with which to ram it but found nothing. Everhard beat and kicked at the door with all of his strength, but it still would not budge. He stood in water up to his armpits when the lights in the passageway went dead. "God help me!" he prayed, but realizing he could do no more for his friend, Everhard pulled himself along the ceiling toward the staircase. Alone and as frightened as he had ever been, the water continued to rise. Somehow, Everhard made it to the stairs, and although numb, climbed until he reached the open deck.

Sergeant Angelo Catalano, dreaming of his future with his sweetheart, Beverly Wilson, celebrated his twenty-first birthday on that fateful Christmas Eve. Far from his Brooklyn, New York, home he spent the day topside with his buddies. Late in the afternoon, he proceeded below deck to retrieve some candy that he had purchased in England. While he was below fetching the candy the torpedo hit and Angelo Catalano was never seen again.

Private First Class Paul Plotkin headed for his compartment to retrieve his life jacket but realized the rest of the men were moving in the opposite direction. Plotkin joined them and stood in the line of soldiers waiting their turn to climb the stairs to the top deck. But when his turn came he saw that the stairs had been destroyed by the blast. There was no panic, and the men reached the top deck by climbing up ladders. Paul Plotkin wandered about the top deck in a daze. He could hear the cries of those trapped below. He met the Company Lieutenant, Roddy A. Martin, of Mullins, South Carolina, who gave him his life jacket. Lieutenant Martin would later go down with the ship.

Captain Gangwere sent messengers around the ship several times to see whether they could get any information as to when help would be on the way. But each time, they returned with nothing to report. Remembered Captain Gangwere, "It was now clear to me that no one was in command of the ship or knew what was going to happen." Gangwere stood in front of his men with his back to the water and, bellowing as loudly as he could, called on the men to stay calm and assured them that somehow they would be picked up and saved. Several of his company officers had arrived on the scene, and he directed them to go through the entire group and make sure that each man was wearing a life jacket. Having accomplished that task, all they could do was wait. Captain Gangwere continued to implore his men to remain calm even as the *Leopoldville* listed more and more.

When Private First Class Tom Schottelkotte looked up from the deck, he too saw that the mast was listing. He watched as the British escort destroyer *Brilliant* pulled alongside the *Leopoldville*. He could see the *Brilliant*'s spotlights trained on the troopship's deck, and he leaned over the railing where he saw the huge, jagged hole in the *Leopoldville*'s hull, right at the waterline. "You could drive a pickup truck through that hole," said Schottelkotte. He watched as crewmen from the *Brilliant* threw a line over, growing ever more apprehensive as the two ships heaved wildly in the heavy seas, banging together. The increasingly anxious Schottelkotte, and with three other soldiers stood on the deck and sang Christmas carols as they waited to be rescued.

Captain Hal Crain, like Lieutenant Colonel Rumburg, spent the time that the *Leopoldville* remained afloat working frantically to save others. It was reported that in the end he gave his own life preserver to one of his men.17

Years later, Lieutenant Colonel Dettre wrote of Captain Crain, "At the age of 26 he had achieved his life's ambition to live a soldier's life and to serve with distinction. He left the memory

After 52 years, Captain Crain was posthumously awarded the
Silver Star on May 17, 1997. The medal is on permanent
display at the National Infantry Museum, Ft. Benning, Georgia.

of an unsullied life filled with high ideals, courage, and strength to meet every issue squarely, even to giving his life that others might live."

Walter Blunt spent part of the day wandering the open deck with his closest friend, Private First Class Harold Decell. They paid scant attention to the other ships in the convoy and had little thought of danger from enemy action. They assumed that they would reach France safely in a few hours. The time not spent topside was spent in their compartment talking, reading, playing cards, or trying to catch a little sleep. Blunt lay down on his back using the seat portion of a table while Decell lay down on the floor beneath him. Both soldiers dozed off to sleep.

Walter Blunt would later recall, "I was awakened by a deafening noise so great it is difficult to find words to fully describe its awesomeness." Almost immediately he was engulfed in water in total darkness. As the water buoyed him upward, he felt equipment and objects bumping against him. Said Blunt, "I heard screams and muffled cries as my head surfaced the water. I could taste the oil in the water and smell the stench of gunpowder smoke. I was dazed but aware enough to wonder if I was now doomed to die. I said a short prayer, thinking of my wife and baby."

Walter Blunt never gave up hope and told himself that there must be a way out. Waves continued to break over him and he grew weaker, but during a pause in the breaking of the waves he spotted light piercing through the darkness and headed toward it. The light was a hole through which Blunt pulled himself until he became stuck around the chest and could go no further. Wedged in the hole, with his head and part of his shoulders above the floor, he was unable to move. Waves washed over him, and he held his breath, but each wave held him down longer as the water got deeper. Suddenly, a light was shining down on him and he recognized the voice of his Company Commander, Captain Howard Orr. "Give me your hand, son, you'll be all right." Captain Orr assured him. The Captain pulled as Blunt struggled to free himself. After a few minutes, Captain Orr lifted him from the hole that had held him fast. Blunt would later say, "I never felt more grateful in my life than I did right then."

His face bloodied, his glasses gone, and thinking that his hip was smashed, Private First Class Arthur Winslow still managed to lead Blunt who was in a state of shock through a maze of twisted

Walter Blunt

wreckage and debris to the sick bay. Only slightly aware of what was going on around him, Blunt watched, as if in a dream, medics who scurried about ministering to the various wounds of his comrades. After about half an hour, he was taken to a lifeboat that was being prepared for launching. A soldier in the lifeboat sitting opposite him had a badly smashed knee. The young man, who was in great pain, asked him to hold his leg so that it could not move and intensify his suffering.

As the lifeboat was lowered, the ropes caught on one end, stopping the pulleys and dropping the other end down sharply, leaving the boat dangling at a dangerous angle. One of the Congolese crewmen scrambled up the rope with great agility, hand over hand, until he dropped back onto the deck of the ship. He then released the rope that caused the lifeboat to drop toward the water in a nose dive. Blunt watched as the twelve foot waves reached up to engulf the plunging lifeboat. He thought that the boat would surely go under and sink but as it hit the water, pontoons around the inside of the boat caused it to right itself.

A Coast Guard cutter pulled near them and, after much difficulty because of the rough seas, managed to secure the boats together. Blunt and the others were taken aboard and down to what appeared to be the engine room. Blunt welcomed the warmth generated by the engines but suddenly became quite nauseous. He vomited the oil and seawater he had ingested. Other survivors were coming into the room, including some who were wounded severely.

When they reached shore, the men were removed by ambulance to a hospital in Cherbourg. After undressing in a ward room Blunt discovered that his trousers were torn completely at the seams, probably while he was being pulled through the hole between E and F decks. Many wooden splinters pierced his long underwear and trousers, but Blunt's only visible wound was a small cut on his right index finger.

Walter Blunt apparently had been removed from the ship in one of the only lifeboats that carried GIs. There were sixty-one men from Company L who were injured. Blunt never saw his buddy Harold Decell again. Private First Class Harold Decell and former Oneida Ltd. employee Staff Sergeant Benjamin Joseph Blaskowski were among the seventy-four men from the company who were killed.

When the torpedo hit, like Walter Blunt, Norman Bullett and his buddies were asleep on the same tables they had eaten from just a short time before. The explosion of the torpedo knocked out both of the *Leopoldville*'s engines almost immediately. It was impossible to inspect the damage below decks, as all escape gangways were destroyed. Within half an hour the ship's stern was below water and the ship listed to port. Initially, the remaining ships in the convoy stopped while the *Anthony* and other escorting warships were ordered to search for the submarine by Commander Pringle aboard the *Brilliant.*

With her engines shut off the troopship was drifting and there was danger of the already damaged vessel hitting a mine. At approximately 6:15 PM a signalman standing next to Commander Limbor signaled to Pringle by hand torch that the *Leopoldville* was sinking slowly by the stern. One minute later, Pringle, fearful that the troopship might hit a mine, ordered Limbor to drop anchor. Pringle had solved one problem, but had created another; with the *Leopoldville* anchored and listing, it would later prove impossible to tow the crippled ship to port.

Pringle's next move was to bring the *Brilliant* alongside the troopship's port side, but that was impossible because the crew had already turned the lifeboats out. It was necessary to go around to the starboard side of the *Leopoldville,* causing a 15 minute delay before the *Brilliant* was in position to take on survivors. The wait for additional rescue craft from Cherbourg began. The British Board of Inquiry later criticized Pringle's decision to use the *Brilliant* to take on men. It was the board's determination that by so doing, Pringle as convoy commander, had handicapped himself in directing the hunt for the submarine, obtaining the assistance of ships operating in escort group 2, and properly evaluating the extent and nature of the assistance that could be expected from Cherbourg.

Pringle reported the torpedo assault to Portsmouth Headquarters within two minutes of the attack, but did not signal anyone on the French shore until a half hour after the incident. Incorrectly, he assumed that his message to Portsmouth had been hurriedly relayed to Cherbourg. As a result of bureaucratic delays, Portsmouth Headquarters only received the assistance signal at approximately 6:45 PM and then passed it on to Cherbourg. The Brilliant was transmitting at 2700 kilocycles per second, but the signal was delayed for some 42 minutes because of other traffic. More valuable rescue time had been lost. Tragically, a new radio frequency that could have quickly transmitted the distress signal became operational that very midnight—much too late to save the soldiers aboard the *Leopoldville.*

Remembering that night aboard the *Leopoldville,* Second Lieutenant Henry Balboni, of Norwood, Massachusetts, would later write, "There was no announcement of any kind regarding any action to be taken by the troops. Certainly there was no order to 'Prepare to abandon ship' or 'Abandon ship.' The atmosphere was so relaxed that I finally decided to return to my stateroom to get some personal items. When I returned to the assigned emergency station the whole area where the three platoons of Company E had been were deserted and the H.M.S. *Brilliant* was maneuvering alongside . . . I heard a young British crewman yell, 'Jump you bloody fools—your ship is sinking!'"[18]

Recalled Sergeant Bill Cline, "Some of us were helping the badly injured and the walking wounded move to the side of the ship and board the destroyer. I helped as much as I could . . . there were so many being brought up from the hold below."

Sergeant Al Via and Charley had made a pact to look out for each other. The two soldiers spotted a lifeboat, climbed in, and waited for the crew to lower it down after it was filled. Several minutes passed, when two members of the crew appeared; but instead of filling the boat with soldiers, the crewmen ordered Via and Charley out. Angry, but accustomed to obeying orders, the young soldiers complied. Said Via, "Neither could speak English, but I knew they didn't want us in there. One of them was carrying a briefcase and the other a square box. They got into the boat and prepared to lower it into the Channel—just the two of them.[19]

Meanwhile, the rough sea was making it difficult for the *Brilliant* to remove the troops quickly. Commander Pringle's first attempt to pull alongside the port side of the torpedoed ship was blocked by davits that were out because of earlier launching of lifeboats. He then proceeded to the starboard side only to discover two lifeboats swung out with no crew in sight to haul them back out of the way.

Having been forced out of the lifeboat that was to be their deliverance, Sergeant Via and Charley watched as the *Brilliant* pulled alongside the troopship, creating huge waves. One of the waves ripped the lifeboat from the side of the ship and left it in splinters. Recalled Via, "We saw the sailors hit the water, one face up and the other facedown. Then both floated out of sight." By ordering Via and Charley from the lifeboat and then taking their places, the two dead Belgian crewmen had unwittingly saved the lives of the American soldiers.

With the *Brilliant* alongside the sinking *Leopoldville* and British sailors urging the American soldiers to jump, for about 15 minutes Al Via and Charley watched the successful leaps of some soldiers and the failed leaps of others before making up their minds to attempt the jump themselves. Said Via, "We climbed over the rail and held onto the side as the rough sea moved the destroyer in and out. I wanted Charley to go first to be sure that he made it, but he knew that and insisted that I make the first jump. To this day I can't remember who went first, but we both made it, and afterward we hugged each other like two long-lost brothers."

Private First Class Romeo Mitri, the youth from Cohoes, New York, and his Company I friend Private First Class Orbie Lind, of Lansing, Michigan, decided that they would also make the jump to the *Brilliant*. They watched as some men mistimed their jumps and fell between the two ships. Others grabbed hanging ropes, not realizing that they were not tied to anything, and also plunged to their deaths between the two ships. Mitri and Lind summed up all of their courage, timed their leaps as best they could, and threw themselves outward into space. Both landed safely on the *Brilliant*'s deck.

Crewmen aboard the *Brilliant* continued to call at soldiers to jump from the stricken transport ship, but many that went to the rail thought it too dangerous, as both vessels continued to heave in the swells. Some of the troops refused to jump. The harbor could be seen only a short distance away, and some soldiers preferred to await the arrival of the tugboat that was to tow them to shore.

Private William Boggs had no intention of waiting to be towed to shore. He climbed over the side holding onto a cargo net. The ships were heaving up and down, as much as fifteen feet, in the swells. Boggs hesitated, and just as the destroyer reached the crest and started to drop, he jumped. Boggs landed on his hands and knees and rolled forward into a gun turret. His steel helmet fell off his head and rolled down the deck. Moving on impulse, Boggs chased the helmet, catching it just before it went over the side.[20]

While others hesitated slightly, like Boggs, George Miller—who was alive because he preferred to brave the cold rather than remain in his stuffy compartment—decided to risk the jump. Miller climbed over the railing and placed his feet on the edge of the deck where it extended past the railing. He reached back with his right hand and held the railing for balance. When the *Brilliant* rose toward him on the next wave, he crouched and jumped. Said Miller, "Even though I was weighted down with a heavy army coat, a life jacket, and a steel helmet, I jumped so far that I landed up against the cabin (or bulkhead) of the destroyer."

Miller and others who jumped were ushered below deck where there was about a foot of water. The *Brilliant*'s pumps worked continuously in an attempt to bail out the water coming in through the hull plates, which had been loosened by banging up against the hull of the *Leopoldville*. Continued Miller, "We sat on benches and were offered pea soup, which we ate out of our steel helmets."

As Private First Class Romeo Mitri and Private First Class Orbie Lind had observed, certain death awaited if a poor jump caused a soldier to land in the water between the ships. With the memory still vivid, Richard Dutka would say 50 years later, "As the ships came together the soldiers were flattened like pancakes. There was blood all over the side of the ships. It was awful . . . sickening."

Gus Ferrare also witnessed the tragic failed leaps of soldiers who were then crushed between the two ships. Recalled Ferrare later, "The *Brilliant* was taking a beating. I had worked my way down the nets on the outside of the *Leo*. I was all set to jump when I saw the bodies floating between the ships . . . Sergeant Dan Gallagher had made it safely to the *Brilliant*. He yelled to me that he would tell me when to jump. The sea swells made it very tricky. After a few false starts I jumped. I just managed to grab the top deck railing of the *Brilliant*. If Sergeant Gallagher hadn't pulled me over the railing just seconds before the two ships crashed together, I would have been another floater."

Thomas A. Cobb

With the sight of soldiers falling between the ships still clear in his mind and the sounds of death still ringing in his ears, Keith Simons would record fifty years later, "I can hear their screams as I write."

Tom Schottelkotte watched as a soldier missed his jump and fell between the two ships. For a moment the young man's head bobbed in the water . . . then the two ships came together and the soldier disappeared. Schottelkotte climbed over the railing and hung on the outside, timing his leap as best as he could. The ships came together three or four times. Then summing up all of his courage, as the *Leopoldville* was high in the water and the *Brilliant* was riding a swell to meet it, he jumped! Schottelkotte dropped a good 10 feet and hit the deck hard. Although he landed on his feet, Schottelkotte sprawled forward, head first across the deck. "Nice jump, Yank!" shouted a British naval officer.

Frank Haugh, of Millvale, Pennsylvania, and Thomas A. Cobb, of Ridgewood, New Jersey, waited in the fourth rank for evacuation and were therefore able to observe several mistakes made by those soldiers who jumped ahead of them. Thought Haugh to himself, "God was with me when I had pneumonia, and He was with me as my car spun out of control. Surely, he didn't save me then only to see me die now!"

Frank Haugh and his friend Thomas A. Cobb, who had just turned twenty-two on November 20, stood motionless at the troopship's rail. As the two friends waited their turn to make the leap for life or death, Thomas Cobb believed that he would never again return to the Old Lighthouse, tend to the Dauntless, or ever again romp with his beloved Tannie.

"Frank," said the frightened Cobb, "If anything happens to me, visit my family because I'm not coming back."

"Don't worry about it, I'm going to get off and so are you," Frank Haugh assured his friend.

Haugh noticed which ropes did not break under a soldier's weight. He kept his mind on two or three of them and when his turn came he knew the rope he would choose. "Remember, you don't want to hit the side of the ship. And wait till the ship starts its drop," Haugh instructed Cobb.

"Remember your promise to me. I'm not going to make it," was Cobb's fatalistic reply.

When he stepped to the railing, Haugh let the *Brilliant* rise above him and jumped as it descended. Haugh landed perfectly on the *Brilliant*'s deck, convinced that the same God who had watched over the infant who lay dying of pneumonia and the teenager who skidded toward a head-on collision with a trolley was with him as he leaped from the doomed *Leopoldville*.[21]

When Haugh picked himself up from the *Brilliant*'s deck and looked back, his comrade Thomas Cobb was nowhere in sight nor did he ever see him again. "He must have panicked," Haugh said years later. "He must have been too afraid to do anything. I was too afraid not to."[22]

Like Frank Haugh, Private Lee Potter was a religious man, who served as the Chaplain's Assistant and as organist to his battalion. Tightly holding onto a stanchion, Potter stood on a railing while trying to properly time his leap to safety. A buddy who was next to him jumped just as the two ships moved apart and Potter watched helplessly as the soldier fell between the two hulls and was crushed. Knowing that he had no choice, Potter hurled himself from the rail and landed belly first on the *Brilliant*'s metal deck. The force of hitting the deck knocked him out and although he had no broken bones, he would suffer from painful bruises for weeks afterward.

The red-haired, Second Lieutenant Edwin "Rojo" Aldrich, carrying the Company E, 264th Regiment payroll, in a musette bag, made the perilous leap to the *Brilliant* and saved not only himself but his valuable parcel.

Captain John Van Sickle released those men in Company K who wished to attempt the hazardous leap. Soldiers wearing overcoats, helmets, and life jackets, like Potter's buddy, mistimed their jumps and Private Corlis Holt also watched in horror as several of his comrades fell screaming into the icy waters where they were smashed between the hulls of the two ships that the sea hurled together in deafening throes. Holt knew that he had to make the jump. He climbed up on the rail and waited until the destroyer's deck was at its nearest point and just beginning its downward plunge. From the deck of the destroyer an officer lifted both arms and shouted, "Jump, lads, jump! Ye may never have another chance like this!" The officer's reassurance provided Holt with the conviction that he could do it, and he leaped from the doomed ship to safety.[23]

Chapter 4

Final Moments Aboard the Leopoldville

"This damn thing is gonna sink!"
. . . Jerry Crean

Vincent Codianni lay in his bunk resting while Private First Class Richard F. Sansone of Buffalo, New York, along with some of the other boys, sang Christmas carols. Suddenly there was a big bang, and everything stopped. A sergeant came down from the upper deck and told them to put on their coats, life preservers, cartridge belt, and helmets and report on deck.

When the torpedo struck, Lieutenant "Pete" Wood, of Bethesda, Maryland, was resting in his bunk. The force of the explosion threw him against the ceiling, but he was not hurt. In response to the alarms that sounded, Wood headed for his assigned boat drill station.

Private Raymond Avery was below deck in his hammock when a loud rumble ran through the ship. Avery and the rest of the men in his compartment were told to put on coats and life jackets and proceed to the deck. As the *Leopoldville* jerked about in the choppy seas, like Raymond Avery, few men on deck realized the awful turmoil and human agony that was taking place below. Soldiers stood by quietly waiting for orders and, for the most part, were unafraid and in good spirits. They smoked, as they joked about the delay in reaching Cherbourg. Only when the dismembered and wounded men were brought up in litters, groaning in pain, did the uniformed soldiers fully comprehend their dire situation. They then displayed acts of compassion by giving up their overcoats to those who were suffering from exposure. Others placed blankets around the shoulders of soaked and freezing men who huddled in small groups shivering, as they braced themselves against the cold wind.

About 1,500 yards from the stricken troopship, Vincent Codianni could see ships with spotlights shining on the water and on the *Leopoldville*. Sergeant Elmer A. Baker, of New Bloomfield, Missouri, walked up to Codianni and the small group huddled with him. "Why don't you go to the end of the deck; it's warm there—it's enclosed by glass windows," he suggested. Without any hesitation, the group of about twenty young soldiers, including Private First Class Martin F. Anderson, of San Diego, California, Private First Class Harold H. Dantinne, of Salem, New Jersey, Private James C. Foester, of El Paso, Texas, Private First Class Steven T. Lester, of Pharron, Oklahoma, Private Edgar C. Moore, of Washington, Pennsylvania, Private First Class Richard E. Moser, of Youngstown, Ohio, Private First Class Waldron Mosher Polgreen, of Albany, New York, and Private First Class Richard F. Sansone, of Buffalo, New York, headed for the warmth of the glass-enclosed deck area. Little did the young soldiers know that the glass enclosure that offered them warmth would shortly become their tomb.

Meanwhile, the open decks were crammed with the wounded and the dead. The magnitude of the disaster quickly became apparent, and even the most seriously injured were only provided minimal first aid. Soldiers with broken arms and legs could only be given morphine injections. Recalled Staff Sergeant Joseph C. Luhning, Company L, 262nd Infantry, "I came upon a man who had both of his legs broken and even though it was extremely painful for this soldier to be moved, four of us managed to get him to the ship's hospital."

Open wounds were bandaged hastily to stem the flow of blood, but more extensive medical attention was impossible and was postponed for some time later.

As he stood on the deck, Staff Sergeant Donald Gengler could feel the vibrations and hear the cracking sounds below, which he knew meant that the water pressure inside was breaking up the ship. Lieutenant Bill Everhard arrived at his assigned assembly area on deck but could find no one from his company. Everhard, about midship on the high side, could see that the ship was listing badly to port side,

Richard Sansone   Elmer Baker with Sandra

and he had no doubt that the vessel would sink. During the long wait on deck, some of the men had discarded their life jackets while others searched in vain for some. Everhard spotted a man from his platoon. He was just a young boy who was scared to death. Everhard tried to reassure and comfort him. The young soldier sobbed, "I don't know how to swim." Everhard gave the boy his life jacket. Fifty years later, the memory of the look on the young soldier's face remained vivid to Everhard, but he never saw the frightened young man again. He was among the missing.

Everhard described the soldier as, "a nice kid" and noted that a friend of the youth, Private First Class Carson Kirk, told him, "His mother always set his place at the table for a long time after the war, thinking that someday he would return."

Waiting his turn to make the leap for life to the *Brilliant*, Private Alfred Corti later described the anti-submarine attack he observed from the deck of the sinking troopship. "In the distance, naval ships were dropping ashcans into the water. When an ashcan went off, a huge geyser of water shot upward and when the reverberation and waves hit the *Leopoldville*, our ship would shake like hell. I don't know how many ashcans were dropped but there were a lot of them."

Everhard watched as men jumped to the safety of the *Brilliant* and tried to determine the best moment to attempt their leaps. He told those who would listen to remove their coats and helmets but keep their life jackets. However, dozens of men threw their helmets overboard, and they rained down on those soldiers still alive in the water between the ships. Everhard convinced a few men to stand on the railing and wait for his order to jump. His method worked, and soon more men took their places on the rail. With each successful jump, more soldiers lined up to take their turns. The best moment to jump was when the two ships were at the greatest distance apart and were just beginning to close. Some men hesitated too long before jumping and were lost.

Everhard had plenty of help in organizing the jumpers. The troops were ready and eager to be told what to do. Soon, soldiers were jumping in groups of ten to fifteen men. Aboard the *Brilliant*, crew members lined up at the rail to reach for the men as they landed. Some of them who fell just short of the destroyer's rail were grabbed and pulled to safety.

Everhard watched as several men carried a badly injured, but still conscious, soldier strapped into a stretcher, up to the rail. Patiently, they waited. When the time came, they straddled the rail and threw the stretcher as hard and as far as they could . . . but they missed. As the dark angry waters swallowed up the stretcher, the cries of the helpless soldier were soon silenced. Only the ominous grinding, crunching sounds of the two hulls banging together were heard by those who witnessed, in awe, the doomed soldier's final gasps as the waters of the Channel claimed him.

It was time for Everhard to leave. He leaned forward, let go, and pushed out. He landed on the destroyer's deck, looked back, and, literally sick to his stomach, vomited. What he saw was the upper deck of the *Leopoldville* crawling with hundreds of men. The jump from the upper deck was a distance of twenty-five to thirty feet, and many who made it broke arms and legs in the process. Said Staff Sergeant Bob Hesse of Company D, 264th Regiment, "To me, it seemed like I was jumping off the Empire State Building." Meanwhile, Everhard had picked himself up from the Brilliant's deck and resumed directing soldiers jumping from the doomed vessel.

Lieutenant George Rehder watched as men who missed their jumps thrashed in the water only to have tons of steel squash their bodies like melons as the two ships came together. He made the decision that he would stay with the troopship no matter what.

It was later reported that Captain Limbor had given the order in Flemish and, not understanding, the soldiers stood patiently on deck waiting to be rescued. It should be noted that the Belgian authorities vehemently deny that Flemish was spoken.

Yet many survivors interviewed said that they were not told to abandon ship and, except for taking thirty men on stretchers with them, no attempt was made by the crew to help the soldiers left behind. Although there were enough lifeboats for 799 men, most of the boats were left hanging in their davits, and no effort was made to cut the lashings of life rafts and floater nets that were secured on deck.24

Recalled "Pete" Wood, "When some of the crew started lowering lifeboats, there was cheering from the troops who thought the crewmen were getting the boats ready for us to use, but it stopped when we realized that they were abandoning ship themselves . . . The seas were quite heavy, and even the crewmen had a hard time with the lifeboats. They kept getting the ropes snarled and had trouble lowering the boats to deck level so they could get in. One boat tipped over and spilled the crew into the sea. There didn't appear to be any rescue attempts even for them by their fellow crewmen. They just kept trying to lower more boats."

It has been reported that as the ocean liner *Titanic* sank, the band played, "Nearer Thy God To Thee." As the *Leopoldville* was sinking, according to Pete Wood, an extraordinary event occurred. A soldier standing by the rail watched as the lifeboats pulled away or became entangled and realized that they had been abandoned by the crew and their situation was hopeless. Said Wood, "The soldier started singing "The Star-Spangled Banner." Soon, everyone was singing. It didn't matter that not many knew all the words. I didn't, but I could hardly sing anyway because I kept choking up. I still do, even now, almost fifty years later."

About this time, a man on the deck above pointed down at Wood and bellowed into a megaphone, "Lieutenant, line up your platoon and bring them up to this deck." Wood wasted no time in carrying out the command. Soon, his men had all climbed the ladder to the deck above where they joined a line leading to the area from which soldiers were jumping to the

Brilliant. There was a gap in the railing that permitted one man to jump at a time. Supervising the jump were two friends of Lieutenant Wood's—Lieutenant Ben Thrailkill and Lieutenant George Washko, both from Company K, 264th Infantry. The two lieutenants stood on either side of the gap, and doing their best to judge the movements of the two ships, gave the signal, and sometimes a shove, to each man at precisely the moment when the two decks were at the correct distance for a reasonably safe jump. Both the vertical and horizontal distances had to be considered, which was no easy task, as the distances of the two ships changed constantly.[25]

Most of Wood's platoon got off safely but as far as Wood knows, five did not. Says Lieutenant Wood today, "I never found out what happened to the five who didn't make it. They were presumed drowned when the ship finally went down. My best guess was that somehow they didn't make it to our assigned spot on deck during the boat drill, possibly because of being on kitchen or latrine duty, away from the platoon, when the torpedo hit. I have always regretted not making more of an effort to find out."[26]

When Lieutenant Pete Wood made his leap, he landed on some sort of depth-charge device and turned his ankle. Wrote Wood, years later, "My jump was made a little easier because I had given my life jacket to a man who had left his on his bunk in the hold and said he couldn't swim. I remember being reprimanded by someone for not having mine on, but it was too late to do anything about it; nobody was going back down into the hold to look for one."

At 7:29 PM, with darkness casting a shadow over the scene, the *Brilliant* had safely taken aboard the maximum number of troops, cast off, and steamed toward Cherbourg harbor. Lieutenant Rehder strained his ears to hear a sailor aboard the *Brilliant* who yelled into a megaphone, "We'll be back after we unload. Don't worry, the ship won't sink. We'll pick up the rest of you on the next load."

Later, at the British Board of Inquiry, Pringle was asked if as a result of the signal he received from Commander Limbor he thought the situation aboard the *Leopoldville* was deteriorating. "Yes sir," was Pringle's reply, "but not so serious as it now appears . . . the appearance of the *Leopoldville* herself didn't appear to cause anxiety."

As the *Brilliant* pulled away from the troopship, Pringle described to the Board of Inquiry, "a stream of lights, like a line of traffic," coming from the entrance to Cherbourg harbor. In response to this vivid picture of advancing rescue craft, Pringle was asked if it did not occur to him that the use of a destroyer going alongside the troopship could more expeditiously remove personnel rather than a large number of small craft. "Yes sir," he agreed, but his main concern was still hunting for the submarine. He then noted the difficulty in pulling alongside the *Leopoldville*. But if the larger destroyers struggled to approach the troopship, it seems obvious the task would prove much more difficult and dangerous for the smaller craft that were nearing the scene.

More than thirty small rescue craft eventually searched the area, darkened by nightfall, where hundreds of soldiers floundered in the icy Channel waters. Some of those soldiers who cried out for help were inadvertently run down by the same boats sent to save them. Pringle also told the Board of Inquiry that when he asked Limbor how many troops were on board, he was given the impression that there were 4,000 men. Said Pringle, "That number seemed quite impossible to carter, even with destroyers, and therefore, I immediately hoped that the only real solution was for the tugs to take her in tow and bring her in." But with the troopship anchored, having admitted that the situation was deteriorating, and with most of the crew gone, how could any tug be expected to tow the sinking ship to shore?

Most incomprehensible, however, is that at about the time the *Brilliant* was puling away, Limbor signaled by hand torch, "Imperative that we abandon ship." The Board questioned, "And you know that signal was made because it is now in your log? "No, I am not sure," answered Pringle. "But this was told to me by the Yeoman of Signals when I checked with him afterward. He told me this signal came through just as we were shoving off." "Can you think of any explanation as to why he didn't see that you got that message?" Pringle was asked. "No sir," he replied. The exchange of questions and answers continued. "It seems to have been rather an important one?" "Yes, sir," was Pringle's response. That concluded his testimony, but Pringle elected to remain during the rest of the proceedings. After deliberations, the board concluded that Pringle did not fully obtain the necessary information regarding the condition on board the *Leopoldville* while he was alongside and that he made an error of judgment assuming that the rescue craft from Cherbourg would adequately deal with the situation. The Board noted in its findings, "The fact that he believed there were 4,000 troops on board should, in our opinion, have emphasized the need for action rather than the reverse . . . There were five ships of the First Escort Group in the vicinity, which he might well have summoned to his assistance had he appreciated the situation more correctly."

Private First Class Joe Holl, Company C, 264th Regiment, was seasick, outside a bathroom, when the torpedo hit. The 19 year-old's life jacket was missing, and a friend, Private First Class Bill Foster from Oregon, paused during his own escape attempt to help Holl locate another jacket. The two young men made their way up to the deck where soldiers waited in line for the jump to the *Brilliant*. The British destroyer, however, could take on no more men and pulled away before their turn came.

As the *Leopoldville* was sinking, Holl, weighted down with an overcoat, two shirts, and two pair of pants, plus the life jacket Foster found for him, jumped into the water. He was picked up later. However, Bill Foster did not survive, and Holl reflects with feelings of guilt that if Foster had not stopped to help him, he would have been among the soldiers who jumped aboard the *Brilliant* to safety.

Lieutenant Everhard looked for the last time at desperate men who swarmed down the side of the *Leopoldville* in a vain attempt to board the destroyer before it left. The water was infested with men. Everhard would later say, "Everywhere you looked, you saw men bobbing in the waves calling for help and waving their arms trying to be seen." Everhard was led below by a crewman, where he flopped on the floor, exhausted, next to Captain Raymond Novak, his Company Commanding Officer.

It took 38 minutes for the *Brilliant* to enter the harbor and moor alongside the *Avant Port*. She then required an additional 45 minutes to land the rescued troops. At 7:40 PM, arriving small rescue craft found a scene illuminated only by the light of a half moon and their own lights, which played on the sinking vessel. Crews aboard the small boats could scarcely see through the darkness the troops in overcoats and full packs that stood mustered in perfect order at the rail of the sinking ship. The small crafts removed the soldiers as fast as possible as the escorting warships hunted the sub.

Lieutenant Rehder fumbled through the darkness to his cabin and managed to find his overcoat. Then he felt his way back up the corridor until he reached the deck. It was then that he noticed empty lifeboats hanging on both sides of the ship.

"Why not launch a lifeboat?" he thought to himself. Although he had received no instructions on how to lower a boat, Rehder convinced another lieutenant to help him make the attempt. Rehder called out to groups of soldiers to join them, but only seven men, including the other lieutenant, heeded his words.

After much trial and error, during which time it appeared that the men might tumble into the sea, the lifeboat was finally lowered successfully into the water. Rehder and his crew pushed off from the *Leopoldville*'s metal hull, but without any lifeboat training they simply spun in slow circles at the mercy of the wind and waves. The men did their best to use the 20-foot oars properly, but in Rehder's words, "It looked like a Laurel and Hardy comedy." With each rise and fall of the waves, the lifeboat drifted farther away from the crippled vessel into the darkness of the cold night.

About an hour after the ship was torpedoed, the boilers blew. The resulting explosion knocked out the wooden stairs with such tremendous force that pieces of wood were imbedded into the steel sidewalls of the ship. Recalled Sergeant Frank Sieplinga of Company B, 264th Regiment, ". . . the boiler blew . . . and a tall stack of lifeboats broke loose and slid across the deck, killing many troops that were in its path."

Said Lieutenant Robert Wurdeman, "The deck beneath our feet began to list more and more to port. We knew than that the ship would sink, and we all waited for the order to abandon ship . . . We never received that order."

After helping many men jump to the *Brilliant,* Sergeant Bill Cline walked to the bow and contemplated his next move. Said Cline, "We were listing badly, and I knew by then that the ship would sink. I ended up in the water, sliding down a rope and scared as hell because the water was rough and bitter cold."

A short time after the *Brilliant* left, another ship from the Port of Cherbourg arrived. It was a U.S. Navy sea-going rescue tug, the *ATR-3*. The auxiliary tug/rescue ship was 160 feet long and had a wooden hull to prevent the attraction of magnetic mines. The *ATR-3* had seen duty during the Normandy Invasion, pulling landing craft from Utah and Omaha beaches. The tug also towed disabled ships and the "Mulberry" artificial harbor units prior to and during the assault. The Mulberry units formed a breakwater protection from the two beaches. On the night of June 5, 1944, the *ATR-3* anchored off Utah Beach, along with the heavy towing rigs. Aboard were divers and fire-fighting provisions. The tug was armed with only two 20mm gun placements and a 3-inch 50mm main battery. Recalled Gunner's Mate 2nd class, Richard E. Freeburg years later, "The skipper told us, 'Well boys, we're on the fifty yard line of the biggest invasion ofthe war and we are expendable.'"

Despite the hazardous duty of freeing ships that had become grounded at low tide on both Utah and Omaha beaches, the *ATR-3* and its crew survived that momentous battle.

Late that Christmas Eve afternoon, RM1C Hugh T. Jones was standing watch in the tug's radio room monitoring the ship to-shore radio and the shore frequency at Cherbourg. He heard radio traffic between the approaching convoy and Naval Headquarters in Cherbourg. He listened to a report that a small boat had deposited American soldiers at the harbor landing and left without any communication. A member of the Shore Patrol asked the landed soldiers where they had come from. The soldiers responded that they were from the torpedoed *Leopoldville.* One of the rescued men remembered seeing a buoy near the ship but none on the trip to shore.

The buoy the soldier saw was Buoy H, 5 miles out of Cherbourg. Hugh Jones immediately sent a messenger to bring the captain of the *ATR-3* to the radio room. Captain Lewandowski arrived soon afterward and was apprised of the situation. All radio traffic on the frequency was copied into the communication log. An officer was heard dispatching three 83000 series U.S. Coast Guard Patrol boats to head to the area and investigate. When the fast-moving patrol craft reached the position, they reported back that an anchored troopship loaded with American soldiers had indeed been torpedoed.

Captain Lewandowski sprang into action. He ordered the fire room to light the other boiler and prepare to get under way. Although the tug still did not have sufficient steam pressure, Lewandowski nevertheless gave the order to weigh anchor and depart. Even as the craft headed toward Buoy H, the *ATR-3* received official Shore Headquarters orders to move out as soon as possible. The Captain replied that they were already proceeding to the scene at top speed (12 knots). It took them 45 minutes to reach the stricken *Leopoldville.*

Sergeant Walter Brown thought that it might be a tug, but whatever it was, it flew the American flag from its bow and . . ."It was a welcome sight," said Brown. As the vessel pulled alongside, a lifeboat containing about six people came between the tug and the sinking troopship.[27] Hugh Jones was on the bridge of the *ATR-3* with Captain Lewandowski. Using a Bogen 80 watt" bullhorn," the Captain yelled, "Get that damn boat out of the way." The Captain's order was ignored.

Sergeant Brown could see that the water was seeping rapidly onto the deck of the *Leopoldville* and the stern was below the surface. Like Captain Lewandowski, Brown and the other men awaiting rescue on the deck yelled at those in the lifeboat to pull away. As they did so, the lifeboat came broadside to the tug, and it almost capsized. As the bow of the tug moved into it, the lifeboat rolled around the other side of the rescue tug and righted itself.

The tug came alongside the *Leopoldville,* but another fifteen to twenty minutes was wasted before Sergeant Brown was finally able to catch a line thrown from the *ATR-3* and secure it to the troopship. The water was creeping farther up on deck, and Brown knew if he was going to get off, the time was now. Sergeant Brown climbed over the railing. Although his arms were not in the sleeves, the overcoat that the unknown soldier had given him still covered his wet shoulders. Brown listened to the *Leopoldville*'s creaking, cracking, and shuddering while he timed the rise and fall of the rescue tug. When he felt that the tug was almost on the crest of a wave, he threw the overcoat backward and jumped toward the ship that would be his salvation.

Brown reached the gunwale, and two sailors took hold of him and pulled him aboard. When he reached the rescue tug's deck, he fell. After getting to his feet, Sergeant Brown looked over the side just in time to see a giant whirlpool of water, and through its center a lifeboat shot up and floated bottom up.

Twenty-one-year old Gunner's Mate Richard Freeburg, known as "the Swede" by his shipmates, gripped one of the tug's rope ladders and assisted men out of the water and onto the vessel's deck. One of those pulled from the Channel was Sergeant Bill Cline. Recalled Freeburg many years later, "The tug's floodlights were trained on the *Leopoldville*. Men were yelling and screaming in the water. It was really chaos." Freeburg witnessed the sight of soldiers being crushed and drowned. "You couldn't do a thing," he would later say. Then he added with disgust, "If the *Leopoldville* hadn't dropped anchor, the *ATR-3* could have towed it to shore."[28]

Hugh Jones watched as soldiers who had jumped into the water were pulled out by the crew of the *ATR-3*. Jones saw one soldier go under for the third time when a carpenter's mate grabbed him by the hair and yanked him out of the water just as the rubbing strake of the *ATR-3* hit the side of the *Leopoldville*. Said Hugh Jones, "If the carpenter's mate hadn't given that extra effort, the man would have been crushed to death. They took him in to the mess deck and pumped the water out of him and he came around and lived."

The tug's cooks made hot soup, which they distributed to the shivering survivors. One of the cooks even jumped into the 48-degree water and saved a soldier's life. It was when the rescued men were taken to the engine room and given tomato juice that Sergeant Walter Brown and Sergeant Bill Cline met for the first time. From their experience aboard the *Leopoldville*, they developed a friendship that has remained intact to this day. The two friends later learned that what they thought was tomato juice was actually just ketchup and water. When told about the makeshift drink, Bill Cline said, "At the time it was tomato juice, and no one could have told us it wasn't."

Hugh Jones watched a soldier walking through the debris on the *Leopoldville,* carrying his buddy on his shoulders. The unconscious soldier was transferred to the tug, and then his buddy made the jump. The tug's crew asked, "What happened?" Replied the rescuer of the unconscious soldier, "I knocked him out! I told him the ship was sinking. He said it wasn't sinking and he wasn't going to leave. We were standing in water over our knees. When the torpedo hit, the ladders collapsed. Later someone threw down a rope ladder. So I hit him and had a hell of a time getting him up that ladder."

"Johnny," the *ATR-3*'s Chief Machinist Mate, was helping men out of the water. As he prepared to release a life raft so that they would have extra lines to hold onto, he yelled, "Move away!" The men in the water complied. But as Johnny released the life raft, an anxious soldier swam into the immediate area and the pointed bow of the life raft killed him instantly.

Captain Lewandowski kept close watch on how fast the troopship was sinking. Up on the *Leopoldville*'s bow, about 100 men were standing at attention. The Captain gave orders to them to start climbing down the cargo nets on the *Leopoldville*'s side into the water. No one moved. The Captain continued to shout as the *Leopoldville* listed badly to port. The troopship was about to sink. From the ship's bow, a soldier calmly cast off the *ATR-3*'s line. The tug carefully backed away so as not to run over the men climbing down the cargo nets into the water.

As men were pulled from the water they were asked if they had come from the bow. Many said that they had. "Why didn't you climb down as the Captain ordered?" asked Jones' crewmates. Replied an angry soldier named Jim, "There was an American Army officer with a gun, and he said the ship was not sinking, and that he was in charge and would shoot any man that made a move to go over the side."

Cold, wet, soggy clothes were removed from the rescued soldiers, and the crew of the *ATR-3* freely gave up some of their own dry clothing to the freezing men. The crew's quarters were transformed into a sick bay. Said Hugh Jones sadly, "We could have rescued all of the men that were standing on the bow if they had obeyed Captain Lewandowski's order and gotten into the water and swam around to our starboard side. As the *Leopoldville* was going down, it caused a great suction, which pulled the men under. Many drowned. Of those that were on the bow, only a few survived. It was believed that the officer who held the men back was one of those who drowned . . . We took on a total of sixty-nine survivors that night . . . and it would have been many more if they had obeyed the Captain's orders."

Another boat that participated in the rescue effort was *Patrol Craft 564*. The complement for a PC is 60 to 70 men, including five officers. Recalled Wes Johnson, of Indianapolis, Indiana, "The

Leopoldville was huge when compared with the much smaller rescue vessels attempting to come alongside her, which was a most difficult task, because of the extremely rough water in the open sea. The very high waves caused a noisy grating and banging between the ships, with deck levels changing precipitously to as much as 10 to 20 feet constantly, and the space between them opening 15 to 25 feet without notice . . . it was scary. These conditions were a challenge to seamanship."

Tied up at a pier in Cherbourg, *PT 461* had taken on fuel during the day. Normally operating with a crew of nine to eleven sailors, on this festive Christmas Eve, only three men, including Lieutenant Sydney Garner, of Gary, Indiana, were on board.

Syd was lost in his thoughts about his wife Sally and baby Susan when someone called out, "The duty shack up above reports there's big trouble at No. 9 and No. 10 buoys." As *PT 461* sped away from the pier, Syd Garner thought to himself, "How the hell can we help with just three men!"

Approaching the crippled *Leopoldville*, Lieutenant Garner and the two sailors with him found the area lit up like a Christmas tree by searchlights from all types of boats that had already arrived. Garner was shocked to see hundreds of men in the water and hundreds more on the troopship's deck waiting to be rescued. Recalled Garner later, "You had everybody in the world out there, trying to do something but screwing up." Lieutenant Garner maneuvered *PT 461* as close as possible to the sinking troopship while keeping far enough away to avoid getting caught in the *Leopoldville*'s rigging.

He cut all of the rescue boat's engines except for one to prevent the boat's propellers from cutting the men who floundered in the water. Said Garner, "There is nothing worse than that sound—Plumph! You knew you hit a guy." Lieutenant Garner had one man steer the craft while he and the other sailor threw lines to the men in the water. The lines were then pulled back until the men could be dragged on board. Garner particularly remembered one youth who shouted to his rescuers to take care of others first. The soldier was hanging onto a line right under the craft's exhaust stacks. Garner was concerned that the young man might die from the exhaust fumes before he made it aboard, but eventually he was pulled to safety from the water.

On deck, the rescued men were stripped of their wet clothing, given blankets in which to wrap themselves, handed small bottles of liquor, and sent below. When *PT 461* finally headed for port, she had rescued 15 to 18 men. Said Syd Garner, "If we could've done anything more, we would've stayed out there, but we had people below who needed medical attention."

The next day, Garner noticed an Army officer's jacket that was left on the deck. He was sure it belonged to the young man who was hanging under the exhaust stacks, but he never saw any of the rescued men again.29

At 8:30 PM, with more than 1,000 soldiers still to be rescued, an explosion probably caused by the collapse of a bulkhead, resounded like a thunderclap. Following the second explosion, there was chaos as it became every man for himself. Using only small penknives, GIs made frantic but pathetic attempts to hack heavy ropes that would release the life rafts.

Recalled Sergeant Daniel Rosenberg, Headquarters Company, 2nd Battalion, 262nd Regiment, "All hell broke loose. Men were running, sliding, and jumping overboard from all directions. Stairways, posts, cables, and many other parts of the ship came hurling through the air." Continued Rosenberg, "I tried to grasp the top rail but missed, and my foot was caught underneath a roll of wire cable. I tried to pry myself loose but couldn't, and it seemed as if the end had come for me." But at that perilous moment, the part of the ship where Rosenberg was caught lurched forward, and his foot was released. Rosenberg slid down the side and, just before hitting the water, managed to reach for and grasp a piece of stairway still attached to the remains of the ship. Said Rosenberg, "I straightened up and jumped into the water as far from the ship as I could manage. Most fortunately, a wave carried me farther away from the wreckage and suction."

The boy from Butler, New Jersey, Sergeant Jerry Crean, along with his men, was having problems clinging to the deck. "This damn thing is gonna sink," Crean thought to himself. He ordered his group down a landing net on the side of the ship. "Hey Sarge, this water's like ice," hollered the first man to reach the water. "Get the hell in the water," Crean yelled back, and kicked the cold and frightened youth into the sea . . . Sergeant Jerry Crean never saw the youth again.

Large rafts that had broken loose from the deck floated nearby, and soldiers scrambled to climb aboard them. Crean observed the chaotic scene and ordered those in the water with him to drift away from the rafts. Sergeant Jerry Crean, Private First Class Cliff "Kip" Tranter, and Private Nevin Herman swam, dog-paddled, and floated farther and farther away from the desperate men, who were pushing and shoving to climb aboard the rafts. Crean grabbed a duffel bag that floated by. It was full of clothes, which trapped air in it, and Crean, Tranter, and Herman clung to the life-saving bag. Chilled to the bone, Tranter and Herman started to slip beneath the water. The weakened Sergeant Jerry Crean did his best to brace up the two men but he could barely support himself. Then, unable to withstand the paralyzing cold any longer, Private Nevin H. Herman, Jr., from York, Pennsylvania gave up his fight for life and disappeared from view . . . gone forever.

The *Leopoldville* was listing so far to the port side that it was impossible for the men to stand on deck. Private First Class Allen Parker and his platoon buddies climbed up and sat on the railing. Private Edwin Malczyk was on his left, along with Private Robert Swanson, Sergeant Coy Craig, and someone Parker didn't know. Parker decided to shed his ammo belt and steel helmet. Not wanting to hit the men in the water, he dropped the ammo belt and helmet on the deck behind him. Said Parker, "When I started to take off the belt the water was at least ten or twelve feet below me, but by the time I had gotten rid of the belt and turned around the water was up to my feet."

With all of his strength, Parker thrust himself into the water and began swimming as hard as he could to get away from the suction of the sinking ship. He looked back once and saw that the ship was standing on end with her bow sticking up out of the water. Said Parker, "I could see there were men still clinging onto her."

Wearing his overcoat, boots, and a life preserver, Staff Sergeant Donald Gengler grabbed a railing and attempted to pull himself over, but the heavy foot of a soldier from a deck above hit his right shoulder. Gengler almost lost his grip on the rail but somehow held on and climbed over the side of the ship and jumped. Unable to swim, Gengler was very frightened.

When he hit the water he kept going down. Gengler could hold his breath no longer and thought that he would drown. Suddenly, however, he found himself back on the surface. It was dark and cold. He could see lights from tugboats but none close to him. He grabbed a piece of lumber that he found floating in the water and held onto it tightly. He could see men on a life raft nearby, but it was already overcrowded and partially underwater. He could only pray that a boat would spot him before the icy waters drained the last spark of life from his freezing body.

Secure in the warmth of their glass enclosure, Private First Class Vincent Codianni and his comrades waited for orders that never came. Suddenly, the ship lurched forward, and the men dashed for the open deck. Some made it, and some, like Codianni, did not. Codianni saw a soldier fall and bang his head. He was bleeding, and Sergeant Elmer Baker and Private First Class Richard Sansone tried in vain to pick the young man up. Private First Class Harold Dantinne and Private First Class Steven Lester smashed the glass and water gushed in. Somehow, Codianni escaped from the enclosure, which for others became a crypt. Codianni managed to get off the ship and swam as fast as he could to escape the suction that was pulling him under! All around him were the bodies of soldiers with their hands out, faces down, bobbing in the water like boards.30

As the ship began to sink rapidly, Lieutenant Wurdeman heard a mighty hiss of escaping steam. Said Wurdeman, "The majority of the men dashed to the starboard rail in a panicky attempt to clear the ship as soon as possible. I am sure that a number of my men were killed at that time." Continued Lieutenant Wurdeman, "Just as the waters began to wash across the deck, I jumped into a raft that was lying on the deck. The water lifted the raft free of the ship, and I pulled five other men into the raft with me."

As the bow rose from the sea, soldiers retreated from the advancing water and, finally, in desperation, climbed guy wires toward the mast. Many could not hold on and fell into the angry sea, which demanded many human sacrifices before the waves would be stilled. Soldiers, turning blue with cold, were dying or already dead.

When it became clear that the *Leopoldville* would sink, Private First Class Keith Simons and the men around him realized that their heavy combat boots would drag them down and drown them. Therefore, they loosened their boots so they could be kicked off easily. Suddenly the *Leopoldville* shuddered and rolled quickly to port.

Simons and about ten men with him clambered over the rail, which proved to be difficult because of the tilted deck. Several lines led from the rail across the almost level side of the ship and dropped off the bottom. Clad in a life preserver, Keith Simons grabbed a line, walked down the side of the ship, and slid down along the vessel's exposed bottom.

As he struggled to kick off his boots, a soldier above him screamed, "Let go! Let go!" Simons then realized that the line was pulling him up as the ship rolled farther and farther to port. With his boots finally off, he pressed his glasses to his face, let go of the line, and dropped into the freezing water of the Channel. The cold sea crashed over him and he came up gasping for air.

Waves slapped at his face causing him to swallow a considerable amount of saltwater and he started to panic. Then, Simons was able to calm himself, and he began timing his breathing with the waves so that he took in air instead of water. After side stroking for a time, Simons glanced back at the troopship.

The *Leopoldville* was standing on its sinking stern. A mass of men in olive drabs had slid down the perpendicular deck and snagged themselves on the ship's superstructure. Above the chaotic noise, Simons could hear the wails of dying young soldiers calling for their mothers! Said Simons, "This sight is burned into my memory as though recorded on film by a flashbulb in pitch darkness. How strange when men face death in desperate circumstances that they should appeal to the mother who gave them being. 'God!' I cried out, 'please help them! Please!' Then I started to swim away as fast as I could."

Private First Class Guy Petty, of Lawrenceville, Illinois, had given his overcoat to a buddy whose clothes were wet. He even gave the soaked soldier the leather gloves his mother had sent him for Christmas. As the ship continued to list precariously, Petty waited for the order to abandon ship, which never came. Finally, as if out of nowhere, a sergeant took it upon himself to order the men near him to jump from the ship before it went down.

Guy Petty climbed the ship's rail and walked down the side of the ship until the onrushing water caught him. Petty was dragged under until the water pressure became so great it caused his eardrums to burst. Then a rope swept across his face and he snatched it. Fighting for his life, he climbed hand over hand, up the rope. But a sudden lurch from the sinking ship jerked the rope from his grasp. Said Petty later, "I thought I would die for air. I took in a lot of saltwater. Soon I was exhausted and gave up. Then there was air—lots of air—and my senses came back."

Somehow Petty had made it back to the surface. He grabbed onto a six foot-long plank that floated past. Then he managed to take hold of still another floating plank. He put a plank under each armpit and locked his legs around the ends. But while trying to reach a lifeboat, he lost one of the planks. The young Petty, who had been a Sophomore at the University of Illinois before he enlisted in the Army, would say of his experience in the water, "My heart burned; my chest burned and ached. I couldn't feel my legs. I was alone. I prayed. I prayed for a long time."

Twenty-seven-year-old Sergeant Ira Frye, the soldier whose company was originally assigned to a compartment at the lowest level of the ship, but whose berth was changed after he stopped for breakfast, watched in horror as some of the men who missed their jump to the *Brilliant* were sucked into the ship's propeller. Eventually, Frye and others climbed down the side of the sinking troopship and jumped into the water. Said Frye, "Me and another fellow . . . I don't know who he was . . . we stayed by ourselves about 100 yards from the other ship and just waited for things to settle down."

Frye clung to a life preserver for about forty-five minutes before a small rescue craft located him and he was pulled from the water.

Just prior to going over the side, Sergeant James Noakes and Captain John Van Sickle shook hands and wished each other well. As Captain Van Sickle started down the cargo nets, a soldier behind him knocked off his glasses. Van Sickle kicked off his combat boots and, once in the water, found and held onto a flotation cask.

Private Gerald Raymond, unable to find a life preserver, stood on deck and realized that with the crew gone his chances for survival were slim. He had been raised in a Christian home, but until that day his faith had never been tested. Although he had been an active church member, he would later say, "My relationship with the Lord was not a vital one. Still, I believed in prayer, and I asked God to protect me . . . I was convinced that only God could save me now."

The dying ship's loudspeaker blared, "The ship is sinking; every man for himself . . . " The fatal words sent a chill down Gerald Raymond's spine. Then he remembered that he was not alone. Recalled Raymond, years later, "God was with me even on that cold, black night. I felt He was telling me to crawl to the high side of the ship. As I did so, it listed further, and I felt myself slipping. But God was with me; I fell right on top of a small, 4-foot square life raft."

At that same moment a soldier floated by on a barracks bag. Gerald pulled the young man across the raft. Then the two of them pulled yet a third soldier into the raft that was their salvation. Panting from exhaustion, in the midst of a surrealistic scene of unbelievable turmoil, the three men in the tiny raft floated away from the condemned vessel. All the while they were on the water, Gerald Raymond thanked God for providing the raft. Raymond and his raft companions spent 45 minutes drifting in the frigid darkness before they were picked up by a rescue ship that took them to shore.

Meanwhile, the *Leopoldville* had settled to the bottom at about 8:40 PM![31] Sergeant Cornelius Burk went down with the ship but managed to surface about one-hundred yards from where the ship had gone down.

Perhaps as many as 1,000 soldiers—clustered together in small knots, many clinging to one another as they tried to escape the suction of the sinking ship—were left floating in 48 degree water. From his vantage point on the raft, a soaked and freezing Private Richard Dutka watched the death plunge of the troopship. The memory was forever etched in his mind and heart. "Everything became very bright, like the sun was shining.

It was the phosphorescence churned up in the sea by the sinking ship. Her stern went down first, then her cockeyed bow, sticking up like the Statue of Liberty. Then, bubbles joined on the water's surface, and everything was quiet."

Recalled SOM First Class Melvin L. DeWitt, aboard *PC 564*, "We tied lines to the large ship to hold us close enough to take personnel aboard. In a short time we were being pulled down with the sinking ship. We cut the lines and the raft bobbed up out of the water like a cork. As we moved away, the GIs were yelling for us to come back, but we couldn't. The *Leopoldville* sank very fast . . . The bow raised several feet out of the water like a giant suffering whale. The sound of screaming men is one that I'll never forget, as we watched them jump over the side and slide down the sloping hull, trying to slow themselves using their feet as brakes. Within a few minutes the ship disappeared beneath the waves and all was silent except for men in the sea calling for help.

Chapter 5

Salvation for Some

"God, make me a man! God, make me a man!"
. . . Capt. John C. Van Sickle

At Saint-Pierre-Église, Medic John V. Corrigan, filled with the Yuletide spirit, shaved and combed his hair in the privacy of his washroom. On that Christmas Eve, he would attend his first Midnight Mass in France. He emerged from the room joyfully humming the first few bars of "White Christmas." Suddenly, Captain Levine burst into the room. The Captain was perhaps the most pleasant man that Corrigan had met in the Army, but at this moment, he stood before him with a harsh expression etched on his face as he broke the news that a troopship had been torpedoed out in the Channel and survivors were being brought into Cherbourg. "Have the boys stand by and be ready to go," shouted Levine, already halfway down the hall racing for a phone.

Corrigan found most of the men in his unit lounging around the Day Room enjoying the holiday mood and each other's company. A few were fortifying their "Christmas spirit" with liquid spirits. Corrigan's grave announcement brought angry epithets and curses directed at the Nazis. Captain Levine returned and everyone sprang into action. Men dashed for their first-aid kits, overcoats, pistol belts, and canteens. "Bring all available morphine!" Captain Levine shouted. Men pinned Red Cross armbands to their field jackets and headed in the direction of the roaring motor and squealing wheels of the weapons carrier ambulance that had just arrived. Captain Levine and Medic Smith scrambled into the front seat while Medics Corrigan, Jepson, Hall, and Hardin piled into the back.

Recalled Corrigan, "Cherbourg was roughly twelve miles distant, but we covered it like it was twelve blocks." The road was devoid of traffic, and Smitty drove as fast as he could. As the ambulance raced toward Cherbourg, Corrigan and the others in the back of the vehicle checked their equipment. Their hatred of the Nazis was now replaced with concern for the lives of the American boys that hung in the balance. Sorrowfully, Corrigan remembers of that urgent ride to rescue, "Hall uttered a remark I was to hear hundreds of times within the next 5 hours, 'What a way to spend Christmas Eve!'"

Many men were lost because they were not instructed how to use their life jackets or helmets in case of an emergency.

Although the ship carried life jacket lights, they had not been distributed to the men. Once in the water, the lack of the life jacket lights meant that soldiers who could have been saved died from exposure because they could not be seen by the rescue craft criss-crossing the scene. Unable to see them, these same craft would also run them down.

The soldiers also were not instructed that it was necessary to hold the collar of the Kapok life jackets down as they hit the water to prevent the collar from whipping up and snapping their necks. Dozens of frightened soldiers jumped from the sinking ship unaware of the danger they faced from the collar, and died instantly of broken necks as their life jackets became death harnesses. There were also some soldiers who did not realize that they should unfasten the straps on their steel battle helmets before they jumped. Like the young men who did not hold the collars of the Kapock life jackets down, soldiers with helmets still strapped on broke their necks when they hit the water. Warm overcoats that provided them with protection from the cold aboard ship became lead weights that pulled many below the surface drowning them. All through the black night many small crafts searched the area and managed to pluck several hundred men from the frigid water.

Because the men were weakened by the frigid water temperature, in most cases it was necessary for rescue crews to jump into the water and fasten a line around each exhausted soldier before he could be hauled on board. This delay undoubtedly resulted in lives lost. Nevertheless, the crew of the small rescue crafts did an excellent job in saving as many lives as they could.

One such example of extraordinary courage concerned the actions of *PC 564* crewman Melvin DeWitt. The vessel had rescued several men and was trying to pull up next to a soldier to help him, but the wind blew the boat away each time it got close enough for the crew to throw him a line. The soldier could not hold onto the line because the flesh had been ripped from the palms of his hands. DeWitt felt that he had to do something to help the struggling youth and, without a thought, handed a line to a young officer. "Hold this," he said, "I'm going in after him." Wearing a Mae West life jacket, DeWitt jumped overboard. He swam to the young man who clung to him so tightly that DeWitt, himself, was pulled under. DeWitt finally managed to tie a rope around the soldier's chest. The exhausted, half drowned youth was ready to be hauled aboard. Just then, someone shouted, "Man overboard! Throw him a line." Said DeWitt, years later, "I can still see the glare of the floodlight and the line coming at me like a coiling snake . . . the young officer had thrown me the other end of the line I already had!"

DeWitt struggled to untangle the mess as *PC 564* came alongside and a hand reached over and pulled the soldier aboard. Another crewman threw over a life preserver and tied it to the rail. DeWitt passed his left arm through it and hung on for dear life. Each time the ship rolled, DeWitt was pulled out of the water in front of the exhaust, so instead of fresh air he was breathing exhaust fumes. Then the ship rolled back and dunked him like so much dirty wash. After a few minutes, DeWitt became groggy, let go, and slid into the dark sea.

Said DeWitt later, "I could see myself rolling under the ship as if in a dream. I remember seeing the 16-inch-wide stabilizer fin that ran the length of the vessel and caught me and spun me from underneath the ship; I remember seeing many bright lights like stars, and my family as clearly as if they were standing there before me. I felt peaceful, and suddenly I was very warm."

The next time he surfaced, DeWitt was under the cork float ladder hanging over the side. He fought his way from under it and rolled over on top of it. As the ship pitched from side to side, he nearly rolled off the float. Somehow, he managed to hang on until someone finally helped him aboard. Captain Spencer handed him a bottle of whiskey and ordered him to drink it. Said DeWitt, "I was as blue as my dungarees . . . that water was cold as an iceberg."

After changing into dry clothes, DeWitt went topside and helped work on the soldier he had pulled from the sea. It was hopeless. Like the permanence of a sculpture carved in stone, the memory remains forever chiseled in DeWitt's mind. "We worked on him for 3 hours, but he was gone. We had lost him . . . I still wake at night sometimes and see it all happen again."

Like Mel DeWitt, *PC 564* crewman Wes Johnson is still haunted by the memory of his own experience that Christmas Eve. When the *Leopoldville* sank, Johnson was standing alone, aft on the port quarter, near the cargo net. He was in a state of shock as a result of the appalling scene he had just witnessed. In his state of mind he was not aware that he was standing directly above the 4-inch exhaust vent that held the water coolant for the auxiliary engines that produced the craft's electric power. The discharge was boiling hot and could spew out some distance when it came under pressure as the ship rolled, causing it to be submerged.

None of the crew gave much thought to this condition because it was never a problem before that time. At sea, they were never near it . . . it was just there . . . a fact of which they were all aware . . . and understood. Johnson was mesmerized by the great whirlpool created by the sinking troopship, but then he spied a swimming soldier. He signaled to him and the soldier responded. Then, just as Johnson was ready to heave him a line, the ship rolled to starboard, and the soldier was struck with the full force of the hot water discharge. He screamed and went under . . . unconscious. With no one near to help, and without a life jacket, Johnson dove into the water immediately to save him. The unconscious soldier proved to be dead weight, and Johnson was unable to secure a firm hold as he grappled with him in the rough water. The two young men bobbed like corks in the frigid sea. Johnson labored there for some time until suddenly he was overcome with exhaustion. Johnson struggled back to the cargo net. He rolled on it and managed to climb up to the deck. Wrote Johnson many years later, "There were other men on the net at the time . . . but who they were I have never known . . . nor cared . . . then!"

Johnson was totally exhausted. He wandered aft to a hidden spot near the 40mm gun and lay down on the deck. Wrote Johnson, "I don't know how long I lay there . . . then I returned to the fray."

When the *Leopoldville* made its final plunge, Private Raymond J. Avery just walked down the side of the ship into the sea. He was dragged under, and weighted down with all of his winter gear, he struggled desperately to swim back toward the surface.

Raymond Avery succeeded in reaching the surface. Eventually, he was picked up by the crew of a tugboat. Remembered Avery of his harrowing ordeal, "There were three or four other survivors in the small cabin—it seemed to be the kitchen, as there was a large coffee urn on the stove. I drank many cups of coffee on the trip to shore, where we landed and were sent to abase hospital."

Sergeant Daniel Rosenberg and several other men attempted to swim as far away from the wreckage as possible. He was struck by debris twice, but not too severely. Although spotlights from rescue vessels shined down on him, no one saw him. Recalled Rosenberg, "I knew then that I would have to conserve my energy and hope for a stroke of good fortune." Shortly, that good fortune smiled on him. He spotted a lifeboat close by and made for it, along with the other soldiers. Said Rosenberg, "I was able to climb over the side. It was a cord-bottom raft. We were tossing around in the open sea for about an hour when a searchlight from one of the craft settled on us. We held our breath as we waved frantically."

Continued Rosenberg, "Suddenly a voice came as if from heaven." "Hold tight, we'll be with you in a minute," the voice called through the darkness. The boat drew close and tossed them a rope. One by one, the soldiers were pulled from the frigid Channel waters and hoisted onto the tug. Dripping wet and quivering from the cold, Rosenberg was stripped of his clothing, wrapped in blankets, and placed in a bunk. Upon reaching the shore, Rosenberg and the others were carried to waiting ambulances and rushed to the hospital.

Sergeant Jerry Crean and Private First Class "Kip" Tranter continued to cling to the lifesaving duffel bag when a table or some piece of wood decking floated past them. The two men managed to climb onto the floating wooden debris. Recalled Sergeant Crean later, "The next thing I knew I woke up next to the engine of a tug, and it felt so good to be warm."[32]

Someone aboard the rescue tug gave Kip Tranter a blanket that provided the two men with the only shelter and warmth they would have during a week spent at a bombed-out airport after being put ashore. As a result of their experience in the water together, Crean and Tranter became lifelong friends. Recalled Jerry Crean of

Tranter's blanket, "It kept us alive for a week. Kip keptthat blanket until the day he died many years later."

Private First Class Jack B. Landovitz, of Brooklyn, New York, and Private First Class Bob Peterson, of Chicago, Illinois, slid over the side of the sinking troopship into the water. Some time later, Landovitz and Staff Sergeant Bob Gianfresco, of Providence, Rhode Island, became separated from the others and floated aimlessly in the frigid water waiting to be rescued. Apparently hallucinating, Gianfrancesco announced to Landovitz that he was going for a rope and disappeared into the black void.33

Guy Petty, the college kid from Lawrenceville, Illinois, could see ships and lights bobbing about as the hundreds of men in the water struggled to stay afloat. Said Petty, "A man would come to the surface, take a gulp of air, and then grab for anything within reach. Usually it was another GI, and this would cause both of them to go down again. I was actually seeing a nightmare—but I wasn't asleep."

Petty believes that he was in the water for about three hours before he was spotted and thrown a lifeline. Stiff and nearly unconscious, he caught the rope on the third attempt. Guy Petty was pulled from the water; he had escaped death. Before the war was over, the young man from Illinois would cheat death a second time.

Private First Class Allen T. Parker swam toward a boat that was directly in front of him. He tried to take hold of ropes trailing over the side of the boat, but the tide carried him away. Then he tried to reach other nearby boats, but the water moved him still farther away. Said Parker, "I soon found out that there was no use in wasting my strength swimming so I lay on my back." After awhile, Parker saw a group of men floating toward him. One of them called out to him, "Hey, buddy, grab a rope and hang on." Parker realized that the men were grouped around a life raft. He seized the rope and hung on.

Finally, a U.S. Army tug passed nearby, and they all began to shout. Sailors aboard the tug heard their cries and threw them a line. So numb were the men from the freezing water that it was difficult for the tug crew to pull them on board. When they were all safely rescued from the water, the tug continued to cruise the area in search of additional survivors. As Parker sipped hot coffee offered by the crew, he was told that he and the others had drifted into an allied mine field. Disregarding their own safety, the men on the tug had maneuvered through the mine field to snatch them from death's grasp.

Private Frank Sample, of Jeffersonville, Indiana, quit high school at the age of sixteen to work on towboats on the Ohio River. Two years later, eighteen year-old Sample was lying on his bunk when the troopship *Leopoldville* suddenly jerked. Sample compared it to a towboat running aground. "It just sort of stopped," he would say. When the ship listed dangerously and began to sink, Sample, with long johns beneath his uniform and wearing an overcoat, strapped on a bayonet and a full canteen. He dropped C-rations into each pocket and crawled across the tilted deck. Like others before him, Sample witnessed the terrible sight of soldiers who missed their jumps to rescue vessels and were crushed.

He crawled to the other side of the ship and attempted to board a lifeboat, but it was packed with injured men. Sample had never learned to swim, but as soldiers tumbled over him into the water, he began to lower himself precariously down a rope. Men and gear dropped on him, and fearing that his back would break, Sample finally let go and plunged into the freezing water and sank. His heavy clothing dragged him deeper and deeper into the black void. Thought Sample, "Why not die?"

It was then that he saw a vision of his kind and loving mother opening the telegram reporting his death. Her screams reverberated in his ears, and at that moment he managed to surface and gulp a breath of air. Sample clawed through the bodies between him and the surface. Finally, his head popped above water, and the gasping youth clung to a lifesaving duffel bag until he was hauled aboard a French tug.

Looking back on that dreadful night, Norman Bullett said, "I will never forget my experience of going down with the ship. I was pulled down for some time, when the boilers, or something, blew up and sent me back to the surface." Continued Bullett, "It was a terrifying time in the water. Looking around, all I could see were men calling for help. I saw the bow of the *Leo* sink, with men jumping off of it. I don't know how long I was in the water, but I began to freeze. I looked around for something to hang onto, and some stairs floated by, so I got on them. Others had the same idea."

Before long, a Coast Guard cutter pulled alongside the half-drowned soldiers, who were chilled to the bone. Sailors from the cutter threw them ropes to grab onto and instructed them to wrap the ropes around their bodies. Bullett's fingers were so numb he could not do it, and he

Norman Bullett

slipped beneath the waves, exhausted. Just then, a big wave brought him back up to the surface, close to the cutter's rail. Three sailors managed to grab him and haul him onto the deck. Norman Bullett was saved so that he could bear witness to those whose cries were silenced.

Sergeant George Chun Fat could see nothing but foreign flags flying over different rescue craft, as he sat low in the rough water in a lifeboat. Suddenly he saw a small American flag waving briskly from a tug headed in their direction. Said Sergeant Chun Fat years later, "Nothing could beat that beautiful American flag and what it stood for." As the tug drew near, a sailor with a rope in his hand called to the men in the lifeboat to grab the rope, which he then tossed to them. Private First Class Millard Zuber, who was one of those in the lifeboat with Sergeant Chun Fat, caught the rope and secured it. Soon everyone jumped safely to the tug.

Sergeant Chun Fat and the others were led down to the warmth of the engine room. Most of them vomited up the saltwater they had swallowed while being buffeted in the lifeboat by the waves. Afterwards, Sergeant Chun Fat opened the engine room door and went outside for fresh air. He could see the troopship sinking and heard the many voices calling for help. He could not bear to listen to their desperate pleas for salvation and so he went back inside, shut the door, and prayed.

The lifeboat containing Lieutenant George Rehder and his seven comrades bobbed up and down on the choppy Channel waters, a mere speck in a sea crowded with dying young men. Out of the dark, Lieutenant Rehder could see a large tug racing directly toward them at full throttle. "Oh God," cried Rehder, "we're going to be rammed and sunk by the tug!"

The tug's engines screeched as they were thrown into reverse, and it seemed to Rehder that the tug just missed crashing into the side of their lifeboat. Crew members aboard the tug threw ropes to the soldiers, which they quickly grabbed and tied on. The survivors in the lifeboat breathed a collective sigh of relief that their trial was over when they heard with disbelief, "Untie that line and cast off." The tug's Captain had made the correct decision that those in the water must be rescued first.

The soldiers in the lifeboat would have to wait. As the tug disappeared into the night, Rehder and his companions crouched down between the rowing seats and were drenched by each wave that crested over them. The relentless gusts of wind tossed them about without mercy, as they drifted aimlessly on the turbulent sea. Soaked to the skin, they prayed that rescue would come before they were swamped or frozen to death.

A few days before Christmas, three LSTs volunteered to run the submarine ring around Cherbourg to deliver 155mm rifles for use at the Battle of the Bulge. Each vessel took one gun aboard at Southampton and departed that afternoon, unescorted. BMG1, W.D. Keister, aboard the *LST 541*, watched as they passed the large British destroyers tied up at the docks.

Some aboard wondered why they were doing this alone and soon the phrase, "suicide mission," was being circulated. As soon as they left port the men aboard *LST 541* observed three apparent liberty ships, dead in the water, being abandoned.

As darkness fell, *LST 541* blacked out completely and observed radio silence. Recalled W.D. Keister, "As we neared the French coast, a lookout reported seeing sparkling lights on the surface of the Channel. Soon we could see bodies in the water. Some were surely dead in their life jackets; others were not. Some men floated on life rafts and some held onto bits of wreckage. The lights that sparkled were attached to life jackets, and some flashlights gleamed in the night. From the deck of our LST it was not far to the water. I remember they were calling to us and we called back. I don't recall just what was said . . . We did not stop. We probably had orders not to stop for good reason.

Often I have wondered how many survivors were injured by the ship's screws. By this time, we were near enough to see the glow of Cherbourg's lights on the clouds. Upon reaching the harbor, dozens of small boats—some hardly bigger than rowboats—were streaming out to pick up survivors."

Perhaps it was the crew of the tugboat who told Lieutenant Rehder and the others in the raft with him that they would have to wait until the men in the water were rescued. Finally, a tug spotted Staff Sergeant Donald Gengler, who was struggling to stay afloat. Gengler was exhausted and so too was the sailor who reached him for and grabbed his hand. The sailor's strength was sapped from pulling soldiers out of the water. With the tired sailor's help, Gengler somehow pulled himself up and onto the tug's deck. He crawled down to the boiler room, where he became violently ill. A crew member wrapped him in a blanket. His dog tag and his watch, which was stopped at 8:15 PM, were the only possessions he had left.

After some time on the flotation cask, Captain Van Sickle pushed off and tried to swim to one of the many small boats that were searching the area for survivors. A line was thrown from one of the rescue craft, but when Van Sickle grasped it, he found that it was not attached to anything. There were tires on the side of the boat, serving as fenders, and he grabbed one but was too weak to hold on. He tried several times to seize a tire but each attempt met with failure. Captain Van Sickle had depleted all of his energy when a sailor reached over the side of the boat, grabbed the seat of the Captain's pants and pulled him on board.

Sergeant Jack C. Randles was a member of Company I, 262nd Regiment. The disaster holds a special meaning for Randles, because in his words, "It was my privilege to see one man face his own crucial hour of testing." Randles described the moment when the *Leopoldville* sank. "The ship suddenly lurched and listed to such a degree that we knew instantly it was going down. I walked down the side of the listing ship and a short jump put me into the cold water."

Randles could not recall how long he was in the water before he was picked up by a Coast Guard cutter. One of the crewmen pulled him from the water and took him to his own bunk, where he helped remove

Randles' wet clothing and wrapped the shivering young soldier in a blanket. The sailor then quickly returned topside to help others.

Soon Randles' benefactor returned with another soldier. It was Captain John C. Van Sickle, Commander of Company K, 262nd Regiment. Although he had never met Van Sickle, the proximity of their companies had given Randles the opportunity to observe the Captain on many occasions. Before the war, Van Sickle had been a school teacher from Akron, Ohio. Randles later wrote, "He impressed me as a dedicated and decent man. Like many of us, Captain Van Sickle had entered the military in response to an emergency call from his country for the duration and 6 months." (The military service at the time was for the duration of the war plus six months.)

Like Randles, Captain Van Sickle was wet and shivering, and in a semiconscious state caused by fatigue and exposure. Said Randles, "I told the seaman I would take care of the Captain, and he could go back to search for others." As Randles removed the Captain's wet clothing he discerned that Van Sickle was saying something. Continued Randles, "I listened intently and realized that he was repeating the phrase, "God, make me a man! God, make me a man!" I knew immediately what he meant by that prayer. As the leader of more than 200 men, he did not want to fail in this hour of testing. On this highly emotional evening, Captain Van Sickle decided that living up to his idea of manhood was more important than removing himself from harm's way. His basic character decreed that he do the right thing, regardless of the consequences."[34]

Chapter 6

The Ordeal Finally Ends

"I came up and I thought my head was going to explode. Hot water was coming out of my ears and all around me were bodies and guys screaming."
. . . Vincent Codianni

Staff Sergeant P.J. Casadonte, assigned to the 1073rd Engineer Port Repair Ship, had made the Channel crossing several times without any major incident. He was the repair ship's Chief Radio Operator. The rest of the crew was composed of seamen, divers, electricians, machine shop operators, and carpenters. On the morning of December 24, the Repair Ship sailed from the Isle of Wight and joined the convoy bound for Cherbourg. Radio silence was maintained during the voyage.

When the Repair Ship arrived at Cherbourg, the Captain received word that a vessel in the convoy had been hit a few miles out. The Repair Ship was immediately ordered to a nearby pier to set up portable lighting on the dock to which survivors would be brought.

The *YMS 305*, a 136-foot American wooden hull minesweeper was moored in Cherbourg while routine maintenance was performed. The mess deck was decorated with what Christmas frills could be found in the town. As late afternoon turned to early evening, Captain C. Denis (Denny) Gilchrist and the other captains of YMS and PT boats at Cherbourg were ordered to stand by to get under way. Sailors on liberty were rounded up and returned to the ship.

Coast Guard Yeoman First Class Wesley J. McEntarfer was assigned clerical duties at the naval base in Cherbourg, but as the full measure of the tragedy became apparent, he was among the personnel pressed into rescue service. Said McEntarfer, "I recall making many trips back and forth to the disaster area. On the first couple of trips we brought back survivors . . . on the rest of the trips we just brought back bodies."

Waiting to be rescued, as the troopship filled with water and tilted dangerously, Corporal Vernon Lindahl, along with hundreds of other soldiers, ran from one side of the deck to the other. When the *Leopoldville* tipped upward, just before making its death plunge, sailors from nearby boats attempted to throw mesh ropes to the soldiers for them to climb down and escape the sinking ship. But by the time the ropes reached Lindahl, they were of no use. Looking back, Lindahl would say, "I didn't need them . . . I just walked down and jumped into the water. I went straight down and I thought, Oh well, I'll never come up. I just sank deep into the water with all my clothes and gear on."

After what seemed like an eternity, Lindahl's life jacket brought him back up to the surface. Rafts floated nearby, but when he reached out for one the tide swept it away. "So I just lay there in the water," Lindahl later said. "I passed out. The next thing I remember I was in the hospital in Cherbourg with blankets piled on top of me and saltwater in my stomach."

Providence had smiled on Lindahl twice that night. First his Captain called him from his compartment where the torpedo hit moments later. Then from his hospital bed he learned that anyone in the water with his head down who looked like he was dead was left there.

Many years later, Lindahl recalled his experience in the icy, turbulent Channel. "I don't know how I got out of the water. I get all choked up when I talk about it. It's still very vivid in my mind."

Technician 5th Grade Joseph Matusiak was unable to leave the vessel before it went under. Suddenly, he found himself struggling for survival in the frigid Channel waters. A boat that he believes was a tug spotted him and pulled him aboard, saving him from certain death. He passed out immediately after being rescued and spent three days in the hospital.

Lieutenant Wurdeman and his raft mates were picked up at approximately 9:30 PM. The sailors on the tug that rescued them gave them cigarettes and warm blankets; afterwards the compassionate sailors permitted the soldiers, exhausted and freezing, the use of the crews' cabins.

Private First Class Richard Dutka and the others on the raft were picked up by a Coast Guard PC. Despite the threat of Uboats in the area, the skipper ordered a spotlight trained on the American flag flying from the mast. Recalled Dutka, "It was very inspirational."

There were six or eight Coast Guard PCs in the harbor that were used for routine patrols, mail trips, and for ferrying personnel to England. Said Wesley McEntarfer, "We had never been on these boats before. But that night, if you were 'Navy,' you were a sailor. We wrestled with the lines in the cold and wind and got under way out of the harbor."

On each mission of mercy, using any method he could—boat hooks, arms, and lines—McEntarfer grabbed at the men and bodies in the water. The crew tried to maneuver through the disaster area in an organized way, but the scene was chaotic.

Said McEntarfer, "I remember one body; it was bare from the waist down with a big gash in the hip. That poor guy must have been in the exact spot where the explosion occurred."

The wind and current carried bodies southwest toward the Channel Islands. Rescue craft were forced not to approach the Islands because the Germans were still holed up there with artillery. The boat with Wesley McEntarfer aboard picked up twelve or fourteen men, mostly dead. One of the craft's propellers malfunctioned, and it became necessary to operate on half power. This condition slowed down their runs back and forth to the pier, and the crew was concerned about the safety of the ship. Later, back at Cherbourg, the cause of the malfunctioning screw was determined . . . the body of an American soldier had become fouled in the propeller.

Private First Class Walter Beran, the youth from Texas who found the ASTP at Baylor University preferable to picking cotton, had made it to the troopship's deck where he waited for orders. Near the end, his battalion commander issued the abandon ship order, and Walter Beran literally walked down the vessel's side into the cold water. Recalled Beran later of his experience in the water, "There was a crowd of us in the water—some very frightened and in a frenzy, clinging to whatever they could, including their colleagues . . . I was able to wrestle myself free from another soldier who was clinging to me. The suction of the ship dragged me under, but at some point the buoyancy of my life jacket brought me back to the surface of the water. The last thing I remember was swimming toward a little boat, and several hours later waking up in the hospital screaming, "Get me to land!" Moments later, I looked up and there was this absolutely beautiful nurse assuring me that I was on land; I'll always be indebted to her, because she proved to be one of the most reassuring experiences in my life . . . and she *was* beautiful."

Walter Beran later learned that his rescuers found him floating unconscious in his life preserver. After recovering, he was released from the hospital and rejoined his unit some 30 days later. The *Leopoldville* disaster confirmed principles that have guided Beran throughout his adult life. Reflects Beran, "It made me appreciate the value of human life and how short life can be."

Thomas Kay had joined the Royal Navy early in 1941. Kay was a gun layer in a gun crew assigned to a branch called DEMS (Defensively Equipped Merchant Ships). Twice, Kay had been aboard ships sunk by torpedoes, and he had sailed aboard a ship sunk by bombs. Once again, Thomas Kay struggled for survival in frigid waters. He had been on watch in the bow when the torpedo struck. Just before the boat went down, Kay heard a deep rumble throughout the ship and felt the bow lifting beneath him. He saw the mast move to a 45-degree angle and shouted amid the commotion, "Right lads, it's time to go!"

Kay threw off his duffel coat and kicked off his sea boots. He climbed over the guard rail and slid down the side of the bow, tearing the skin off the back of his legs, buttocks, and hands on the rough plates under the bow. When he hit the water, Kay swam away from the ship as fast as he could. Once, he looked back and saw the bow of the *Leopoldville* sticking straight up in the air and men dropping off her like flies. Thomas Kay tried to hold on and wondered if, like a cat, he had used up all of his "nine lives."

After about 15 minutes in the water, Kay was spotted by the U.S. Coast Guard *PC 564*. A scrambling net hung over the side, and Kay grabbed it and held fast. Said Kay, "I could neither climb up the net nor let go; I hung onto the net as the ship rose and fell with the waves." Two American seamen scrambled down the net and somehow dragged Kay up onto it.

Safely aboard the PC, an exhausted Kay collapsed in a heap on a large canvas on the deck. "Don't lay there buddy," one of the sailors called out, as he lifted a corner of the sheet. Beneath the canvas, Kay could distinguish the forms of two or three dead soldiers.

Like Thomas Kay, Private First Class Arnold Dahlke half walked, half-slid down the side of the *Leopoldville* into the freezing Channel waters. Dahlke was born and raised in Detroit, Michigan. He had been drafted after his eighteenth birthday and entered the Army at Fort Sheridan, Illinois, on May 1, 1944, before he had completed high school. After basic training, Dahlke was assigned to bugler training, but all of the schools were closed in July; so instead of becoming a bugler, he became a rifleman. Then at Fort Rucker, he joined the 66th Division, Company I, 262nd Regiment.

The trip across the Channel had been uneventful, and just a few hours before, like so many of his comrades, Arnold Dahlke had been sleeping in his hammock. Now, weighted down by his wool underwear, trousers and shirt, sweater, and field jacket, he was in a fight for his life as he struggled to stay afloat in the icy waters. Dahlke had swallowed so much saltwater that he vomited blood. Just 1 week had passed since he celebrated his nineteenth birthday on December 17. It did not appear likely that he would see his twentieth birthday. The weight of his clothing was pulling him under, and it seemed that only a miracle could save him. Arnold Dahlke's miracle was *PC 564,* which spotted him barely managing to stay afloat.

Dahlke's hands were cut from rope burns, and with his heavy wet clothing and his body limp from exhaustion, it required four sailors to haul him out of the water.[35]

Private First Class Keith Simons had accepted the fact that he was going to die when the same *PC 564* that had saved Kay and Dahlke appeared out of the darkness and caught him in their lights. A sailor threw him a line from the bow, but Simons' hands were so stiff from cold that he could not grasp it. Simons wrapped the line around his right arm several times until it was clear up to his armpit. Then he clamped his arm against his side. The sailor tried his best to pull Simons, weighted down by his wet clothing, from the water, but he could not. "I can't pull you up," the sailor shouted down at him, "Hang on and I'll take you alongside. There's a cargo net there." Simons hung on for dear life until the sailor was able to move him around to the starboard side of the craft and, with the help of two other sailors, drag him over the rail and haul him in. Said Simons, "They dumped me, like a sack of wet, frozen potatoes, on deck." A sailor started to remove Simons' glasses, but somehow Simons managed to moan through lips numb from the cold, "No! No! I need 'em!" The tension of the moment was broken, and the three sailors who had saved his life burst out laughing.

During his time in the water, Simons nearly panicked and drowned, but he regained his composure with the thought that he was not going to make a widow of his bride Flora. His joy at being saved, however, was short-lived. There were twelve soldiers besides him who had been pulled from the Channel alive. *PC 564* had also hauled aboard three bodies. Simons' mind flashed back as he remembered the pledge he made to his friend Fred Schlerf, "Your damn right we're going to make it!"[36] But, before him on the deck of *PC 564* lay the lifeless bodies of Harry C. Robison, Dessie W. Brown, and his hunchbacked buddy Fred Schlerf. Keith Simons buried his head in his hands and sobbed uncontrollably.

When *YMS 305* arrived at the site of the disaster, the sailors found the area lit by searchlights from ships that were already on the scene. Captain Gilchrist turned his searchlights on survivors wearing the type of life jacket that had a portion in front and a portion in back. The soldiers in the water appeared to be waving, and Captain Gilchrist maneuvered his boat alongside and threw lines to them, but they did not respond. Captain Gilchrist then realized their waving arms were only caused by the motion of the waves. A saddened Gilchrist ordered cargo nets over the side and pulled several soldiers from the water. Artificial respiration proved futile. Although none of the soldiers was injured, all were dead from hypothermia. Their will to live had not been strong enough to overcome the icy, bitter cold winter waters of the Channel. With a heavy heart, Captain Gilchrist maneuvered his craft from man to man . . . twenty-six bodies were eventually picked up.

The deck space of his boat was limited, and Gilchrist ordered the bodies stacked in groups of three and four. *YMS 305* returned to port where Army personnel claimed its cargo of bodies. Years later, Captain Gilchrist would write, "Apparently, it had been thought that the *Leopoldville* could be towed into port and that's why we were not dispatched to the scene earlier."

Captain Jack Gangwere was later credited with saving many lives because of a simple precautionary measure that he took. "I didn't think much of it at the time. Later though, I remembered telling many of my men to make sure that their life jackets (Mae Wests) were secure and the laces on their combat boots untied," he said.

With their boots tied loosely the soldiers were able to kick them off in the water so that they could swim and stay afloat.

One of the last orders given on board the sinking vessel was for someone to turn off the gas in the ovens to prevent a fire. Recalled Gangwere years later, "Our Christmas dinners went down with the ship. The turkeys were roasting, and we were supposed to have a holiday meal before landing in France."

When the *Leopoldville* sank, Captain Gangwere went down with the ship. "I remember when I hit the water I seemed to go down . . . down . . . down. In my mind the thought was, 'Boy, my wife is going to be mad at me. There she is at home with a new 1-month-old baby who I haven't been home to see yet and here I am floating around the English Channel!'"

When Captain Gangwere finally broke the surface, all around him he saw and heard men yelling, groaning, and struggling. Captain Gangwere shouted to the men in the water as loudly as he could, doing his best to calm them and assure them that they all would be picked up. Colonel Ralph Martindale, who was in the water near Gangwere and heard his booming voice of reassurance above all the rest, would in fact later recommend Captain Gangwere for the Bronze Star and Purple Heart.

After floating aimlessly for what seemed like an eternity, a tugboat appeared alongside the group of half-drowned soldiers. A sailor called from the tug, "Boy are we glad to see you guys . . . we've pulled in thirty-two dead men. You're the first live ones that we've found."

The men were pulled from the freezing Channel waters and brought to the engine room, where they found warmth. Totally exhausted, Captain Gangwere passed out.[37]

Lieutenant George Rehder stood at the bar of the English pub, the pretty young waitress by his side. He raised his glass and offered a holiday toast to the men of Company H. "Good cheer and a Merry Christmas to all!" he said and down the hatch went his "Gold Wedding" bourbon. Lieutenant Rehder coughed, gagged, and choked as his vision evaporated in the spray of the waves that continued to whip over the side of the lifeboat. Instead of the smooth taste of the "Gold Wedding" bourbon, it was only the spray of saltwater and oil from the sinking *Leopoldville* that he had ingested.

The sweet voice of the pretty waitress that he had planned to romance faded into the darkness to be replaced by the rumbling throb of a PT boat engine above the scream of the wind. A single spotlight flipped back and forth over the waves. An almost inaudible voice called out repeatedly, "Hey, anybody in that lifeboat?" Heads popped up from the gunnels of the boat and hands and arms waved frantically.

The PC gunnels were approximately 6 feet higher than the lifeboat. The rough sea would make the transfer to the PC hazardous. Skillfully, the PC Captain alternated his motors until finally he was able to come alongside the lifeboat and throw ropes to the waiting men. Anxious to reach the safety of the larger craft, one young soldier climbed onto the small wooden platform of the lifeboat's bow. The wobbly, shaky youth stood on the moving pedestal and hurled himself toward the PC boat when he thought it had come within range . . . He missed. The youth hit the water with a loud splash, his head and body disappearing beneath the waves.

Before the soldier resurfaced, a sailor from the PC had already dived in after him. The sailor immediately grabbed the floundering youth, spun him around, and swam to the rear of the PC, where helping hands pulled them both from the Channel's frigid waters. The others all jumped aboard the rescue craft without incident. It was Lieutenant Rehder's turn next.

Lieutenant Rehder had removed his overcoat and was not wearing a life preserver. He was determined not to duplicate the first soldier's experience in the water. Carefully he gauged the best moment for his leap. As the two vessels came together he dove for the PC and appeared to fly like a bird through the air. He landed flat on his belly with a thud on the deck of the PC. As several sailors helped him to his feet they broke into uncontrollable laughter. Lieutenant Rehder saw no humor in being soaking wet, freezing, and sprawled on his belly on the deck of the PC. Rather than amusing him, their continued laughter was arousing his anger. Then Rehder felt something strange on his face and ran his hands back and forth over it not knowing what to expect. Still the crew of the PC doubled over with laughter.

That very afternoon, the PC had been freshly painted. When Lieutenant George Rehder stood up, he was covered with gray paint from head to toe. Some of the crewmen of that PC boat referred to George Stanley Rehder gleefully as "the gray ghost!"

The injured Colonel Chris Rumburg made his way to the top deck and prepared to jump from the sinking ship when he observed one of his men about to enter the water without his life vest. Colonel Rumburg removed his own vest and gave it to him. Rumburg then jumped into the water and swam around helping soldiers reach the rafts and keeping them calm. He observed one soldier having difficulty getting to a raft. Rumburg helped the soldier over to the raft and used all of the great strength that God gave him to shove the soldier onto the raft. Colonel Rumburg's hand then slipped from the side of the raft and sank from sight.

When the *Leopoldville* made its death plunge, Lieutenant Donald MacWilliams rolled down the steeply sloping deck until he became caught beneath the stanchion of a life raft.

MacWilliams went down with the ship to a depth of some thirty or forty feet before he finally managed to free himself and rise to the surface. A member of the West Point swimming team, MacWilliams had learned how to use his oxygen sparingly. After his head popped above the waves, MacWilliams took several deep breaths and then managed to swim about fifteen or twenty feet to a large life raft, where he joined several survivors who already occupied it.

A harbor boat was approaching, and a deckhand threw a large heavy rope to the men in the raft. After they secured the rope, the men began the difficult climb to the rescue craft. As MacWilliams prepared for his own climb to the safety of the boat, he spotted a man floating on the water at about the same point where he himself had surfaced just moments earlier. The soldier was wearing his life preserver but was obviously unconscious, as his head was rolling under the waves, and MacWilliams knew that he could not live long in that position. Tired and very cold, Lieutenant MacWilliams wept as he realized that he could not abandon the unconscious soldier. He dropped back into the water and managed to drag the unconscious soldier back to the raft, where waiting hands hauled him safely out of the water into the harbor boat.

The exhausted and freezing MacWilliams then managed, with considerable difficulty, to climb aboard the bouncing craft. All of the survivors were quickly taken below, where they found every available flat surface covered with pies cooling.

The harbor boat's cook had spent hours baking the pies for the sailors' Christmas dinner, but before they reached shore, the sick and chilled survivors had covered every inch of the mess hall with vomit. Recalled MacWilliams many years later, "Then, some very fine company commanders among us led the men in prayers of Thanksgiving and prayers for our lost comrades . . . mingled with many tears."

An excellent swimmer, like MacWilliams, nineteen year-old Vincent Codianni alternated between swimming and floating for what he is certain was an incredible two long hours. He swam to conserve body heat and floated in an attempt to listen for the calls of rescuers. Codianni could not believe he was still alive. He would later say, "The ship was almost gone, and I just walked right off . . . The water was up to my waist and I started swimming like hell!"

But within seconds the great suction pulled him under, and he went down in a swirling whirlpool, like he was being churned in a giant washing machine! He felt himself tumbling around upside down, disoriented, and almost out of air. "I don't know how I got out of there," he would later say, "I just swam like hell." Miraculously, however, he suddenly found that he had returned to the surface. He felt a burning sensation from the saltwater and realized that his neck and arms had been cut by broken glass. Codianni had also lost his front teeth, and his tongue was split in half right down the middle. Later, he reflected, "I came up and I thought my head was going to explode. Hot water was coming out of my ears, and all around me were bodies and guys screaming."

Unable to talk or cry out to any rescuers because of his split tongue, Codianni was sure he was going to die. Adding to his misery, the strong currents in the English Channel began to sweep him away from the scene of the sinking. Helplessly he watched the lights of Cherbourg, representing safety and warmth, just a short five miles away. His body wracked with pain, chilled to the bone, and totally exhausted, Codianni was overwhelmed by a desire to sleep. But sleep meant death, and relying on his strong faith in God, Codianni held on and kept himself afloat.

Suddenly, out of the dark, he spotted a ship and swam toward it. Codianni used all of his skills as a strong swimmer and closed the distance between himself and the ship that would be his salvation. Then, just when he had almost reached the vessel . . . it left.

When all hope seemed lost, a French tugboat passed by. Unable to speak, Codianni raised his hand and was spotted by a young French boy, who threw him a rope. Codianni could see two black men on the tug's deck, who he assumed were members of the *Leopoldville*'s Congolese crew. A soldier whose face was covered with blood clung to the side of the boat. The two black men and the French boy tried to haul the wounded soldier aboard unsuccessfully. Then Staff Sergeant Jan Paczkowski appeared and pulled the injured infantrymen from the freezing Channel. Next, Paczkowski grabbed Codianni and pulled him from the water to the safety of the tug's deck.

"Codianni, I'm glad you made it," Sergeant Paczkowski said trying to smile. The shivering Codianni was taken down to the boat's boiler room, which was crowded with soldiers, some of whom appeared to be dead. "I just flopped down and lay there," he would say. "I was in a hell of a lot of pain and I thought I was gonna die."

After the tug docked at Cherbourg, Sergeant Paczkowski carried the limp Codianni up the stairs on his back, like a sack of potatoes, and placed him on a waiting stretcher.

When Codianni arrived at a French hospital, most of the medical staff was off at a holiday party. Two prisoners of war (POWs) took him up to a ward, but because no bed was available, he was left in the hallway on a stretcher. A couple of hours passed, and a bed was finally located. Vincent Codianni has never forgotten the compassion shown him by a POW and a black soldier, who were present in the ward that night. "I was shaking like a leaf. A POW was passing by and noticed me; he went over to one of the soldiers and told him that I looked like I was dying . . . I was shaking. This soldier, with his leg in a cast, came over. He was a black soldier from one of the ordnance companies in the area, and he had been injured while on duty. He asked me what the problem was. When I told him, he went and got some blankets and threw them on me."

Returning to Cherbourg, the tug *ATR-3* drew too much water to dock at the fleet landing. Recalled Hugh Jones, who had operated the bridge radio throughout the rescue, passing information back to shore headquarters, "We had to send the survivors over in a Landing Craft Mortar (LCM). Some of them were terrified of making the short trip to shore and I don't blame them one bit. They had already been through "hell" that night!"

Recalled Keith Simons of his arrival in Cherbourg, "I'll never forget walking up that dock in the dark in my stocking feet. There was a big sign that said, 'Merry Christmas.' I thought, how ironic. Then I thought, what a gift—*Life.*"

The PC carrying Lieutenant George Rehder bumped against the dock at Cherbourg and cut its engines. Lieutenant Rehder and those with him in the lifeboat had made it to safety. For the first time that night, a humbled Lieutenant Rehder stepped onto solid ground. Years later, he would write, "The scene that I witnessed was indelibly pressed into my mind . . . There were small boats, tugboats, pleasure boats, and work craft all tied on either side of us, under giant floodlights. It was like daylight even though it was past midnight. Backed up just behind the dock, with their doors wide open, was a long line of ambulances—ambulances with a big Red Cross painted on each of them. The process of loading these ambulances with bodies and the injured was proceeding rapidly. As fast as one ambulance would take on its load and leave, another would come up in its place. That was the vision that hit me as I came on deck . . . We didn't talk, we just watched."

"He [Leslie Hoffman] was outgoing and fun-loving and enjoyed life.
He really hadn't had a chance to live as he was only 24 when lost." . . .
Alison Hoffman (sister of Lieutenant Leslie Hoffman).

Doctor Fran Shields was a very close friend of Lieutenant
Leslie E. Hoffman, Jr., of Herkimer, New York. He knew that
Hoffman was with the 66th Division and that the Division was
scheduled to go to Europe. He has said of Lieutenant Hoffman,
"We spent many happy hours together before the war." Recalling
that Christmas Eve, Dr. Shields wrote, "I was stationed at a field
hospital in Normandy—probably fifteen to twenty miles west of
Cherbourg. On Christmas Eve, 1944, while we were celebrating
Midnight Mass (I was serving the Chaplain), we were alerted that
an American ship had been torpedoed in Cherbourg harbor. We
interrupted mass immediately and sped toward the area in our
ambulances. There, we joined other Army outfits in bringing
survivors on shore and to local hospitals. It was during the rescue
operation that I learned the torpedoed ship (the *Leopoldville*) was
carrying the 264th Regiment of the 66th Division—Lieutenant
Hoffman's outfit.

However, he was not among the known survivors. I, of course, inquired about him among the survivors and eventually found a soldier who said that Lieutenant Hoffman was among the officers who remained on board until his enlisted men were off the ship. He obviously never made it himself. Because of wartime censorship I was not able to pass this sad information on to his mother until the war was over."

Sergeant Cornelius P. Burk was also one of the fortunate ones who was rescued.

When Private William Kalinowski reached the docks, they were lined with soldiers. Kalinowski had lost his clothes in the disaster, and as he hurried to a waiting ambulance he tripped and the blanket that covered his nakedness fell to the ground. Kalinowski covered himself again and the ride to the hospital proceeded without further incident.

Sergeant George Bigelow remembered being placed on a stretcher and being put into an ambulance, but then he blacked out. Lying in one of the beds in the hospital at Cherbourg he regained consciousness as a nurse brushed back his hair and told him to rest.

Staff Sergeant Donald Gengler was also placed in an ambulance and raced to a hospital. He was treated for cuts on his legs and for pneumonia, which kept him hospitalized for eight days. But Gengler had survived. A number of young men from his company had not.

Along with many of his fellow crewmen, Staff Sergeant P.J. Casadonte was ordered to the unloading area where survivors were arriving in ever greater numbers. Recalled Casadonte, "I assisted survivors off the small craft that picked them up. I will always remember the look of horror mixed with a kind of relief on their faces knowing that they had made it to safety. We put them in vehicles that transported them to an area field hospital. Some members of our crew were sent out to see whether they could find any survivors or bodies. They found a few bodies! Other craft that were on the scene had picked up most of the bodies and any survivors that remained. We returned to our ship about midnight. Coming across the Channel earlier in the day we were planning a little Christmas celebration for that evening . . . It never happened!"

There were three general hospitals in the immediate vicinity, and a plan was hastily conceived to rush the injured soldiers directly to them. Captain Levine and his medics were to speed the wounded survivors via ambulance to the 165th, 167th, and 280th general hospitals. Commanded Captain Levine, "Leave your kits here. They'll be coming in so fast we won't have time nor room to work on 'em. But bring all the morphine!"

Surgical Technician Sergeant John V. Corrigan threw a blanket over a soaking wet young man and led him to a waiting ambulance. "You'll be OK. How are you feeling?" Corrigan asked. "I'm cold," the youth stuttered.

When Corrigan returned to help the next survivor, the fellow waved him off, "I'll be all right, thanks. Please help some of the other guys." Corrigan could see that more help was needed on the boats that arrived rather than on the pier itself. When he boarded the first ship, he tossed a blanket around a good-looking boy and said, "Here, wrap this around yourself. Say, Bud, what state are you from?" The youth reacted immediately and beamed with pride as he replied, "Pennsylvania!" It was just a little remark, but Corrigan knew it was all the youth needed to bring him to his senses and regain his confidence and self-control. The question worked like a charm. The next boy Corrigan helped was from Texas. "Come on Texas!" Corrigan yelled and the youth leaped up onto the dock.

In addition to his medical bag of tricks, Corrigan also found his sense of humor to be a valuable tool. "Come on, dirty face," he called to a lad with an oil-smeared face. From this bleak occasion in which he had a near fatal experience, the phrase provided a cheerful, reassuring note to the youth. Said Corrigan later, "Instead of telling a nervous and naked boy that he would go into shock if he wasn't wrapped in blankets, I would say, 'Listen pal, there are a lotta people out there, so you'd better put something on.' Many, who only moments before felt that they might not laugh again, broke into grins, which eased the tension that naturally gripped their bodies."

After the survivors had all left the ship, Corrigan scampered back onto the wharf just as Captain Levine ordered two sailors to set down a lad who appeared dead. The Captain took the boy's hand and checked his pulse. Corrigan tore open the front of the youth's coat, sweater, and shirt. He lifted his undershirt so that Levine could listen to his heartbeat. Captain Levine adjusted his stethoscope and moved it around the boy's chest, but there was not even a murmur. Corrigan read his dog tags. "I figured if he was a Catholic, I might help him make a final Act of Contrition," recalled Corrigan sadly. In the lower right-hand corner of the tag was the letter "P," for Protestant.

"Cover him up, Jack, and leave him, he's gone," Levine whispered. Corrigan complied but not before he said a prayer over the body of the young soldier. Remembered Corrigan, "It was the first dead body I had ever handled . . . the first body set over in a dark corner of the pier. It was not the last I handled, nor the last set aside that night!"

As Corrigan turned to leave the area where the dead youth lay, he noticed a Navy Lieutenant lift the blanket and bend over the body. "He's probably checking to see if he recognizes the boy," Corrigan thought to himself. Corrigan's attention was diverted to the scores of survivors, many naked and shivering, arriving at the dock. If any of the survivors showed the slightest sign of going into shock, Captain Levine immediately ordered a stretcher for the freezing soldier. As they worked throughout the night, rank meant little. Helping hands could belong to a Major, a Captain, a Sergeant, or a Private. What mattered was the careful, speedy handling of the cold and injured soldiers on the litters. Saving lives was the only concern.

As fast as Captain Levine and Jack Corrigan passed the boys onto the pier, men carried or helped them to waiting ambulances and trucks. The rows of dead soldiers grew steadily. Recalls Corrigan, "As Captain Levine searched for heartbeats and peered into their glassy eyes, some were beginning to turn slightly blue. I noticed that practically all of the lifeless forms had one thing in common . . . a huge quantity of clothing. Some actually wore heavy overcoats, pistol belts with canteens, cartridge clips, first-aid pouches, combat jackets, fatigue jackets, regular olive drab shirts, heavy woolen undershirts, and cotton undershirts. Their own clothing had pulled them under to their deaths. Panic seized many of them when they hit the water, and they completely forgot to shed that extra weight. Somehow or other I believe the memory of their faces will live with me always. One lad had bitten a piece out of his life preserver and the fluff from it stuck in his mouth and covered his body. Many of them clung to wallets, fountain pens, and small kits, but the most pathetic sight I saw was one young boy who lay with his hands clasped over his chest. Beneath his overcoat and jacket and under his shirt there rested a solitary box of K-rations."

Captain Levine and Corrigan continued to move from body to body, confirming that each soldier was dead. Corrigan noticed that the same Lieutenant who had studied the first body that he had handled was examining all of the bodies that he and Captain Levine had just completed checking. Corrigan became angry. "Doesn't he accept Captain Levine's decision? Who does he think he is? Why does he keep rechecking? Why doesn't he go where he's needed?" Corrigan thought to himself, his resentment mounting.

The tide began to ebb, and the larger craft ran the risk of running aground near the floating dock. An urgent cry turned Corrigan's attention away from the annoying Lieutenant. "Got twelve survivors on board, but I can't bring this ship in any closer. Send out a doctor! We'll need more blankets too."

Within minutes, Levine, Hall, and Corrigan were climbing out of the motor launch and onto the ship. An officer led them to the sleeping quarters, speaking rapidly as they went. "We have about a dozen on board. There are four men in this cabin here, Doctor. There is one on the top deck aft, but he's gone, I'm sure."

Captain Levine stepped into the cabin to examine the first four soldiers. Just then, Corrigan saw the familiar but enigmatic Lieutenant race up the stairway in the direction of the top deck aft. Once again, however, Corrigan's attention was diverted from the Lieutenant by an urgent appeal. "Hey, we got one in bad shape in the galley." Corrigan went to the galley immediately and found what resembled a human form covered by a pile of blankets on the floor. Corrigan reached under the layers of blankets and extracted a chilled arm. He would later say, "I began to feel for a pulse. Suddenly a head belonging to a black-haired lad of about 20 shot out from between the blankets. On his face was the broadest and most welcoming smile I have ever seen.

"Nothing wrong with you, Bud, is there?" Corrigan inquired.

"No, I'm feeling OK, except I'm a bit cold," was the reply.

"Where in hell are your clothes?" Corrigan asked jokingly.

The young soldier simply smiled as Corrigan wrapped another blanket around him and assured him that dry land and a pretty nurse to hold his hand were just minutes away.

Shortly after they returned to the dock and the young soldier was safely on his way to the hospital with the promised pretty nurse, Captain Levine, Hall, Jepson, Smith, Hardin, and Corrigan were once again skimming across the waves of Cherbourg Harbor aboard a PC bound for another errand of mercy. About a mile out, they drew alongside a sub chaser. They were informed by the crew that all of the survivors whom they had rescued had been picked up by smaller craft except for two who were too seriously wounded to be moved. As Corrigan descended the steep stairway, he saw a sailor giving artificial respiration to one of the boys. Captain Levine delegated Hall, Jepson, and Smith to alternate in the life-saving process. Meanwhile, Hardin felt for a pulse. There was none. In a last effort to save the youth, a shot of adrenaline was administered. It had no effect . . . Another body was placed on a litter and covered with a blanket.

Corrigan arrived at the bunk where a lad with a back injury rested. The sailors wisely had not moved him for fear of severing his spinal cord. Captain Levine made a swift diagnosis of a possible fractured pelvis. The medics now faced the problem of moving the youth without aggravating his injury. Under Captain Levine's direction, the medics picked up the entire mattress on which the injured lad lay. Jepson wedged himself beneath the mattress, supporting the youth's back. The soldier was then eased out of the cabin into the narrow aisle. Next he was placed into a wire basket-type stretcher and secured with straps. Ever so carefully, the lad was hoisted up the almost vertical passageway. Soon, he was aboard the PT boat, speeding toward the shore. Corrigan accompanied the youth all the way to the waiting ambulance. Just before the ambulance pulled away, the lad turned to Corrigan, and in words of parting he expressed concern for his mother. "I hope Mom doesn't hear about this, because she will worry about me." Corrigan assured him that wartime censorship would guarantee that she would not know a thing.

At about this time, a loud, bossy MP Captain arrived on the scene. Remembered Corrigan, "With a flourish of his arms and a wagging of his tongue he attempted to organize an operation that was already functioning smoothly. For his efforts he received scant attention from some and outright contempt from others. Today he is probably bragging about how he mastered the situation completely."

Private Gerald Raymond struggled to keep warm. He was taken to an Army hospital and, like so many others, was treated for pneumonia. All around him were young men coughing and gasping for breath. His mind drifted back to the small snow covered Iowa town where his family, unaware of his plight, was celebrating Christmas. He had lost everything he owned when the ship went down, but the Red Cross gave him writing paper, shaving cream, and other personal items. His most precious gift that Christmas, however, was a copy of the New Testament that he received from an Army Chaplin. He would later say, "What a help it was in overcoming my loneliness and discouragement!"

Those survivors who did not require hospitalization were to be brought to the huge mess hall at the Hotel L'Atlantique. Lieutenant Colonel William Ennis was ordered to prepare for housing survivors. He had a dozen semi trailer trucks deliver bedding, cots, and mattresses. Told that he could expect 2,000 men by morning, the beds were stacked side by side in the mess hall. Remembered Lieutenant Colonel Ennis, "We put gallons of coffee on the fire. We cut up hundreds of loaves of bread, and split open dozens of cans of corned beef and spam."

Technical Sergeant Bob Hesse found himself on a pier waiting his turn for the trip to the hospital. He noticed piles of wooden C—and K-ration boxes, which he stacked and set afire to dry the wet and freezing survivors. Perhaps it was at that fire started by Bob Hesse where Private First Class Romeo Mitri and Private First Class Orbie Lind would recall they sat to keep warm. Said Hesse, "We watched for hours as bodies, dead and alive, were brought to the pier. Some live ones were stacked up with the dead ones. Some were so frozen, they could only move their eyes, but that was enough to save their lives."

Yeoman Wesley McEntarfer described how the "bodies" were placed under sheets in a sheltered area of the dock when the preliminary examination indicated that death had occurred. "In more than one instance, I saw a sheet get up and walk, indicating that the severe cold had slowed body functions to the point where it appeared the person was dead but really had a spark of life remaining."

But for William A. Dallas, who participated in the rescue effort that Christmas eve, it was the memory of death, not life, that tortured him for the remainder of his life.

"I thought I was in hell. There were hundreds of bodies lying all over the beach with full packs still on their backs. They were frozen because it was a bitterly cold night, but as they thawed out, their arms slowly came down because they apparently had them raised as they sank under the water and drowned. Their legs straightened out and I was sure hundreds of them were still alive, but the doctors and the medics went from man to man and said, 'This one's gone,' 'there's no life here,' and so on down the line. I wanted to scream at them,' They're still alive, can't you see that?' but what I saw was the bodies thawing out and they were all dead . . . row upon row and all piled up like stacks of wood in our backyard at home . . . When I saw the constant movement, I was sure they were still alive, but their arms came down slowly and they gave a final sigh and collapsed into the sand on the beach."38

Private Ralph Drew, of Midlothian, Maryland, hit the icy, choppy water and lost his life preserver. When he popped up, the water was full of diesel oil and every time he tried to get a breath of air, he got a mouthful of oily saltwater instead. He managed to cut off his boots with his trench knife. He held onto a rope in the water with several other young men but then realized it was not attached to anything.

Drew blacked out and, when he came to, found himself lying on land, naked and protected only by a raincoat. Off in the distance he heard a faint voice. "Throw him up there too!" said the muffled voice. Drew realized that the soldiers thought he was dead and so he yelled, "Hey, I'm alive!"

When the rescue boats rushed to pull men from the freezing water there was no time to properly minister to their urgent needs. Limp soldiers were simply pushed, dropped, or slung out of the way on the decks of the rescue boats. Those who could, crept below decks on their own. Many simply remained where they were until the boats returned to Cherbourg. Once on shore, medics reported that untreated injuries had led to unnecessary deaths.

The medics also found soldiers who had died from "dry land drowning." Young men, who were laid on their backs while still full of saltwater, had vomited and choked on their own tongues. Had they been turned on their stomachs, they might have been saved. There were others who might have been spared had they received artificial respiration. In fairness, the crews aboard the rescue boats were not skilled in life-saving techniques, and their speed in pulling men from the water probably saved many more lives than were lost.

Millard P. Rummel was the senior noncommissioned officer of a unit that controlled a German POW stockade in the Cherbourg district. Rummel's unit was assigned to perform support tasks for the area's American Military Hospital. Rummel "buttoned up" the POW's for the night and proceeded to his quarters, where he contemplated how he would celebrate Christmas. Before he could decide, he was told of the torpedoed troopship and ordered to have his POWs made available for emergency litter-bearer ser vice. By now, it was known that GIs plucked from the frigid waters of the Channel were being brought ashore in great numbers. Many of them were unable to walk.

The magnitude of the emergency soon became apparent, and as the night wore on it became impossible to supervise the POWs properly. If any of them had wanted to escape, they had only to walk away. Instead, they faithfully labored through the night carrying litters. Maybe it was the enormity of the tragedy, maybe it was the Christmas spirit, but whichever it was, nearly 44 years later, Rummel would write, "My memories of that Christmas Eve are of a long line of litters passing en route to a ward or the morgue and the fact that our POWs chose to help and notescape."39

Lieutenant George Stanley Rehder was taken to a small wooden warehouse, where approximately 200 soldiers gathered around a couple of red-hot potbelly stoves. It was somewhere between two and three AM on Christmas morning. Wooden tables had been lined up, end to end. Soldiers with blankets thrown over their shoulders talked in low tones, as they sat in small groups, while others rested their heads on the tables. Still others wandered around aimlessly, searching for their buddies. Perhaps this was the hall where Private First Class Romeo Mitri remembered years later that cheers were heard as new survivors were brought in and recognized.

Lieutenant Rehder looked around him, and the full impact of the catastrophe struck him head on. He was overwhelmed with a sense of bewilderment and guilt. "Why was I spared?" he thought. He remembered an old adage from his military training, "Yours is not to reason why, yours is but to do or die." So powerful was his full realization of the enormity of the disaster that Lieutenant Rehder, half conscious of what he was doing, suddenly climbed up onto one of the tables in the hall. Addressing the dazed and bewildered young soldiers who had survived the night, Rehder said in a strong but compassionate voice, "I think somebody ought to say something right now." The mess hall grew quiet. "Lord God in heaven, for the protection you have given us this night, we thank you. We ask your love and blessing for those who are not with us."

A hush came over the mess hall in the warehouse. A pin dropping would have echoed through the room. Unaware that his mother lay in bed, nauseous and filled with a sense of foreboding, Lieutenant Rehder stepped off of the table. As he did, his eyes filled with tears. There, in a corner across the room he viewed a Christmas tree identical to the one they had decorated with such tender loving care back at camp in Dorcester, England. From the branches of the scraggly tree hung the same homespun ornaments of cigarette packages, balls made from Christmas wrapping paper, and colorful postcards from home. Chains of silver from chewing gum wrappers and cigarette packs formed garlands that circled the tree. At the top of the tree was the same homemade star, fashioned from a flattened tin can. Never again in his lifetime would Lieutenant Rehder behold such a beautiful Christmas tree, which would inspire such compelling sentiments of the true spirit of Christmas.

Trembling and choked with emotion, tears flowed freely down his cheeks. "Thank you, Lieutenant," a blanket-covered GI said as Rehder handed the youth one of the two cups of hot coffee he held in his hands. "We all felt it had to be said."

The light of Christmas Day finally parted the darkness, but it was clear that of the 2,235 soldiers aboard the transport ship, nearly 800 brave souls were lost. There were also 650 soldiers from the *Leopoldville* who suffered injuries. Like so many others that Christmas Day, Sergeant Bob Gianfrancesco's body washed ashore. Upon his release from the hospital, Private First Class Allen T. Parker learned that forty men from his Company were lost. Of the men who had been with him on the deck of the *Leopoldville*, Private First Class Babiel and Coffee had managed to board the destroyer, but Chace, Malczyk, Swanson, and Sergeant Coy Craig had drowned.[40]

Second Lieutenant Robert Blank, aboard the *Jonas Lie*, with its cargo of Sherman tanks, quickly realized that there was submarine activity in the area, as the ship arrived at the western approaches to the British Isles.[41] The escort vessels were dropping depth charges and moving rapidly along their flanks. Lieutenant Blank was advised to scan the water to detect possible torpedo wakes.

As a result, all were very much relieved when, on Christmas Eve, they passed through the torpedo nets and entered the Solent, which is the English body of water that lies between the Isle of Wight and Southampton. An impromptu Christmas celebration was in progress when a launch appeared next to the *Jonas Lie*. A young British woman in uniform, referred to by the British as a Wren, clambered up the ladder and presented sailing orders to the Captain. Lieutenant Blank was surprised to be told that they were leaving at once and that their destination was Cherbourg across the English Channel. The *Jonas Lie* hoisted anchor and headed out into the Channel, where it was soon joined by two other liberty ships. The Navy gun crew was on high alert, having been notified of a sinking of great magnitude some hours before.

Recalled Lieutenant Blank of that crossing, "There was an enormous full moon overhead, which seemed to illuminate the entire sea, so we were astonished when a huge shape appeared off our starboard side, which we later learned was the French heavy cruiser *Lorraine*. Later, we realized that a report of the torpedoing of the *Leopoldville* had been transmitted to the high command, and this French vessel had been hurriedly sent to guard us against attack in the submarine-infested waters." Continued Lieutenant Blank, "It was quite early, but after sunrise, when our ship and two others sailed into Cherbourg on Christmas morning. But before we entered the harbor we saw the horrific sight of hundreds of helmet liners, knapsacks, and other floating objects bobbing in the water. We understood then that there had been a great marine disaster."[42]

P.J. Casadonte, who had assisted survivors the night before, recalled, "We awoke to a very sad situation on Christmas morning. There on the dock were Army personnel, loading dead soldiers aboard Army trucks. They loaded them . . . a line of men at the feet, another line at the heads . . . and there were a lot of them!"

Sergeant Miguel Velez, who had missed sailing on the *Leopoldville* because he was fighting his own life-and-death battle with double pneumonia, later wrote in his diary, "On Christmas, a rumor that the 66th Division was crossing the Channel was spreading, and that night, a sailor said he saw a torpedoed boat and that he had been told that either the 262nd Regiment or the 264th, had gone down. That gave me a big shock, but I wouldn't believe it. Yet, at the time, it was always in my head . . . I couldn't get away from it."

Remembered Lieutenant Pete Wood, "The first real indication of the magnitude of the tragedy came to me a day or so after our landing [at Cherbourg]. We were standing on the dock, as other survivors were being brought in. A small rescue vessel pulled up to the dock and five or six men got off, among them a former classmate at OCS, a platoon leader of Company F, 262nd Infantry. He was apparently unharmed physically but was thoroughly shaken. "My God! This is all that's left of Company F—five men?" The men of Company F had been in the compartment where the torpedo hit. Recalling how he checked the roster of those men missing, Norman Bullett said, "It was a sad time for the men of the 66th Division."

Chief Warrant Officer Kaplan of battalion supply was a busy litter-bearer throughout that night. On Christmas morning, John Corrigan learned from Kaplan that the Navy Lieutenant who had puzzled and irked him when they tended to the wounded and dying was in fact not a medical doctor, but a Navy Chaplain. Corrigan's feelings of annoyance toward the Navy Lieutenant changed to admiration when he realized why the officer bent over each boy on a litter. The Lieutenant was a Catholic Chaplain conditionally administering the last rites of the Church. Wrote John Corrigan years later, "I am sure that it would be a source of some comfort to the hundreds of bereaved parents to know that a man of God was on the scene. Never will I forget the manner in which that Chaplain seemed to be everywhere at once on that Christmas Eve." Continued Corrigan, "As a whole, our unit performed exceedingly well, despite the fact that it happened to be our first really large-scale emergency. Perhaps our months of association with Captain Levine had groomed us for the task. It's true, we didn't render much actual first-aid treatment, as our role was chiefly to speed up the evacuation to the hospitals; yet we went to bed early Christmas morning content that we had been of vital service to hundreds of our fellow servicemen. Frankly, I was proud of the manner in which I had behaved. Perhaps it was my years of participating in athletics and in public speaking that aided me in remaining calm, cool, and collected. In handling the dead bodies, I felt myself growing callous until I grabbed the belt of an overcoat to lift a body. As I did, the face rolled into full view, and glassy eyes stared up at me as water gurgled out of the mouth. After that, I handled each body as if it were the body of my closest friend."

Only 17, including the Captain, of the 235-man Belgian crew and British Armed Guard were lost. The submarine responsible for the disaster, *U-486*, slipped away and on December 26, 1944 while still operating off the French coast near Cherbourg, sank the British *Capel* and damaged the *Affleck*.43 Captain Gilchrist, aboard the *YMS 305* once again arrived on the scene of sunken ships. He ordered his minesweeping gear in and put out his small boat to pick up survivors. This time, Gilchrist rescued four injured sailors but also removed three bodies from the Channel's frigid waters.

On Christmas Day, many of the transport ship's survivors enjoyed a turkey dinner with all the trimmings, but few would recall that Christmas meal as fondly as Sergeant George Chun Fat. Near Cherbourg, a black Quartermaster outfit was stationed who handled all the freight moving into the harbor area. In 1944 the Army was still segregated, and black soldiers believed that they were fighting not only the Axis powers but deep-rooted racial hatred as well.

On Christmas Day 1944, however, there was no thought of race—only compassion for the men of the 66th Division who had lost everything, and who in many cases were left literally naked. And so George Chun Fat remembers, with a lump in his throat, the black soldiers of that Quartermaster outfit who shared their turkey dinners, candy, and cigarettes with their white comrades in arms.

That night, glad to be alive, many of those soldiers sang carols as they gathered around the same Christmas tree in the corner of the warehouse on the dock where Lieutenant Rehder had offered his brief prayer for those who were lost. Singing along with the rest, Staff Sergeant Bob Desnoyer, of Granada Hills, California, could hardly believe that just a few hours before many of these men were showing gifts and cards to each other that they had received from family and friends. The passage of fifty years has not lessened Desnoyer's sadness over the loss of a sweater that his wife Rita had knitted for him.

Private Earl Jacobs survived the icy waters of the English Channel that Christmas Eve. He had no serious injuries but spent a week in the hospital recovering from the trauma of the disaster, which left him destitute. Yet, Earl Jacobs remembers that Christmas Day as fondly as does George Chun Fat. Jacobs could not have received a better present than the one he received on that Christmas 1944. Raymond Jacobs, Earl's brother, took part in the rescue efforts that terrible night, and while searching desperately through the survivors list, Raymond discovered Earl's name. The two brothers were reunited in the hospital. Said Earl Jacobs, years later, "We shared the Christmas package that he got in the mail. I never got mine."[44]

When West Point graduate, Second Lieutenant Donald G. MacWilliams, awoke in a Cherbourg hospital he momentarily thought that he had died and gone to heaven. Recalled MacWilliams years later, "Then a small radio by my bed emitted the lovely sound of Jo Stafford singing 'I'll Be Home For Christmas' and I realized that I was a very lucky man."

The next day MacWilliams and many others were moved to neighborhood houses because yet another ship was sunk. Fuel aboard the vessel caught fire, and many men jumped into the flaming seas and were badly burned and required immediate attention and beds. Said MacWilliams, "The French people were very kind and caring and welcomed us into their homes."

Red-haired West Pointer, Second Lieutenant Edwin "Rojo" Aldrich, faithfully carried the musette bag containing the Company E, 264th Infantry payroll that he had rescued from the sinking *Leopoldville.* When he arrived at the assembly area in France, he could find no one qualified to relieve him of the bag. Rojo, therefore, personally held the money for more than a week until a finance officer was located who could accept it. Rojo arranged for guards to protect him and the money while he slept. He would later say, "The payroll was more trouble than surviving the torpedo attack."

Anthony Cacace

Three days had passed since the tragedy. It was December 27, 1944, the birthday of Staff Sergeant Anthony Cacace. Back in Brooklyn, New York, his loving mother sat down and wrote him his V-mail birthday greeting. The passage of more than 52 years has not dimmed the light of her beautiful sentiments and well wishes for her son's birthday.

"December 27, 1944 . . . Dear Son, Happy Birthday and God bless you. I hope we can have lots of fun your next birthday. How are you, son. I guess you must have moved because you have your old A.P.O. number back. Lots of luck wherever you are. Son, did you have a nice Christmas? I had a very quiet one. We are all well at home and in another couple of weeks Dad will be able to go to work. Today he went to the doctor for a checkup. Gramma and all of your aunts send you their love. Brother, did you get Sonny's letter yet? He wrote and told me that he wrote to you. Ginny is still home. Nothing happened yet. I was hoping it would happen today, and so did she, but the day isn't through yet. Gee, but I miss you and did I ever tell you how much I love you. Brother, Christmas Day uncle Johnny and your uncles on Dad side were here, but I had gone to wish Gramma a Merry Christmas, so Dad and I missed them and uncle Johnny had his stepson with him. He came home from overseas. Something is wrong with him. Gee, I get through so fast with this paper, so son, I end with lots of love and kisses and again Happy Birthday. Love Mom, I love you X."

Louise Cacace was confident that her son and the other young men of the 66th Division had spent a pleasant Christmas somewhere in England. She was happy and certain that by Christmas 1945 she and her sons would all be reunited.[45]

Meanwhile, the young men of the 66th Division in Cherbourg, France, grateful to be alive, mourned the deaths of their comrades. One such young man was Technical Sergeant Bob Hesse. To pass the censors, his letter of December 30 to his parents could only hint at the terrible tragedy that had transpired just a few days before. "I hope to be able to tell you how we all spent our Christmas Eve before long. I can't tell you anything except that in one way it was the best Christmas I have ever spent in my whole life and then again it was the worst . . . Don't worry about anything because everything is OK."

In one of the many coincidences concerning the disaster, survivor Alex Yarmosh knew that his brother John, was stationed with the Navy in Cherbourg. Alex asked a sailor if he knew John Yarmosh. "Yeah," replied the sailor, "He's peeling potatoes in the tent for Christmas dinner." Thus, the two brothers were reunited on that Christmas Day. Bob Hesse's parents received yet another hint that something was wrong when they read John Yarmosh's letter dated December 31, 1944. "I am the brother of Sergeant Yarmosh who is in your son's platoon. Your son looks fine and is in great shape . . . Don't worry about him, he is safe and sound."

Vincent Codianni, who could not call out for help because his tongue was split in half, spent two weeks in a French hospital before he regained his strength. But he remained haunted by the memory of that Christmas Eve nightmare.

A tent city alongside a hill was erected to house the 66thDivision survivors. It quickly became known as "Purple Heart Hill." Private William Kalinowski still remembers that on December 26, it was announced that a late Christmas Mass would be held for the German POWs working at the hospital. He went to the mass and remains convinced that he was the only GI who participated. The chapel was filled with Germans. Remembered Kalinowski, "As they went up for communion and when they sang 'Silent Night,' I kept choking and swallowing hard!"

Angelo Catalano

Chapter 7

Missing in Action

"Christmas was now the memory of death, not the joy of the birthof Christ."
. . . Jerry Catalano

Perhaps the three most phenomenal telepathic experiences on that Christmas Eve happened to Della Olson, wife of Chaplain Arnold Olson; the mother of Robert Banks from Chicago, Illinois; and the mother of Staff Sergeant Gregory G. Jurlina, the young lad who was born in Yugoslavia but raised in Donora, Pennsylvania. Della Olson would later write, "My heart ached even to the point of actual physical pain all afternoon and evening on that December 24, 1944." At first, she dismissed it because it was the first Christmas that she and her husband were separated. Her feelings of foreboding were compounded by not knowing where he was, but she concealed her fears to provide their children with the joy of a traditional Christmas celebration. Despite the shortage of butter and sugar, Della managed to prepare for her children some of their favorite goodies. With the opening of gifts and the evening meal completed, the children were tucked into bed.

Della herself soon retired and very quickly fell sound asleep. Later she would recall, "It could not have been long afterward when I found myself sitting bolt upright in bed fully awake as if someone had called my name and said, 'Arnold needs prayer right now!' It was not until almost a year later when Arnold had returned home and we were discussing our respective experiences [that] I learned [why] I was awakened so suddenly—Arnold was in shock as the reality of the night's terrible disaster hit him as mangled and dismembered bodies of his men were still being retrieved from the sea."

Gregory Jurlina was one of the 72 soldiers from the state of Pennsylvania killed in the disaster. He met Joseph Jordan while they were members of the ASTP at the Colorado School of Mines. Jordon so admired Jurlina that he named his son Gregory in honor of his 66thDivision buddy.

Robert Banks was among the hundreds of young men between the ages of eighteen and twenty-one floundering in the forty-eight degree waters of the English Channel crying out in desperation for their mother's to save them from the darkness that was about to cover them forever! All around him, Banks watched drowning men slip silently into the depths. As he awaited his own fate, he screamed into the void at the top of his lungs, "MOTHER, MOTHER, HELP ME MOTHER!!!"

Thousands of miles away in Chicago, Illinois, Annette Banks, like Della Arnold, suddenly was jolted from her sleep. In a state of panic, she rose from her bed and after pacing the floor for several minutes stared out the window into the bleak winter night. Then she woke her sleeping husband. Consumed with fear, she told her husband, Joseph, "Something is terribly wrong; in my sleep I heard Bob calling out to me!"

However, the most incredible telepathic experience that occurred on Christmas Eve of 1944 concerned the mother of Company F, 262nd Regiment Staff Sergeant Gregory Jurlina. At the family's traditional Christmas Eve dinner, supper candles were lit that symbolized God's safekeeping over Greg and the rest of the family. Greg's candle, however, would not light and kept sputtering out. His sister, Mary

Steranko, recalls that her father swallowed hard and explained it was the wax on the wick, but neither her mother nor her father could hide their concern for their son. Even more strangely, on Christmas Eve 1944, Greg's mother dreamed that he was knocking at the door. When Greg came home on his various furloughs he would knock on the door and then hide at the side of the house. When his mother answered the door, he would jump out and happily surprise her. So real was the dream that she dressed and went outside looking for him but found nothing. 46 That Christmas morning, her footprints were still visible in the fresh snow on the ground.

o o o

The first letter received from her soldier husband by Margie Cycon in the new year of 1945 was dated January 11. Staff Sergeant Joe Cycon was now in France. Many years later, Joe Cycon's daughter Karen would write, "I believe he loved Bill Donnelly as a brother and was totally devastated by his death."

"I would have liked to be in Walton [New York] with you on Xmas Eve. I bet the kids had a good time . . . I hope we can all be together next xmas. I wish I could tell you how I spent Xmas Eve, but it will have to wait . . . the censors wouldn't pass it . . .

. . . Darling, don't talk any more about Bill—he's gone and I want to forget it. Don't worry about me, as I'm alright and I'm taking good care of myself. All I'm waiting for is to be with you again. It seems like an awful long time since I last saw you. Don't forget to send me some pictures of yourself. I lost all the others I had."

Joe Cycon continued to write Margie on a regular basis, but the mood of his letters did not change and hinted that something terrible must have happened that past Christmas Eve.

"January 26, 1945 . . . The weather is miserable right now. It's raining like hell, as if we didn't have enough mud here. Honey, don't send me any cigarettes as I have enough . . . You can get me a pipe. I lost the one I had. I lost my identification bracelet too; don't think I was careless with it because I liked it. I can't tell you how I lost it because it wouldn't pass the censors.

"January 29, 1945 . . . I got a letter from you tonight in which you asked me, or rather told me, about the phone call you received from Mrs. Neely. It's true about Howard De Martini and the other guy . . .

they were good friends of mine. The same thing happened to Bill and that wasn't easy to take. You know how much I thought of Bill, but I can't give you any more information about it as the censors will not let it go thru [sic]. Call up Mrs. Neely and tell her that as soon as I can, I'll tell you all about it . . . You see I was with him at the time."

Staff Sergeant Howard W. De Martini, Company F, 262nd Regiment, was from Northvale, New Jersey, and his body was never recovered. Sergeant Fred L. Neely, Company K, 262nd Regiment, resided in Clarinda, Iowa. The disposition of his body is unknown by me at this time, although it may have been returned to his family in the United States for permanent burial. Joe Cycon's buddy, Staff Sergeant William O. Donnelly, Company F, 262nd Regiment, lived in Cincinnati, Ohio. His body was never found. Company F was housed where the torpedo struck the troopship. Joe Cycon and his other good friend Staff Sergeant Walter T. Brown were alive because the "slop" that had passed for dinner made them sick and both had left their quarters in search of the latrine.

Pvt. Salvatore C. Cuccia

There were 175 men assigned to Company F of which nineteen survived. Joe Cycon was one of five men from the 2nd Platoon who lived. The bodies of the remaining thirty-three soldiers in his platoon were never recovered. Walter T. Brown was one of three soldiers from the Weapons Platoon to survive. The bodies of the remaining twenty-six were never found. In all, there were only four known dead: First Lieutenant Norman U. Bradenback (Hillsboro, Illinois), Private First Class Lucius E. Jackson (Lincoln, Massachusetts), Private Salvatore C. Cuccia (Silver Creek, New York), and Staff Sergeant Marvin L. Rilling (Seligman, Arizona). The bodies of the other 152 men were never found.

Joe Cycon's next letter home was written on February 2. The pain of the *Leopoldville* disaster remained evident from his message. "I hope that when this war ends they'll forget about censorship right away. I got a lot to tell and keeping quiet just drives me nuts and I know how much you'd like to know what I'm doing. All I can say is I'm still healthy and kicking . . . glad to be alive. I just want to get home to you as soon as possible. I love you darling more than ever."

He again hints at the enormity of the *Leopoldville* disaster in his letter of February 5. "Honey, Bill isn't here anymore . . . he's gone, along with De Martini and Warner [Private First Class Edwin R. Warner, Utah]. I can't tell you anymore about it so you explain it to Mrs. Neely . . . and it's not a good feeling talking about Bill all the time."

Joe Cycon's next two letters expressed his deep feelings of homesickness and his yearning for Margie. "I just keep dreaming of the good old days we used to have and I sort of go through them all in memory . . . I'll never want to leave home when I get back honey . . . When you talk about our future in your letters it really makes me homesick. It sounds so nice . . . I'll just keep looking forward to the day when I can be with you again darling and then I'll be the happiest guy on earth."

Then, on February 11, he wrote the letter that would explain all that had happened. ". . . I thought that since the latest one you got [letter] was dated Jan. 22 you knew about Bill, but in the letter today you asked about him. Honey, he's gone like H. De Martini and the other guy that Mrs. Neely called you about. It's not very easy to talk about it. I hope you know what I mean . . . Honey, I'm sending you a pair of handmade lace gloves that I bought from some French woman . . . They are expensive. I hope they get to you alright."

When Margie Cycon received Joe's letter she did not attempt to try on the gloves for several weeks. She had been receiving numerous letters and phone calls from anxious relatives of men in Joe's company asking her if she could obtain information from him about their sons and husbands whom they had not heard from since Christmas. Margie was therefore very depressed and had put the gloves aside. One day, when she finally picked them up and attempted to try them on, one finger refused to go all the way into the glove. Something was stuck inside it. Wedged into the glove was a small rolled up newspaper item. It was a short article concerning the troopship *Leopoldville,* which had been sunk.

London, January 14. The German radio speculated today that the 11,509-ton ship *Leopoldville,* a former Belgian passenger liner, had been sunk between England and France while in use as an Allied troop transport.

Berlin said two lifeboats bearing the liner's name had been washed ashore in the Channel Islands and that one of the boats held military equipment, establishing that troops of the 262nd United States Infantry Regiment had been shipwrecked. There was no Allied report of such a happening.

Thus, did Joe Cycon outwit the censors and inform his wife Margie that he had survived the sinking of the *Leopoldville* while his good friend Bill Donnelly and many others had apparently been lost.

o o o

During 1944 the Post Office struggled to maintain mail service at a time when it faced an increasing shortage of available manpower. Even though he was just 14 years old, Jerry Catalano had successfully applied to assist in mail delivery. While performing those duties during the Christmas holidays he caught pneumonia. The end of January 1945 saw the teenager still home recovering from his illness. Jerry Catalano still recalls vividly the day an old man appeared at their door and handed the telegram to his mother informing her that his brother Angelo was missing. Even though his mother could not read or speak good English she immediately grasped what the telegram meant. She ran through the house, screaming out for her son, her cries of anguish resounding in young Jerry's ears.

Peter Acri with Velma and Jim. Velma had a portrait taken of her with baby James Douglas. Later, she had that picture superimposed on a portrait of Peter

When his father came home, he was devastated by the news. During that Christmas season of 1944, Private First Class Roe Catalano was fighting in Belgium, where he was wounded. Roe was sent to Paris for a period of rest and recuperation. While there, he met members of the 66th Panther Division. From them he learned of the disaster and that his brother's company was hard hit. A worried Roe Catalano asked a chaplain to inquire about his brother, only to have his worst fears confirmed. He already half expected the dire answer to his question since his letters to Angelo were being returned unanswered. A desolate Roe wrote home that he wished he could have taken his brother's place in the troopship because of Angelo's plans to marry Beverly.

With the pain over the loss of his beloved brother still intense, Jerry Catalano would write 50 years later, "Our entire family was never the same again . . . Christmas was now the memory of death, not the joy of the birth of Christ. It was many years before we would celebrate Christmas as we should. Everyone grew up and had families, and that required a change in our lives to celebrate again with our families the joy we once knew."

It was January 17, 1945, when the doorbell rang and the Western
Union boy handed Velma Acri the telegram that sent her into shock.
Her husband was reported missing in action in the English Channel.
She had no idea of the circumstances, and every night she sat by
the radio hoping for news that possibly he had been taken prisoner.
Day after day, week after week, Velma would slump into her favorite
living room chair and tearfully read over and over again Pete's last
letter home. "December 21, 1944 . . . Southern England . . . Dearest,
Yesterday was a very good day for me. I received four letters from
you and a card. I also got letters from Mom, Mrs. Crump, my local
union, and a church paper. I had quite an enjoyable hour or so
reading them. Gee Hon, I could almost win this war single handed
after reading a few of your letters.

They make me feel so proud of you and Jim [their son]. I sure
am the luckiest fellow in the world to have such a swell family waiting
for me when I come home. It seems as if I've been away for years
instead of just a few months. I'm storing up an awful lot of loving
for you and Jim. Hon, I would like to keep a diary like you said, but
it's against regulations. That's because they don't want the enemy to
get a hold of any information that might be of help to them. A diary
would trace one man in a certain unit and naturally wherever that
man has been so will have been the rest of the outfit. See what I'm
driving at Hon? Looks like the diary is out. Darling, tell your folks
I appreciate their thoughtfulness, but there really isn't anything I
need that they could get me for Xmas. Tell them to use the money
somewhere else where it will do the most good. If the feeling is
there then the present doesn't really matter. In Mrs. Crump's letter
to me she told me how Muzz died. Muzz was buried in France, or
did you know? If I ever get over in that direction I'm going to try
and visit his grave. He's buried somewhere near Rouen. I thought
he died at sea, but her letter tells me he died in a British Hospital
at Rouen, probably from shock. I'll send the letter a little later
on . . . then you can read all the details. Hon, I've got an awful lot
of other mail to catch up on so you'll have to excuse me if I drop
this off now.

All my love & kisses . . . Your faithful hubby, Pete P.S. Please send
me some food."

"It wasn't fair," Velma sobbed out loud biting down hard on her
lip. Mrs. Crump and her husband Fred did not have any children

and so they idolized their nephew, Martin (Muzz) Miller. A few years older than Pete, Muzz was in the Navy. On September 25, 1944, his minesweeper was torpedoed, and Muzz was badly burned. Muzz, the apple of his Aunt's and Uncle's eyes, was gone. And now Pete. "Dear God! Bring him home safe," Velma prayed.

A second telegram arrived on March 7, 1945. It confirmed Peter L. Acri's death. Velma later wrote, "*This was the worst day of my life! His older brother and I went to tell his parents that Pete's death was confirmed . . . it was so traumatic. I tried to hold up for them, as I know it would be a terrible thing to lose a son. I know God gave me our son [so that I would] have a part of Pete.*"

o o o

Christmas morning, the twins mother, Dorothy Lowry, went to visit the home of her neighbor and good friend, Mrs. Hazel Zundel. As was her custom, she came bearing Christmas gifts for everyone in the house, including Hazel's husband and daughter-in-law, Mrs. Helen Zundel. Dorothy's husband was not with her because she wasn't planning to stay for a prolonged visit. She was awfully upset and extremely nervous. It was clear to all present that something was terribly wrong. Everyone noticed that Dorothy just couldn't sit still. Dorothy herself expressed to those in the room that she didn't know what to do with her self and felt like she was going crazy that morning.

When questioned by her friend Hazel what was wrong, she told her that she felt something had happened to her boys. It was obvious to everyone in the room that Dorothy was truly grief-stricken. Overcome with emotion, Dorothy cried out, "Something terrible has happened to my boys!" Hazel shot back, "Oh Dorothy! Don't act like that. I have two boys over there. I'm praying for them to come home, but you don't see me acting like that and falling apart!" The heartbroken Dorthy, crying openly, with tears streaking down her face, blurted out, "You don't understand Hazel . . . Your boys are coming home, mine aren't!" Everyone in the house became so overwhelmed with Dorothy's genuine anguish that all began to cry. At the time they thought she was just another mother missing her boys over the Christmas holiday.

Glenn & Jack Lowry with their mother while home on leave

o o o

On Christmas Day 1944, Helen Appleby and her husband Walter
celebrated the holiday with dinner at his parent's home. Walter's mother
asked everyone to join her in a prayer for Preston's safe return. Then,
before dinner was served, as a highlight for everyone seated at the table
for the festive occasion, Helen Appleby shared Preston's most recent
letter. "Somewhere in England . . . December 2, 1944 . . . Dear Mom and
Dad, Hello folks, how is everyone? Do you know that in 6 more days I will
be 30 years old. I feel as though I am getting quite aged. I have finally
gotten settled down here and think I will enjoy myself. The country here
is really beautiful. Every part of it seems to be cared for by someone. The
fields, as far as you can see, look as smooth as the lawns in our front yards.
The country is dotted with small villages in picturesque spots. Quite a
few of the houses have thatched roofs, which adds to the quaintness
of the place. I wish you both could make a trip over here sometime as
I believe you would really enjoy traveling through the country. By the
way Dad, I rode on one of their trains and it was quite an experience.
Each car is partitioned off into several compartments, which open out
onto the platform but have no connection. They have first-, second-, and

third-class compartments. The passenger and freight cars are quite tiny in comparison to ours. How are Walter, Helen, and Davy? I hope the war is over soon. The news looks pretty good and it looks as though it won't be too long now. I am planning on visiting London soon and am looking forward to seeing the place. I may also have a chance to visit Southampton some time soon. I must close now. Write soon. Lots of Love, Bub"

Helen joked with the other family members gathered at the table about Preston's turning thirty and feeling that he was getting so ancient. Little did Helen realize that when Preston wrote those words he had only twenty-two days to live.

Following the New Year, Preston's father wrote him on January 3, 1945. "Hello Preston, You don't know how glad we all were to get your letters and to know you made the trip OK. Bub, I got a kick out of your ride on the English train. Mom and I went to Western Union and cabled you $50. The operator said you should have it in 2 days. I do hope you get it that quick. We wanted to mail it sooner, but Western Union would not send it to the first A.P.O. that you gave us. We all had a very nice Christmas . . . I got to see David on his first Christmas morning. Of course he did not guess what it was all about but he was pretty well excited as he got so many things to play with. I wish you could see him. He is a fine little fellow and looks as much like you as he does Walter . . . Bub, always be on the alert and be as careful as you can. Mom is writing you tonight; also she is writing to Mrs. Cass and Margorie. Emily was here for a couple of days at Christmas and asked all about you . . . Preston, the old Ford is still going. I have to be real careful and take care of it all that I can, as I don't know when I can get another one. As soon as the war is over, I am going to buy a new Ford. Well Bub, write to us as quick as you can and take as good care of yourself as you can. Mom will write often and I will when I can. With lots of love from both of us. Dad"

With her cup still overflowing with the joy of the Christmas season, Preston's mother wrote him a V-mail letter on January 5, 1945. "Dearest Bub, Your letters came. They have made us so happy. I'm sending you Chas's address. I hope you can see him and Roudy. Bub, write us V-mail by airmail as they come much faster that way. Your letters were 1 month in coming. We cabled you $50 on January 3rd. Let us know if you get it. Take care of yourself and please write as often as you can. Worlds of love to you, Mother"

Carl Carlson & Clarence Carlson

o o o

Three days afterward, perhaps because her motherly intuition sensed danger, Preston's mother wrote him again. "Dearest Bub, Let me know if you are getting my letters—also if you have received the money we cabled you. You didn't mention getting any letters from us. We are all average. David is fine. Will have his picture made in a few days and want to send you some of them. I received a letter from Mrs. Cass. She had gotten your letter and was really thrilled. They say these V-mail letters go faster so that's how I'm sending this one. I sent you Chas's address by V-mail a few days ago. Please write as soon as you can. Worlds of love from us all, Mother"

Several days later, his parents were torn with grief when a telegram arrived from the War Department with the news that Preston was dead. Margie Cass' dream of life together with her young love, Preston Appleby, died with him, and she along with her mother, shared the anguish of his heartbroken family.[47]

As painful as the loss of Lieutenant Preston Appleby was to his family and his fiancée Margie Cass, a double loss now appeared imminent for Mr. and Mrs. Carl A.J. Carlson of Jamestown, New York. An Army major from the Buffalo office arrived at their home on the morning of January 26, 1945, with the terrible news that both of the twins were "missing in action." Weeks, and then more than a month, passed, but still there was no word of their fate. That "word" finally was received by Colonel John M. McDowell, Commanding Officer of the Western New York Military District. He directed an Army Captain from the Second Service Command to deliver the message from the War Department to the parents of the twins. Late on the afternoon of Friday, March 9, 1945, the Army Captain arrived at the home of Mr. and Mrs. Carlson and informed them that their only children, both 19 years old—Private First Class Carl Henry, the budding artist, and Private First Class Clarence Helmer, talented accordion player, were both dead.

o o o

The same tragic news of the death of two sons was delivered to two other families who had boys aboard the troopship. Killed when the *Leopoldville* sank were Privates Dan and Sam Borovich, the two former

Sam Borovich   Dan Borovich

coal miners from McDonald, Pennsylvania. They were survived by their parents and four sisters. For their grieving mother and father, there was the added anxiety concerning the safety of their three remaining sons, who were still serving in the Armed Forces. Like Dan and Sam, Pete and Nick Borovich were in the Army and Bert Borovich was serving in the Navy.

O O O

Also lost were twin brothers, Privates First Class Glenn E. and Jack N. Lowry of Belle Vernon, Pennsylvania. Recalled Guy Clark Sawyer of the Lowry brothers, "Jack and Glenn did not want to be separated. After they went into the water, they were never seen again."[48]

It is obvious from the condolence letters received by John and Dorothy Lowry that their twin sons were truly loved by all who knew them. The twin's cousin Wooda Van Hixenbaugh was aboard the U.S. amphibious ground force ship, the *Auburn*, bound for Iwo Jima, when he wrote the following letter of sympathy. "February 6, 1945 . . . Tuesday night . . . Dear Uncle John and Aunt Dorothy, Yesterday, I received a letter from Dad, and in that letter he informed me of the tragic news relating to the twins. I was stunned and for a time speechless and motionless. I did not know what to say, for I began to think of the days that we had spent together, of the times we had, and of our many visits. Right now, there is nothing much that I can say. If I could do anything to make your burden lighter I would do so. If I could say anything to make your great loss seem easier, then I would say it. Perhaps it might be in this. Your faith in Christ and your devotion to that faith will render the load somewhat lighter to carry.

"This note is written rather hastily for I wish it to make the next mail. I will write to you again soon. May the Eternal Father help you now and ever. Yours affectionately, Sonny"

During the battle of Iwo Jima from February 19 through March 16, 1945, the *Auburn* served as the flagship for Rear Admiral H.W. Hill, Commander, Amphibious Group 2. The *Auburn* then saw action at Okinawa from May 31 through June 30, 1945 with Admiral Hill, Commander, 5th Amphibious Force. The *Auburn* departed Okinawa on July 1, 1945, and steamed to Pearl Harbor for repairs.[49] Wooda Van Hixenbaugh survived the terrible kamikaze attacks during the fierce battles on Iwo Jima and Okinawa and was discharged from the Navy on May 20, 1946.

Dorothy Lowry also received a personal condolence message from the Captain of Company I, dated February 23, 1945, which read in part, "A thorough search has failed to recover their bodies. Therefore, it was impossible for us to have a burial service for them. The loss of your sons is keenly felt by all of us. I realize that there is little we, the friends and comrades of Jack and Glenn, can say or do to lessen your great sorrow, but I do want you to know that we share your grief and wish to extend to you our deepest and most heartfelt sympathy. If I can be of service at any time, please do not hesitate to call on me. Sincerely yours, Jack F. Gangwere, Captain, 262nd Regiment"

Perhaps the most deeply moving condolence letter regarding the loss of her sons that Dorothy Lowry received came from Army Chaplain Edgar Douglas who remembered the brothers from their training days back in the States.

"March 6, 1945 . . . Dear Mrs. Lowry, I think nothing I have heard recently has given me a greater shock than your letter received yesterday. Of all the men I've known in the Army the memories of Jack and Glenn and our fellowship together stand out above all others. I have discussed them with Mrs. Douglas, perhaps more than any other two men I've worked with. My interest in them deepened and I learned to appreciate them more each day I was with them. Many, many nights Jack and Glenn would drop in my office and sit and talk with me—of home, of you and of their father, of their church, and their pastor. I think I have never known two boys who loved and appreciated their mother more than they did . . . They were two of the finest, most wholesome Christian boys I have ever known. They reminded me so much of my own sons, and for some reason I was drawn a little closer to them than most of the men I worked with in basic training.

"There come times in our lives when words are not adequate to express our feelings. I can only say to you and their father that you have my deepest sympathy and my earnest prayers in this trying hour . . . There are some things we must accept by faith. We can only put our trust and faith in the Lord at a time like this . . .

"Again let me say that you have my deepest sympathy . . . Very sincerely yours, Edgar L. Douglas Chaplain (Captain) AUS."

o o o

Tragedy also struck the Truelock family back in Sullivan, Indiana. Like his Company I buddies, Glenn and Jack Lowry, the body of Ralph A. Truelock was never found. His daughter Vicki was born on December 29, 1944, just 5 days after his death. Bonnie Truelock posed with her new baby girl next to a small table on which a photo of Ralph was displayed, proudly wearing his 66th Panther shoulder patch. The picture of Bonnie and Vicki was intended as a gift to show him his new daughter, but joy quickly turned to grief when the family read a German report in the back section of the *Terre Haute Tribune* concerning lifeboats of the 66th Division that had floated to the Channel Islands. Said Bonnie, "We knew then that he was gone." Some two weeks later, the dreaded telegram arrived reporting him missing.

Bonnie and Vickie Truelock

Adding to Bonnie's misery, her allotment was stopped by the Army and she could not receive a pension because Ralph was not officially dead for one year. Bonnie lived with Ralph's parents for two years. Said Bonnie, "His mother went off the deep end, and I couldn't leave her. Vicki was all she had. She received the Purple Heart and everything . . . I didn't take the medals till after she died." Continued Bonnie of those sad days, "The boys he ran around with collected pennies to send to me. We bought things for Vicki with them."

o o o

In one of his letters home, Waldron Polgreen considered the possibility that he might be killed during the fighting in Europe. He wrote his wife, "When I go I want to go triumphantly!" He lived life to the fullest and loved nature. In yet another letter he wrote, "When you are lonesome look at the sun by day and the stars by night and I will be watching with you." He enjoyed the Helderberg mountain range located southwest of Albany, New York, and hoped to build a home there with his family after the war. He enjoyed the sunsets and would sit for a long time watching them. He liked long hikes, picnics, and camping trips with his children. He loved his home and wrote his wife, "When I come in and shut the door I am content." He often said that his home was his castle. He wrote, "I miss most you and the boys and the details of home."

He wanted a large family and thoroughly enjoyed all the work and details of bringing them up. When the third baby was born he cared for the two boys himself for a week, not wanting anyone to help him. He wanted to hand down to his sons the rich heritage of his family. For this reason he was interested in his family history and also the history of Albany itself. He had material collected for a history of Albany, weaving in much family history. Although quiet and reserved he enjoyed talking about his antiques, stamps, old prints, and pictures. He was older than most when he married, but by his careful planning and dreaming he was able to make the 6 years a wonderful experience in love and companionship.

Reverend Hobart Goewey, pastor of the Trinity Methodist Church in Albany said of him, "He was gifted with the capacity to love deeply. He had such hope for the future. In all of his letters he spoke of this period as only an interruption of his plans and dreams. He thought a

Frances and Waldron Polgreen and their three children

great deal of this place of worship. From England he wrote, wanting memorial flowers for Christmas for his father but the letter arrived after Christmas."

The body of Private First Class Waldron Polgreen, Company K, 262nd Regiment, was recovered and buried in France. On February 25, 1945, Frances Polgreen wrote a touching letter to her college friends that spoke of her husband's death and of her life without him. "Dear Gang, I have heard from all of you personally and I appreciate your sympathy and affection. It has been a trying time for so many of us. I am getting along quite well . . . Sometimes, I have to get a friend to stay with the boys. Nothing is settled yet. I get the insurance and pension by the month. I know I will manage somehow. We will stay right here . . . This is all I know. On January 15, I had a telegram saying that Waldron was killed in action on December 25 in the European area. In 2 weeks I had a letter from the War Department saying that they had been informed of the destruction of a troop transport ship in the European Theater of Operations and that [my] husband was listed with a small group who were killed in action due to this sinking . . . The report in the Army Office here says it was in the English Channel . . .

Two weeks later, Captain John C. Van Sickle wrote, saying that Waldron was buried in Normandy and that a chaplain of his own faith officiated at the services. On Friday I received a letter from Secretary Stimson, saying that Waldron had been awarded the Purple Heart, posthumously, and that I would receive it soon.

. . . I just have to keep going for the boys' sake . . . Everyone has been so nice to me. I have about 150 letters and cards. It helps to know that so many are thinking of me . . . At Christmas time I expected to send snapshots to all but did not get around to it. It just seemed I could not make any headway with Christmas.

Well, the best of kindly thoughts to each of you. Love, Frances"

o o o

New York City resident Staff Sergeant Dominick Cappello, Company A, 264th Infantry, was one of the 80 men from New York State who was killed in the catastrophe. His father was one of the few parents who actually learned the true circumstances of his son's death. He received a letter from Dominick's Army buddy, Staff Sergeant Henry Dubowski.

Dominick Cappello was apparently struck by a lifeboat that broke loose. He was killed instantly or knocked unconscious, causing him to drown.

"June 29, 1945 . . . Dear Mr. Cappello, . . . I have been wanting to write to you sir for a long time. So please excuse me for waiting so long. I am one of Dominic's buddies. He was with me until the last time I seen him on the boat. I will try an explain as much as I know about what I think happen to 'Cappe.' When we were hit on the 24th of December, Dominic and I ran up on deck together. We had our life preservers on us and we were standing on a staircase going to the ship's headquarters when we noticed that the ship sort of tilted to one side. Then we got near the railing of the ship, when we seen the ship was going down. There was a lifeboat, which was still tied to the ship, and Dominic and I got in it, but the ship tipped over and the boat went down before we had a chance to get the lifeboat loose. After that I went down so deep in the water that I thought I would never get up again. But I finally shot up out of the water and got rid of some of the salt water, which gave me a little hope. I got up on top of the water, the first thing I yelled was 'Cappe, Cappe.' I nick named him that way back in Florida. But I did not hear or see him. What I think is when we got in the lifeboat and the boat went down, it sorta turned over on one side and the lifeboat that was still tied to the boat went down and I think Cappe was hit by the lifeboat. It's funny, I can't swim a stroke, but Cappe was a darn good swimmer, so you see I am sure he was hit by something. I cannot forget Dominic because he and I had a lot of fun together. The boys used to call us the big three. Cappe, Chapman [Staff Sergeant Donald Chapman], and myself. We always palled around together. I used to always like to hear Cappe sing songs, he sure had a nice voice. Mr. Cappello, I sure did not want to bring any sorrow or memories back. But I wanted you to know, I loved Cappello and he and I were like brothers. You can be proud of having such a nice son. He sure was a good fellow and a great guy. Mr. Cappello, have you a picture of Cappe? I would like to have one. I had one but it went down in the Channel.

"I hope you are well and the rest of your family is the same. Give my regards to Mrs. Cappello and the family. So until I can hear from you, may God bless you all. A buddy of your son, Henry"

o o o

That Christmas of 1944, Gerald Raymond lay in a hospital bed in Cherbourg. The 30-year-old father of two children, whose business had been selling livestock minerals and feed to farmers, read the Christmas story from his copy of the New Testament as he had never done before. Gerald Raymond came to the 23rd verse and found himself reading it over and over.

"Behold, a virgin shall be with child, and shall bring forth a son, and they shall call his name Emmanuel," [which means God with us].

He found special comfort in the phrase, "God with us." This verse became his guiding light for the rest of his life. Years later, Gerald Raymond wrote, "I realized that because of Christ's birth, He had been with me during the night, and He was with me in my hospital bed. Feeling His presence gave me a peace and joy I'd never known before."

On a Saturday in early January 1945, Gerald Raymond's outfit reassembled at the Cherbourg fairgrounds. They were addressed by a Lieutenant, who admonished them, "Tomorrow is Sunday. I'm sure some of you made promises out there in the water you'll want to keep." That Sunday the churches were filled to overflowing. Not long after that, it was off to the front and the waiting German soldiers . . . The killing resumed.

But Gerald Raymond had discovered a new course in his life. War and the *Leopoldville* disaster had brought him to a crossroads in his earthly journey. Reflected Gerald Raymond some 36 years later, "I carried my New Testament with me and read it at every opportunity . . . God had spared my life, bolstered my faith, and created in me a desire for more active service in His work . . . Christmas is 'God with us'—through every circumstance!"

Members of the 66th Infantry Division in France 1945

Chapter 8

Aftermath

"I led patrols up into no man's land . . . I took chances that I wouldn't think about taking today."
. . . Norman Bullett

The survivors of the *Leopoldville* were issued new clothing, and preparations were made to move out. Because their M1 rifles were lost in the disaster they were issued World War I 03 rifles. The weapons were loaded with cosmoline, which had to be cleaned out entirely before use. Only one bullet at a time could be loaded into the 03. Said Sergeant Donald Gengler, Company K, 262nd Regiment, "We were relieved when we received new M1s just prior to shipping out."

Following the *Leopoldville* disaster, its fighting strength vitally sapped, the 66th Division was chosen to replace the men of the 94th Infantry Division. The relief began on December 26, in the Lorient Sector, and on New Year's Day 1945, full responsibility for containing the German pockets at Lorient and St. Nazaire passed to the 66th Infantry Division. That they were not considered part of the "big picture" was small consolation to the men of the 66th who were injured fighting the Germans or to the families of the soldiers killed in battle while serving in France.

o o o

Frank M. Caldarone, Technician 5th Grade, Company I, 262nd Infantry, Stamford, Connecticut, was one of those killed. On April 19, 1945, Caldarone was a member of a support squad of a combined Tank-Infantry attack against a strong German force. The tanks passed through the Infantry, and as the assault squads pushed forward it was discovered that the assaulting tanks had overlooked a well-fortified pillbox on the American right flank.

Disregarding his own personal safety, Caldarone worked his way forward under intense small arms fire to an opening in the pillbox, firing directly into it as he went. He then threw a white phosphorous grenade into the aperture but was hit by return enemy fire and killed. As a result of his actions, the balance of Caldarone's support squad was able to move forward and destroy the enemy position. For his aggressiveness, initiative, and outstanding courage, Frank Caldarone was awarded the Silver Star posthumously, which was accepted by his widow, Betty Caldarone.

o o o

During one attack on the German lines, *Leopoldville* survivor Sergeant George Chun Fat and his squad moved forward directly behind one of the attacking infantry-tank forces. The mission of his squad was to be ready to reinforce the attacking squads in case of unexpected enemy resistance.

As the American tanks approached the enemy bunker directly to Sergeant Chun Fat's front, the bunker from his left flank opened fire. The tanks engaged the new target immediately. As the tanks swung around to aim their guns on the bunker that was firing on them, the enemy soldiers occupying the strong point directly to Sergeant Chun Fat's front opened fire at the assault squads following the tanks. One infantryman was cut down in the first burst.

Unless silenced, the enemy bunker threatened to decimate the entire assault squad. Sergeant Chun Fat tried to attract the attention of the tanks, but the din of battle made it impossible. The only solution was to conduct a personal assault on the bunker. George Chun Fat crossed a hedgerow, spotted the entrance to the bunker, and tossed in three phosphorous and three high explosive grenades, knocking out the gun responsible for spattering lead at the patrol. He then captured two prisoners he discovered in a communications trench.

After leading the prisoners back toward the American lines, Sergeant Chun Fat again returned to the other side of the hedgerow in search of more Germans. Having placed a member of his squad at the entrance of the silenced bunker, George Chun Fat spotted three more enemy soldiers in the far end of the communications trench. When the Germans refused to surrender, Sergeant Chun Fat blasted them with his grease gun, killing all three.

o o o

Remembered Private First Class Norman Bullet of those terrible days, "Up on line there were many fire fights. What the Krauts didn't have in armor, they made up for in artillery . . . One evening about 5 PM the Germans opened up with 340mm coastal artillery batteries that could hurl a 700-pound shell twenty-one miles inland. It took 1 minute after the gun was fired for the shell to hit our lines. The breach of the gun [was so big it] had to be loaded with a crane." Continued Bullet, "I led patrols up into no man's land to check out what the Germans were up to. On one patrol, the Germans tried to pin us down, but I was able to get our patrol back through our lines with no casualties. I took chances that I wouldn't think about taking today."

o o o

It was during one of the shellings of the 88mm guns in the St. Nazaire sector that Al Via, the Mess Sergeant who had abandoned his Christmas turkeys when the 66th division was ordered out on December 23, was wounded by fragments from a German shell. However, Via's life was saved again, this time by his steel helmet.

Donald Earl Gengler, promoted to Platoon Sergeant, along with his men, was deployed on the front lines at St. Nazaire, like Al Via. The weather was cold, with snow and rain. The men lived in dugouts protected by sandbags, rocks, and logs. They had to cross a dangerous area to retrieve their supplies and keep in contact with the platoon on their left. A huge camouflage net hung over the area, and Sergeant Gengler's men would run and crawl behind it. The Germans had an 88mm gun set up, and they shot at anyone they saw crossing the location. Recalled Sergeant Gengler of the perilous tract of ground, "We crossed mostly at night. They shot it [the 88mm gun] like they were shooting a rifle, low to the ground. They never hit any of us, but we were always repairing the net."

Continued Donald Gengler, with his memories of the fighting in France, "There was constant artillery fire from both sides going over our heads. On some nights I went on reconnaissance missions of three to four men to a patrol to locate enemy positions. It was dangerous as we crept along the hedgerows. We never knew if any Germans were on the other side. I went on a daytime combat patrol with eleven other men to knock out a German pillbox. My job was to cover with fire as our bazooka and BAR [Browning automatic rifle] men moved in close to fire on the pillbox. We were successful. As we were moving back to our line the German mortars started coming at us. One soldier was wounded."

o o o

Following the S.S. *Leopoldville* disaster, survivor Jack B. Landovitz, of Brooklyn, New York, was resting with his unit in an orchard. He was stationed in the Bretagne-Loire sector outside Lorient, on April 26, 1945, when an enemy barrage began. During the shelling, Jack Henriot, a gunner from Seattle, Washington, sustained a severe leg wound. Landovitz, who had watched helplessly as Staff Sergeant Bob Gianfrancesco disappeared into the dark freezing Channel waters, along with Captain Sam Dudderar, grabbed a litter from a nearby ambulance and evacuated the critically injured soldier while under fire. Henriot survived his injury but lost his leg at the hip and was returned to the States. Jack Henriot overcame his handicap and later became a naval architect, and worked in the Puget Sound area. He never forgot Jack Landovitz, and over the years the two men continued to exchange holiday greetings.

o o o

The shelling on April 26 wounded sixteen soldiers from Company C while taking the life of Private Clinton Owens, of Crowley, Louisiana. His body is buried at Brittany American Cemetery.

o o o

On May 11, French and American troops from the 66thDivision marched into St. Nazaire for the official surrender ceremonies. Private First Class Guy Petty, of Lawrenceville, Illinois, who had cheated death in the English Channel by locking floating planks under his arms until he could be rescued, participated in the disarming of surrendering

Germans. Petty noticed a German prisoner scrutinizing him so intently that he became annoyed. "What are you staring at?" Petty demanded of the German prisoner. The captured soldier handed Petty his rifle and replied, "Yesterday, I held you in my gun sight but I didn't shoot you because the war was over and another shot would have been useless." A stunned Guy Petty, who had cheated death twice, gave the German soldier a pack of cigarettes.

o o o

The vast majority of the 66th Division members did not return to the States with any spectacular tales of valor. They had simply gone to war and done their duty. They were more than happy to hang their uniforms in the closet and put the memories of their hardships and heartaches behind them. It was time to dress in civilian attire once again and resume their normal lives. One such member of the 66th was Dominick Scala, of New Hyde Park, Long Island, New York. He entered the Army at the age of 21 and served from November 17, 1942 through March26, 1945. He had three brothers who also served during the war, and all of them returned home safely.

o o o

Rescued by the crewmen of the tug *ATR-3,* Sergeant Bill Cline spent two days in the 280th Hospital. With the pain still reflected in his voice, Cline notes, "I froze both feet, which have been numb for fifty years."

o o o

For Walter Beran, who had been plucked from the Channel waters as he floated unconscious in his life preserver, the *Leopoldville* disaster remains a large part of his memory, and like many survivors of the tragedy, he has come to believe that the sacrifice of his comrades spared him from later death. The Battle of the Bulge took more lives than the Normandy Invasion, and Walter Beran, reflecting on that ill-fated voyage, has said, "If we'd gone to the Bulge, I probably wouldn't have survived . . . I'm like the Korean soldier who was asked what he wanted the most, and answered—'Tomorrow!'"

o o o

Private First Class Keith L. Simons, who was plucked from the freezing water by the crew of *PC 564,* survived yet another brush with death during the fighting in France. On March 6, 1945, a piece of shrapnel from a German 88mm gun stopped one-eighth of an inch from his spine. That fraction of an inch had been the difference between life and death, or at best becoming a paraplegic!

Simons views his trial in the water in a positive light. "It made me want to do something for mankind, and that's probably why I became a teacher." He wrote of the catastrophe, "Far too many good men on that ship didn't make it. When I think of them I weep."

o o o

While participating in the fighting in the St. Nazaire and Lorient sectors, *Leopoldville* survivor Private First Class Walter Blunt, like Keith Simons, was wounded when a mine exploded on March 10, 1945. Eventually he was transferred to Kennedy General Hospital, in Memphis, Tennessee. Over a year later, on May 16, 1946, he received a Medical Discharge and resumed his college studies.

Walter Blunt became active in his local American Legion Post and served as its Commander during 1948 and 1949. During this period, many families had the bodies of their loved ones shipped home from overseas for burial in local cemeteries. Several times a week Walter Blunt and the other members of his American Legion Post provided the Honor Guard that met the trains carrying the mortal remains of local heroes.

o o o

Lieutenant Morton "Pete" Wood was discharged in early 1946. Civilian Wood was hired by a consulting engineering firm, where he eventually became a senior partner. However, there was one interruption in his career . . . Korea. In late 1950 he was recalled for service in the Korean War. After several months of stateside duty, he was shipped to Korea as a First Lieutenant. Before daylight on the morning of September 30, 1951, Lieutenant Wood led a rifle platoon on an attack called "Operation Commando."

Seventeen days of bitter fighting followed on the approaches to Hill 346 ("Old Baldy") and then on the hill itself. By the time the men made their fourth assault on the hill, Wood's platoon consisted of only about ten of the original forty men. There were also about ten more men, remnants of the 1st Platoon, whose commanding officer had been killed several days before. During the assault, a Chinese machine gunner shot Lieutenant Wood through the right hip. He was airlifted by helicopter to a MASH (Mobile Army Surgical Hospital) unit and after spending about a year in various hospitals, was retired with a disability.

Said Wood, "Like the S.S. *Leopoldville* disaster, the event got little publicity, being described by historians as merely a 'line straightening' operation. However, the 1st Cavalry Division was mauled so badly during the operation that less than 2 months later it was withdrawn from Korea, to be replaced by the 45thDivision. I'm not sure how many of those men ever reached the top of Old Baldy."

o o o

Lieutenant Fred Pisano, abandoned by his mother when he was less than two years old, and whose completed adoption on December 24, 1923, provided the Pisano family from Brooklyn, New York, with the best possible Christmas present, was plucked from death's grasp as he floundered in the frigid waters of the English Channel.

o o o

After he recovered and was released from the hospital, Vincent Codianni was given the option of staying and fighting or returning to his home in Waterbury, Connecticut. He remained and fought. He would say, "If you were there and saw your platoon wiped out you would stay and fight too. It was the only thing I could do."

Thus, he saw action in Normandy until the war ended, fighting the pockets of Germans left behind after the D-Day assault.

The Surrender Ceremony took place at St. Nazaire on May 11, 1945, at 10:30 AM. The memory of the *Leopoldville* nightmare, however, has never ceased to haunt Codianni. For his service, Codianni earned a Bronze Star and a Purple Heart.

Brothers, Pals During Life, Die Together as Ship Sinks

Transport Sunk on Christmas Day

They were together in life, and in death they were not separated.

This sums up the tragedy of two McDonald brothers, sons of Mr. and Mrs. Joe Borovich.

Sam was 25 and Dan a year younger, and both worked in the Pittsburgh Coal Co. mine at McDonald before the war began.

Both were single and, shortly after Pearl Harbor, both were called to service. They were inducted together in April, 1942.

Served as MPs

They had their basic training at Ft. Riley, Kan., together, and together they were stationed in New York as military police for a time.

Then there was an urgent need for copper miners, and both were honorably discharged in September, 1943, to go and work in Butte, Mont.

But they didn't want to mine copper, and they came home to their old jobs in the coal mine. And the following May they were inducted into the Army again, and last September they went to England with an infantry unit.

Brothers Scattered

They left their parents and four sisters, Zora, Sophia, Bessie and Marie at home, but their brothers were scattered all over the world.

Pvt. Pete Borovich was in the South Pacific area with the Air Corps. Pvt. Nick was in France

DAN and SAM BOROVICH
Even death couldn't separate them.

and Seaman Bert was in the Navy.

Still Sam and Dan were together and they never will be separated now.

For their father has received a War Department telegram which said:

"The Secretary of War desires me to express his deep regret that your sons .... were killed when a transport carrying troops was sunk in the English Channel, Dec. 25."

Chapter 9

Forgotten

". . . Without fanfare, official reports were classified as secret and locked away . . . It was as if the ship and the soldiers never existed."
. . . Edward Snow

The 66th Division Orchestra was extremely popular at Camp Rucker, Alabama. One warm August evening in 1944, the orchestra, along with four other Division bands, packed several thousand people into the Rucker field house in a never-to-be forgotten, "Royal Battle of Music." The orchestra director, Lieutenant Francis X. Coakley, was responsible for also hosting Jerry Wald and his band. The Division's smash show, "You're in the 66th," was a huge success. The show even played in Jacksonville, Florida, where it helped raise $4.5 million in war bonds. This phenomenal sum of war bonds sold became the legacy of Lieutenant Francis X. Coakley, who was one of the soldiers lost in the sinking of the *Leopoldville*.

o o o

Fifty years later, Technical grade 5 Jack Chvat, Headquarters Company, 262nd Infantry, who was ordered off of the *Leopoldville* and directed to transport a jeep across the Channel in an LST, still remembered the Lieutenant he knew from his hometown back in New Jersey. Wrote Chvat of Lieutenant Coakley, "He was already on the top deck and could have transferred to the safety of the British destroyer . . . He chose to return to the hold to search for several members of his platoon who were not accounted for."[50]

Cornelius D. Winters, Jr., was one of the 23 soldiers from the state of New Jersey who were killed. His body was never recovered.

Private First Class Cornelius D. Winters, Jr., of Paramus, New Jersey, a member of Company F, 262nd Regiment, was from a large family with ten brothers and sisters. Winters' mother passed away in January 1996, never knowing the truth about the disaster that took her son. Cornelius' sister, Kathy Kurhanewicz, of Lawrenceville, Georgia, has said of her brother, "My mom and Junior had a special relationship, as I did with him. He was the best young man, loved everyone, helped my mom and us, and brought home stray animals even though we were poor. We all helped him to feed them. He joined the service for his country and to help the family."

o o o

Vincent Codianni has not forgotten men like Steven Lester of Oklahoma, a soldier with a wife and three children. Using his bare hands, Lester broke panes of glass that freed his comrades from the watery grave that claimed him as the price paid for the lives of others. Thus, every Christmas Day, Codianni dedicates a mass at the Immaculate Conception Church for the men who died on the *Leopoldville*.

As tragic as the deaths resulting from the sinking of the *Leopoldville* were, the disaster was not the worst troopship loss of life for the Allies during World War II. That dubious distinction belonged to the British troopship *Rohna*. The catastrophe occurred slightly more than a year before that of the *Leopoldville*. Built in 1926, the 8,602-ton former liner *Rohna* left Oran on November 25, 1943, in a convoy bound for India. Like the *Leopoldville*, the British troopship carried some 2,000 American soldiers and was loaded to near capacity.

In yet another ironic similarity, whereas the *Leopoldville* was attacked just before Christmas, the *Rohna* was attacked just after Thanksgiving. On November 26, 1943, the convoy was attacked repeatedly by a formation of German bombers. The attack continued for several hours, but then a single aircraft carrying what at that time was a new weapon, a guided bomb—somewhat like a V-1 buzz bomb in appearance—was dropped off the port side of the *Rohna.* The bomb struck above the water line immediately over the engine room, causing the after portion of the vessel to burst into flames. The intense fire either destroyed the lifeboats on the port side or prevented them from being launched.

The lifeboats on the starboard side were used to get away, but some of the overloaded boats were swamped by the soldiers in the water who desperately tried to clamber into them. The *Rohna* remained afloat for an hour and a half, but by that time the ship had settled so far by the stern that the engines and boilers broke loose. The hull of the *Rohna* was ripped apart, and the ship sank. The complement of 195 sailors lost 5 officers and 115 crewmen. Captain Murphy, unlike Captain Limbor, survived the disaster. Of the American soldiers aboard, 1,015 were killed.

Despite the enormity of the loss of life, the sinking of the *Rohna,* like that of the *Leopoldville,* was not reported to the news media. Allied censors shrouded both disasters in secrecy. Family members back in the States were told only that their loved ones died in battle.

o o o

On January 14, 1945, Evelyn Sansone of Buffalo, New York, received the Western Union telegram that was the dread of every World War II wife.

> The Secretary of War desires me to express his deep regret that your husband Private First Class Richard F. Sansone has been reported missing in action since 25 December in European area. If further details or other information are received you will be promptly notified.
>
> . . . Adjutant General

o o o

The following day, January 15, Mary Lester, of Pharoah, Oklahoma, received an identical telegram regarding her husband, Private Steven T. Lester. Similar telegrams were being sent to wives and mothers throughout the nation. Some will maintain it was a necessary censorship of a heavy wartime loss. But, because the Germans had already provided news of the troopship sinking to the AP News Agency, it would appear that the only ones not aware of the catastrophe were the families and friends of the young boys who gave their lives. The parents, wives, sweethearts, and friends of the victims of the *Leopoldville* disaster now clung to the false hope that their loved ones were still alive and prayed for the day when they would be found safe. The Army, in fact, knew full well that they were all dead. The War Department's letter to Mrs. Angelina Sgroi concerning her son Paul, Company H, 262nd Regiment, was typical of the cruel hoax played out over several months.

> 25 January 1945 . . . The War Department was recently notified of the destruction at sea on 25 December 1944 of an American transport which was carrying troops in the European Theater of Operations.
>
> Although a large number of survivors was reported, a smaller group was reported as being missing in action as a result of this sinking. Your son, unfortunately, was in this latter group, and it is with deep regret that I must confirm my telegram of recent date which informed you that he was missing in action.
>
> I know that added distress is caused by failure to receive more information or details. Therefore, I wish to assure you that at any time additional information is received it will be transmitted to you without delay, and, if in the meantime no additional information is received, I will again communicate with you at the expiration of three months.
>
> The term "missing in action" is used only to indicate that the whereabouts or status of an individual is not immediately known. It is not intended to convey the impression that the case is closed. I wish to emphasize that every effort is exerted continuously to clear up the status of our personnel. Under

war conditions this is a difficult task as you must readily realize. Experience has shown that many persons reported missing in action are subsequently reported as prisoners of war, but as this information is furnished by countries with which we are at war, the War Department is helpless to expedite such reports.

Paul Sgroi was one of the 80 young soldiers from New York State killed in the disaster. His body was never found.

Private Paul S. Sgroi was born in the upstate New York village of Frankfort on November 25, 1925. At the age of 17, his mother signed the necessary consent papers permitting him to work as a laborer for the New York Central Railroad. He was inducted into the Army on January 18, 1944. Left with only the faint hope that her son might be a prisoner of war, Angelina Sgroi fought back the tears as she once again read his last letter home.

"December 18, 1944 . . . Somewhere in England . . . Dear Mom, Just a few lines to let you know I am feeling fine and hope to hear the same from you. I received the birthday card you sent me. Thanks a lot for it. Too bad I couldn't be home for it. I also got a letter from Vito and one from Josephine [his sister]. Glad to heard that everything back home is OK and that you are all in good health . . . Hope you had a good Thanksgiving, . . . Have you gotten any of my letters yet? Did you get the money I sent you? Let me know if you did . . . Well I don't have any more to say, so I will be signing off now . . . My best reguard [sic] to you all. So long, be good, God bless you all. Take it easy.

Don't worry about me. Please answer soon. Your Son, Paul"

Although Paul Sgroi wrote his mother that she should not worry about him, the reality was that Paul Sgroi was dead and that Angelina Sgroi would never see her son again. The true facts were known to the Army in a casualty report dated December 29, 1944. There were thirty-six soldiers in the 3rd Platoon of Company H, 262nd Regiment, and only five survived, including Second Lieutenant George Stanley Rehder. There was one known dead, First Lieutenant Harry Cybak, Jr., of Nemacolin, Pennsylvania. The body of Private Paul S. Sgroi was among the thirty bodies of soldiers of the 3rd Platoon never found. A dedication ceremony was held at the Frankfort High School auditorium on Friday evening, May 4, 1945, honoring the sixteen former students, including Paul S. Sgroi, who made the supreme sacrifice during World War II.

o o o

Not until March 7, 1945, did both Mary Lester and Evelyn Sansone once again receive identical telegrams verifying their worst fears. Shortly after Christmas, like Mary Lester and Evelyn Sansone, the mother of Private First Class Paul R. Viets received a telegram from the War Department that he was missing. A letter from the Adjutant General's Office two months later confirmed that he was dead. His mother died in 1948 without ever knowing the circumstances surrounding his death. Only after reading an article 40 years later, written by Vincent Codianni for the *Waterbury Republican,* did Roland A. Viets, of Thomaston, Connecticut, learn of the sinking that took his brother's life.

o o o

When Louise M. Cacace, of Brooklyn, New York, was notified that her son Staff Sergeant Anthony F. Cacace was missing, she refused to accept the possibility that he might be dead. Fortified with a strong faith in God and a mother's love, she wrote her son letters almost every day, which she intended to mail him once word was received that he had been found safe. "February 6, 1945 . . . My Darling Son, I just had to write to let you know how I pray night and day to God and St. Anthony to find you and I only hope I won't have long to wait because my Son

I think of you night and day and cry every time. One day last week I received a telegram for Dad. At the shipyard they wanted him to go to see a doctor and I was scared stiff to open it up. I was afraid it would be about you . . . although Son I know you are safe. God will be good to me and send you back. In fact, even your father got scared and he told them in the yard never to send another telegram because he is afraid of what it will do to me . . . and don't think he doesn't cry because he does. I never saw your father cry as he did for you. The girl upstairs got a telegram that her husband was wounded. Even that would satisfy me. Your brother Vin keeps writing to me asking why you don't answer his letters, and I tell him you are too busy or you would write . . . You had to miss everything, your brother's engagement, his wedding, and now even the news that you are an uncle. But Mom will try to make it all up to you when you do get home and it better be soon because I'm going crazy from worry. Well son, I'll end now with lots of love and hopes in my heart St. Anthony will find you with the help of God. I love you son. Nobody but me knows how much. Lots of Love, Mom."

Word of his safety never came—only the confirmation of his death.

o o o

An account of German broadcasts reporting a troopship sinking in the English Channel appeared in the *Times-Herald,* Washington, D.C., on Monday, January 15, 1945. This report forced the Army to finally acknowledge, on January 25, 1945, that a transport ship had been sunk in, "European waters somewhere in the European Theater." However, the Army only admitted to 248 dead with 517 missing. The article stressed that "more than 1,400 were saved" and went on to say the sinking was "recent" but gave no particulars as to the date or other circumstances.

Instead of acknowledging the truth surrounding the events of Christmas Eve 1944, the Army hid the magnitude of the disaster from the general public and the families of the soldiers who were killed in the catastrophe. On January 26, 1945, Ten Eyck Remsen Beardsley, an attorney from New York City, wrote a letter to Secretary of War Henry L. Stimson, stating that he was ". . . much concerned . . . assume that the loss of the transport ship in European waters announced over the news ticker yesterday, and in yesterday afternoon's and this morning's newspapers, referred to the *Leopoldville,* which I understand was sunk in the British Channel on December 25, having on board 2,200 soldiers, comprising the 262nd Infantry Regiment."

He then requested the answers to eleven questions, which he raised, including the following: "(1) Is there any reason to suppose or to believe that some of the 517 reported as missing have escaped? (2) Is an investigation being made in order that responsibility for this catastrophe may be definitely fixed? (3) Are steps being taken immediately, or have they been taken, to remove the officer or officers responsible on the premises?"

He then continued, "If there are any military reasons why these questions should not all be answered, please answer those that you can answer at this time, and advise me as to when they can all be answered. From the meager information that I have, it would seem to me that there has been incompetence on the part of those who are in charge of the transportation of the troops that may be criminal either upon the part of the officers themselves, or those who appointed them."

Byron Babb pictured with his wife Louise, was one of the six soldiers killed from the state of Kansas. His body was never found.

Reaction by the Army to Mr. Beardsley's letter was swift. The letter was forwarded to Major Herbert G. King, Chief, Security Branch Intelligence Division, and Beardsley was investigated by Army Intelligence who determined that Beardsley had written his letter on behalf of his heartbroken daughter. SergeantRichard Claybrook, his son-in-law, and a friend Private First Class Byron Babb, Jr., both of the 262nd Infantry Division, were listed as missing in the disaster.

A series of letters followed, but Mr. Beardsley's attempts to learn the circumstances that took the life of his son-in-law Richard, who resided in New York City, and that of his young friend, Byron, who resided in Wichita, Kansas, all proved futile.

On March 5, 1945, a totally frustrated Beardsley wrote to Major General J. A. Ulio:

"In response to the letter I received from the War Department purporting to be signed by you, I wish to advise you as follows: I think I have a right to have at least some of my questions answered. My son-in-law Sergeant Richard A. Claybrook was on the ill-fated *Leopoldville* when she was sunk, and also a young friend, Byron Babb, both of the 262nd. When I wrote to Secretary Stimson, I asked that the matter be either taken care of by him, or someone other than a merely routine subordinate. I don't think that the letter of February 24 was written by you. It is not necessary for you to either confirm or deny my statement that the *Leopoldville* was sunk in the English Channel, because I already know that. Of the eleven questions I asked, possibly the answer to only two of them, numbers 2 and 3, could be of any use to the enemy. The point is that I do not think there was any excuse for the catastrophe. I think there has been criminal incompetence somewhere, and that is my reason for pressing this matter. Two officers from the War Department called to see me after I wrote my letter, and I gave them considerable information. This information should not have been necessary, because the War Department ought to have been aware of the sources of my knowledge. I think there has been some lack of courtesy on the part of the War Department. I wrote on January 26, and my letter was not answered for almost a month, although you very promptly sent your representatives to see me to obtain such information as I had, and I think that if you will inquire from Colonel Charles E. Newman and Captain Frederick Suydam, the

Ten Eyck Remsen Beardsley   Virginia & Richard Claybrook

representatives that called to see me, you will learn from them, that they were treated with courtesy and given all the information that I had and sources. I am serious about this matter, and do not intend to drop it, and such a letter as yours of February 24 merely makes me more determined to obtain the information I seek and to take action based upon such information should I then consider further action justified."

The response to Mr. Beardsley's determined quest for the truth solicited the following brusque letter from J.A. Ulio, Major General, The Adjutant General. It was dated March 15, 1945.

"Dear Mr. Beardsley, I have your letter of March 5, 1945, in further reference to your inquiry concerning a ship used in transporting troops in the European area. I regret exceedingly that nothing further may be added to my letter of February 24, 1945 at this time."

It appears this abrupt reply by the Adjutant General ended the "Beardsley case." At the time of the tragic death of his son-in-law, Mr. Beardsley was 69 years old. He and his daughter never learned the true magnitude of the disaster that took the life of the young man they both loved. It should be noted that the bodies of both Sergeant Richard Claybrook and Private First Class Byron Babb were never found.

Byron Babb, assigned to the ASTP program, was sent to Northern State Teacher's College, Aberdeen, South Dakota. He and Louise, his high school and college sweetheart, were married on March

4, 1944. One month later, the ASTP program was canceled and he was transferred to the 66th Infantry Division. Louise wrote of that time, "We realized how every moment we were together was important." The couple became close friends with Dick and Virginia Claybrook.

o o o

An official wall of silence persisted regarding the disaster even after the war ended and censorship was no longer justified. On October 8, 1945, *Leopoldville* survivor, Lieutenant Robert M. Wurdeman, wrote of his personal experience aboard the Belgian troopship in a narrative titled, "My Best and Worst Christmas Eve." It began, "I say it was my best Christmas Eve because I was fortunate enough to be among the survivors of the most tragic sinking in the European Theater of Operations." The two-page typed story concluded as follows, "Of the sixty two men from Headquarters Company who boarded the ship, twenty-one died on 'My Best and Worst Christmas Eve.'" Robert Wurdeman's chronicle was to be broadcast on the radio program "We the People," his arrival in New York on or about November 1, 1945 . . . On the day of the program, it was canceled with no reason given.

Another victim of the *Leopoldville* was 29-year-old Jim Coen. Had he lived, he would have been the uncle of Pat Hurtek, of Garfield Heights, Ohio. Hurtek was not born until 7 years after Coen's death, but over the years she heard a great deal about her mother's only brother. During the war her mother worked at the Pentagon and was told only that her brother was missing in action. The bureaucracy refused to give her any details, and Jim Coen's sister was "bitter and angry." Said her daughter Pat, "I think it became an obsession with my mother to find out why the government was hiding it. But even working for the Pentagon, knocking on every door in Washington, didn't help.

It was only about 5 years later when, out of the blue, she met this soldier who had been a witness to the sinking, then she found out."

Jim Coen's sister always kept her brother's memory alive, and although Pat Hurtek never met the young man who would have been her uncle, she said, "I almost feel like I know the man. I grew up with this as kind of a diet. It came up every Christmas."

o o o

Jerry Catalano was reading his local newspaper when he spotted an article concerning reunions of units from World War II. One concerned the 66th Panther Division. Forty-four years had passed since the disaster that took his brother's life, but Jerry instantly dialed the number that led him to Robert Hesse, of Linden, New Jersey. Bob Hesse, president of the Panther Veterans Organization (PVO), invited Catalano and his brothers to accompany PVO members on their September 1989 European trip.

Three of Angelo Catalano's brothers, Roe, Fred, and Jerry, along with their wives, attended the PVO European reunion. The highlights of their London stay included a tour of Westminster Abbey, St. Paul's Cathedral, Piccadilly, and Parliament. On the afternoon of September 24, they arrived at Portsmouth. From the same Portsmouth docks where *Leopoldville* had begun its final journey, the Catalano family boarded an overnight ferry that transported them to France. Unlike the troops of the ill-fated ship, this time, as noted in their itinerary booklet, they were to "sail the night away in the comfort of a private, 2-bedded cabin."

Arriving in France on September 25, they toured St. Lo, where they saw the Carillon Tower and Major Howe Memorial. Over the next 2 days, the Catalano brothers, their wives, and 66th Panther members visited the submarine pens at St. Nazaire and various former battle areas. The trip included a tour of Cherbourg, Utah Beach, and its D-Day Museum.

As part of their healing process, on September 29, they boarded a French warship that took them over the site of the sunken *Leopoldville*. There, a "burial at sea" ceremony was held. As the French ship rose and fell on the waves, a sailor blew taps on his bugle, as Angelo Catalano's brothers cast a floral wreath upon the waters. Although their hearts remained broken, the Catalano kin had found a measure of peace.

Some of the *Leopoldville* dead were buried in graves in France, and some were returned to the States. However, many families never learned the fates of their loved ones. At Omaha Beach Military Cemetery there is a large rose garden surrounded by an 8-foot-high semicircular marble wall. At the top of the wall is inscribed, "Comrades in Arms, Whose Resting Place Is Known Only to God." It is the "Garden of the Missing," honoring American soldiers whose bodies were never recovered. Listed alphabetically, the deeply carved inscriptions indicate each soldier's name, rank, company, regiment, and division. On September 29, 1989, the cemetery caretaker filled in Angelo Catalano's inscription with wet sand so that his name was the most prominent one seen. Angelo Catalano's brothers and their wives stood before the wall, their eyes fixed on the wet sand that highlighted his name. Reverently they laid a floral wreath at the base of the wall below his name, knelt, and prayed. After 44 years, the family was finally able to provide a proper burial ceremony for their lost brother.

o o o

Robert Hesse organized the PVO in 1968 and served as its president for 24 years until his death in July 1992. His friend Vincent Codianni likewise devoted his life to ensuring that the sacrifice of the *Leopoldville* soldiers should never be forgotten. Codianni wrote letters to congressmen, senators, and presidents in a vain effort to have a monument erected in Arlington Cemetery. He also failed in an attempt to create a U.S. postal stamp dedicated to the tragedy. Both Hesse and Codianni appealed unsuccessfully for a Presidential Citation to recognize the many acts of bravery that occurred that night. As the years passed Codianni became an unofficial historian of the disaster and gathered survivors' accounts of the sinking. He amassed sworn statements from survivors, which were then presented to Army historians. At his home can be viewed dozens of scrapbooks documenting his correspondence with soldiers, widows, and politicians.

o o o

Survivor Bill Cline has said of the disaster, "The crew leaving the ship . . . no English being spoken . . . yet no panic . . . just a brave one hell of a bunch of 66th men . . . who should never be forgotten. I love and respect them all . . . the best of the best! I live with this sinking, and combat loss of life every day of my life."

o o o

General George C. Marshall was advised by memo on January 6, 1945, of the details of the tragedy. The report stated in part, "Had this disaster occurred in peacetime, it would have been regarded as a shocking scandal." Author Edward Snow wrote of the calamity, "No sea disaster in history has ever received less publicity. Without fanfare, official reports were classified as secret and locked away . . . It was as if the ship and the soldiers never existed."

o o o

No less an authority than well-known best-selling author and researcher Clive Cussler, referring to the *Leopoldville* disaster, coined the phrase, "Forgotten by many, remembered by few!" Cussler has also written of the disaster, "The *Leopoldville*, despite its seemingly senseless toll of human life, is an underwater monument to the heroism of the unsung and ordinary soldier, the little publicized GI. The rusting hulk is as important a resting place for our nation's dead military heroes as the cemeteries of France, the Philippines, and Arlington—only there are no white crosses on neatly trimmed grass to mark their graves."

o o o

The soldiers aboard the *Rohna* were told that the lifeboats and emergency equipment were the crews' responsibility and soldiers died because the lifeboats could not be lowered and life belts were issued in a haphazard manner with no instruction regarding their proper use. The largely Congolese crew fled the *Leopoldville*, just as the Indian lascars fled the *Rohna*. Like the *Leopoldville*, the story of the *Rohna* has remained cloaked in secrecy.

It has been said that if we do not learn the lessons of history, we are condemned to repeat our mistakes. The *Rohna* was sunk just over a year before the *Leopoldville*. Had the lessons of the *Rohna* catastrophe been learned through an exhaustive inquiry into the disaster and appropriate corrective measures taken, who knows how many soldiers' lives aboard the *Leopoldville* might have been spared. Murphy's Law states that whatever can go wrong will go wrong. Sadly, this axiom was never more true than in connection with the sinking of the *Leopoldville*. The radios aboard the vessels in the convoy were tuned to a frequency only heard in England. The Cherbourg-based boats used a different radio frequency only receivable at the French port.

It was therefore impossible to have radio communication between the ships in the convoy and the French port just 5.5 miles away.

Furthermore, junior ranking officers at Cherbourg Harbor were not about to incur the wrath of the top brass, who left word that they were not to be disturbed at their Christmas celebrations unless an emergency was absolutely verified.

No matter how vaguely, at least the disaster was reported by the British and American news media during the latter part of January 1945. As the French local populace discovered bodies washed ashore, however, they were told by the authorities that they should not discuss their findings with anyone, as the matter was highly secret. While researching old French newspapers for the year 1945, as part of his study of the disaster for a proposed TV documentary, Reuters investigative news reporter Lawrence Bond was unable to uncover any—not even one—French newspaper article concerning the catastrophe. Many questions concerning the disaster remained unanswered because the British and American military authorities filed the investigate inquiries concerning the tragedy away, marked "Secret."

The search for the truth only began to be acknowledged some 15 years later when documents became available under the Freedom of Information Act. The answers to sought-after questions proved to be more distressing than the allegations of negligence that were raised.

Survivors of the *Leopoldville* have been told that the death toll from the tragedy was 802 soldiers, and this number is listed on the PVO monuments located at Camp Blanding, Florida, and Camp Rucker, Alabama. The first available casualty reports indicated 264 soldiers known dead with 538 missing, a total of 802 lost, and it is this figure that has come down through the years. As the passenger and casualty lists were scrutinized more closely, however, the final death toll noted in a memorandum dated January 5, 1945, was 248 known dead and 517 missing, for a total of 765 lost. Newspaper reports from January 1945 acknowledged 765 lost in the Christmas Eve troopship sinking. I have reviewed all released casualty lists as carefully as possible and found a total of 763 confirmed dead and missing. An Army report from 1947 claimed 493 soldiers still missing, and it is this figure that I agree with as being the most accurate.

From documents I have studied from the National Archives, these are the facts. Lieutenant Colonel Milton W. Witt, Inspector General Division, in his report dated January 3, 1945, indicated that at least four ships arrived in Cherbourg during December 1944 without passenger lists. It was evident from the testimony in the case that the procedure for handling passenger lists prior to embarkation was not being followed by the Port at Southampton. Post officers were not present at the gangways during the embarkation to assist the unit commanders in checking the men aboard ship. Although the *Cheshire* carried in excess of 2,000 soldiers, it arrived at Cherbourg that fateful Christmas Eve without a passenger list. A certified passenger list delivered to Cherbourg headquarters from Southampton on December 25, 1944, contained a number of errors.

Furthermore, the passenger list of the *Leopoldville* contained so many errors that a large number of people worked long hours to try to verify the names of the casualties. The statements of survivors of the *Leopoldville* all pointed to a lack of discipline and training on the part of crew members.51 Said Lieutenant Colonel Witt in his official report, "It is a little difficult to understand just why the Master of the Ship, Captain Limbor, did not give the order to 'abandon ship' after the ship was torpedoed.

Since the ship remained afloat for over two hours after being struck, it would seem that all personnel could have been removed and that the loss of life could have been held to a minimum."

The only ones praised in Lieutenant Colonel Witt's report were the soldiers of the 66th Division. "The discipline and training of the soldiers aboard the *Leopoldville* is to be commended and was certainly of much higher caliber than that of the ship's crew in this emergency."

A review of a memorandum dated January 6, 1945, from Captain M.C. Jackson, U.S. Naval Reserve, to Admiral Harold R. Stark highlighted the following, "Both engines were stopped at or immediately after the explosion and the vessel lost way quickly. The blast opened No. 4 hold to the sea and collapsed G deck and part of F deck, in addition to destroying the escape gangways, thus effectively sealing off the only escape from G deck and possibly F deck as well. This would account, assuming troops were in their assigned space, for 129 men on G deck and possibly 124 on F deck. Some statements indicate that E deck also collapsed and the escape gangway was destroyed; if so, this would account for an additional 140 lives lost. No inspection was possible of the lower decks in No. 4 hold, apparently, as all escape gangways had been destroyed.

"Approximately 500 troops were removed and carried to the beach by the *Brilliant*. Small craft, including PT boats, Coast Guard cutters, PCs, tugs, and others, including the *ATR-3,* were arriving about the time the *Brilliant* pulled away. The *Leopoldville* was then in darkness, except for the lights played on her by various rescue craft. It is believed that the troops aboard did not realize their immediate danger. This is based on the fact that the Coast Guard officers had a substantial amount of difficulty in getting the troops to jump from the ship's rail to the decks of the Coast Guard cutters (3 to 4 feet), and, further, that a good many of the troops were still passing personal gear to the weather deck from their troop compartments shortly before the *Leopoldville* slipped beneath the waves."

Kept "secret" until declassified in late 1958 and 1959, the testimonies of the survivors before Lieutenant Colonel Milton W. Witt regarding numerous incredible acts of heroism were heartbreaking. Yet the Presidential Unit Citation, which Bob Hesse, Vincent Codianni, Bill Everhard, and other members of the 66th Panther Division have sought for more than 52 years, has been withheld.

o o o

The following excerpts are from that classified debriefing:

"The first I knew that we had been hit was the explosion I heard. Almost before it died out I was underwater. I thought I was at the bottom of the ocean because for a few moments I could not move and water had covered me completely. I thought it would only be a few moments before I would be dead, so I lay and waited . . . A few men who were in the compartment were screaming because they were hurt . . . The stairs had been blown down and there was nothing left but a mass of wreckage. . . . Tables that had held meals only an hour before were completely smashed to bits . . . Steel beams had been snapped like toothpicks, and there were heaps of boards and equipment scattered all over the place.

The men were magnificent. They were calm and very orderly. Not one of them pushed or yelled. Sergeant Furgeson was helping them onto the ladder and keeping order. To try to explain how calm the boys were is impossible. I think that seeing them act as they did made me feel that these men were real men and were acting as they should."

Sergeant Albert J. Montagna, Company L, 262nd Regiment

"In spite of the fact that men were sleeping on tables and in hammocks, some without life jackets, the men did not at any time become panicky when the water rose, but rather broke into emergency supplies of jackets or picked up jackets and went immediately to the upper deck. As I passed through the debris, I found the twisted bodies of three men killed by the explosion. There was one man buried up to his waist, pleading for help, so released him. The men in the compartment were looking for the exit in a half-dazed manner, so by my directing them, they each filed calmly and coolly to the deck to their previously designated emergency areas. Some filed out with bleeding heads, some with torn clothing and shattered limbs, but no one displayed any panic whatsoever. When passing from the forward to the rear exit, the officers aided and saw men helping other men get onto their feet and free them from beneath the wreckage; the explosion had caused tables, benches, and all wooden structures to collapse, which pinned many men to the floor. Because the water rushed in with such fury, the men did not even have a chance to maneuver for the exit; some were pinned to the walls and others to the ceilings. Evidently, the explosion had torn loose and collapsed the stairways and cable ladder that were in the stairwell, further preventing escape from the lower compartments."

Second Lt. Rowdney W. Boudwin, Company L, 262nd Regiment

"As the destroyer passed alongside, it collided with the extended lifeboat already half-full of crew members and two wounded soldiers. In so doing, the boat tipped, causing one lad to jump directly into my arms onto the open deck where he was immediately carried off by two aides. The second wounded man dropped between the lifeboat and the railing but was able to hold onto the gunwale of the lifeboat and to the railing of the ship. While he was suspended in this position, the destroyer closed in against the lifeboat, crushing the soldier at the waist as the lifeboat splintered against the railing. Hauling this man back onto the open deck, I turned around and was again met by two aides, who immediately carried the man to the aid station. Later in the 280th Station Hospital I met this soldier and was amazed to find him still alive even though his left leg had been amputated . . . During the transferal of patients, unbelievable daring and bravery were exhibited by soldiers who leaped from our ship to the Coast Guard cutter in an effort to help receive the patients who were literally thrown from one ship to the other. Several persons misgauged the distance and were crushed as they fell between the ships . . . We decided to remove the litter cases from the bulkhead and hold them in readiness for any eventuality. Moving aft along the starboard rail with a line of litters, we called ahead for the men in formation to stand by for litters, at which time they automatically opened a path and let us pass through. Again, perfect discipline was displayed by the men even though it was practically impossible to stand upright on deck, these men parted their formation, allowing ample room for the litters to be passed forward. Before we could reach an opening, the deck was awash, and the onrush of the water upset all of the litter bearers and washed the patients out into the sea."

Captain Howard C. Orr, Company L, 262nd Regiment

Colonel Ira C. Rumburg, Headquarters 1st Battalion, 264thRegiment, as previously mentioned in an earlier chapter of this narrative, was one of those lost. He was, in fact, one of eight soldiers killed who resided in the State of Washington.

"Hrvot [sic] came up, and as he got to the top of the ladder, I pulled him out. He limped to a bulkhead and nearly fell over. His foot was completely crushed so he could hardly stand on it. How he got up the ladder is another one of the many miracles that will never be explained . . . I noticed that someone was coming up the ladder very slowly. Not thinking that he might have been hurt I yelled for him to hurry. He looked up at me and stopped. When I looked at his face I hardly recognized him at all. It was Uppinghouse. I thought my stomach had done a barrel roll. His face was smeared with blood, and he had a terrific cut over his forehead and on his nose. I thought for sure that he was a walking dead man. He had been in the compartment below us, and he didn't know how he got to the ladder. It was completely underwater, and he must have gone through plenty . . . He was one of the last men to try to come out of the compartment under his own will power.

"I saw one man trying to crawl to the ladder. His arm was broken and he could not use his legs. I tried to help him over to the ladder, but when I got him there he couldn't climb up. It was then that Captain Orr came down into the compartment. Colonel Rumberg [sic] was also there, along with Lieutenant Boudwin and Lieutenant Blaney. We started to carry the man to the wrecked stairs, but before we got there he had passed away. He must have been beaten up terribly inside because he could hardly move."

Sergeant Albert J. Montagna, Company L, 262nd Regiment

"I was greatly impressed with the manner in which officers and non-commissioned officers gallantly directed their men to abandon ship, especially during the last 10 minutes, when there was a degree of panic and when most of the ship was underwater except for the bow. Also while in the water it was not uncommon to hear such commands as, 'Move your arms and feet.' 'Raise your head when you breathe.' 'Keep your mouth closed.' It is the strongest conviction that most personnel were more concerned with the safety of others than their own well-being."

Capt. William E. Pursley, Headquarters 2nd Bat 262nd Regiment

o o o

In response to the board of inquiry question, "What was your opinion of the attitude and method of performance of the ship's crew in this emergency?" Some of the answers were as follows:

"It seemed to me that the crew was interested only in themselves and nobody else."

Sergeant Billy Burga, Company E, 264th Regiment

"When the ship was struck, I happened to be in my cabin. I went forward to the area where my troops were along the right side of the ship, starboard along C deck. However, I didn't get there because each time I made a move to go down, part of the crew would shout for me to keep away."

Captain Raymond J. Novak, Company B, 264th Regiment

"At no time did I see any member of the ship's crew, officer, or seaman take control of any one situation."

Captain Howard C. Orr, Company L, 262nd Regiment

"I would say it was very unsatisfactory . . . We were never given orders to abandon ship, [and] the lifeboats were not launched by the ship's crew. Had we been told more about the condition of the ship—that it was likely to sink—we could have gotten most of the men off on life rafts and saved quite a number of lives."

Captain Sam K. Dudderar, Company C, 264th Regiment

"The preparations for loading were very unsatisfactory. The instructions given were insufficient and the action of the crew during the accident should warrant every last one of them being hanged, and I can substantiate my statement with evidence from all of the men in my company who survived. Two platoons were in the fore part of the ship and two platoons aft. This should never have been done in the first place. However, I never had all my men under my control. Most of the men that were in the aft end of the ship went down with the ship. It was a definite lack of information and control, and no help whatever was received from any of the ship's crew."

Captain Arthur A. Freidberg, Company E, 264th Regiment

o o o

The next question was: "Did you hear any order to abandon ship?"

"No, sir," replied Sergeant Billy Burga, Company E, 264th Regiment.

"No, sir," said Technical Sergeant Cornelius P. Burk, Company E, 264th Regiment.

"No sir . . . I was not aware that the ship was going down until it took the final slide and started to slide toward the back." Said Second Lieutenant Houghton T. Stevens, Company C, 264th Regiment. "We never received an order to abandon ship, nor did any of the men who went down with it . . . I took my company, which was in the fore part of the ship, on my own initiative, up on deck and we got aboard one of the destroyers.

I did not receive any order to do that. Had orders been given, I believe every last man might have been gotten off that ship.

In the opinion of my men, the ship's crew members were not performing their duties. If they had been, many of the men could have been saved. I think the officers of the ship were negligent in not getting information out to troops on board the ship. The crew members were packing their suitcases when they should have been maintaining their posts."

Captain Arthur A. Freidberg, Company E, 264th Regiment

o o o

It was not until May of 1996 that documents concerning the *Leopoldville* disaster were finally released by the British Admiralty. The handful of documents so far provided me by a friendly source represent only the tip of the iceberg. A secret report, dated April 9, 1945, containing a summary of the Board of Inquiry conclusions, included the fact that as a result of the explosion the starboard shaft appeared to have been fractured and the steering engine put out of action. The troop accommodation in the after part of the ship on E, F, and G decks flooded immediately. Water also entered the engine and boiler rooms.

The level of the water rose in the engine and boiler rooms despite the use of all available pumps, with the result that they had to be abandoned. The sinking of the ship was directly attributed by the Board to the flooding of these compartments.

In the early stages, Captain Limbor had hoped that the pumps would be able to deal with the situation in the engine and boiler rooms but 1 hour after being torpedoed he realized that the ship was in danger of sinking. The chronological list of signals and events records that at 1856 [6:56 PM], the *Leopoldville* signaled the *Brilliant*, "Water coming in on engine room. We won't be able to stay much longer." [Same message shouted verbally.]

When it became evident that the *Leopoldville* might sink, the Board concluded that energetic action on the part of the Master, Captain Limbor, and the officers to clear the port side by releasing the lifeboats would have enabled one of the other escorts standing by to come alongside and to embark more troops. Captain Limbor, however, was reluctant to release the port lifeboats and did not do so until he finally gave the order to abandon ship at 1930 [7:30 PM]. Limbor then appears to have released four boats from the port side of the boat deck in which the crew had been placed.

Parts of *Brilliant* Commander Pringle's own report dated January 1, 1945, follow.

"Initially the escorts consisted of the [British] ships, *Brilliant* and *Hotham*. H.M.S. *Anthony* joined off F Buoy at 1212 [12:12 PM], and later [the French] F.S. *Croix de Lorraine* joined [at] about 1720 [5:20 PM] when the convoy was near Buoy.

H8 . . . In view of information received from the Commander in-Chief, Portsmouth, that sinkings by submarines had been reported off Buoys H2 and H10 on December 23, 1944, I had requested the Commander [Limbor] to zigzag after entering Channel H, and zigzag No. 16 had been ordered. At 1720 [5:20 PM], the convoy passed close to Buoy H8. At 1754 [5:54 PM], the direction of the zigzag and increased tide as the coast was approached had brought the convoy 3.5 miles east of the Channel, and a signal was in the process of being passed to the Commander giving the bearing and distance of Buoy H10, when an explosion was observed on the *Leopoldville*, near her stern. As seen from the *Brilliant*, the spout of water appeared to be on her starboard (far) side, and I at once formed the impression that she had been hit aft by a torpedo fired from the west. She was then in position 49° 45' 20" N; 01° 34' W, 5.5 miles from the entrance to Cherbourg harbour . . . I ordered H.M.S. *Hotham* and H.M.S. *Anthony* to screen H.M.S. *Cheshire* into harbour, and F.S. *Croix de Lorraine* to hunt while H.M.S. *Brilliant* closed onto S.S. *Leopoldville*. I had first intended to hunt in H.M.S. *Brilliant*, but while drafting the signal, one was received from F.S. *Croix de Lorraine* saying she was carrying out observant, so I altered my orders to let her continue . . . In case she had been mined and in order to bring her head to sea, I ordered her to anchor, which she [*Leopoldville*] did at once in a position about 1 mile to westward (leeward) of her position on being torpedoed . . . At this time, I felt that it would have been wiser to have detailed one of the other ships to stand by S.S. *Leopoldville,* but having made the original signal, I decided to go through with the matter as arranged rather than alter the dispositions . . . I had these concerns in mind: (a) To get H.M.S. *Cheshire* safely into Cherbourg; (b) to hunt the submarine; and to get S.S. *Leopoldville* into harbour or take off survivors. These were catered for in my signal at 1802 [6:02 PM], but when H.M.S. *Anthony* sighted a torpedo track and started hunting also, another signal at 1820 [6:20 PM] predisposed her to hunt with F.S. *Croix de Lorraine* instead of continuing with H.M.S. *Cheshire.*"

Lieutenant A. Leach, the Commanding Officer of the *Anthony,* in his own report of the incident, dated December 29, 1944, stated that as he was steering to join the *Leopoldville* after the attack, the asdic [Anti-Submarine Detection Investigation Committee/Sonar] operator reported a torpedo approaching on the starboard beam. This was successfully avoided and the torpedo track was seen to pass clear astern. The *Anthony* was then ordered by the *Brilliant* to go alongside the wreck's portside. This proved impossible as a number of lifeboats were alongside and partially lowered, filling up with survivors [crew members] so the *Anthony* was ordered by the *Brilliant* to join the *Croix de Lorraine* carrying out hunting of the sub around the wreck. Noted Lieutenant Leach, "The arrival of numerous tugs and other small rescue craft, which clustered around the wreck and inshore of her, eventually made 'observant' impossible due to loud diesel noises swamping the asdics and the impossibility of penetrating amongst them at more than slow ahead without collision . . . It is considered that the U-boat could easily have escaped by keeping inshore amongst rescue craft and drifting west on the tide."

Continued Commander Pringle in his report, "As H.M.S. *Brilliant* was casting off, the large number of shore boats approaching appeared to put the rescue situation well in hand, and I did not order F.S. *Croix de Lorraine,* who was close by, to go alongside. It was with surprise and distress that I learnt next morning that some 500 men were still missing, but until it is known whether any of these could have perished in the explosion or went down with the ship, it is difficult to assess the failure of our rescue efforts. This was the first occasion upon which these ships had been employed all together in the Channel."

o o o

The chronological list of signals and events indicates that the *Brilliant* signaled the *Leopoldville* to drop anchor at approximately 1816 hours (6:16 PM). Since the *Anthony* had clearly previously signaled that a "torpedo passed astern, hunting," why did Commander Pringle signal to drop anchor, making the *Leopoldville* a "sitting duck" for further submarine attack?

Captain W.G. Bowles, Ships Adjutant of the *Leopoldville,* in his report dated December 28, 1944, claimed that Captain Limbor's orders and bearing were in the highest tradition of the service. He acknowledged that the behavior of the Belgian crew was "fair" but criticized the rescue efforts from other ships as "bad." Wrote Captain Bowles, "Many ships arrived on the scene, but with the exception of the *Brilliant,* none came close enough to give the help required."

Admiral Charles Little, the Commander-in-Chief, Portsmouth, in his report to the Secretary of the Admiralty dated January 5, 1945, acknowledged that the First Escort Group, consisting of the British ships *Affleck, Gore, Bentley, Capel,* and *Garlies,* was operating in the immediate vicinity and closed the scene an hour after the torpedoing of the *Leopoldville.*

Admiral Little reported, "It seems that the number of missing could have been much reduced if the situation had been handled differently and with better judgment." After reviewing the results of the Board of Inquiry's findings, he wrote on January 26, 1945, "It would appear that the Commanding Officer of H.M.S. *Brilliant* considered that the main thing was to hunt the submarine, and that he relied on the ships and craft coming out from Cherbourg to take off the remaining survivors. As pointed out by the Board of Inquiry there were sufficient ships available in the vicinity to carry out both objects. I consider that Commander Pringle handicapped himself as Senior Officer present by not making himself fully acquainted with the state of affairs on S.S. *Leopoldville* and thereby failing to allow another vessel alongside . . . This situation contributed to the loss of 300 additional lives. The failure to appreciate and deal with the real situation constitutes a serious error in judgment but not in my opinion one which amounted to negligence, nor could such a charge be substantiated. I recommend Commander Pringle should receive a measure of Their Lordship's displeasure."

The recommendations were acted upon on April 18, 1945, by the British Admiralty. "I am to state that My Lords concur with your submission and I am to request that for his errors in judgment and mishandling of the situation, you will convey to Commander John Pringle, R.N., an expression of Their displeasure. I am to state that this officer is at present appointed to HMS *Hargood.*"

o o o

The British Admiralty had relieved Commander Pringle of his command of the *Brilliant* and transferred him to the *Hargood*. A reprimand indicating a measure of Their Lordship's displeasure also became part of his personnel file. Commander Pringle died several years ago, and former Brilliant crewman Angus Currie is just one of the ship's crewmen who adamantly defend Pringle's actions, stating that he handled an extremely difficult and hazardous situation as best as he could.

On April 9, 1946, The Naval Attache, British Embassy, Washington, D.C., sent the following supplication to the Director of Naval Intelligence, Admiralty, London.

"It is requested that I may be supplied with the above particulars [information concerning the *Leopoldville* disaster] for transmission to the War Department and any other details that may be available concerning this sinking. It is understood that these facts are required for purposes of record and in answer to a Congressional inquiry."

The brief reply from the Director of Naval Intelligence, Admiralty, to the Naval Attache, Washington, was dated May 7, 1946, and concluded, "It is emphasized that the information from the Board of Inquiry is not for publication."

Thus, not even elected officials of the United States government were permitted access to the full facts concerning a disaster that claimed 763 confirmed lives of our brightest youth from forty-six of the then forty-eight United States.

The Chief of Naval Information, in response to a request for information regarding the disaster by *New York Times* military reporter Hanson Baldwin and the Reuters News Agency, wrote on March 1, 1946, "Several weeks ago, Reuters asked for information following up on a request from Boston, and were informed that the ship was torpedoed while proceeding under escort to Cherbourg and that the incident was one of the normal hazards of war. In view of the events following the sinking, the matter will clearly have to be handled with discretion. It is, however, thought most desirable that we should avoid being accused of hiding anything, and the Divisions to whom this paper is marked are therefore requested to state what information can be given."

This was followed by a memo dated March 19, 1946, from Admiral Powell, Head of Military Branch II.

"The story of the *Leopoldville* does not reflect any great credit upon us, and I should be adverse to disclosing it unless the need is very strong. To issue anything publicly in America might only serve to revive a controversy that would be better allowed to die."

A second memo regarding the request for information was written by Admiral Powell on March 23, 1946.

"I remain of the opinion that to provide the *New York Times* with material for a special article would be most undesirable, which would only serve to foment further controversy on a matter which would be better left to die of inanition. If Reuters must be told anything, I recommend that they should be informed that the loss of the *Leopoldville* was a normal hazard of war and that the Admiralty has no special statement to make on the circumstances of the loss."

Retired *New York Times* military reporter Hanson Baldwin died in 1991. He never succeeded in uncovering the genuine facts from the British Admiralty. However, despite the best efforts of the American, British, French, and Belgian authorities to bury the pertinent inquiry documents to forgotten recesses of their archives, the story of the *Leopoldville* and the search for the truth remained very much alive!

Fort Benning, Georgia *Leopoldville* Disaster Monument

Chapter 10

Remembered

"Those . . . that lost their lives deserve the proper respect and remembrance for their sacrifice, and those that survived need to be recognized for their valor."
. . . New York City Congressman Gary L. Ackerman

By April 11, 1945, advance tanks of the Ninth Army reached the Elbe, south of Magdeburg, and forces of the Third Army took Weimar. Meanwhile, the British crossed the Leine near Celle, and the Russians had reached the Danube Canal, near the center of Vienna. Victory in Europe was less then a month away. The victory that was now within the grasp of President Roosevelt, however, was denied him. The man who had led the nation first through the Great Depression and then a World War died of a cerebral hemorrhage at Warm Springs, Georgia, on April 12, 1945.

That same day the German submarine *U-486* also met its end. On April 12, 1945, a torpedo from the British submarine *Tapir* sent Lieutenant Gerard Meyer and the crew of the *U-486* to the bottom!

On April 9, the German *U-486* left its base at Bergen, Norway, for its second war patrol. The submarine had not proceeded very far when snorkel trouble developed and Commander Meyer made the decision to return to base. It was a decision that sealed his fate.

At 0730 hours (7:30 AM) on April 12, 1945, the British submarine *Tapir* was patrolling off the mouth of Fejeosen Fjord when the *Tapir's* sound equipment detected noise from an engine of a U-boat. It was confirmed that the sounds were indeed from the engines of a submerged U-boat and that the sounds clearly indicated that the

German U-boat of the U-486 type.

sub was moving toward the entrance of the fjord. Captain Roxburgh brought the *Tapir* to periscope depth in the hope that the Captain of the U-boat would be rash enough to surface before clearing the entrance of the fjord.

At 0749 hours (7:49 AM) the U-boat was indeed surfacing and proceeding toward the fjord's entrance. At 0753 hours (7:53 AM), just 4 minutes after the U-boat was first sighted, the *Tapir* fired a salvo of eight torpedoes. Two minutes of tense waiting passed, and then an explosion was heard. Through his high powered periscope, Captain Roxburgh saw the U-boat hit amidships and literally explode. Roxburgh watched in awe as bits of the U-boat flew through the air and a large column of brownish smoke rose straight up to a height of some 500 feet. Apparently, some powerful explosives aboard the U-boat triggered the awesome blast. Breaking-up noises were reported by the *Tapir*'s sound man, and when the smoke cleared the U—boat was gone![52]

Lieutenant Gerhard Meyer had met his destiny just three days before his 30th birthday. The U-boat and crew responsible for so much suffering and death on the *Leopoldville* that previous Christmas Eve had perished in one monstrous and hellish fireball.

Father "Dick" Tellers, of St. Joseph R.C. Church, Sharon, Pennsylvania, a former 199th General Hospital Army Chaplain, crossed the English Channel aboard the *Leopoldville* just one week before the troopship was sunk. According to rumors heard in France, Father Tellers, Nurse Helen Murphy Livesey, and the rest of the 199th General Hospital Group believed that there were no survivors when the *Leopoldville* went to the bottom.

Haunted by the question, "Why was I spared?" Father Tellers never told his brother John or his closest friend Father Goodell anything about the *Leopoldville*. He passed away in August 1993, not knowing that more than 1,400 young men had survived the Christmas Eve catastrophe.

o o o

The years passed, and parents struggled to cope with the losses of their sons. On May 29, 1946, the Joseph Thiery Flower Fund of the Allenport Mill, Pittsburgh Steel Co., sent a wreath of flowers to the

John Lowry, the father of the Lowry twins, died in 1949. Dr. Loretta Graves Brown, of Birmingham, Alabama, had dated Jack Lowry. She believes that John died of a broken heart.

Belle Vernon American Legion Post, along with a note indicating that the flowers should be placed at the Honor Roll in memory of Jack and Glenn Lowry.

As a result of inquiries they made in an attempt to comprehend their loss, John and Dorothy Lowry received a letter from the Army dated May 20, 1949, which stated in part . . ."Although many survivors were rescued, I regret to inform you that your sons were listed as missing. Since that time a complete search of the area has been conducted in an attempt to locate remains that could be associated with your sons, and every effort has been made to correlate their [remains] with those of unknowns interred in U.S. Military Cemeteries and reported isolated burials. However, all efforts have proven futile. The circumstances surrounding their deaths have been thoroughly reviewed, and based on information presently available, the Department of the Army has been forced to determine that their [remains] are not recoverable . . . Realizing the extent of your grief and anxiety, it is not easy to offer condolences to you for your loved ones under circumstances so difficult that there are no graves at which to pay homage. May the knowledge of your sons' honorable service to their country be a source of sustaining comfort to you. Sincerely yours, James F. Smith, Quartermaster Major, QMC Memorial Division.

Nowhere in the letter from the Army were the parents of the Lowry twins told of the enormity of the disaster that took the lives of their children.

Young newly married women, widowed by the *Leopoldville* tragedy, also grappled with the heartache of rebuilding their lives. Peter L. Acri's widow Velma wrote in 1996, "In my eyes he has never grown old, I can only remember him as that handsome young husband that I adored."

When Sergeant Richard A. Claybrook and Byron Babb were sent to New York at the end of October 1944, in preparation for shipping overseas, Louise Babb and Genny Claybrook followed them and stayed at the home of Genny's parents, Mr. and Mrs. Ten Eck Beardsley, in Brooklyn. While on leave in New York, Byron and Louise went to a nightclub. Remembers Louise, "We didn't care what it cost because he was leaving and I was going home. We had dinner and I requested all our favorite song ('You Would Be so Nice to Come Home to'), and all the rest. When we got ready to leave and asked for the check, we were told no charge, no tip. I couldn't believe it. New York was great. That was the night we decided to have a child."

Dorothy Lowry Clyde Wyatt died at the age of 93 on April 13, 1996—just one day after the 51st anniversary of the sinking of the U-486.

When Byron reached England at the end of November 1944, he was able to visit his brother Dean, who was stationed with the Army Air Corp. That Christmas eve, Louise Babb became ill and sensed that something was terribly wrong. Louise gave birth to a daughter on July 30, 1945. Byra was named in honor of her father.

Sisters of the young soldiers killed mourned the loss of their brothers no less than their widows did. Celine Cobb of Poughkeepsie, New York, has written of her brother Thomas A. Cobb, "As Tom grew older, he became engaged in intellectual pursuits, experiments in biology, physics, mechanical inventions, etc. It was as though he knew his life would be short, and it was a race against time to learn about everything. He was never idle."

When Thomas Cobb's mother was officially notified of his death, Tom's waterlogged wallet was among the personal belongings his grieving family eventually received from the Army. His body was originally buried in France, but later it was returned to the United States for permanent interment. Thomas Cobb grew up and spent his happiest years in Pennsylvania. His mother therefore decided that her son's final resting place should be in Pennsylvania.

Originally buried in the military cemetery at Ste. Mere Eglise, France, Sergeant Elmer August Baker was finally home to stay when on September 18, 1948, he was reburied in the Baker family plot at Riverview Cemetery in Jefferson City, Missouri.

The survivors of that tragic night likewise struggled to put the painful memories behind them and get on with their lives. Wrote *Leopoldville* survivor Fred G. Pisano in a letter of September 16, 1945, to his girlfriend Virginia Lagergren, "Monday December 24, 1945 . . . Linz, Austria . . . My Dearest Ginnie, This is Christmas Eve all over the world; to me it seems just like any other ordinary day. The old home spirit is missing. I should not complain . . . I have lots to be thankful for. Last year at this time I was on the *Leopoldville* sailing across the Channel. It was also a year ago today that the *Leopoldville* met her fatal end taking with her 768 men. Sixteen of those men were [in my unit]. I was very fortunate indeed to have been fished out of the Channel. I wish I could meet the boys in the U.S. Navy who picked me up. Perhaps someday back in the States we will meet."

Even forty-one years later, Henry Balboni of Norwood, Massachusetts, still could not block out the vivid sight of the inert bodies in the water after they had been crushed by the hulks of the *Leopoldville* and the *Brilliant.* Joseph Matusiak returned home and married the girl he had been dating during the war. Despite the passage of fifty years, Matusiak, when vacationing still cannot bring himself to board a cruise vessel and will always fly instead. For Joe Holl, who survived because Bill Foster stopped to help him find a life jacket, the disaster remains vivid in his mind. "I'll never bury that memory. I'll always see myself in the water. I can picture it today as if it were yesterday."

As Christmas Eve 1996 approached, *Leopoldville* survivor Melvin F. Whaley, of Modesto, California, wrote, "For 52 years the *Leopoldville* has been foremost in our memory and cast a dark and gloomy shadow over the holidays."

Survivors' wives tried their best to understand the mood swings, the sleepless nights, the recurring nightmares that tortured their husband's very souls. Reverend Arnold Olson, who was then a Chaplain, has no memory of what happened and how he escaped. There are several hours of his life that are a total blank. Family members report that on Christmas Eve he would wake from his sleep screaming.

William Kalinowski would experience depression without knowing why and foster feelings of guilt just for being alive. He could not even bring himself to discuss the tragedy with members of his family until 1983, and then in no great detail.

Kalinowski was released from the hospital just before the New Year of 1944 and was returned to his outfit, Company L, 262nd Regiment. The soldiers were being treated to an Esther Williams movie, and beautiful girls in bathing suits were performing a water ballet. Kalinowski stood in the back of the large tent and watched the film for five or ten minutes. He began to enjoy the picture until his whole being was consumed with guilt.

Years later, Kalinowski wrote, "I broke down and cried and thought of all the dead guys. I couldn't take it. I walked out."

When told by his Sergeant that he was to be awarded the Silver Star for helping in the rescue of men in hold F-4, Kalinowski replied, "Big deal. I get a Silver Star and those guys get a burial at sea. It just ain't fair." Kalinowski proceeded to Company Headquarters and requested that his name be removed from the list.

Al Via and Melva on their honeymoon. "Why you're gorgeous! I'm going to marry you!"

Albert Via, of Frostburg, Maryland, often reflects on the fact that he is alive because two Belgian crewmen ordered him and his friend out of the lifeboat, that ironically became the tomb of the crewmen when it was shattered into splinters as the *Brilliant* pulled alongside. "Why was I spared?" questions Via.

So strongly forged were the bonds of friendship among comrades of the disaster that they could even reach beyond the grave. Bob Letts was devastated by the loss of his hometown buddy Joseph McKinney, who was killed as a result of the *Leopoldville* catastrophe. Letts always wanted to do something in Joe's memory and finally ordered a headstone for his long-lost pal.

While stationed at Aberdeen, South Dakota, Walter Blunt and First Sergeant Harold S. Bailey also forged a friendship that would last a lifetime. Bailey lived in Florissant, Missouri, and after the war Blunt visited him frequently. Through the years, the two men never discussed the *Leopoldville* until their last visit in August 1992. Only then did Harold Bailey discuss the tragic recollections that had plagued him for nearly forty-seven years. Walter Blunt would recall, "I think he knew it would be our last visit together, as he was suffering from heart disease."

Finally, through the efforts of the PVO spearheaded by Robert Hesse, E. Arthur Gillespie, and Vincent Codianni, a memorial was erected at Camp Rucker, Alabama, where the 66th Division had trained. On May 11, 1988, exactly forty-three years after the German Surrender Ceremony at St. Nazaire, some one-hundred-twenty veterans and their wives gathered to dedicate a memorial to those members who lost their lives in the sinking of the *Leopoldville* and the subsequent action against the Germans.

The sacrifice of the 66th Panther Infantry Division soldiers during World War II was now immortalized in stone. Sadly, outside of this tribute and one at Fort Blanding, Florida, for which the members of the PVO themselves were responsible, there remained no memorial dedicated to the *Leopoldville* catastrophe that included a relief of the sinking ship or a list, by state, of all the names of the soldiers lost.

During a visit in 1989 by *Leopoldville* survivor Morton "Pete" Wood to the Tomb of the Unkown Soldier at Arlington National Cemetery, he observed that the Trophy Room at the memorial contained over fifty plaques of infantry, armored, and airborne divisions that saw combat during World War II. The 66th Division, however, was not represented. Pete Wood immediately set about the task of designing an appropriate plaque, which he had crafted that same year. After approval by the cemetery superintendent, the 66th Division plaque was then suitably placed alongside the others in the Trophy Room.

In 1967, Robert Neilson, a former Washington State University wrestling coach, was named chairman of a statewide committee to establish the Chris Rumburg Memorial Fund. The fund's purpose was to provide wrestling scholarships and to pay travel expenses for Washington State University wrestlers. The fund was officially established on June 26, 1974. When wrestling ended at WSU in 1986, the fund also ended. Jason Krump, editor of *"Butch's Beat"*, the official publication of Washington State University Athletics, has written of Ira Rumburg, "Rumburg's life does not need a fund in order to validate his heroism. It may be impossible to absolutely quantify the positive significance of Rumburg's life. Perhaps it can be measured each time the Cougar football team steps on the field, or when the WSU student leadership gathers for its weekly meetings, or when the ROTC conducts its morning training sessions. Or maybe it is realized from the contributions made by the 100 souls, and their future generations, which he saved on that Christmas Eve in 1944."

Still, the story of the 66th Division remained little known. Encyclopedias and history books, even those considered to be authorized accounts of The Battle of the Bulge, did not even mention the *Leopoldville* calamity as a footnote. However, after fifty-one years of denial, the official wall of silence began to crack. On March 20, 1996, New York City Congressman Gary L. Ackerman delivered a moving tribute to the tragedy of the *Leopoldville* before the House of Representatives. Congressman Ackerman concluded his remarks by noting, "The most tragic and troubling part of this story is the American public's general ignorance of the facts. All of us, and particularly the family members of the lost soldiers, should be told the full story of their loved ones' valiant efforts in their fight to preserve democracy." Congressman Ackerman then issued the following challenge to his associates. "Therefore, I ask my colleagues to join me in remembering and honoring those who gave their lives in protecting the ideals that all Americans cherish. I would also like to remind my colleagues that this story should hold a special place in every state's history. Simply put, the 802 soldiers who lost their lives deserve the proper respect and remembrance for their sacrifice, and those who survived need to be recognized for their valor."

Congressman Ackerman's tribute was entered into the Congressional Record the following day.

The survivors of the disaster struggled for over half a century to bring the tragic story out of the darkness of concealment into the revealing light of truth. Responding to Congressman Ackerman's challenge that the *Leopoldville* story should be an important chapter of each state's history, on May 26, 1996, Mayor Philip Giordano of Waterbury, Connecticut, dedicated that city's Memorial Day Commemoration Ceremonies to the memory of the *Leopoldville* Disaster and directed that all city government flags be flown at half-staff. Since then a number of local and state government officials have issued proclamations, citations, commemorations, and resolutions honoring the sacrifice of the young men lost in the *Leopoldville* disaster and the valor of those who survived.

On May 27, 1996, in New York City, *Leopoldville* survivors and families who lost loved ones in the disaster led the Manhattan American Legion Memorial Day parade from West 79th Street and West End Avenue to the Soldier's and Sailor's Monument at West 90th Street and Riverside Drive. At the monument, the *Leopoldville* catastrophe was remembered with an appropriate ceremony. The Honor Guard was provided by sailors from the British warship *Cumberland,* and guest speakers included Manhattan Borough President Ruth W. Messinger, Arthur Flug, representing Congressman Gary L. Ackerman, and Deputy Grand Master of Masons in the State of New York, Stewart C. McCloud.

The Grand Chapter of the Order of the Eastern Star, State of New York, presented New York City Municipal Archives Director, Kenneth R. Cobb, with two beautiful plaques honoring those killed in the disaster who were from New York City. World War II Navy veteran Joseph Carinci, of Oneida, New York, accepted one plaque honoring Oneida orphan Staff Sergeant Benjamin Joseph Blaskowski on behalf of Oneida American Legion Post 169. The other plaque, designed by *Leopoldville* survivor Vincent Codianni, was presented by

Preston Appleby who resides in Richmond, Virginia. Appleby and his son made the trip to New York City to honor the memory of the uncle for whom he is named.

A number of *Leopoldville* survivors attended the ceremony including Gerald Crean, of Bloomingdale, New Jersey, Frank Haugh, of Fairview Park, Ohio, and George Chun Fat (86 years young), who flew across the continent from San Diego, California, to say goodbye to his former comrades.

Also in attendance was Federal Court Artist Richard Rockwell, nephew of America's beloved illustrator, Norman Rockwell. Richard Rockwell's sketch of the sinking *Leopoldville* appears on the plaque presented to the City of New York, which lists by borough the names of the thirty-nine city residents killed in the catastrophe.

The most prized possession of Sandra Cardens, the daughter of Sergeant Elmer Baker, is a cardboard 78-rpm record of her father's voice. During World War II, as their contribution to home-front morale, Pepsi Cola Corporation made 78-rpm cardboard records available to servicemen, who then recorded brief messages on them, which were mailed home to loved ones. One of those courtesy records contained Sergeant Elmer August Baker's 1944 Mother's Day greeting to his wife and young daughter.

"Hello Sandy. How does Daddy's baby feel after being without her mommy for so long?

"Sweetheart, I sure miss you, so write often. I can never tell you how much your letters mean to me. They bring back so many pleasant moments we spent together, and make me feel so swell.

"This record is to wish you a Happy Mother's Day. I hope you like it. When you get lonesome, you can shut your eyes and pretend I'm there.

"Give Sandy a big kiss for me and tell everyone hello.

Don't worry sweetheart, if I don't write as often as I did, because I expect it'll be pretty busy.

"Darling, each of the months that have passed seem like years to me, but I hope we can soon be together again to make all our dreams come true.

"I love you so much sweetheart. All my love and kisses to Sandy and you. Goodbye."

Sergeant Elmer August Baker mailed home his Pepsi Cola courtesy record Mother's Day greeting to his wife Geneva and daughter Sandra.

There were forty young men assigned to the 2nd Platoon of Company K, 262nd Regiment. Seven months after Sergeant Elmer August Baker mailed home his Pepsi Cola courtesy record Mother's Day greeting, on Christmas Eve 1944, he crossed the English Channel aboard the Belgian troopship *Leopoldville*. Both Staff Sergeant Donald E. Gengler and Private First Class Vincent Codianni, although hospitalized, were among the 2nd Platoon's twenty-four survivors of the torpedoed ship. Sergeant Elmer August Baker and Private First Class Waldron M. Polgreen were among the ten young men from the 2nd Platoon whose mortal remains were recovered. The body of Private Richard F. Sansone was among the six from the 2nd Platoon that were never found.

On Veteran's Day, November 11, 1996, a ceremony sponsored by the American Legion in remembrance of the *Leopoldville* disaster was held at the Eternal Light Monument, West 24thStreet and Broadway, New York City. During their remarks, New York City Mayor Rudolph Giuliani, Manhattan Borough President Ruth Messinger, and New York City Councilman Andrew Eristoff all paid tribute to those New York City youths killed in the *Leopoldville* disaster.

The following day, Queens Borough President Claire Shulman issued a Commemoration in honor of the six young men from the Borough of Queens who died.

On December 19, 1996, New York Governor George Pataki issued a Proclamation honoring all of the young soldiers killed in the S.S. *Leopoldville* disaster who resided in the State of New York. By his Proclamation, Governor Pataki became the first governor in the United States to honor the memory of the American soldiers killed in the Christmas Eve 1944 catastrophe.

At the request of John L. Behan, Director, New York State Division of Veteran's Affairs, memorabilia from families of *Leopoldville* victims were displayed at the New York State Vietnam Memorial. The memorial museum and gallery are housed inside the New York State Justice Building in Albany. The exhibit was opened to the public from December 23, 1996 to January 24, 1997.

As a result of seeing the exhibit "*Leopoldville*—Never Forget," Tobias Polgreen wrote the following: "I was only nine months old when my father died, the youngest of three boys, so I have no recollection of anything about my father firsthand. Having no father in my life was a part of growing up and I accepted it. I missed out on having a dad to talk to in my life but in my book dad died a hero. He did not want to go to war and could have gone to the farm to work. He didn't and when the draft board needed some men for the war effort, he did his part and happened to be one of the many who didn't come home to his family. He was buried in France and it is my hope that someday I will be able to visit his final resting place. For fifty-two years, I have known very little about the death of my dad and how it happened . . . January 1997 proved to be a very informative month in regards to the sinking of the *Leopoldville* and the tragedy it was not only for my dad but many others. I have talked to men who were there. I have read numerous personal accounts of what happened in the eyes of many survivors . . . I have met and talked to a man [Robert Langavin] who lives a mile from where I live who was on the *ATR-3* rescue tugboat. We have lived this close and never knew it. I have shed a few tears recently thinking about all of this. It is as if dad came alive for a brief moment and I have dealt with it on a more personal basis."

Leopoldville survivor Vincent Codianni, who escaped from the glass enclosure with Waldron Polgreen only to become separated from him in the frigid water, in 1996 organized the *Leopoldville* Memorial Association, with the help of Colonel John G. Chiarella, Ret., of Waterbury, Connecticut, and Donna Hesse, of Linden, New Jersey, widow of Robert Hesse, the founder of the PVO. The Association's purpose is to create public awareness of the horrific but still little known catastrophe.

Another of the association's goals was to raise the necessary funds for a *Leopoldville* Monument that would include a relief of the sinking ship on the stone and a list, by state, of all the soldiers who were killed in the *Leopoldville* disaster. It was decided that the monument should be placed at the National Infantry Museum, Fort Benning, Georgia.

Z. Frank Hanner, Director, National Infantry Museum, in his letter of support for the proposed *Leopoldville* Monument wrote Vincent Codianni, on January 29, 1996, "History is the thread that binds us together as a nation and makes us unique. We must ensure that generations to come have the opportunity to remember and reflect on those who made the supreme sacrifice while protecting our country. I can think of no better place for your monument than here on the grounds of the National Infantry Museum where our soldiers will be reminded of other infantrymen who have gone before them. It will also let our citizens who visit the museum recall that freedom is never free—someone has to pay the price."

The widow of Peter Acri, Velma DiMartile, spoke from the depths of her soul when she wrote why she felt the monument was so important. "I'm sure I speak for all the widows, that it[monument] would help the hurt we have carried all these years.

. . . It would mean so very much to me and my son to be able to see his father's name engraved, along with all the others lost that most fateful day, which lives in our hearts forever . . . My heart cries out to be able to see my late husband, Peter L. Acri of Company E, 262nd Regiment, have his name honored, along with all the other "boys" lost in the tragedy"

A *Leopoldville* Benefit Concert was held at the Kennedy High School auditorium, in Waterbury, Connecticut, on November 2, 1996, to raise funds for the proposed monument. The concert was sponsored by the Mayor's Council on Culture, the Waterbury Region Convention and Visitors Bureau, the Waterbury Veterans War Memorial Committee, the newspaper *Waterbury Republican-American,* the Dante Alighieri Society, Clive Cussler, author/historian, and of course the *Leopoldville* Memorial Association.

A letter of greeting from then U.S. Presidential candidate Bob Dole was read to those attending the concert. "It is a distinct pleasure to send greetings to those in attendance at the *Leopoldville* Benefit Concert. I offer a special salute to two *Leopoldville* survivors participating in today's events: Ret., Brigadier General Donald G. MacWilliams and former Army Chaplain Jack C. Randles.

"My thanks go to all present for promoting remembrance of the *Leopoldville* tragedy through creation of a *Leopoldville* Memorial . . ."

Informed about the erection of the *Leopoldville* Monument in Fort Benning, Georgia, John P. Fievet, President of the *Rohna* Survivors Memorial Association wrote *Leopoldville* survivor Vincent Codianni, "I'm elated that the *Leopoldville* Memorial will be located at Fort Benning. What could be more appropriate than to have our memorials located within a few miles of each other. The *Rohna* Memorial is in Fort Mitchell National Cemetery, which adjoins Fort Benning."

The Leopoldville disaster monument was dedicated on November 7, 1997. The ceremony was attended by an estimated 150 people from at least 22 different states from as far away as Arizona, California, and Washington. A plaque containing the names of five Leopoldville survivors later killed in the fighting in France was dedicated and added to the monument on October 22, 1999. Copies of a Leopoldville tribute read before the United States Senate by North Dakota U.S. Senator Byron Dorgan were distributed to everyone present at the ceremony.

Leopoldville survivor, Vincent Codianni is a jeweler by profession. In 1994, at his own expense, he designed and minted a 50th anniversary Leopoldville disaster commemorative medal.

Ironically, Senator Dorgan's uncle, Pfc. Allan J. Dorgan from Regent, North Dakota was a Leopoldville victim. His body was never found.

Since Governor Pataki became the first governor in the nation to honor those killed in the calamity, the governors of Florida, Georgia, Iowa, Maryland, Massachusetts, Michigan, Mississippi, Missouri, New Jersey, Pennsylvania, Tennessee, and Utah have followed his lead with similar proclamations honoring those soldiers killed from their respective states. The Virginia State Legislature also recognized the *Leopoldville* disaster and honored the sacrifice of the seven Virginia members of the 66th Division killed in the catastrophe. Virginia State Legislature Resolution NO. 956 commemorating the loss of the American soldiers aboard the *Leopoldville* was adopted on February 19, 2007.

On November 15, 2004, the 60th anniversary of the 66th Division sailing from New York Harbor to England and their destiny aboard the Leopoldville, the bipartisan White House Commission on Remembrance held a beautiful wreath-laying ceremony at the Tomb of the Unknowns, Arlington National Cemetery. Survivors and families of soldiers killed from 23 different states, 160 people in all, attended the solemn tribute.

United States Senator Byron Dorgan (ND) escorted Lucy Ruggles, the 85 year old widow of Pfc. Harold J. Decell down the rotunda steps to place a Leopoldville floral wreath in front of the Tomb of the Unknowns. Lucy Decell Ruggles gave birth to their twin daughters, Leslie Ann and Linda Lee, on April 26, 1945.

Antonio Martinez, from Arroyo Grande, California, represented the Leopoldville survivors and was escorted up to the tomb by White House Commission on Remembrance director, Carmella LaSpada. At the conclusion of the ceremony, everyone present was invited to attend a luncheon/reception at Fort Meyer, Virginia, located next to Arlington Cemetery.

Since Christmas Eve 1994, the 50th Anniversary of the Leopoldville catastrophe, over 125 Leopoldville related articles have appeared in newspapers and magazines all across the country. One such article that appeared in the New York Daily News on December 22, 1999 written by reporter Karen Zautyk was headlined,

"A Tragedy Too Long Secret." The Leopoldville disaster is a secret no longer and the survivors and families of soldiers killed have finally received the recognition they so justly deserved, but for so many years were denied.

Professional divers prepare to dive to the Leopoldville wreck in order to film it for a television documentary.

Chapter 11

Protected

". . . It's like going to a cemetery and taking a headstone."
. . . Dan Wellen, nephew of Leopoldville victim, S/Sgt. John Klein

During early July, 2000, I received an e-mail message from French diver/researcher Bertrand Sciboz alerting me that the Leopoldville wreck was being looted by so called "sport divers". Bertrand Sciboz requested my help in bringing the desecration of this World War II American underwater gravesite to the attention of the American public in order to protect the wreck from further looting.

I began my efforts to achieve that goal by writing over 200 letters to Leopoldville survivors and the relatives of Leopoldville victims urging them to write their respective congressmen and senators demanding that the wreck be protected. I also wrote to a number of government officials myself as well as various news media. I also e-mailed numerous messages on the internet regarding this issue. As a result of this letter writing campaign, at least 65 elected United States officials from at least 20 different states received letters from their constituents demanding that the necessary steps be taken to protect this underwater gravesite where so many of their loved ones died.

Charles Anderson from Meyersdale, Pennsylvania, in his letter to his Congressman and Senator wrote, "My wife's brother (Pfc. Jay Warren Taylor) was one of the brave soldiers who gave his life when this vessel was sunk off the coast of France. I am deeply saddened to hear that the final resting place of our nations soldiers is being used in this manner. Every military memorial cemetery deserves our greatest respect and the final resting place of so many soldiers should also be treated with great honor and respect."

Sandra Cardens, the daughter of Leopoldville victim Sgt. Elmer Baker wrote to her senator, "It is an insult to me and the memory of my father and the fathers of so many others who lost their lives that night, that their very bones are being picked over by these vultures. Although it has been fifty-six years since the tragedy, there is still a wound that will never heal. We owe these men! My father just celebrated his 22nd birthday in New York in November 1944 . . . These boys went proudly to help their country. Don't we owe them some respect now? I beg you to help by bringing this to the attention of whomever it takes to get a quick response before it is too late."

Frank DiMola From Ramsey, New Jersey lost his brother, Pvt. Nicholas J. DiMola, in the Leopoldville tragedy. His letter to his congressman and senator stated in part,"How long will it be before American soldiers helmets, rifles and other gear and equipment are removed from this underwater gravesite if it has not already occurred?"

Evelyn C. Harzinski, the sister of Cpl. Reginald J. Clark Jr. whose body was never found wrote to her congressman, "In 1997 my husband Anthony and I, two daughters and two grandsons visited Cherbourg, France. I always said before I die I wanted to place flowers in the English Channel where the Leopoldville went down."

The body of Pfc. Grant P. O'Neil from Pawcatuck, Connecticut was among the 493 never found. His sister, Frances M. O'Neil in her letter to the authorities at American Normandy Cemetery wrote, "Our family like many others, is trying to find out what happened to our family member. My sister and I have asked that the remains of the buried unknown dead from the Leopoldville be some of the first to have DNA testing done in hopes that we may have some closure, which has been denied to the families of these men. None of us would like to go to an antique store, or flea market someday and find dog tags or anything else belonging to these men . . . Protect this site and let the dead rest in peace."

Survivors also responded to the call for action. Miguel Velez from Little Rock, Arkansas wrote to his elected representatives, "As a Company I survivor, half of my immediate patrol died in that tragedy. I personally find this is an outrageous insult and I am very angry about this issue. Such desecration, sport diver looting at my buddies final burial gravesite, is not right. Nothing seems to be sacred anymore. These heroes cannot rest in peace. In fact, my GI duffel bag is down there, which I have never recovered."

New York Long Island Congressman Rick Lazio became one of the first elected officials to urge then Secretary of State Madeleine K. Albright request that the French government take the necessary action to stop the desecration of the Leopoldville wreck site.

The New York State American Legion at their annual convention in Niagara Falls from July 20-22, 2000 adopted Troopship Leopoldville Resolution #48 calling upon the United States Congress to take immediate and appropriate action to prevent further desecration of the Leopoldville troopship. Further, at the National American Legion Executive Committee meeting held in Indianapolis, Indiana from October 16-19, 2000, Resolution #24, "Preserving the SS Leopoldville" was passed. The resolution encouraged all American Legion departments to contact their governor's office to memorialize the soldiers killed when the ship was sunk and that their state congressional delegates take action in the United States Congress to prevent further desecration of the Leopoldville or any of its contents.

Banger, Maine TV stations WABI and WLBZ on August 1 and August 4, 2000 respectively aired segments on the looting of the Leopoldville wreck. The segments included interviews of family members of Leopoldville victim, Pfc. Edward Stone.

Globe-Gazette, Mason City, Iowa newspaper reporter, Kristin Buehner wrote an article concerning the problem that appeared in the August 22, 2000 issue of the paper. The page One article was titled, *"Respecting the dead, Family of war casualty wants looting to stop at grave on the bottom of the English Channel."* Reporter Buehner wrote two other articles concerning the looting that appeared on page two of the paper. *"Close army buddy calls soldier Quite a Man. Family contacted*

Grassley (U.S. Senator) for help. "The second article was titled, *"Detective wants wreckage protected."*

Next, newspaper reporter Staci Hupp, wrote an article regarding the looting for the *Des Moines Sunday Register.* The page One article titled, *"Iowa family joins move to end looting of WWII shipwreck"*, appeared in the paper on September 3, 2000. Dan Wellen, a nephew of Leopoldville victim S/Sgt. John Klein stated, "It's like going to a cemetery and taking a headstone." Margaret Wellen, Klein's sister, contacted Iowa U.S. Senator Charles Grassley for help. Senator Grassley notified the State Department and told reporter Staci Hupp, "Our government needs to resolve this issue with the French government as quickly as possible. Family members have waited decades to learn the fate of their loved ones. I intend to continue pressing for a solution that will stop the desecration of the grave site and ensure respect for the lives that were lost for the freedoms enjoyed today in Europe and the United States."

During September 2000, Leopoldville survivor Fred Brent and I appeared on the Long Island, New York TV12 news program, *"Morning Edition"*, and discussed the looting problem. During October 2000, NBC Syracuse, New York Action News TV-3 also aired a segment on the looting issue.

On October 3, 2000, South Carolina State House of Representative Thomas G. Keegan lead a ceremony at the State Capitol honoring the South Carolina soldiers killed in the Leopoldville disaster. Leopoldville survivor, Ben Thrailkill, who previously held Keegan's legislative seat made a presentation to Margaret Loftis Gallman, the sister of South Carolina Leopoldville victim, Sgt. James Loftis.

Back in France, newspaper reporter, Sophie Jeanne, wrote an article about the looting issue that appeared in the Cherbourg paper, *La Presse De La Manche.* The paper devoted the entire second and third pages of the newspaper to the Leopoldville disaster and the looting issue.

By this time, the story had caught the attention of *People Magazine* Reporter Anne Driscoll. Her two-page article appeared in the December 11, 2000 issue of the magazine on pages 203/204. The article included both color and black and white photographs and was titled. "Sacred Trust: Families of U.S. Soldiers killed in a World War II sea disaster fight to keep divers from looting the wreck."

Also during December 2000, Providence, Rhode Island TV news reporter, Glenn Laxton, aired a segment on the issue. The piece aired over WPRI TV 12 on December 18, 2000. Families and friends of Leopoldville victims from Rhode Island were interviewed for the segment. Yet another major TV network, ABC TV News, aired a story about the looting issue. Leopoldville survivor Fred Brent, Jerry Catalano, the brother of Leopoldville victim Sgt. Angelo Catalano, and myself were interviewed by ABC TV NYC Channel 7 *"Eye Witness News"*. The segment aired on December 23, 2000 in the New York City, New Jersey, and Connecticut tri-state area as well as the "feed" to affiliate ABC TV stations across the country.

On Christmas Day 2000, the Rhode Island newspaper *"Providence Journal"* printed an article titled, *"Christmas Eve 1944: 7 RI men die on torpedoed ship"*. Lending his name to supporting the effort to stop the looting of the Leopoldville was Robert D. Ballard, PhD and President Institute for Exploration, Mystic, Connecticut. His letter to me read in part, "I applaud your efforts and wish you the best with your project. I constantly give lectures supporting your point of view and will continue to do so in the future."

The 200 plus letters I wrote to Leopoldville family members were not in vain. In a letter dated August 17, 2000, to Mary Mueller, sister of Leopoldville victim Pfc. John Killeen, West Virginia United States Senator John D. Rockerfeller IV wrote in part, "As the ranking minority member on the Senate Veterans' Affairs Committee, your concerns have special significance to me. I have always felt strongly about ensuring that those who have so nobly served our country are treated with the dignity and respect they deserve. For that reason, I am forwarding a copy of your letter to the State Department, along with a personal request for information on this matter . . . I feel that contacting this agency's representatives will be a positive initial step in resolving this situation."

Mary Mueller also contacted her West Virginia congressman, Alan B. Mollohan. Congressman Mollohan brought the issue to the attention of the American Embassy in Paris, France. The reply he received from Embassy Consul General Larry Colbert dated August 31, 2000 stated in part, "I and my colleague, the U.S. Navy Attaché at this embassy, have been in contact with several French and American government organizations with the aim of finding an appropriate and certain means to protect what is in effect a grave site of American servicemen."

In a letter dated January 11, 2001 to Jospeh T. Reichert, the son of Michigan Leopoldville victim, T/4 Wilmer Poupard, United States State Department International Relations Officer, Frank Ostrander wrote in part, "We have urged France to accord the Leopoldville appropriate treatment and protection as a . . . war grave of the U.S. soldiers . . . who died on it. In addition, we have asked the Government of France to prevent the removal of artifacts from the wreck and to seize any artifacts previously removed without approval so that they may be displayed in an appropriate military museum in the United States, France, the United Kingdom, or Belgium. We have also approached the British and Belgium governments to seek their support to declare this vessel a war grave to be accorded appropriate protection from sport divers.

France, the United Kingdom and Belgium are sympathetic to our view. Belgium is exploring whether it remains the legal owner of the vessel and France is examining its domestic legal authority to protect the Leopoldville and its artifacts. We will continue to work with the concerned governments to promote full protection for the Leopoldville."

It was ironic that at the same time American citizens were seeking to raise over 100 million dollars for the World War II Memorial in Washington, DC to honor the memory of those men and women who saved the world from tyranny that the undersea final resting places of thousands of World War II soldiers and sailors were at risk of looting and desecration. The United States Department of Veterans Affairs dedicated the year 2000 to thanking American veterans. A policy statement stated, "Thank you 2000 aims to recognize the men and women who preserve our freedom by serving in our Nation's armed forces. Citizens are invited to join in making 2000 the year our nation thanks more than 24 million American veterans living today and remembering the legacy of those who died."

Yet, at the same time that we proclaimed veterans should be thanked for their sacrifice, their underwater graves around the world were being looted by "sport divers". Nearly fifty-seven years after the Leopoldville catastrophe, the families connected to the calamity finally were assured that their loved ones underwater shrine would be safeguarded. In a letter dated June 29, 2001 to the family of Leopoldville victim Pvt. Edward Stone, Washington DC French Ambassador PierreHenri Guignard wrote that the Leopoldville wreck would now receive protection from further looting and desecration. A decree by the French Ministry of Culture and Communication dated March 08, 2001 declared the wreck of the S.S. Leopoldville as a, "bien cultured maritime pour raisons historiques", a cultured asset for historical reasons. The Leopoldville wreck was officially registered under # 01/2001 DRASSM. The French decree and registry meant that the French maritime authorities had immediately prohibited all diving operations inside the wreck and strictly restricted these activities in the proximity of the site.

The "squeaky wheel gets the grease" and the outcry from the Leopoldville survivors, relatives of victims, and United States government representatives and agencies succeeded in ensuring that an appropriate agreement to protect the Leopoldville wreck was concluded.

The relatives of Leopoldville victims, through their many letters to their elected officials expressing the urgency to bring the issue to a quick resolution have won a great victory. This underwater shrine where so many American soldiers died has received the protection it deserves. Further, the strategy that succeeded in protecting the Leopoldville wreck now stands as a model for others to follow concerning how to preserve wrecks in every ocean of the world from similar looting and desecration.

When the Fort Benning, Georgia Leopoldville disaster monument was dedicated in November 1997, Tom Cordle, the nephew of Leopoldville victim Pfc, Ferrel McDonnell read a poignant poem he had composed honoring his uncle and the other Leopoldville victims who for so long had been forgotten. His poem concluded,

But death was not the end of things
For some still feel its searing sting
In wounds they will forever feel
In hearts that never really heal
In faded photos, black and white
In haunting voices in the night
In endless days spent asking why
A son or husband had to die?

But does it matter, after all
What place a dying soldier falls?
What matters is the answered call
For freedom

Who measures sacrifices made
Or faults the charging Light Brigade?
Who dares deny the price was paid
For freedom

There will be channels yet to cross
And wars to fight that can't be lost
And some will pay the final cost
For Freedom

But let there be no bitter tears
Remember all the better years
And those whose blood has bought and paid
That men might live lives unafraid

So honor all the valiant men
And let the word go forth again
There is but one thing worth the price
Of such unselfish sacrifice
"Freedom!" "Freedom!" "Freedom!"

Normandy American Cemetery Colleville-sur-Mer, France

Chapter 12

Revisited

" . . . Think not only upon their passing remember the glory of their spirit."
. . . Inscription on north chapel wall, Memorial Chapel,
Normandy American Cemetery

During the first week of April, 2008, I had the fantastic opportunity to retrace the steps of the 66th Infantry Division from their base at Camp Piddlehinton near West Dorset, England to the pier at Southampton where they boarded the *Leopoldville* and sailed to their destiny off of Cherbourg, France. I was accompanied by *Leopoldville* survivor George Bigelow, Tom Cordle whose uncle, Pfc. Ferrel McDonnell was killed in the sinking and Barbara Shaw whose grandfather, Pfc. Joseph Thibodeau also lost his life in the catastrophe. When we revisted the old 66th Division army barracks at Camp Piddlehinton, 83 year-old . . . survivor George Bigelow met for the first time former HMS Brilliant sailor Bob Clothier who participated in the rescue effort.

This journey of a lifetime was made possible by the Canadian television company, Northern Sky Entertainment Ltd. which at the time was in the process of filming a television documentary about the *Leopoldville* disaster. After two busy days revisiting Camp Piddlehinton and the pier at Southampton, we left our accommodation in Poole and boarded a large car ferry for the trip across the English Channel to Cherbourg, France. The weather was clear and sunny and as we neared Cherbourg we passed close to the 52 foot research vessel *Triad* from which professional divers were diving the *Leopoldville* wreck to film it.

Leopoldville survivor George Bigelow at the rail of the *Triad* looks out over the water above the Leopoldville wreck and reflects on the loss of his comrades that Christmas Eve so long ago.

Once in Cherbourg, we settled in at the Hotel Mercure Cherbourg Plaisance. The following day we sailed on the *Triad* to the exact spot where the Leopoldville sank 63 years ago just a short distance outside the breakwater of Cherbourg harbor. George Bigelow after saying a few reverent words in honor of his comrades who died that night tossed a floral wreath on the water. Then Barbara Shaw spread some dirt from her father's grave back in Massachusetts on the water as her tribute to both her father and her grandfather, Pfc. Joseph Thibodeau. Barbara later described the moment as overwhelming. She felt tears of sadness for not knowing her grandfather, a man who Impacted her life so much, but she also felt tears of joy for the opportunity to be aboard the *Triad* 180 feet above his final resting place and pay tribute to his memory. The dive crew with their cameras then dove to the wreck beneath us. On a computer monitor in the wheelhouse of the *Triad* we watched as sonar images of the wreck slowly appeared on the screen. As I looked out from the boat and strained my eyes to look for land in the distance, it became clear to me that no one could possibly have completed the swim to shore that Christmas Eve while struggling against the darkness, tossing waves and the freezing 48 degree Channel waters.

When I first began my research into the *Leopoldville* disaster back in the early spring of 1994, I never in my wildest dreams thought that one day I would find myself standing on the deck of a vessel at the exact location where the *Leopoldville* sank. It was both exciting and humbling as I reflected on the confusion, panic, and unbelievable acts of courage and faith that unfolded as the doomed ship listed and finally disappeared from sight on that mournful Christmas Eve. When I closed my eyes I could almost see the faces of the teenage soldiers bobbing in the waves as they pleaded for their mothers to save them. My ears rang with the voices of British sailors shouting, "Jump Yank, Jump!" Although I battled sea sickness aboard the *Triad*, the opportunity to retrace the journey of the 66th Division soldiers to the point where 763 of them perished and changed forever the lives of the survivors and those who participated in the rescue effort was an experience I will remember and treasure for the rest of my life.

The most memorable part of retracing the journey of the 66th Division however was to revisit the final resting place of so many of the young soldiers who I have come to know and respect as a result of my research into the catastrophe.

The American Battle Monuments Commission is charged with the responsibility of being the guardian of America's overseas commemorative cemeteries and memorials. Its mission is to honor the service, achievements and sacrifices of our armed forces. The ABMC was established in 1923 as an agency of the executive branch of the federal government. The agency maintains 24 permanent American military burial grounds on foreign soil. There are presently 124,913 U.S. war dead interred in these cemeteries including 93, 242 dead from World War II. Normandy American Cemetery and Memorial is one of 14 permanent American World War II military cemeteries on foreign soil.

Normandy American Cemetery near Colleville-sur-Mer, France is located on a cliff overlooking Omaha Beach with spectacular views of the English Channel. The cemetery's 172.5 acres contain the graves of 9,387 American military dead. Most of them lost their lives in the D-Day landings and the operations that followed. The cemetery is basically rectangular in shape.

After leaving the Visitors Building at the entrance to the cemetery and before arriving at the graves area is a beautiful, semi-circular memorial filling most of the eastern end of the cemetery with a memorial garden and Tablets of the Missing to its rear. The semi-circular colonnade of the memorial has a loggia (a roofed gallery) of French limestone housing battle maps showing the Normandy invasion beaches and air operations over Normandy from March to August 1944. The floor of the open area within the arc of the memorial is surfaced with pebbles taken from the invasion beach below the cliff and imbedded in mortar. Centered in the open arch of the memorial facing toward the graves area is a beautiful 22-foot bronze statue of a handsome young man with outstretched arms lifted upward. The statue represents the "Spirit of American Youth Rising from the Waves". Encircling the pedestal of the statue on the floor in bronze letters is inscribed, "Mine eyes have seen the glory of the coming of the Lord".

Behind the memorial structure is the Garden of the Missing. Engraved on the stone tablets of the semi-circular wall are the names of 1,557 missing American armed forces personnel lost in the region whose remains were never recovered or if found were unable to be identified. Large sculptured laurel leaves separate each tablet on the wall. It is ironic that nearly a third of the names engraved on the tablets in the Garden of the Missing are of 66th Infantry Division soldiers lost in the sinking of the *Leopoldville.*

Tom Cordle from Tellico Plains, Tennessee, the first member of his family in 63 years to return to France slowly walked along the path that followed the wall reading the names on the tablets until he found his uncle's name. Head bowed, struggling with emotions of both anger and sadness that were welling up in his mind and heart, he placed his hand over the name of Pfc. Ferrel McDonnell. Standing quietly alone, Tom Cordle reflected on his uncle's life and the circumstances of his death.

Pfc. Ferrel Franklin McDonnell was born on January 2, 1926, the second of eight children born to Frank and Sara McDonnell. The McDonnell children grew up in Muskegon, Michigan during the "Great Depression" years of the 1930's. Ferrel's sister, Beulah, has recalled of that period, "We were really, quite happy kids. We didn't realize we were poor. Everyone we knew lived about the same as we did."

The McDonnell's were a musical family. Ferrel's great uncles had been musicians in a well-known band and his grandmother had been a piano teacher. The family would gather round the radio and listen to country music. They had an old piano and at about the age of twelve, Beulah learned to play a few chords. In the evenings, they would all sing together. On those occasions, Ferrel would always say, "When we grow up, I'm going to see that you get piano lessons and I'm going to get saxophone lessons." It was a dream that would not be realized by Ferrel.

In April of 1943, Beulah met and married the man of her dreams, Thomas Lambert Cordle. Tom and Ferrel became inseparable. Ferrel and his childhood sweetheart, Ellie Hite, were Best Man and Maid of Honor at Beulah's wedding and they also became engaged.

But with America at war, and although he was only seventeen, Ferrel begged his mother to sign the necessary papers so he could join the army. His departure was delayed for some time however, because he was quarantined with the measles and it was May 4, 1944 before he entered into the armed forces. Ferrel's brother, Harvey, still ponders if Ferrel's fate may have been altered due to the measles.

Tom Cordle stands in front of the panel on the Wall of the Missing upon which his uncle's name is engraved. Note the single rose he placed on the ground in honor and memory of his uncle, Pfc. Ferrel McDonnell.

Beulah still vividly remembers the day that Ferrel left home. "We were all standing on the sidewalk, waiting for his bus. We were crying and carrying on, when Ferrel turned to me and said, "What are you crying for? You'd think I was never coming back."

Assigned to Company F, 262nd Regiment, while awaiting his orders to go overseas, Ferrel received a letter from Ellie. She had met someone else and would soon be married. Ferrel's heart was broken, as he confided to Harvey in his letters home.

On December 22, 1944, just two days before the voyage that would lead to disaster and claim so many American lives, Ferrel McDonnell wrote his parents, "Dear Mom & Pop & Tom & Boots (nickname for Beulah), I wrote a letter yesterday so there really isn't much to say. I think I'll make this my Christmas card. Merry Christmas and a Happy New Year to all of you. Ferrel."

On December 29, 1944, just five days after the catastrophe, Sara McDonnell wrote her son, "Dear Ferrel, I want you to write even if its ok & every day or so sign your name so I know you are all right . . . What did you do Xmas. Did any of your packages get there near Xmas? Have a letter saying you got one around the 12th of December," Ferrel was still heartbroken that Ellie had married someone else. Continued his mother's letter, "Don't feel too bad about Eleanor . . . There are lots of girls and lots of time." Sara McDonnell had no way of knowing when she wrote those words that for her son, time had run out.

Ferrel loved to paint pictures of the sea and ships. In every painting, he included a body of water, a ship, or both. His last painting, left unfinished, was of a shipwreck. While his brother Harvey still wonders if the measles altered Ferrel's destiny, perhaps his fate was not altered at all.

Tom Cordle stepped back from the wall, knelt and placed a single rose on the ground in front of the tablet bearing his uncle's name. Then he stood up straight and saluted. His pilgrimage from Tellico Plains, Tennessee to Colleville-sur-Mer, France completed, Tom Cordle turned silently and slowly walked away.

West of the memorial is a large reflecting pool and two flagpoles flying the American flag followed by the graves area and the chapel. The Circular chapel is constructed from limestone except for its granite steps. Directly above the chapel's door is engraved a replica of the Congressional Medal of Honor, America's highest award for valor. Entering the chapel, one is immediately drawn to the black and gold marble altar. Across the front of the altar is the inscription, "I give unto them eternal life and they shall never perish". Immediately above the altar table is a Star of David with a dove in the center of the Star. Directly behind the altar is a tall window. On the glass around the edges of the window are 48 stars representing the then 48 states. Affixed to the lower half of the window is a thin teakwood Latin cross. The altar is flanked on both sides by flags of the United States, France, Great Britain, and Canada.

Leon Kroll of New York City designed the chapel's beautiful and colorful mosaic ceiling. The mosaic symbolizes America blessing her sons as they depart by sea and air to fight for freedom, and a grateful France bestowing a laurel wreath upon American dead who gave their lives to liberate Europe's oppressed peoples. An angel, dove, and a homeward bound ship illustrate the return of peace.

The main paths through the cemetery are laid out in the form of a Latin cross. The path along the central mall that forms the cross passes through ten plot areas, five on each side of the east-west mall. The plots are numbered from A thru J. Each plot area has a number of rows and then an individual grave in that row. Thus, to locate a particular soldier's grave it is necessary to know the plot, row, and grave number. Cemetery staffs at the Visitors building are available to answer questions and there is a comfortably furnished room where visitors can register and pause to refresh themselves.

Each grave is marked with a white marble headstone, a Star of David for those of the Jewish faith and a Latin cross for all others. Of the 9,387 interred in the cemetery, 307 are unknowns, 3 are Congressional Medal of Honor recipients, and 4 are women. Buried side by side are father and son and 38 pairs of brothers.

Like Tom Cordle, Barbara Shaw from Raynham, Massachusetts became the first member of her family in 63 years to return to Cherbourg and Normandy American cemetery. After well over a half-century, Barbara Shaw could now pay a final tribute to the grandfather World War II and the *Leopoldville* took from her.

Joseph E. Thibodeau was born in Haverhill, Massachusetts on October 25, 1910. He married Lillian Dunbar in early 1931 and worked on the tugboats in Boston as an electrician until he entered the army. Lillian Thibodeau received a letter from the government stating that her husband was killed in the European area and nothing more. It was not until the year 2000 that the family of Joseph E. Thibodeau finally learned the true circumstances of his death. Barbara Shaw's father, Joseph, was only thirteen years old when his father died. The young boy adored him and Christmas time in the Thibodeau house was not a happy time. Throughout Barbara's childhood, her father was extremely sad at Christmas. She remembers, "It was like a dark cloud hanging over the holiday. My father went to his grave never knowing what happened to his father."

As Barbara Shaw walked along the rows of white marble crosses, she felt as if she was at a funeral not only for her grandfather but for all the young soldiers who gave their lives for our freedom. "I took it personal", she later said. After passing through many rows of crosses mixed with the Star of David, her pilgrimage ended in front of plot D, row 14, gravesite 14. As the cool early April breeze blew back her hair, she knelt and rubbed dirt from her father's grave onto the white marble cross-engraved with the name, Pfc. Joseph E. Thibodeau. With tears welling up in her eyes, Barbara spoke softly almost to herself, "Now my father is at peace." Barbara too was now at peace. She would later say, "Resting in Normandy American cemetery, I know my grandfather is treated with the honor and respect due him." Reflecting on the trip to Europe Barbara would write months later, "I had many different emotions, like being on a roller coaster. It was a thrill and dream of a lifetime."

Barbara Shaw at Normandy American Cemetery walks along plot D, row 14 past rows of white crosses searching for her grandfather's name.

George M. Paden from Sand Springs, Oklahoma was unable to make the trip with us to Europe and revisit the path taken by the 66th Infantry Division and his father, Pvt. George W. Paden. Born on September 13, 1939, George M. Paden was only five years old when his father crossed the Channel that fateful night. Pvt. George W. Paden was assigned to Headquarters Company, Ammunition and Pioneer Platoon, 3rd Battalion, 262nd Regiment. There were 19 survivors from his platoon of which 14 were hospitalized. The bodies of 2 soldiers from his platoon were never found. The body of Pvt. George W. Paden was one of 3 recovered. His son sent me a personal letter honoring the father he barely knew and requested that I read it for him at his father's grave.

Tom Cordle stood with me in front of Pvt. George W. Paden's white marble headstone at plot C, row 14, grave 24. The morning had been cold and although it was early April, there had been a brief snow shower. I stood as straight as I could and saluted. Then I read in a clear loud voice the following poignant letter from a son to his father.

"Dad, It's been almost 65 years since we last had conversation and, of course, I remember very little of what was actually said between us. Lots of events have filled these years and due to your premature death you've missed all of them. However, I write today just to let you know that while you were never physically present the significant impacts for good that you have left upon me have influenced my life every single day.

Growing up in our hometown brought me into direct contact with many who held you in the very highest esteem and they were always faithful to remind me of what a great heritage I have in your being my father. They spoke so highly of you and all who knew you were so sorry that you were killed Christmas Eve, 1944, while in the service of our great nation. While I did not at that time fully understand the loss of you in my life I surely do now.

Throughout my adult life I have tried to hold high the standards for which you gave your efforts to and ultimately to which your life was given: God, Family, Country, Honesty, Integrity, Ethical Behavior, Hard Work, and Service to your fellow man. I have often wondered as an adult what life would have been for me had you returned home from WWII when I was still a child. I know that war has a strange way of changing people and yet I almost know for sure that your return to

us would only have made life so much better for us all. But, that was
not to be and you died honorably a hero's death and down through
these years I have been proud to say that I am a 'Gold Star' son of
a WWII hero.

Life for me has been good. I have been married for almost 47
years and we have made you the grandfather of two sons, both of
whom are happily married and each has two children which makes
you the great-grandfather of four, three girls and one boy, ages 13
years to 3 ½ years and the boy is the youngest. They of course, fill
our lives each day with much joy and are the center of our universe.
I am now retired from a forty-year career as a public school educator,
still live in our hometown less than a mile from our very first home,
and fill my days with lots of activities that give me satisfaction and
meaning.

Dad, you and I both know that someday soon we will be together
once again for eternity and that's a long, long, forever!! Those will
be 'happy days are here again' times I am certain. In the meantime
I desire for you to continue to rest in peace knowing fully that both
your life and your sacrificial death have had meaning and purpose
for me and for all those whom your life touched. I am proud to be
your son and in that fact I find motivation to become the best man
I possibly can be. The legacy you left me and the strong name you
carried while in my life have left big footsteps for me to follow and for
that I shall be forever grateful. I love you still. Your son, George."

When Congress established the American Battle Monuments
Commission in 1923, President Warren G. Harding appointed
General John J. Pershing as its first chairman. Gen. Pershing
commanded the two million soldiers of the American Expeditionary
Force (AEF) that fought in Europe in 1917. He was the ideal person
to head the commission and held the position until his death in 1948.
Gen. Pershing once wrote of the soldiers he commanded, "Time will
not dim the glory of their deeds."

On the deck of the sinking *Leopoldville* that Christmas Eve of 1944,
Pvt. George W. Paden gave his own life jacket to a frightened soldier
without one. I wrote this account of the *Leopoldville* disaster in the
hope that time will not dim the glory of the deeds of the many 66th
Division soldiers who perished that cold and dark night. The Bible
teaches us that no greater love has a man than that he lays down his

life for another. For Pvt. George W. Paden and the other soldiers who died that Christmas Eve, . . . Rest in Peace.

Pvt. George W. Paden

Pvt. George Washington Paden from Sand Springs, Oklahoma was married and the father of two small boys. He was in his mid-thirties but felt it was his obligation to fight for his country. Leopoldville survivor Pfc. John W. Daves was on deck with Pvt. Paden as they prepared to go overboard when they observed a young frightened soldier. Pvt. Paden gave the terrified soldier his own life jacket and the young soldier in turn gave Pvt. Paden a St. Christopher's Medal. Pfc. Daves last saw Pvt. Paden quietly reading his New Testament. The body of Pvt. Paden was recovered and buried in France. When Pvt. Paden's personal effects were returned to his family, the St. Christopher's Medal was among them

After World War II families had the option to have the body of their loved one returned to the United States for burial in a local family cemetery or a National military cemetery or leave the body buried in an American military cemetery on foreign soil. The following list consists of those 66th Division soldiers whose bodies were recovered and buried in Normandy American Cemetery. It is intended to help family members or friends who previously did not have this information. Families and friends may contact the American Battle Monuments Commission web site at *www.abmc.gov* to make arrangements for floral decoration at the gravesite and if possible, a photograph of the decoration in place.

Normandy American Cemetery

Name Plot Row Grave

Name	Plot Row Grave	Name	Plot Row Grave
Pfc. Michael F. Abatemarco	F-13-6	Pvt. Joseph Alexandrovich	G-10-34
Pfc. Hugh R. Barr	D-7-27	Pfc. Jack N. Bell	A-13-34
Pfc. John W. Brown	J-27-15	Pvt. Leo K. Chalcraft	G-15-37
S/Sgt. Michael Chalkan, Jr.	E-12-34	Pfc. Robert L. Chambers	C-13-24
Pvt. James P. Coen	D-18-21	Pfc. Leonard J. Cross	C-7-23
1/Lt. Harry Cybak	D-27-27	S/Sgt. John K. Dobkowski	C-17-42
S/Sgt. James J. Doherty, Jr.	A-20-25	T/5 Alf G. Ewald	C-20-25
2/Lt. Joseph R. Fierro	C-22-7	Pvt. Harry F. Fogelsonger	D-8-6
Pfc. Earl B. Fox	D-28-19	T/5 Tony A. Frank	B-7-20
Pvt. Henry Freund	A-9-20	S/Sgt. Robert Gianfrancesco	C-16-15
Pvt. Charles W. Goodlet	C-15-13	Pfc. Art S. Head	D-13-14
Pfc. James V. Heim	H-3-42	Pvt. Nevin H. Herman, Jr.	C-18-24
Pfc. Whiton L.E. Jackson	C-6-34	T/Sgt. Floyd J. Johnson	C-15-27
Pfc. Frank J. Kuchta	C-20-27	Pvt. Stanley J. Lapinski	F-21-22
T/Sgt. Luther M. Lawrence	D-27-19	Pfc. William E. Leftwich	E-23-23
1/Sgt. Harry Lutz	B-9-20	Pvt. John MacGowan	F-19-12
S/Sgt. Raymond B. Martinsen	H-22-19	Pvt. Gerard L. Mason	F-2-16
Pvt. Arthur T. Mathieu	B-23-30	S/Sgt. Arlo R. Mathison	D-21-29
Pfc. Glen P. McGhan	D-17-37	Pvt. George W. Miller	A-12-19
Pfc. Charles Molinsky	A-16-19	T/4 Herbert C. Moyer	E-2-44
Pvt. James W. Nolan	E-5-17	Pvt. William E. Nolan	D-7-13
S/Sgt. Charles P. Ofsonka, Jr.	A-5-25	Pfc. Joe B. Ortega	D-11-21
Pvt. Vincent Paci	C-3-20	Pvt. George W. Paden	C-14-24
S/Sgt. Thomas H. Patterson	D-17-21	Pvt. Carl R. Perry	C-21-34
Lt. Col. Victor E. Phasey	D-15-14	Pfc. Waldron M. Polgreen	A-11-19
1/Sgt. Lawrence E. Privett	D-27-6	T/5 Seth W. Reed	C-12-34
Pfc. Ernest C. Reichle	E-17-37	S/Sgt. Marvin L. Rilling	C-22-34
Sgt. Wardell J. Roberts	A-11-35	Pfc. Harry C. Robison	D-4-21
T/Sgt. Paul M. Rodal	F-13-12	Pfc. Don T. Rose	C-23-24
Pvt. Wilbur L. Rouch	C-25-6	1/Sgt. Jack Russell	C-8-39
Pfc. Edward W. Rzenek	C-8-44	Pvt. Arthur Schiller	F-5-12

Pfc. Hartselle B. Scholl	C-28-27	Pvt. James S. Scribner	C-7-20
Pfc. James E. Shand	E-21-34	S/Sgt. C.D. Smith	D-3-29
Pvt. Joseph J. Solotes	F-28-26	Sgt. Charles F. Sullivan	C-23-27
Pfc. Joseph E. Thibodeau	D-14-14	Pvt. Claude C. Thompson	G-28-34
Pfc. Robert L. Thompson	D-13-6	Pfc. Frank W. Vojir	C-28-39
S/Sgt. Carl J. Walz, Jr.	D-9-27	Pvt. Donald E. Williams	D-20-27
Pvt. LaVere R. Williams	H-24-27	Pfc. John J. Zubal	F-3-14

Epinal American Cemetery is located approximately four miles southeast of Epinal, France. The cemetery's 48.6 acres are on a plateau 100 feet above the Moselle river in the foothills of the Vosges mountains. Most of the 5, 255 graves found at Epinal American Cemetery are soldiers who lost their lives in the campaigns fighting across northeastern France to the Rhine and beyond into Germany. Although the cemetery is a few hundred miles from the beaches at Normandy, for reasons unknown to me, the body of one Leopoldville victim, T/5 Eugene R. Temple from Indianapolis, Indiana instead of being buried with his comrades at Normandy American Cemetery was buried at Epinal American Cemetery in plot A—row—5—grave 27.

Bibliography

Bayside High School, NY. *Triangle* Yearbook January 1944

Shirley W. Dunn & Allison P. Bennett. *Dutch Architecture Near Albany—The Polgreen Photographs* Purple Mt. Press, Fleishmans, NY, 1996.

Rolland E. Kidder. *A Hometown Went To War, Remembrances of World War II* Sandy Bottom Press, Chautauqua, NY, 1996

Arnold Olson. *Give Me This Mountain.* Arnold Olson, Minneapolis, MN, 1987.

Gerald Raymond. *Torpedoed!* Power for Living, Scripture Press, Colorado Springs, CO. December 14, 1980; Vol. 39 (1)

George Stanley Rehder. *The Night Before Christmas* Wilmington, NC (unpublished).

Raymond J. Roberts. *Survivors of the Leopoldville Disaster* Raymond J. Roberts, Bridgman, MI.

Jacquin Sanders. *A Night Before Christmas* G. P. Putnam's Sons, New York, NY, 1963

United States Army—40,000 Black Panthers of the 66th Division, Published 1946

Siinto S. Wessman. *66th—A Story Of World War II* Army & Navy Publishing Co., Baton Rouge, LA. 1946

Paul Willis. *Remembering World War II West Dorset At War,* Published by The Bridport Heritage Forum, England 2005

National Archives

British Admiralty—*Leopoldville* documents and investigative reports

United States National Archives, College Park, Maryland, numerous declassified *Leopoldville* documents and investigative reports including the official U.S. army *Leopoldville* casualty lists prepared on December 29, 1944 and January 5, 1945

American Battle Monument Commission

American Battle Monument Commission American Memorials and Overseas Military Cemeteries—Publication Normandy American Cemetery and Memorial—Publication American Battle Monument Commission web site—www.abmc.gov

Newspaper and Related Articles

Brig. Gen. J.W. Nicholson (Ret.) *"Off the Beaten Path"*
Army Magazine, November 2005, pgs. 41-44.
Diane Fischler, *"Remembering the SS Leopoldville"*
Army Magazine, November 2001, pgs. 44-46.
Assembly, Association of Graduates, USMA Vol. XIV 7/1955, p. 91.
Lew Moores. *"Memories Still Haunt WWII Vet."* The Cincinnati
Enquirer (Cincinnati, Ohio), December 22, 1994. Used with permission from The Cincinnati Enquirer/Lew Moores, *"Memories Still HauntWWII Vet."*
Cumberland Sunday Times-News (Cumberland, MD). *"Six Allegany County Servicemen Met Tragedy on Christmas Eve 1944,"* December 25, 1988.
Staci Hupp, *"Iowa family joins move to end looting of WWII shipwreck"*
DesMoines Sunday Register, Des Moines, Iowa September 03, 2000 pg.
1AAlison Bay. *"'44 Ship Survivor—Lucky to Be Alive. Transport Was Torpedoed On Christmas Eve."* The Denver Post (Denver, CO), 1994.
Brian K. Pitzer. *"Bonded by Art, Tragedy"*, Alumni News pgs. 2-4,
Edinboro University of Pennsylvania, Winter 1999
Stephen Drew. *"Englewood Resident—A Survivor of WWII Ship Disaster."*
Englewood Independent (Englewood, OH), January 4, 1995.
Phillip Tardani. *"One Fateful Night—He Still Hears Sounds of Death at Christmas."*
Loveland Daily Reporter-Herald (Loveland, CO), 1994.
Kristin Buehner, *"Respecting the dead . . . Family of war casualty wants looting to stop at grave on the bottom of the English Channel"*, Globe-Gazette, Mason City/Clear Lake, Iowa August 22,2000 pg. 1A
William Gordon. *"Ex-GI's Recall Horror Of Troop Ship Tragedy."*
Newark Star-Ledger, Newark, NJ. December 24, 1994.
Karen Zautyk. *"A Tragedy Too Long Secret."* New York Daily News December 22, 1999 Oneida Ltd. Employee Wartime Newspaper, *The Community Commando.*
Vol. 1 (13); April 24, 1943, p. 3. (Courtesy of Oneida, Ltd.)

Melvin L. DeWitt. "Torpedoing of the *Leopoldville*" "The Day Before Christmas, 1944." Patrol Craft Sailors Association Newsletter, Wes Johnson, Indianapolis, IN.

Wes Johnson. *"This Is My Story."* Patrol Craft Sailors Association Newsletter (provided from files of *Leopoldville* survivor Vincent Codianni).

P.C.C. News, (Pittsburgh Coal Company) Vol. 6 Number 1 April 1945 In Memoriam page to Sam and Dan Borovich

Ann Driscoll, *"Out of the Past . . . Sacred Trust . . . Families of U.S. Soldiers killed in a World War II sea disaster fight to keep divers from looting the wreck"* *People Magazine,* December 11, 2000, pgs. 203,204

James A. Ross. *"Soldier's Gift Was Escape From Sinking Ship."* The Plain Dealer, December 18, 1994, p. 1J. (Reprinted with permission from The Plain Dealer.)

The Post-Journal (Jamestown, NY), *"Local Twins Give Lives In Action— Brothers, 19 'Died At Sea' On Christmas Day, Parents Told,"* March 9, 1945, Second Section, p. 9.

Charles Birmingham. "Memory of Ship Sinking Is Bond for Area Men Who Met Recently." The Post-Journal (Jamestown, NY), December 24, 1969, p. 1.

Millard P. Rummel. *"1944—More Than 800 American Troops Were Lost That Night."* St. Petersburg Times (St. Petersburg, FL), September 3, 1989, p. 36J.

Doug Clark. *"Carols Renew Memories of Allies' Cowardice—WWII Vet's Wish for Christmas: Only the Truth."* the Spokesman Review December 25, 1994.

Salatheia Bryant. *"The Nightmare Before Christmas."* Tribune (Sun City Center, FL), December 24, 1994, p. 1 (provided from file of *Leopoldville* survivor Norman Bullett).

Corlis Holt. *"When Disaster Struck"*, VFW Magazine pages 24-25, December 1988

Ellen Kranick. *"It Was A Christmas Eve Etched In Horror."* Warren Times Observer (Warren, PA), December 23,1995.

Jason Krump *"The Epitome of Courage"*, Butch's Beat Washington State University Athletics Volume 13 Issue 6 July 11, 2007 pgs. 8-12.

"Whom Shall We Send?" West Point 50th Reunion Book Class of 1944. West Point, NY. p. 91.

Heidi Russell. *"A Real Hero."* York Sunday News (York, PA), December 25,1994, pp. C-1, C-2.

Testimonial Letters and Personal Accounts

Henry Lawrence Balboni, Norwood, MA. Testimonial Letter, May 2, 1985; provided from files of *Leopoldville* survivor Vincent Codianni.

George E. Bigelow, Ann Arbor, MI. Testimonial Letter, January 16, 1985; provided from files of *Leopoldville* survivor Vincent Codianni.

Surgical Tech. Sergeant John V. Corrigan. "My Christmas Eve in '44" (personal account of the disaster).

E.P. Bill Everhard. *"SNAFU—Christmas Eve, 1944"* (personal account of the disaster)

Jack F. Gangwere, Wheeling, WV. Testimonial Letter, March 21, 1985; provided from files of *Leopoldville* survivor Vincent Codianni.

Donald E. Gengler, *"Memoirs of World War II".* June 28, 1971

C. Denis Gilchrist. "Cherbourg 1944—Christmas." (provided from files of *Leopoldville* survivor Vincent Codianni).

Hugh Jones, San Bernardino, CA. Testimonial Letter, January 1988; provided from files of *Leopoldville* survivor Vincent Codianni.

William Kalinowski, Swansea, MA. Testimonial Letters, February 14,1985 and April 4, 1985; provided by *Leopoldville* survivor Vincent Codianni.

Colonel John C. Van Sickle USAR (Retired), Akron, OH. Testimonial Letter, July 18, 1985; provided by *Leopoldville* survivor Vincent Codianni.

Andrew B. White. *"I'm Too Young!"* Memoirs of World War II, July 1, 2000

End Notes

[1] After the war, the *George Washington* was put on reserve. While laid up in Baltimore harbor during January 1951, the *George Washington* was severely damaged by an accidental fire. The once proud troopship was subsequently broken up for scrap metal.

[2] When writing to each other, it was common practice among young lovers of the period to quote the titles of popular romantic ballads that had special meaning for the two of them. "I'll Walk Alone" was a sentimental romantic ballad composed by Sammy Cahn and Julie Styne for the hit show, "Follow the Boys."

[3] Peter Acri's older brother Oscar. He survived the war and went back to Pennsylvania.

[4] The cover of the card from Glenn and Jack Lowry to their father pictured, in color, Cruden Bay Golf Course, the eighth green. Beneath the picture was printed, "Good Luck!" Their mother's card showed a color drawing of Founders Towers, Magdalen, College, Oxford. The inside inscription read, "Once again to bring you with true heartiness, the best of all Good Wishes for Christmas and the New Year. Love, Jack and Glenn"

[5] Cornelie Marie Limbor and her son Jacques survived the war and returned to their home in Belgium.

[6] Christmas morning, 1944, Helen M. Livesey attended mass at the Etretat village church. Her memories of that last Christmas of the war and the days that followed are recorded below.

"We clanked up to the communion rail in field clothes and helmets.

Then we traveled by truck to a railroad yard, where we spent Christmas sitting around on the railroad tracks, eating turkey sandwiches for dinner.

We pulled out at night, the men in boxcars and the girls in compartment cars that were half blown away. Sanitary facilities were extremely poor. It was here that we learned never to be without a roll of toilet paper stuck between our helmets and liners."

Nurse Livesey recalled 4 or 5 days and nights of delays before they moved out. Their food always consisted of cold C and K-rations. The railroad tracks were surrounded by bomb craters that had filled with water. Frozen by the cold temperatures, the craters provided ice ponds for occasional skaters.

"We arrived at Rennes, Brittany, where we were billeted on the second floor of a boarding school. The bathtub was in the basement, and time was allotted to men and women for bathing. Here we took over a hospital, about a block away, from another unit that was moving out. The wards were large, about fifty beds, with one or two rooms for the sicker patients. Again, there was a rigid blackout at night. Getting hot water was a problem; it had to be carried to the wards.

"Nurses, as officers, were allotted one bottle of whiskey every month or two for a nominal sum. When V-E Day came, my colleague and I wanted to give each patient a drink of our whiskey to celebrate—ours was a ward of skin conditions and trench foot, so there was no clinical contraindication— but we couldn't get permission. Everyone we asked replied that he or she did not have the authority. We decided to give drinks anyway!"

Former Army Nurse Helen M. Livesey can look back to the indecision of those in authority with laughter. But, for the young American soldiers aboard the *Leopoldville* when it was torpedoed in the English Channel, indecision, errors, and omissions by those in authority played a major role in adding to the immeasurable heartache and terrible loss of life.

7   When Sergeant Via was told the turkeys "stay," a number of Panther soldiers left some of their clothing behind to allow room to stuff the turkeys in their duffel bags. Only after the *Leopoldville* was torpedoed and orders were given to put on long johns, was it discovered that some men had replaced that warm item of clothing with a turkey. The birds went to the bottom along with the ship and perhaps the absence of the long johns contributed to the freezing deaths of some of the young soldiers.

8   That Christmas Eve of 1944, Captain George E. Plott, Company H, 262nd regiment, from Waynesville, North Carolina, was one of the soldiers who would not survive the sinking of the *Leopoldville*.

9   Edward Haas would later write, "As we entered the harbor we were somewhat surprised to see that there was a lot of small boat activity in both directions, especially since it was Christmas Eve. The *Chesire* docked in what I recall was a timely manner and we disembarked

orderly. I don't believe at that time that I or anyone else knew what had befallen our comrades on the *Leopoldville.*"

[10] Corporal James Hawkins was the brother of Robert E. Hawkins. James was also killed during World War II. The two brothers are buried alongside each other in Arlington National Cemetery.

[11] Private First Class Bill Donaldson perished in the sinking of the *Leopoldville.*

[12] Sergeant Carl Miller did not survive the sinking of the troopship.

[13] Sergeant Glanton, of Emmett, Arkansas, was one of those lost when the troopship sank.

[14] Private First Class Alfred Corti was able to escape from the sinking *Leopoldville* by jumping to the deck of the *Brilliant.* In later years, he moved to Ossining, New York.

[15] Frederick Perkins was one of thirteen men from his company who was rescued by the destroyer. Perkins was sent to the hospital for a cut foot.

Although he had survived the tragedy, Perkins' wife back in upstate New York was notified that her husband had, "met a sudden death."

Distraught by the news, she was taken by her father to see Red Cross officials, who straightened the matter out; they determined that Frederick

Perkins was indeed alive and was not one of those who perished in thatterrible Christmas Eve calamity.

[16] Kalinowski clearly writes Marman, but the name Marman cannot be found in any lists of survivors or deceased.

[17] At the U.S. Military Academy, West Point, New York, Captain Hal F.

Crain's name appears in the Memorial Hall on a large bronze plaque thatlists all of the graduates who were killed in action during World War II.

[18] A few days after the tragedy, Second Lieutenant Henry L. Balboni visited the Cherbourg Harbor Entrance Control Post (HECP) and spoke with Lieutenant Colonel McConnell. He knew the Colonel when they were both assigned to the Harbor Defenses of New York. Colonel McConnell advised Lieutenant Balboni that his HECP was never advised by the British that the *Leopoldville* had been torpedoed. Colonel McConnell told him that he had dispatched personally local army rescue boats on his own authority because sight observations showed that the troopship had ceased to proceed toward the entrance to the harbor. Balboni added, "I cannot report a single instance of any aid or direction being offered to the troopship passengers by any member of the *Leopoldville* crew, Belgian or British. The men of the 66th Division were pretty much left to make their own individual decisions."

19   There were at least four lifeboats rendered useless during the early phase of the disaster; two were destroyed in the initial blast, and two were shattered by the *Brilliant*. It was estimated that, at most, 100 soldiers left the vessel aboard lifeboats, and the actual figure probably was less. About 23 British gunners and staff of the some 40 British Armed Guard aboard the troopship made it into the boats. The rest of those in the 10 remaining lifeboats were the crew. Counting crew, British Armed Guard, and soldiers, there were in all about 300 men and 2 female nurses who left in the available lifeboats, which had a capacity of 590. This simple math demonstrates clearly that the lifeboats pulled away from the disaster scene approximately half full, leaving behind many soldiers who could have been saved.

20   William Boggs later learned that seven of his platoon comrades were lost in the disaster.

21   Frank Haugh never saw a Corvette ship like the *Brilliant* again until one summer when he and his wife vacationed in Nova Scotia. In Halifax harbor was a World War II Corvette tied up at the dock. Although no longer seaworthy, it was available for a tour. Wrote Haugh afterwards, "I never realized how small this ship was, and the very tight area we had for landing when we swung over. Had I realized it that night, I am sure it would have made the task much more difficult."

22   After the war, Frank Haugh visited Thomas Cobb's home in Ridgewood, New Jersey, and honored his former army friend's last request. Haugh met his friend's mother and brother, Richard, and explained to them the circumstances surrounding his death.

23   After the war, Corlis Holt attended Hardin-Simmons University in Abilene, Texas, from which he graduated in 1948. He began a 40-year career as a journalist, mostly as a sportswriter, for several Texas dailies, including the *Fort Worth Star-Telegram, Port Arthur News, Houston Post*, and *Houston Chronicle*. He never forgot that incredible Christmas Eve, and the influence of those events remained strong throughout his life. In his own words, "Surviving that catastrophe as well as the subsequent action against the Germans has influenced my life substantially. It has served to bolster my confidence. Often, when facing a tough situation, I say to myself, This can't be as bad as what I endured in the service, and the Lord brought me through that all right. I can whip this, too."

24   The official position of the Belgian Government is that the crew of the *Leopoldville* acted properly; they deny completely the accusations

to the contrary by some of the *Leopoldville* survivors. Lieutenant Pete Wood would write years later, "Looking back, it is hard to criticize the crew too much. They had probably seen a lot more of the war then we ever would, and many had probably been through other sinkings. Our feelings at the time, however, were not too kind."

25 Both Lieutenant Ben Thrailkill and Lieutenant George Washko of Lieutenant Wood's platoon, who directed the jumping to the *Brilliant,* survived the sinking of the *Leopoldville.*

26 Lieutenant Pete Wood confirmed the names of the five men lost from his platoon, Company T, 264th Infantry. They were Private First Class Marvin J. Barton, Poughkeepsie, New York; Private First Class Gregorio V. Contreras, Del Rio, Texas; Staff Sergeant James J. Doherty, Jr., Connecticut; Private First Class Thomas J. English, Jr., Pittsburgh, Pennsylvania; and Private First Class John A. Worden, Battle Creek, Michigan.

27 It was not until 51 years later at a reunion of the members of the 66thDivision, held in Danvers, Massachusetts, that Walter Brown and Bill Cline learned that it was the tug *ATR-3* had rescued them. At the reunion, Walter Brown and Bill Cline met, for the first time, the *ATR-3* crewmen who had saved their lives. They were Art Bilotas, Quincy, Massachusetts;

Carl Fiorenza, Lothian, Maryland; Richard Freeburg, North Warren, Pennsylvania; Herb Horner, Francis town, New Hampshire; and Robert Langervin, Binghamton, New York.

28 For almost 50 years, Freeburg repressed the sight of the men he saw perish. But the memories and the cries of those in the water would not be silenced. Beginning in 1993, he coordinated annual reunions with his former shipmates. He also wagged a fight with the federal government to officially acknowledge the disaster and recognize the efforts of those who tried to help.

29 The Army officer's jacket left on the deck of PT 461 was always displayed in Syd Garner's office in a place of honor. Syd spent the rest of his life trying to locate its owner without success. Frequently he would say, "I have it where I can look at it and wonder who the hell the guy was."

Sydney E. Garner, forever linked to the 66th Panther Division, died on September 22, 1994, at the age of 79.

30 Private First Class Martin F. Anderson, Private First Class Harold H. Dantinne, Private Edgar C. Moore, Private First Class Waldron Polgreen, and Private First Class Richard E. Moser were killed. The bodies of Sergeant Elmer A. Baker and Private First Class Waldron Polgreen

were both found in the water. Private James C. Foester's body was never found. Private First Class Richard F. Sansone's body was also never recovered.

[31]   A discrepancy exists regarding the exact time that the *Leopoldville* sank.
The official Belgian time is 8:05 PM, whereas the 66th Division puts the time at 8:20 to 8:25 PM. The U.S. Navy report records the sinking at about 8:30 PM. The men at Fort L'Ouest, France, listed the sinking in their record book as 9:05 PM, whereas the U.S. Army at Cherbourg kept no record at all of the time of the sinking. The British Admiralty refused to give any time to Jacquin Sanders, author of *A Night Before Christmas*, who estimated the sinking as no earlier than 8:20 nor later than 8:40 PM.

[32]   At the time of the sinking, Jerry Crean was 23 years old. Looking back he says of the disaster, "When you are training with people that you know your life will depend on someday, you get very close, and to lose so many all in one shot . . . and then go to the cemetery in France where they are laid out like sticks in a row . . . and a lot of them are your friends . . . the *Leopoldville* tragedy will never leave me. I find a place and cry every Christmas Eve."

[33]   Jack Landovitz was eventually picked up by a U.S. Coast Guard vessel, taken to Cherbourg, and placed in a military hospital. The day after Christmas, he rejoined elements of Company C, which were reassembling at a dog race track in Cherbourg.

[34]   In March 1994, Jack Randles' interpretation of Captain Van Sickle's prayer was verified during a telephone conversation with John Van Sickle's widow. She affirmed that her husband had lived his life as, ". . . a man of unfailing integrity." John Van Sickle had never told her about his encounter with Jack Randles. She said the only personal thing he ever related about his experience that fateful Christmas Eve concerned a decision he made while in the water. He told his wife that a ship pulled alongside to retrieve him and others around him. He tried to climb the rope ladder that had been lowered but did not have the strength to do it. Then, realizing that he was in the way of others, he deliberately pushed himself away from the ship. It was a decision, he was sure, that would seal his death. That was Van Sickle's last accurate memory of his rescue. It wasn't until 42 years later at a meeting of the 66th Panther Veterans Organization in 1986 that John Van Sickle learned from Jack Randles that the same person who had rescued Jack Randles was also Van Sickle's savior.

35   After he was saved by *PC 564*, Arnold Dahlke was taken to the 280thStation Hospital where he remained until January 31, 1945. When he rejoined Company I, 262nd Infantry, he first learned that 72 men from the company had been lost.

36   Keith Simons, of Loveland, Colorado, never forgot his friend Fred Schlerf, who was the ammunition bearer for his mortar. He wrote of him, "May his soul and those of the 800 others be in a warm and lovely place."

37   Captain Jack Gangwere's company lost about 50% of their complement (about 100 men) in the disaster. As Company Commander, Capt. Gangwere wrote to the relatives of those who died.

He later said, "All I could tell them was that their relative was missing . . . nothing about the ship or the German sub." Captain Gangwere also criticized the crew. "There were no boats for us; the crew, including the women workers, got to them first."

38   William Dallas served with the 533rd Ordnance Division attached to the a Tank Corps and landed on Omaha Beach on D-Day plus 4 in June 1944 [June 10, 1944]. He drove a tank ashore during the heavy fighting and spoke of it many times during the years he raised his family. But it was not until a warm, rainy Christmas eve in 1991 that told his wife the story of Christmas eve 1944.

"They had wedding rings on and wore watches and were heavily dressed for the bad weather, but they never had a chance. I wondered if their families would ever know the true story of how and where they died. Some were my age, some younger and a few older, but I never had anything hit me so hard."

William Dallas was 25 years old when he participated in the Leopoldville rescue effort.

39   There was concern that German prisoners in camps near Cherbourg might attempt to escape but that did not happen. The Channel Islands were bypassed by the Allies and were not bombed or attacked. A story was told of a raiding party of Germans from the Isle of Jersey, who landed at Granville shortly after Christmas and freed about 100 POWs and took them back to Jersey. The raiding vessels were apparently tracked by U.S. radar, but the raid was coordinated with the low tide so that the PT boats at Cherbourg could not operate safely between the mainland and Jersey. At the time of the raid, U.S. Army guards allegedly had no ammunition in accordance with local policy. The only casualties suffered during the operation were a few Royal Marines who resisted

the Germans. Since Jersey was isolated, the "freed" German POWs could not be returned to combat duty. The raid had only succeeded in "liberating" the Granville POW Camp from the responsibility of caring for and feeding some 100 German prisoners.

[40] Private Robert J. Swanson was one of the 36 soldiers from the state Illinois lost in the disaster.

[41] The liberty ship *Jonas Lie* was itself torpedoed and sunk on January 9, 1945, at the mouth of the Bristol Channel, as it was about to join the convoys coming down from the rivers Mersey and Clyde at Liverpool and Glasgow for its return to the United States. Aboard the liberty ship when it was sunk, Lieutenant Robert Blank was picked up by the British ship *Huddersfieldtown*, an armed trawler, and brought to Milford Haven, Wales.

[42] When Lieutenant Blank arrived in Cherbourg, he did not see any survivors because he had to remain on board the *Jonas Lie* while the liberty ship discharged its cargo. Security was extremely tight because there were rumors regarding German parachutists allegedly dropped on the bluffs over the city. When he finally did go into town, he was subjected to all sorts of inquiries by armed guards. In addition to showing his ID, he was asked who had won the World Series and other questions, which only someone familiar to the American scene would know.

After the sinking of the *Jonas Lie*, Lieutenant Blank stayed in Swansea, Wales, for a week, where there was an American port battalion, and then was ordered to London where he was issued a new uniform and flown back to Washington.

[43] While crossing the English Channel the British frigate *Capel* was torpedoed at approximately 2 PM in the afternoon of December 26, 1944. There were nine officers and sixty-eight seamen killed, including the commander of the vessel, Lieutenant Heslop.

[44] The hospitalized Earl Jacobs, who spent Christmas Day with his brother Raymond, later was awarded the Bronze Star for his attempts to rescue his trapped comrades.

[45] Two weeks after the disaster the families were still unaware of what was happening or even where their sons or husbands were.

"January 12, 1945 . . . Dear Son, Here I am again. How are you? We are all well at home. Brother, another day and no mail from you. I hope you are still in England."

[46] Gregory Jurlina's last letter home mentioned that he had met another Donora boy serving in the 66th Division, Private Ralph Vernile.

Ironically, Private Vernile was also killed when the *Leopoldville* was torpedoed and sunk. Mary Steranko was 11 years old when the telegram reporting her brother's death arrived. She was, in fact, writing him a letter when the notification was received.

Greg's mother remained convinced that by God's grace, her son's spirit was able to reach out from his watery grave and return home one last time in order to say goodbye. Both parents died never knowing the magnitude of the disaster that took their son's life, and like so many others, the body of Staff Sergeant Gregory G. Jurlina was never recovered.

[47] First buried in France along with the other recovered bodies, the War Department gave the Appleby family the option of returning the body of their son to the United States or having his remains permanently interred in France. His grieving parents chose to have his body brought back to the States.

[48] Guy Clark Sawyer, probably the last person to see the Lowry twins alive, was a member of Company I, 3rd Platoon. He celebrated his nineteenth birthday on December 22, 1944, just 2 days before the *Leopoldville* disaster. Sawyer heard a very loud blast right before the ship started to sink. "I was knocked into the water by a big wave." After catching his breath, Sawyer was able to swim away from the ship wearing a life preserver.

Wrote Sawyer later, "I will never forget the sounds coming from everywhere as some were praying and others were calling for their mothers." A tugboat eventually spotted him and he was pulled from the water and saved.

[49] Commissioned on July 20, 1944, the *Auburn*, named for a mountain in Massachusetts received two battle stars for her service during World War II. She served as flagship for Commander, Training Command, Atlantic Fleet, during the early part of 1946. On May 7, 1947, *Auburn* was placed out of commission in reserve at Norfolk, Virginia.

[50] After World War II, the government built a golf link at the Lyons Veterans Medical Center in New Jersey. The link was named for Coakley and another prominent golfer killed during the war—the Russo-Coakley Golf Course. The Francis X. Coakley Memorial Tournament

has been held at Galloping Hill since 1945, and a bronze plaque can be seen in the Pro Shop.

Sergeant Bob Hesse, of Linden, New Jersey, had warned Lieutenant Coakley 10 or 15 minutes before the ship went down to get his remaining men toward the bow since the vessel was sinking by the stern. That was the last time Hesse saw him. Lieutenant Francis X. Coakley died helping his troops abandon ship. His last letter home was dated December 23 and noted that he was preparing a big Christmas party for the kids of Dorchester on Christmas Eve. Many parents and wives received such letters from their loved ones expressing that they would be in Dorchester for the holiday. Devastated relatives therefore could not believe that their loved one was gone and were certain, it must be a mistake.

[51] In yet another ironic twist to the tragedy, the rescued crew of the *Leopoldville* was placed aboard the *Cheshire* on the afternoon of Christmas Day and returned to England without incident. Many of the officers and crew of the *Leopoldville* were then assigned to another Belgian Line ship, the *Persier*. The *Persier* was torpedoed in the channel on February 11, 1945. Ten survivors of the *Leopoldville*, including the First Officer Carl Brognion and two female nurses, lost their lives.

Finally, it should be noted that just 4 days after the *Leopoldville* disaster, at 2:40 PM on December 28, the troop ship *Empire Javelin* with 1,500 soldiers aboard, was torpedoed about 34 miles south southeast of St. Catherine's Point, Isle of Wight. The ship sank after a second explosion. The rescue of the 1,642 survivors was effected by the British destroyer *Brilliant*, the same destroyer that took survivors from the *Leopoldville*. The frigate and the French frigate *L'Escarmouche* also participated in the rescue efforts. The submarine responsible for the attack evaded the anti-submarine search. Although the *Empire Javelin* was struck during daylight hours, which facilitated rescue efforts, only six lives were lost. Unlike the *Leopoldville*, this ship held abandon ship drills. Amazingly, a drill had just been completed a few minutes before the torpedo hit.

[52] The sinking of *U-486* by the *Tapir* represented the last British submarine success in home waters before the war ended. The *Tapir* arrived in the Far East in July 1945, but with the unconditional surrender of Japan in August, Captain John Roxburgh was deprived the opportunity of sinking a Japanese submarine.

The *Tapir* was transferred to the Royal Netherlands Navy in 1948 and renamed the *Zeehond*. The sub, however, was returned to the Royal Navy in 1953 and her name reverted to *Tapir*. The submarine that had avenged the *Leopoldville* was sold to ship breaking industries at Faslane in 1966 and scrapped.

"Elmer [Baker], I do remember well in 1948, when you were returned to us. I know for Mom it was an extremely difficult event to face . . .

For me, a six-year-old, it was a very exciting occasion. I remember that all the furniture was moved out of one of the rooms of our tiny three room house and your casket was placed there, with the flag draped over it. . . . I remember the soldier standing guard, . . . I remember the dog tags fastened to the casket, the one with the filed edge, the one you filed the burr off of during your last visit home, . . . the one that convinced Mom that it was your remains in the casket. The tag that is now in my possession along with that honored flag folded in memory of a brother that fate never allowed me to know.

Your baby brother, Roger [Baker]"

In Memoriam
66th Infantry Division

This In Memoriam list was originally published by me in July 1997. As a result of my ongoing research into the disaster the list has been updated and corrected. Where my research determined the final disposition of the body it is indicated as follows:

[M] body never recovered; [F] body buried in France; [R] body returned to the United States for burial

Alabama (7)

Carlton, Garlan Pfc.	Co. I 262nd Regiment	Stockton [M]
Goodwin, James D. Pfc.	Co. E 262nd Regiment	Anniston [M]
Harris, John W. Pfc.	Co. H 262nd Regiment	Bexar [M]
McCorkle, Roy E., Jr. Pfc.	Co. F 262nd Regiment	Florence
Roberts, Marzell Pvt.	Co. E 262nd Regiment	Empire [M]
Terry, James H. Pvt.	Co. L 262nd Regiment	Cullman [M]
Waldrop, Roy A. Pfc.	Co. K 262nd Regiment	Waverly [M]

Arizona (3)

Rilling, Marvin L. S. Sgt.	Co. F 262nd Regiment	Seligman [F]
Vasquez, John G. Pvt.	Co. B 264th Regiment	Globe
Willis, Waldo M. S. Sgt.	Co. I 262nd Regiment	Show Low [M]

Arkansas (6)

Bell, Jack N. Pfc.	Co. A 264th Regiment	Widener [F]
Field, Henry, Jr. Pvt.	Co. F 262nd Regiment	Doddridge [M]
Glanton, Homer T. T. Sgt.	Co. C 264th Regiment	Emmett
Lutz, Harry 1st Sgt.	Hdq. Co. 3rd Battalion 262nd Reg.	Abbott
Melson, Paul A. T. Sgt.	Co. L 262nd Regiment	Ozone
Wade, Joseph T. Sgt.	Co. I 262nd Regiment	Van Buren [M]

California (29)

Anderson, Martin F. Pfc.	Co. I 262nd Regiment	San Diego
Andrews, William H. Sgt.	Hdq. Co. 1st Battalion 264th Reg.	Alhambra
Aprea, Fred Pfc.	Co. K 262nd Regiment	Los Angeles [M]
Berg, Fred W. Pvt.	Co. K 262nd Regiment	Oakland [M]
Crain, Hal F. Capt.	Co. F 262nd Regiment	[M]

Pfc. Carl Nelson

Twin brothers, Carl and Nels Nelson from San Francisco, California were born on October 24, 1924. Both were outstanding students and Pfc. Carl Nelson was accepted into the ASTP program. He completed the course at the University of Wyoming in April 1944. Nels Nelson was attached to the 8th Army Air Force in England. The two brothers arranged through the Red Cross to meet in Southampton on December 24. A disappointed Nels arrived in Southampton shortly after the Leopoldville sailed. The body of his twin brother, Pfc. Carl Nelson, was never found.

Dominguez, Joe Pvt.	Co. E 262nd Regiment	Los Angeles [M]
Durgy, William D. S. Sgt.	Co. L 262nd Regiment	Bakersfield [M]
Godoy, Arthur C. Pfc.	Co. E 262nd Regiment	Los Angeles M]
Jump, Clifford V. Pfc.	Co. E 262nd Regiment	Selma [M]
Kerr, Ian H. Pfc.	Hdq. Co. 3rd Battalion 262nd Reg.	Los Angeles
Lebensart, Frederick Pfc.	Co. E 264th Regiment	Pomona
Macrorie, Edward J., Jr. Pvt.	Co. K 262nd Regiment	Alhambra
Martinez, Candelario Pvt.	Co. K 262nd Regiment	Los Angeles
Mathews, Richard N. Pfc.	Co. E 262nd Regiment	Los Molinos
Menalo, Charles F. Pfc.	Hdq. Co. 1st Battalion 264th Reg.	Los Angeles
Miller, Carl H. T. Sgt.	Co. I 262nd Regiment	Los Angeles
Murray, Samuel L. Pvt.	Co. E 262nd Regiment	Fresno [M]
Nelson, Carl A. Pfc.	Co. E 262nd Regiment	San Francisco [M]
Olivas, Magdaleno Pfc.	Co. I 262nd Regiment	Oakland
Perry, Joe J. T/5.	Co. L 262nd Regiment	Carruthers [M]
Reeder, Thomas R. Sgt.	Co. I 264th Regiment	San Diego
Robles, Nabor P. Pvt.	Co. F 262nd Regiment	Los Angeles [M]
Stull, Ray S. T/4.	Co. E 264th Regiment	Orange [M]
Taylor, Delbert L. Pvt.	Co. I 262nd Regiment	[M]
Vonder, Mehden Robert Pfc.	Co. A 264th Regiment	[M]
Wells, Donald E. Pfc.	Co. F 262nd Regiment	Berkeley [M]
Williamson, Donald E. Pfc.	Co. F 262nd Regiment	Huntington Park [M]
Young, Fred F., Jr. Sgt.	Co. E 262nd Regiment	Doyle [M]
Zamarripa, Pete M., Jr. Pfc.	Co. L 262nd Regiment	Los Angeles [M]

Colorado (12)

Birkholz, Everett E. Pfc.	Co. F 262nd Regiment	Denver [M]
Bowle, Thomas A. Pfc.	Co. E 262nd Regiment	Delta [M]
De Silva, Philip E. Pfc.	Co. E 262nd Regiment	Denver [M]
Donaldson, William D. Pfc.	Co. I 262nd Regiment	Grand Junction
Lowenhagen, Theodore C. T. Sgt.	Co. F 262nd Regiment	Fruita
Manley, Albert L., Jr. Pfc.	Co. F 262nd Regiment	Crested Butte
McGee, Everett L. Pvt.	Co. L 262nd Regiment	Brighton [F]
Murchison, Rob R. Pfc.	Co. K 264th Regiment	Fort Collins
Ortega, Joe B. Pfc.	Co. I 262nd Regiment	Brighton
Quinonez, Joe J. Pfc.	Co. B 264th Regiment	Trinidad
Reeder, Harold P. Pvt.	Co. L 262nd Regiment	Colorado Springs
Struble, Frank P. S. Sgt.	Co. F 262nd Regiment	Pueblo [M]

T/4 Concetto J. Caracoglia

T/4 C. J. Caracoglia from Hartford, Connecticut was assigned to 2nd Battalion Medical Detachment, 262nd Regiment. It was later reported that many of the men assigned to the medical detachment remained on deck to care for the wounded rather then try to save themselves. There were only 8 survivors from the medical detachment unit of which 3 were hospitalized. No bodies were recovered. The body of T/4 Caracoglia was among the 19 from medical detachment never found.

Connecticut (13)

Berube, Joseph E. Pvt.	Co. F 262nd Regiment	Ballouville [M]
Bruschayt, Herbert W. Pfc.	Co. F 262nd Regiment	Hamden [M]
Caracoglia, Concetto T/4.	Med. Det. 262nd Regiment	Hartford [M]
Carlson, Francis M. Cpl.	Co. H 262nd Regiment	Parana [M]
Dobkowski, John K. S.Sgt.	Hdq. Co. 2nd Battalion 262nd Reg.	Ansonia [F]
Doherty, James J., Jr. S.Sgt.	Co. I 264th Regiment	[F]
Machado, Frank R. Pfc.	Co. C 264th Regiment	Danbury
O'Neil, Grant P. Pfc.	Co. I 262nd Regiment	Pawcatuck [M]
Rowe, Hazlewood Pfc.	Co. F 262nd Regiment	Wallington [M]
Shand, James E. Pfc.	Co. H 262nd Regiment	Bridgeport [F]
Strobel, Robert H. Pfc.	Co. F 262nd Regiment	Bridgeport [M]
Svenningsen, Elmer Pfc.	Co. F 262nd Regiment	Stamford [M]
Viets, Paul R. Pfc.	Co. E 262nd Regiment	Thomaston [M]

Florida (6)

Chalcraft, Leo K. Pvt.	Co. L 262nd Regiment	St. Petersburg [F]
Crawford, William H. Pvt.	Co. L 262nd Regiment	Pensacola [R]
Henderson, Dewey A. Pvt.	Co. L 262nd Regiment	Tampa [M]
Hinton, Frederick D. Pvt.	Hdq. Co. 1st Battalion 264th Reg.	Lake Butler
Nolan, James H. S. Sgt.	Co. K 262nd Regiment	Jacksonville [R]
Wright, Kenneth K. Pfc.	Co. K 262nd Regiment	Crestview [R]

Georgia (8)

Barwick, Eugene H. Pvt.	Co. B 264th Regiment	Cairo [M]
Freeman, Ethell W. Pfc.	Co. F 262nd Regiment	Odum [M]
James, William C. Pfc.	Hdq. Co. 2nd Battalion 262nd Reg.	Savannah
McInnis, James E., Jr. Pvt.	Co. F 262nd Regiment	Columbus
Mobley, Lewfay B., Jr. Pfc.	Co. F 262nd Regiment	Columbus
Russell, Jack 1st Sgt.	Hdq. Co. 3rd Battalion 262nd Reg.	Columbus [F]
Smith, Henry A. Cpl.	Med. Det. 262nd Regiment	Dalton [M]
Zellner, Harold M. Sgt.	Co. I 262nd Regiment	Macon [M]

Pfc. Calvin Glenn Christensen and his wife Anita

Calvin Glenn Christensen was born on December 26, 1916 in American Falls, Idaho. Glenn, as everyone called him, entered the military service in June 1940. A member of Company F, 262nd Regiment, he married Anita L. Nicolaus at the Camp Rucker Chapel on June 30, 1944. Witnesses to their wedding, Company F buddies Pfc. Everett E. Birkholz from Denver, Colorado and Pfc. Antonio DeResta Jr. from Providence, Rhode Island, would both perish in the *Leopoldville* disaster. The bodies of Pfc. Christensen, Pfc. Birkholz, and Pfc. DeResta were never found. Anita L. Christensen never remarried. She died on August 9, 1982 at the age of 64.

Idaho (3)

Buhler, Glen L. Pfc.	Co. E 262nd Regiment	[M]
Campbell, Tez V. Pvt.	Co. K 262nd Regiment	Pocatello
Christensen, Calvin G. Pfc.	Co. F 262nd Regiment	American Falls [M]

Illinois (36)

Baglio, Michael S., Jr. Sgt.	Co. F 262nd Regiment	Chicago [M]
Bradenback, Norman U. 1st Lt.	Co. F 262nd Regiment	Hillsboro
Brisendine, Bruce F. Pfc.	Co. F 262nd Regiment	Pekin [M]
Colo, Joe Pvt.	Co. H 262nd Regiment	Highwood [M]
Colwell, Franklin W. S. Sgt.	Co. I 262nd Regiment	Tuscola [M]
Cross, Leonard J. Pfc.	Co. C 264th Regiment	Chicago [F]
Dalton, Delmar L. Pfc.	Co. A 264th Regiment	Bloomington
Deamantopulos, Andrew Pfc.	Co. F 262nd Regiment	Chicago [M]
De Klyen, John C. Sgt.	Co. B 264th Regiment	Oak Park [M]
Dronenberg, Donald P. T. Sgt.	Co. H 262nd Regiment	Prophetstown [M]
Duhasek, William R. Sgt.	Co. A 264th Regiment	Chicago
Farling, Ernest W. Pfc.	Co. F 262nd Regiment	Magnolia [M]
Ferbus, Baptiste E. Pfc.	Co. F 262nd Regiment	Johnston City [M]
Goble, John W. T. Sgt.	Co. C 264th Regiment	Peoria
Godelas, Peter T. Pfc.	Co. F 262nd Regiment	Chicago [M]
Griffith, George O. Pfc.	Co. F 262nd Regiment	[M]
Johnson, Floyd J. T. Sgt.	Co. K 262nd Regiment	Casey [F]
Kingrey, James P. T/5.	Co. L 262nd Regiment	Harvey [M]
Marcinkowski, Arthur A. Pfc.	Co. H 262nd Regiment	Chicago
McArthur, Kent O. Pvt.	Co. F 262nd Regiment	Chicago
Mikalaitis, Joseph E. Pvt.	Co. L 262nd Regiment	Chicago
Nelson, Eric G. Sgt.	Co. F 262nd Regiment	Lake Forest [M]
Papineau, George J. Cpl.	Co. I 262nd Regiment	Chicago [M]
Pollitt, Joe A. T. Sgt.	Co. F 262nd Regiment	Peoria [M]
Read, Basel O. S. Sgt.	Co. C 264th Regiment	Chicago
Rose, Don T. Pfc.	Co. I 262nd Regiment	Chicago
Scholl, Hartselle B. Pfc.	Co. K 264th Regiment	Chicago [F]
Shub, Abraham Pfc.	Co. I 262nd Regiment	Chicago
Smith, Lewis A. Pfc.	Co. F 262nd Regiment	Berwyn
Steib, Joseph E. Pvt.	Med. Det. 264th Regiment	Mt. Carmel
Swanson, Robert J. Pvt.	Co. C 264th Regiment	Moline
Taylor, Robert H. Pvt.	Co. B 264th Regiment	Ozark
Verbauen, Albert Sgt.	Co. H 262nd Regiment	Chicago [M]

Welch, Donald P. Pfc.	Hdq. Co. 3rd Battalion 262nd Reg.	Chicago [M]
Westbrook, Marion J. Pvt.	Co. E 262nd Regiment	Alton [M]
Willcoxen, Donald E. Pfc.	Co. K 262nd Regiment	Peoria [M]

Indiana (28)

Alvarado, Donald R. Pvt.	Co. E 262nd Regiment	Marion [M]
Bain, Emil Pvt.	Co. H 262nd Regiment	Gary [M]
Bouse, Oren A. Sgt.	Co. C 264th Regiment	Kokomo
Buell, Edwin D., III Pfc.	Co. H 262nd Regiment	Mill Creek [M]
Essex, Aaron W. Sgt.	Hdq. Co. 3rd Battalion 262nd Reg.	Hope [M]
Harman, Cecil C. Pfc.	Co. F 262nd Regiment	Wabash [M]
Houchen, Donald R. Pvt.	Co. H 262nd Regiment	Henryville [M]
Kocsis, Anton Pfc.	Co. F 262nd Regiment	South Bend [M]
Lewis, Emry L. Pfc.	Co. I 262nd Regiment	Tinton [M]
Lottes, Clarence E. Pfc.	Co. K 262nd Regiment	Tell City [M]
McDonald, Buford C. Pfc.	Med. Det. 264th Regiment	Bedford [R]
McIntyre, Robert F. Pfc.	Co. F 262nd Regiment	South Bend
McKain, Harry W. Pfc.	Co. E 262nd Regiment	Terre Haute
McMillen, Furl C. Pfc.	Co. H 262nd Regiment	Indianapolis
Rowland, Elmer D. Pfc.	Co. B 264th Regiment	Indianapolis
Scribner, James S. Pvt.	Co. L 262nd Regiment	Indianapolis [F]
Temple, Eugene R. T/5.	Co. C 264th Regiment	Indianapolis [F]
Truelock, Ralph A. Pfc.	Co. I 262nd Regiment	Sullivan [M]
Verash, Leslie F. Pvt.	Co. H 262nd Regiment	South Bend [M]
Walters, Gerald E. Sgt.	Co. B 264th Regiment	Hagerstown [M]
Wambach, Harold R. Pvt.	Co. L 262nd Regiment	Evansville [M]
Weeks, Ulysses B. Pvt.	Hdq. Co. 3rd Battalion 262nd Reg.	Gary
Weinand, Edward F. T/5.	Co. F 262nd Regiment	Hammond [M]
White, Vernon W. Pfc.	Co. F 262nd Regiment	Milan [M]
Williams, Donald E. Pfc.	Co. K 262nd Regiment	Indianapolis [F]
Williamson, Melvin E. Pfc.	Co. H 262nd Regiment	Valparaiso [M]
Wright, Russell M. S. Sgt.	Co. H 262nd Regiment	Plymouth [M]
Yaeger, George A. Pfc.	Co. C 264th Regiment	Portland

Iowa (20)

Bosch, Gerald Sgt.	Co. I 262nd Regiment	Maurice [M]
Boyer, Gerald L. Pvt.	Co. L 262nd Regiment	Elgin [M]
Campbell, Harold C. Pfc.	Co. B 264th Regiment	Knoxville
Carew, William B. Pfc.	Co. F 262nd Regiment	Dubuque [M]
Cook, Dean L. Pfc.	Co. F 262nd Regiment	Nevada [M]
Fratzke, Melvin L. Pfc.	Co. D 264th Regiment	Independence

Hartwick, Claude H., Jr. Pvt.	Hdq. Co. 1st Battalion 264th Reg.	Des Moines [M]
Hoyt, Robert S. S. Sgt.	Co. E 262nd Regiment	Creston [M]
Hutchens, James E. Pfc.	Co. I 262nd Regiment	Waterloo [M]
Klein, John J. S. Sgt.	Co. E 264th Regiment	Clear Lake [R]
McManis, Orion G. Pvt.	Co. F 262nd Regiment	Keokuk
Mohr, Ray J. Pfc.	Co. I 262nd Regiment	Laurens
Neely, Fred L. Sgt.	Co. K 262nd Regiment	Clarinda [R]
Parry, Charles W. Pfc.	Co. F 262nd Regiment	West Branch [M]
Paulsen, Roy E. Pvt.	Co. F 262nd Regiment	Clinton [M]
Smrkovski, Clarence C. Pfc.	Co. K 264th Regiment	Pocahontas [M]
Swanson, Charles E., Jr. Pfc.	Co. H 262nd Regiment	Council Bluffs [M]
Welbourn, Eldred O. Sgt.	Co. F 262nd Regiment	Underwood [M]
Wiedner, Joseph J. T. Sgt.	Co. F 262nd Regiment	Dubuque [M]
Williams, Lavere R. Pvt.	Hdq. Co. 3rd Battalion 262nd Reg.	Des Moines [F]

Sgt. Arthur Polk with his wife and baby daughter.

Sgt. Arthur Polk from Levenworth, Kansas was born on December 20, 1921. On December 22, 1942, he married the former Pearl Drew. At the time of his death, his daughter, Sharon, was only fifteen months old.

Kansas (6)

Babb, Byron E., Jr. Pfc.	Co. H 262nd Regiment	Wichita [M]
Carrell, Gilbert D. S. Sgt.	Co. F 262nd Regiment	Wichita [M]
Masterson, Lawrence J. Pvt.	Med. Det. 262nd Regiment	Wichita
Polk, Arthur D. Sgt.	Hdq. Co. 2nd Battalion 262nd Reg.	Leavenworth
Samms, Lawrence L. S. Sgt.	Co. H 262nd Regiment	Arkansas City [M]
South, Merle W. S. Sgt.	Co. H 262nd Regiment	Bonner Springs [M]

Kentucky (19)

Bowling, Everett R. Pvt.	Med. Det. 264th Regiment	Beech
Conn, Curtiss Pvt.	Co. H 262nd Regiment	Dana [M]
Cornwell, Clinton J. Pvt.	Co. F 262nd Regiment	Means [M]
Erwin, Ordest H. Pvt.	Co. B 264th Regiment	Hazel
Evans, Luther O. Pfc.	Co. F 262nd Regiment	Covington [M]
Farler, Otis Pfc.	Co. F 262nd Regiment	Viper [M]
Ferguson, Richard J. Pvt.	Co. H 262nd Regiment	Fannin [M]
Garland, James B. Pfc.	Co. I 262nd Regiment	Eubanks [M]
Gilbert, Estill T/5.	Co. H 262nd Regiment	Oneida [M]
Goodlet, Charles W. Pvt.	Co. B 264th Regiment	Louisville [F]
Gulley, Eula T. Pfc.	Co. I 262nd Regiment	Muses Mills [M]
Hatton, Orville Pfc.	Co. H 262nd Regiment	Lee City [M]
Hopkins, Elden G. Cpl.	Co. L 262nd Regiment	Woodbine [M]
Kennedy, Abe H., Jr. T. Sgt.	Co. I 262nd Regiment	Owensboro
Parker, John F. S. Sgt.	Co. F 262nd Regiment	Bonnymam [M]
Sanders, Coleman W. Pvt.	Co. H 262nd Regiment	Cloverport [M]
Schlueter, Harold W. Pfc.	Co. K 264th Regiment	Demossville [M]
Travis, Hoyt L. Pvt.	Co. E 262nd Regiment	Madisonville [M]
Welch, Virgel R. Pfc.	Co. I 262nd Regiment	Rosslyn

Louisiana (3)

Frank, Jony A. T/5.	Co. K 262nd Regiment	Shreveport [F]
Henderson, John M. Pvt.	Co. K 264th Regiment	Baton Rouge
Scheuermann, Joseph F., Jr. Pfc.	Co. F 262nd Regiment	New Orleans [M]

Pvt. Albert J. Arnold

Pvt. Albert J. Arnold from Frye, Maine was married and had two
daughters. His body was never found.

Maine (11)

Arnold, Albert J. Pvt.	Co. I 262nd Regiment	Frye [M]
Auclair, Joseph A. Pvt.	Co. F 262nd Regiment	Westbrook [M]
Baker, Donald A. 2d. Lt.	Co. D 264th Regiment	Biddeford [M]
Cote, Philip G. Pfc.	Co. F 262nd Regiment	Dexter [M]
Higgins, John W., Jr. Pfc.	Co. F 262nd Regiment	Winthrop [M]
Hodgdon, Charles H. Pfc.	Co. I 264th Regiment	Guilford
Lavigne, Alfred G. Pvt.	Co. C 264th Regiment	Lewiston
Lesperance, Paul E. S. Sgt.	Co. K 262nd Regiment	Samford [M]
Otis, Fred L. Pfc.	Co. I 264th Regiment	Bangor [M]
Stelmok, Frank Pvt.	Co. I 262nd Regiment	Auburn
Stone, Edward F. Pfc.	Co. F 262nd Regiment	Brownville

Maryland (6)

Ash, Robert L. S. Sgt.	Co. K 264th Regiment	Flintstone [M]
Berigtold, Raymond E. Pfc.	Co. K 262nd Regiment	Baltimore [M]
Hawkins, Robert E. Pvt.	Co. I 262nd Regiment	[M]
McKinney, Joseph O. Pfc.	Co. E 262nd Regiment	North East
Myers, Harold L. Pvt.	Co. I 262nd Regiment	Hagerstown
Powell, James W. Pfc.	Med. Det. 262nd Regiment	Baltimore

Massachusetts (38)

Alexandrovich, Joseph Pvt.	Co. K 262nd Regiment	Hudson [F]
Bissett, Willett R. Pfc.	Co. I 262nd Regiment	Roxbury
Bouffard, Joseph C. Pfc.	Co. F 262nd Regiment	Marlboro [M]
Chace, Roderick E. Pvt.	Co. C 264th Regiment	Attleboro
Ciekalowski, William P. S. Sgt.	Co. F 262nd Regiment	East Hampton [M]
Cram, Ralph D., Jr. Pvt.	Co. F 262nd Regiment	Jamaica Plains [M]
Dalton, William F. Sgt.	Co. L 262nd Regiment	Roxbury [M]
Daniels, Robert L. Pfc.	Co. F 262nd Regiment	Haverhill [M]
De Piero, Louis A. S. Sgt.	Co. E 262nd Regiment	Dorchester [M]
Dockler, Paul A. Pfc.	Co. B 264th Regiment	Gardner
Fernanndes, Martin, Jr. Pvt.	Co. F 262nd Regiment	New Bedford [M]
Flammia, Anthony J. Pfc.	Co. K 262nd Regiment	Mansfield
Forman, Gerald Pvt.	Co. F 262nd Regiment	Malden [M]
Hope, James H. Pfc.	Hdq. Co. 3rd Battalion 262nd Reg.	Marion
Howard, Edward F. Pfc.	Co. K 262nd Regiment	East Douglas
Irvine, Richard G. Pfc.	Co. E 264th Regiment	Hopkinton
Jackson, Lucius E. Pfc.	Co. F 262nd Regiment	Lincoln [F]
Kibart, Francis E. Pvt.	Co. H 262nd Regiment	Brockton [M]
Krassin, Sumner Pvt.	Co. F 262nd Regiment	Mattapan [M]

T/4 Wilmer C. Poupard

T/4 Wilmer C. Poupard was from Monroe, Michigan. His body was never found.

Lemos, Anthony Pfc.	Co. E 262nd Regiment	Somerville [M]
Luckman, Thomas Pfc.	Co. F 262nd Regiment	Brockton [M]
Maiuri, Peter Pfc.	Co. B 264th Regiment	Malden
Maloney, John F. Pvt.	Co. F 262nd Regiment	Dedham [M]
Mayers, Raymond J. S. Sgt.	Co. H 262nd Regiment	Hebronville [M]
Miscone, Joseph P. Pfc.	Co. F 262nd Regiment	North Billerica
Nolan, William E. Pvt.	Co. K 262nd Regiment	Pittsfield [F]
Patterson, Thomas H. S. Sgt.	Co. I 264th Regiment	Quincy [F]
Pellegrini, Victor Pvt.	Co. F 262nd Regiment	Newton [M]
Peterson, Burton T/4.	Co. D 264th Regiment	Marshfield
Peterson, Lennart W. Pfc.	Co. L 262nd Regiment	North Adams [M]
Skinner, Charles V. Pfc.	Co. F 262nd Regiment	Newtonville [M]
Steele, William J. Pfc.	Co. K 262nd Regiment	Fall River [M]
Stenquist, Helmer R. Pvt.	Co. K 262nd Regiment	Worcester
Sullivan, Charles F. Sgt.	Co. C 264th Regiment	Worcester [F]
Tambascia, Dominic G. Pfc.	Co. L 262nd Regiment	Waltham [M]
Thibodeau, Joseph E. Pfc.	Co. A 264th Regiment	[F]
Vallee, Ernest D. T/4.	Med. Det. 262nd Regiment	Lowell [M]
Wintle, Russell E. Pfc.	Co. F 262nd Regiment	Lowell [M]

Michigan (28)

Abbott, Leslie G. Pfc.	Co. E 262nd Regiment	Maple Rapids [M]
Ambrose, Raymond C. Pvt.	Co. L 262nd Regiment	Hudson [M]
Bannick, Ronald C. Pfc.	Co. F 262nd Regiment	Elkton [M]
Brown, John W. Pfc.	Co. I 262nd Regiment	Detroit [F]
Estlund, Robert O. Pvt.	Co. K 262nd Regiment	Royal Oak [M]
Fauer, John A. Pfc.	Co. D 264th Regiment	Detroit
Furmark, Carl E. Pfc.	Co. L 262nd Regiment	Detroit [M]
Galus, Stanley M. Pvt.	Co. F 262nd Regiment	Bay City [M]
Gutt, Donald C. Pvt.	Co. I 262nd Regiment	Detroit [M]
Heim, James V. Pfc.	Co. C 264th Regiment	[F]
Lewandowski, George J. Pfc.	Co. E 262nd Regiment	Detroit [M]
MacGowan, John Pvt.	Co. K 262nd Regiment	Redford Twp
McDonnell, Ferrel F. Pfc.	Co. F 262nd Regiment	Whitehall [M]
McVety, Robert L. Pvt.	Co. C 264th Regiment	Port Huron [M]
Miller, George W. Pvt.	Co. K 264th Regiment	Pontiac [F]
Monk, John J., Jr. T/5.	Co. L 262nd Regiment	Highland Park
Morehouse, F.R. Pvt.	Co. E 262nd Regiment	Jerome
Poupard, Wilmer C. T/4.	Co. L 262nd Regiment	Monroe [M]
Robeson, Claude C. Pfc.	Co. F 262nd Regiment	Flint [M]

Pfc. Garvis Dillinger

Pfc. Garvis Dillinger from Dumas, Mississippi was born on December 28, 1926. He had two brothers and two sisters. He grew up a farm boy and spent many days in the field helping his father make a living off the land. When he turned eighteen, he quit school and volunteered for military service. The body of Pfc. Garvis Dillinger was never found. His mother was so distraught over the death of her son that she spent a year in a hospital recovering from her loss.

Salata, Edmund P. Pvt.	Co. F 262nd Regiment	Hamtramck [M]
Schramm, Warren C. S. Sgt.	Co. H 262nd Regiment	Bay City [M]
Schurig, Russell E. Pfc.	Co. C 264th Regiment	Ferndale [M]
Shaver, Glen B. Pfc.	Co. F 262nd Regiment	Royal Oak [M]
Smrecak, James J. Pfc.	Co. E 264th Regiment	Munger
Tait, Robert P. Pfc.	Co. L 262nd Regiment	South Haven [M]
Wincheski, Albin J. S. Sgt.	Co. F 262nd Regiment	Ludington [M]
Witucki, Marion A. S. Sgt.	Co. L 262nd Regiment	Bay City [M]
Worden, John A. Pfc.	Co. I 264th Regiment	Battle Creek

Minnesota (10)

Boekhoff, Lawrence A. Pvt.	Co. F 262nd Regiment	Saulk Rapids [M]
Cushman, Glenn L. Pfc.	Co. I 262nd Regiment	Minneapolis
Flurry, Allen R. Pfc.	Hdq. Co. 3rd Battalion 262nd Reg.	Dennis
Gobats, John L. Pfc.	Med. Det. 262nd Regiment	Virginia [M]
Haven, Edwin L. Pfc.	Co. F 262nd Regiment	Appleton [M]
Kinder, Lester W. Pfc.	Co. H 262nd Regiment	West Concord [M]
Lettengarver, Albert L. T/5.	Co. I 262nd Regiment	St. Paul [M]
Mathison, Arlo R. S. Sgt.	Co. B 264th Regiment	Spring Valley [F]
Tarr, John Z. Pfc.	Co. L 262nd Regiment	St. Paul [M]
Tibbetts, Jessee J. Pfc.	Hdq.Co. 3rd Battalion 262nd Reg.	Ball Club [M]

Mississippi (21)

Ainsworth, Harise E. Pfc.	Co. K 262nd Regiment	[M]
Alexander, J. D. Pfc.	Co. K 262nd Regiment	Philadelphia
Biggart, Will O. Pfc.	Co. I 262nd Regiment	Isola [M]
Byrd, Robert S. Pfc.	Co. F 262nd Regiment	Ocean Springs [M]
Carter, Audie L. Pvt.	Co. I 262nd Regiment	Houston [M]
Creed, Robert W. S. Sgt.	Co. I 262nd Regiment	Lauderdale
Crenshaw, Thomas L. Pvt.	Co. H 262nd Regiment	Louisville [M]
Dancy, John B. Pvt.	Co. D 264th Regiment	Coldwater [M]
Dillinger, Garvis Pfc.	Co. I 262nd Regiment	Dumas [M]
Dover, James W. Pfc.	Co. I 262nd Regiment	Sarepta
Fried, Simon Pvt.	Co. L 262nd Regiment	Sidon [M]
Graham, Melton E. Pvt.	Hdq. Co. 3rd Battalion 262nd Reg.	Tiplersville [M]
Gurley, Ben D. T/4.	Co. K 264th Regiment	Tishomingo [M]
Howell, Alton Pfc.	Co. H 262nd Regiment	Lucedale [M]
Jenkins, Robert E. Pfc.	Co. L 262nd Regiment	Meridian [M]
Martin, Ray E. Pfc.	Co. F 262nd Regiment	Wesson [M]
McBay, James D. Pfc.	Co. F 262nd Regiment	Bay Springs [M]
Moncrief, Clifton Pfc.	Co. H 262nd Regiment	Coldwater [M]

Morgan, James L. Pfc.	Co. E 262nd Regiment	Heidelberg [M]
Mortimer, James E. Sgt.	Co. E 262nd Regiment	Winona [M]
Winstead, Rufus B. Pvt.	Co. F 262nd Regiment	Pass Christian [M]

Missouri (31)

Baker, Elmer A. Sgt.	Co. K 262nd Regiment	New Bloomfield [R]
Bathke, Oliver C. Pfc.	Hdq. Co. 3rd Battalion 262nd Reg.	St. Louis
Bence, George R. Pfc.	Co. I 262nd Regiment	Kansas City [M]
Benda, Leonard F. Pfc.	Co. E 262nd Regiment	St. Louis [M]
Canon, Carl L. S. Sgt.	Co. E 262nd Regiment	Kansas City [M]
Davis, Raymond Pfc.	Co. I 264th Regiment	Aurora
Gordon, William I. Pvt.	Co. F 262nd Regiment	Kansas City [M]
Hoover, Raymond B. S. Sgt.	Co. I 262nd Regiment	Lee's Summit [M]
Israel, Philip S. Pvt.	Co. K 264th Regiment	St. Louis [M]
Koenig, Richard H. T/5.	Hdq. Co. 3rd Battalion 262nd Reg.	St. Louis
Korte, Clarence I. T/5.	Hdq. Co. 1st Battalion 264th Reg.	Florissant [M]
Leftwich, William E. Pfc.	Co. K 262nd Regiment	Cardwell [F]
Marriott, Sherman E. Pvt.	Co. E 262nd Regiment	Stover [M]
Martinsen, Raymond B. S. Sgt.	Hdq. Co. 3rd Battalion 262nd Reg.	Monett [F]
Mason, Gerrard L. Pvt.	Co. L 262nd Regiment	Kirkwood [F]
Matthews, Leonard E. T/4.	Co. I 264th Regiment	Sikeston
McDaniel, Everette N. Sgt.	Co. E 262nd Regiment	Long Lane [M]
Moyer, Herbert C. T/4.	Co. E 264th Regiment	Richmond [F]
Parks, Wilbur C. T/5.	Co. K 262nd Regiment	St. Joseph
Price, Chester E. T. Sgt.	Co. H 262nd Regiment	Lockwood [M]
Privett, Lawrence E. 1st Sgt.	Co. F 262nd Regiment	Ava [F]
Rago, Robert J. Sgt.	Co. C 264th Regiment	Kansas City
Rennison, Eugene W. Pvt.	Co. L 262nd Regiment	Kansas City
Rigdon, Norman L. Sgt.	Co. F 262nd Regiment	Farmington [M]
Sexton, Herman B. Pvt.	Co. K 262nd Regiment	Kansas City [M]
Smith, C. D. S. Sgt.	Co. C 264th Regiment	St. Louis [F]
Suntinger, Clarence M. Pfc.	Co. H 262nd Regiment	St. Louis [M]
Tener, Ralph M. Pvt.	Med. Det. 262nd Regiment	Neosho [M]
Tinker, Ira V. S. Sgt.	Co. H 262nd Regiment	Williamsville [M]
Walz, Carl J., Jr. S. Sgt.	Co. I 264th Regiment	Jefferson City [F]
Wilson, Cecil W. Pfc.	Co. E 262nd Regiment	Versailles [M]

Montana (3)

Bonde, Carl R., Jr. Pfc.	Co. E 262nd Regiment	Kalispell [M]
Gillin, John F. Sgt.	Co. F 262nd Regiment	Harlowtown [M]
Rott, Robert J. Pfc.	Hdq. Co. 2nd Battalion 262nd Reg.	Dillon [M]

Nebraska (5)

Doyle, Willis W. S. Sgt.	Co. I 262nd Regiment	Curtis
Elston, Leroy J. Pvt.	Co. L 262nd Regiment	Clearwater
Lemke, Otis C. S. Sgt.	Co. H 262nd Regiment	Bouning [M]
Quinlan, William P. Pfc.	Co. F 262nd Regiment	Omaha [M]
Taylor, Forrest D. T. Sgt.	Co. B 264th Regiment	Platemouth

Nevada (1)

Shaw, William A., Jr. Pvt.	Med. Det. 262nd Regiment	Reno [M]

New Hampshire (4)

Lavigne, Richard M. Sgt.	Co. F 262nd Regiment	Lempster [M]
Mathieu, Arthur T. Pvt.	Co. K 262nd Regiment	Manchester [F]
Miller, Douglas F., Jr. Pvt.	Co. F 262nd Regiment	Rochester [M]
Whittier, Carl F. Pfc.	Co. F 262nd Regiment	Concord [M]

T/4 John Marzotto

T/4 John Marzotto was from Weehawken, New Jersey. Assigned to Company L, 262nd Regiment, his body was never found.

New Jersey (24)

Benson, Edward E. Pfc.	Co. I 264th Regiment	Camden [M]
Christopher, Malcom B. Pfc.	Co. E 264th Regiment	Nutley [M]
Claybrook, Richard A. Sgt.	Co. H 262nd Regiment	Plainfield [M]
Coakley, Francis X. 1st Lt.	Co. C 264th Regiment	Elizabeth [M]
Cobb, Thomas A. Pfc.	Co. D 264th Regiment	Ridgewood [R]
Cywinski, Charles Pfc.	Co. H 262nd Regiment	Jersey City [M]
Dantinne, Harold H. Pfc.	Co. K 262nd Regiment	Salem
De Martini, Howard W. S. Sgt.	Co. F 262nd Regiment	Northvale [M]
De Prima, Frank T/5.	Hdq. Co. 2nd Battalion 262nd Reg.	Paterson
Fierro, Joseph R. 2d. Lt.	Co. H 262nd Regiment	Manville [F]
Gleeson, Douglas C. Pfc.	Hdq. Co. 2nd Battalion 262nd Reg.	Clifton
Goesch, Joseph M. Pfc.	Co. K 262nd Regiment	Long Branch
Hine, Harry C. Pvt.	Co. L 262nd Regiment	Jersey City [M]
Howland, Edward T. Pfc.	Co. I 262nd Regiment	West Caldwell [M]
House, Russell S. S. Sgt.	Hdq. Co. 1st Battalion 264th Reg.	Dover
Juskus, Carl F. Pfc.	Co. L 262nd Regiment	Jersey City [M]
Marzotto, John T/4.	Co. L 262nd Regiment	Weehawken [M]
Miles, Robert F. S. Sgt.	Hdq. Co. 2nd Battalion 262nd Reg.	Camden [M]
Ofsonka, Charles P., Jr. S. Sgt.	Co. D 264th Regiment	Boonton [F]
Schiller, Arthur Pvt.	Hdq. Co. 1st Battalion 264th Reg.	Jersey City [F]
Schlerf, Fred J. Pfc.	Co. I 262nd Regiment	Newark
Steuble, Gilbert J. S. Sgt.	Co. C 264th Regiment	Belleville
Vester, Richard H. Pfc.	Co. E 262nd Regiment	North Branch [M]
Winters, Cornelius D., Jr. Pfc.	Co. F 262nd Regiment	Paramus [M]

New Mexico (3)

Franco, Pablo G. Pfc.	Co. H 262nd Regiment	Loving [M]
Kolb, Marvin Pvt.	Co. E 262nd Regiment	Santa Fe [M]
Spence, Stephen C. Pfc.	Co. L 262nd Regiment	Albuquerque [M]

Pfc. Kenneth J. Turner

Pfc. Kenneth J. Turner from Lee Center, New York was born on October 15, 1925. The body of the nineteen year old was never found.

New York (80)

Abatemarco, Michael F. Pfc.	Co. L 262nd Regiment	Brooklyn, NYC [F]
Aborn, Harold L. Pvt.	Co. H 262nd Regiment	Yonkers [M]
Alania, James V. Pfc.	Co. L 262nd Regiment	Lowville [M]
Aschmann, Frank G. Pfc.	Co. F. 262nd Regiment	Croton-on-Hudson [M]
Bartelena, Dante J. T. Sgt.	Co. F 262nd Regiment	Bronx, NYC [M]
Barton, Marvin J. Pfc.	Co. I 264th Regiment	Poughkeepsie [M]
Bassett, John E. Sgt.	Co. F 262nd Regiment	Rye [M]
Blaskowski, Benjamin J. S. Sgt.	Co. L 262nd Regiment	Verona Station [M]
Borenstein, Jack Pvt.	Co. A 264th Regiment	Brooklyn
Brande, Robert Pfc.	Co. F 262nd Regiment	Brooklyn, NYC [M]
Cacace, Anthony F. S. Sgt.	Co. E 262nd Regiment	Brooklyn, NYC [M]
Calabrese, Vincent R. S. Sgt.	Hdq. Co. 3rd Battalion 262nd Reg.	Corona, NYC [M]
Cammarano, Michael P. Pfc.	Co. K 262nd Regiment	NYC
Cappello, Dominick J. S. Sgt.	Co. A 264th Regiment	Manhattan, NYC [M]
Carlson, Carl Pfc.	Co. F 262nd Regiment	Jamestown [M]
Carlson, Clarence H. Pfc.	Co. F 262nd Regiment	Jamestown [M]
Caruso, Thomas A. Pvt.	Co. L 262nd Regiment	Brooklyn, NYC [M]
Catalano, Angelo G. Sgt.	Co. L 262nd Regiment	Brooklyn, NYC [M]
Coen, James P. Pvt.	Med. Det. 264th Regiment	Bronx, NYC [F]
Crowe, Eugene J. Sgt.	Co. I 262nd Regiment	NYC [M]
Cuccia, Salvatore C. Pvt.	Co. F 262nd Regiment	Silver Creek [R]
Damsky, Daniel S. Pfc.	Co. I 262nd Regiment	NYC [M]
Di Mola, Nicholas J. Pvt.	Co. L 262nd Regiment	Brooklyn, NYC [M]
Ellett, Joseph S. Pfc.	Co. I 262nd Regiment	Elmira [M]
Ewald, Alf G. T/5.	Co. K. 264th Regiment	SpringfieldGardens,NYC[F]
Falci, James L. Pvt.	Co. F 262nd Regiment	Buffalo [M]
Foge, Francis J. Pfc.	Hdq. Co. 3rd Battalion 262nd Reg.	Brooklyn, NYC
Fogelsonger, Harry F. Pfc.	Co. I 262nd Regiment	Buffalo [F]
Freund, Henry Pvt.	Co. A 264th Regiment	Brooklyn, NYC [F]
Grad, Robert A. Pvt.	Co. L 262nd Regiment	Buffalo
Gurtner, Herman T/4.	Co. I 262nd Regiment	Vega [M]
Hattem, Monroe Pfc.	Co. F 262nd Regiment	Bronx, NYC [M]
Hirschel, Howard T. 2d. Lt.	Co. B 264th Regiment	NYC
Hoffman, Leslie E. 1st Lt.	Co. I 264th Regiment	Herkimer [M]
Holleran, James R. Pfc.	Co. A 264th Regiment	Cornell
Hover, James E. T/5.	Co. B 264th Regiment	Elsmere
Katz, Nathan Pfc.	Hdq. Co. 2nd Battalion 262nd Reg.	Bronx, NYC
Kessler, George Cpl.	Co. C 264th Regiment	Bronx, NYC [M]

King, Edward Pvt.	Co. F 262nd Regiment	Brooklyn, NYC [M]
Klosterman, William A., Jr. Pfc.	Co. F 262nd Regiment	Rockville Center [M]
Kraemer, Bernard J. Pfc.	Co. F 262nd Regiment	Brooklyn, NYC [M]
Lamb, Richard B. Pfc.	Co. K 262nd Regiment	NYC [M]
Lapinski, Stanley J. Pvt.	Co. I 264th Regiment	Buffalo [F]
Maksyn, Edward C. Pfc.	Co. K 262nd Regiment	Jackson Heights, NYC [M]
Malczyk, Edwin J. Pvt.	Co. C 264th Regiment	Buffalo
McDonald, Bernard D. Pvt.	Co. F 262nd Regiment	Niagara Falls [M]
Morse, Carlton S. Pvt.	Co. F 262nd Regiment	Rochester [M]
Nassif, Assaph J. Pvt.	Co. F 262nd Regiment	Binghamton [M]
Nigbor, Henry Pvt.	Co. F 262nd Regiment	Dunkirk [M]
Paci, Vincent Pvt.	Co. K 264th Regiment	Solvay [F]
Paterson, Douglas W. Sgt.	Co. E 264th Regiment	Brooklyn, NYC
Perry, Carl R. Pvt.	Co. B 264th Regiment	Binghamton [F]
Peterson, Robert G. Pfc.	Co. K 262nd Regiment	Brooklyn, NYC
Polgreen, Waldron M. Pfc.	Co. K 262nd Regiment	Albany [F]
Reccardi, Victor J. S. Sgt.	Co. A 264th Regiment	NYC
Robbins, Jerome Pvt.	Co. I 264th Regiment	NYC
Rodies, Heinz G. Pfc.	Co. L. 262nd Regiment	Wyandanch [M]
Russell, Kent E. Pfc.	Co. F 262nd Regiment	Clayton [M]
Rzemek, Edward W. Pfc.	Co. I 264th Regiment	Buffalo
Sansone, Richard F. Pfc.	Co. K 262nd Regiment	Buffalo [M]
Sciarra, Robert J. Pfc.	Co. K 264th Regiment	Brooklyn, NYC
Sgroi, Paul S. Pvt.	Co. H 262nd Regiment	Frankfort [M]
Simonetti, John Pvt.	Med Det. 262nd Regiment	Brooklyn, NYC [M]
Smith, Robert J. Pvt.	Co. F 262nd Regiment	Potsdam [M]
Solotes, Joseph J. Pvt.	Co. E 264th Regiment	Lockport
Stern, Lawrence M. Pfc.	Med. Det. 262nd Regiment	Brooklyn, NYC [M]
Stewart, Walter K. Pfc.	Co. I 262nd Regiment	Brooklyn, NYC [M]
Tartaro, Joseph F. Sgt.	Co. L 262nd Regiment	Ozone Park, NYC [M]
Tassi, Louis 1st Sgt.	Co. C 264th Regiment	Woodside, NYC
Tilzer, David Pfc.	Co. H 262nd Regiment	NYC [M]
Turetzky, David S. Pvt.	Co. I 262nd Regiment	Bronx [M]
Turisk, Isadore Pvt.	Co. C 264th Regiment	Niagara Falls
Turner, Kenneth J. Pfc.	Co. H 262nd Regiment	Lee Center [M]

Vogel, Frank S. Pfc.	Co. F 262nd Regiment	Whitestone, NYC [M]
Vojir, Frank W. Pfc.	Hdq. Co. 2nd Battalion 262nd Reg.	NYC [F]
Wilson, Richard J. T/5.	Co. L 262nd Regiment	Brooklyn, NYC [M]
Wolf, Henry H. Pfc.	Co. L 262nd Regiment	Bronx, NYC
Yaccketta, Dominick T. Pfc.	Hdq. Co. 2nd Battalion262nd Reg.	Tully
Young, George F. S. Sgt.	Co. E 262nd Regiment	Nassau, [M]
Zaloga, Edward J. Pvt.	Co. B 264th Regiment	Albany

North Carolina (17)

Barr, Hugh R. Pfc.	Co. A 264th Regiment	[F]
Brogden, Lee R. S. Sgt.	Co. B 264th Regiment	Goldsboro [M]
Clark, William C. Pvt.	Co. B 264th Regiment	Tarboro
Furr, Fred D. Pfc.	Co. F 262nd Regiment	Concord [M]
Hill, George E. T/5.	Co. I 264th Regiment	Wilson
Lawrence, Luther M. T. Sgt.	Co. B 264th Regiment	Colerain [F]
Leopard, John P. Pvt.	Co. I 264th Regiment	Norton [R]
Long, Robert H., Jr. Pvt.	Co. A 264th Regiment	[M]
Massey, Robert B. S. Sgt.	Co. L 262nd Regiment	Mebane [M]
Moore, Clifton B. Pfc.	Co. F 262nd Regiment	Oak City [M]
Plott, George E. Capt.	Co. H 262nd Regiment	Waynesville [M]
Reece, Dole C. Pfc.	Co. K 262nd Regiment	Lenoir
Rogers, Robert A. Pfc.	Co. E 262nd Regiment	Roanoke Rapids [M]
Russ, Paisley E. S. Sgt.	Co. I 262nd Regiment	Bolton [M]
Smith, William F. Pfc.	Co. L 262nd Regiment	Bessemer [M]
Stewart, Roger H. Pfc.	Co. A 264th Regiment	[M]
Tucker, Warren C. Pfc.	Hdq. Co. 2nd Battalion 262nd Reg.	Charlotte

North Dakota (7)

Cuskelly, Richard R. Pfc.	Co. F 262nd Regiment	Dickinson [M]
Dorgan, Allan J. Pfc.	Co. K 264th Regiment	Regent [M]
Gentz, Herbert I. Pfc.	Co. C 264th Regiment	New England
Hendrickson, Chester B. T. Sgt.	Co. K 264th Regiment	Luverne [M]
Kragtorp, Ernest O. Pfc.	Co. L 262nd Regiment	Aneta [M]
Lawrence, Benton L. Pvt.	Med. Det. 262nd Regiment	Rock Lake [M]
McGhan, Glen P. Pfc.	Co. C 264th Regiment	Bottineau [F]

Pfc. Andrew J. Marcinko

Pfc. Andrew J. Marcinko was from Newtown Falls, Ohio. Assigned to Company K, 262nd Regiment, his body was never found.

Ohio (44)

Appleman, Robert B. Pfc.	Co. E 262nd Regiment	Cuyahoga Falls [M]
Bader, Donald W. Pfc.	Co. E 262nd Regiment	Lakewood [M]
Bailey, William C. Pvt.	Co. E 262nd Regiment	Euclid [M]
Bishop, Richard U. Pvt.	Co. H 262nd Regiment	Greenville [M]
Cellura, Angelo T. Pfc.	Co. I 262nd Regiment	Cleveland [M]
Cleelan, Robert W. Pvt.	Co. D 264th Regiment	Springfield
Cottrell, John F. S. Sgt.	Co. B 264th Regiment	Lima
Cummins, Jack C. Pvt.	Co. C 264th Regiment	Piqua [M]
Davis, William J. Pvt.	Co. K 262nd Regiment	Akron [M]
De Soto, Claude Pvt.	Co. B 264th Regiment	Osbourn
Donnelly, William O. S. Sgt.	Co. F 262nd Regiment	Cincinnati [M]
Doughman, William O. Pvt.	Co. B 264th Regiment	Loveland [M]
Eckerman, Arthur E. Pfc.	Co. B 264th Regiment	Cleveland
Ensign, Armand E. Pfc.	Co. C 264th Regiment	Elyria
Ferguson, Robert V. S. Sgt.	Co. I 264th Regiment	Delta
Green, Cecil C. Pvt.	Co. A 264th Regiment	Rock Bridge
Harmon, Edison W. Pvt.	Co. D 264th Regiment	N. Baltimore
Herrman, Robert E. Pvt.	Co. C 264th Regiment	Cincinnati
Hunston, Russell E. Pfc.	Co. C 264th Regiment	East Palestine
Jones, James A. D. Pfc.	Co. C 264th Regiment	Conneaut [M]
Kieser, Marcell V. Pfc.	Co. F 262nd Regiment	Columbus [M]
Kilbarger, Thomas L. Pfc.	Co. F 262nd Regiment	Lancaster [M]
Kopczewski, Anthony W. Pvt.	Co. F 262nd Regiment	Cleveland [M]
Leidner, Oliver C. Pfc.	Co. K 262nd Regiment	Uhrichsville
Longwell, Robert G. Pfc.	Co. I 262nd Regiment	Delphos [M]
MacMillan, Lynn L. Pfc.	Co. H 262nd Regiment	Independence [M]
Marcinko, Andrew J. Pfc.	Co. K 262nd Regiment	Newton Falls [M]
Matwijiw, Robert L. Pvt.	Co. K 262nd Regiment	Cleveland
McCall, Emmett P. Pfc.	Co. B 264th Regiment	Columbia [M]
McDermott, John M. S. Sgt.	Co. F 262nd Regiment	Lakewood [M]
McGlone, Eugene A. S. Sgt.	Co. B 264th Regiment	Niles
Meyers, Donald G. S. Sgt.	Co. B 264th Regiment	Rudolph [M]
Moser, Richard E. Pfc.	Co. K 262nd Regiment	Youngstown
Norris, Guy D. Pvt.	Co. F 262nd Regiment	Belmont [M]
Pancheri, Joseph A. S. Sgt.	Co. H 262nd Regiment	New Philadelphia [M]
Schwitzgebel, Eugene A. Pfc.	Co. B 264th Regiment	Canton [M]
Slusser, Elmer D. Pfc.	Co. B 264th Regiment	Dayton [M]
Stewart, Benjamin L. Pvt.	Co. F 262nd Regiment	Norwood [M]

S/Sgt. Donald G. Meyers

S/Sgt. Donald G. Meyers was from Rudolph, Ohio. He had a recurring infection that dated back to his time at Camp Rucker, Alabama. He was trying to get hospitalized to finally cure the illness but was cleared for duty and sailed on the Leopoldville. His last letter home to his sister was dated December 18, 1944 and spoke of the birth of her son Dan on November 21, 1944. Sgt. Meyer was looking forward to getting home and spoiling his first nephew and the family's first grandchild. His letter concluded, "Don't worry over me, I will be fine, just take care of yourselves." The body of S/Sgt. Donald Meyers was never found. His wife, Marry, eventually remarried and moved to Texas.

Stewart, Donald L. Pfc.	Co. F 262nd Regiment	Troy [M]
Suder, James T. Sgt.	Co. F 262nd Regiment	Marietta [M]
Watts, Jack Pfc.	Co. E 262nd Regiment	Wheelersburg [M]
Weaver, Irvin J., Jr. Sgt.	Co. E 262nd Regiment	Dayton [M]
Wells, Floyd K. Pfc.	Co. H 262nd Regiment	Cincinnati [M]
Witham, Charles W. Sgt.	Co. H 262nd Regiment	Miamisburg [M]

Oklahoma (14)

Bell, William E. Pfc.	Co. H 262nd Regiment	Valliant [M]
Chew, Floyd E. Pfc.	Hdq. Co. 2nd Battalion 262nd Reg.	Ramona
Coble, Wayne H. 1st Sgt.	Co. H 262nd Regiment	Foraker [M]
Craig, Coy C. Sgt.	Co. C 264th Regiment	Pryor
Crowl, Elmer R. Pfc.	Co. I 264th Regiment	Tulsa [M]
Fisher, James O. 1st Sgt.	Co. L 262nd Regiment	Pine Valley [M]
Hargraves, Jeff Sgt.	Co. H 262nd Regiment	Burbank [M]
Lester, Steven T. Pfc.	Co. K 262nd Regiment	Pharron [M]
McKenzie, Daniel W. Pfc.	Co. E 262nd Regiment	Moyers [M]
Paden, George W. Pvt.	Hdq. Co. 3rd Battalion 262nd Reg.	Sand Springs [F]
Reisig, William L. Pfc.	Hdq. Co. 2nd Battalion 262nd Reg.	Shattuck
Ritthaler, Frank, Jr. Pfc.	Co. F 262nd Regiment	Perry [M]
Simpson, Bernard W. Pvt.	Co. B 264th Regiment	Ponca City
Wellborn, Charles B., III Pvt.	Co. I 262nd Regiment	Tulsa [R]

Oregon (2)

Foster, William S. D. Pfc.	Co. C 264th Regiment	Pendleton
Neiderheiser, Daniel Pvt.	Co. C 264th Regiment	[M]

Pfc. Edward H. Heumann

Pfc. Edward H. Heumann was from Mckees Rocks, Pennsylvania. Assigned to Company H, 262nd Regiment, his body was never found.

Pennsylvania (74)

Acri, Peter L. Pfc.	Co. E 262nd Regiment	Harrisburg [M]
Berger, Robert Pvt.	Co. K 262nd Regiment	Norwood
Billger, Paul L. Pvt.	Co. I 262nd Regiment	Huntingdon
Bixler, Bruce E. Pvt.	Co. C 264th Regiment	Valley View [M]
Borovich, Dan Pvt.	Co. I 262nd Regiment	Mcdonald [R]
Borovich, Sam Pvt.	Co. K 262nd Regiment	Mcdonald [R]
Burkhart, Ralph E. Pvt.	Co. F 262nd Regiment	Myersdale [M]
Cavalcante, Edward M. Pfc.	Co. H 262nd Regiment	McClellandtown [M]
Chalkan, Michael, Jr. S. Sgt.	Co. A 264th Regiment	Mahanoy City [F]
Chambers, Robert L. Pfc.	Co. I 264th Regiment	Rochester [F]
Clark, Reginald J., Jr. Cpl.	Co. H 262nd Regiment	Swayerville M]
Constantine, Tony T/4.	Hdq. Co. 3rd Battalion 262nd Reg.	Chestnut Ridge [M]
Cronk, Rolland D. Pfc.	Med. Det. 262nd Regiment	Pleasant Mount [M]
Cybak, Harry, Jr. 1st. Lt.	Co. H 262nd Regiment	Nemacolin [F]
Daugherty, Mervin R. Pfc.	Co. E 262nd Regiment	Apollo [M]
Debuski, Michael Pfc.	Co. E 264th Regiment	Morea
Downing, Frank P., Jr. Pvt.	Co. B 264th Regiment	Lewistown [R]
Dreisbach, Richard T. Pvt.	Co. A 264th Regiment	York [R]
Drivick, Joseph J. Sgt.	Co. F 262nd Regiment	Philadelphia [M]
English, Thomas J., Jr. Pfc.	Co. I 264th Regiment	Pittsburgh
Fisher, Howard I. Pvt.	Co. F 262nd Regiment	Erie [M]
Fox, William T/5.	Med. Det. 262nd Regiment	Philadelphia [M]
Gable, Wayne W. Pfc.	Co. A 264th Regiment	Walnutport [M]
Gilbert, Harold Pfc.	Co. A 264th Regiment	
Gorham, Donald R. S. Sgt.	Co. H 262nd Regiment	Wilkes Barre [M]
Grazier, David O. Pfc.	Co. F 262nd Regiment	Tyrone [M]
Hayes, Albert T. Pfc.	Co. H 262nd Regiment	Allentown [M]
Herman, Nevin H., Jr. Pvt.	Co. B 264th Regiment	York [F]
Heumann, Edward H. Pfc.	Co. H 262nd Regiment	Mckees Rocks [M]
Hoffenberg, Jennings L. Pfc.	Co. E 264th Regiment	Sharon
Jaspan, Ralph L. Pvt.	Co. H 262nd Regiment	Philadelphia [M]
Jurlina, Gregory G. S. Sgt.	Co. F 262nd Regiment	Donora [M]
Kane, Thomas J. T/5.	Co. F 262nd Regiment	Philadelphia [M]
King, Charles R. Pvt.	Co. L 262nd Regiment	New Freedom [M]
Kluciar, Milos Pfc.	Co. F 262nd Regiment	Ford Cliff [M]
Kozielski, Joseph V. Pfc.	Co. B 264th Regiment	Philadelphia [M]

Kuchta, Frank J. Pfc.	Co. I 262nd Regiment	Greensburg [F]
Lagana, Joseph G. Pvt.	Co. D 264th Regiment	Lattimer Mines
Lowry, Glenn E. Pfc.	Co. I 262nd Regiment	Belle Vernon [M]
Lowry, Jack N. Pfc.	Co. I 262nd Regiment	Belle Vernon [M]
Makowski, Stanley E. Pfc.	Co. I 262nd Regiment	Larksville
Martynowski, Edward H. T/5.	Med. Det. 262nd Regiment	Philadelphia [M]
Maryan, William N. Pfc.	Co. F 262nd Regiment	Erie [M]
McDermott, Thomas J. T. Sgt.	Co. C 264th Regiment	Philadelphia [M]
McVey, Walter F., Jr. Pfc.	Co. I 262nd Regiment	New Providence
Miller, Emory R., Jr. S. Sgt.	Co. I 264th Regiment	Harrisburg [M]
Molinsky, Charles Pfc.	Co. A 264th Regiment	[F]
Moore, Edgar C. Pvt.	Co. K 262nd Regiment	Washington [R]
Mosako, Alva G. Sgt.	Co. F 262nd Regiment	Chestnut Ridge [M]
Nolan, James M. Pvt.	Co. A 264th Regiment	[F]
O'Donnell, John H. T/5.	Hdq. Co. 3rd Battalion 262nd Reg.	Milroy [M]
Pispeky, Joseph Pfc.	Co. K 264th Regiment	Lansford
Pukas, Herbert A. Pfc.	Co. K 264th Regiment	Minersville [M]
Reed, Seth W. T/5.	Co. K 262nd Regiment	Herndon [F]
Ross, William C. Pvt.	Co. I 262nd Regiment	Laurel Run Boro [M]
Sanborn, Charles J. Pfc.	Med. Det. 262nd Regiment	Philadelphia [M]
Sapovchak, Nick Pfc.	Co. I 262nd Regiment	Ambridge
Saska, Harry J. Pfc.	Co. K 262nd Regiment	Houston [M]
Schokowitz, Morris Pvt.	Co. L 262nd Regiment	Philadelphia [R]
Schramm, Jack A. Pfc.	Co. L 262nd Regiment	Pittsburgh [M]
Secich, Joseph G. Pvt.	Co. L 262nd Regiment	Verona [M]
Sellers, Benjamin F., Jr. Pfc.	Co. C 264th Regiment	Steelton [M]
Shevera, Edward T/5.	Co. I 264th Regiment	New Boston
Skibinski, Walter J. Pfc.	Co. F 262nd Regiment	Scranton [M]
Sloan, Wilbur J., Jr. Sgt.	Co. I 264th Regiment	New Castle [R]
Sweet, Robert C. Pfc.	Co. C 264th Regiment	Erie [M]
Taylor, Jay W. Pfc.	Co. E 262nd Regiment	Elizabeth [M]
Van Belle, Daniel J. Pfc.	Co. I 262nd Regiment	Philadelphia [M]
Vernile, Ralph R. Pvt.	Co. F 262nd Regiment	Donora [M]
Vierling, David E. Pvt.	Co. K 262nd Regiment	Knox [M]
Vince, John M., Jr. T/5.	Co. L 262nd Regiment	Hannastown [M]
Welsh, Robert D. Pfc.	Co. B 264th Regiment	Kappel [M]
Zeigler, Charles E. Sgt.	Co. B 264th Regiment	Herndon [M]
Zubal, John J. Pfc.	Co. B 264th Regiment	Johnstown [F]

Rhode Island (8)

Bennett, Lynwood F. Pvt.	Med. Det. 262nd Regiment	Riverside [M]
Carson, Marshall Pvt.	Med. Det. 262nd Regiment	Providence [M]
Celentano, Peter Pfc.	Co. F 262nd Regiment	Johnston [M]
Costa, William Pfc.	Co. K 262nd Regiment	Providence
De Resta, Antonio, Jr. Sgt.	Co. F 262nd Regiment	Providence [M]
Gianfrancesco,Robert M. S. Sgt.	Co. C 264th Regiment	Providence [F]
Hodosh, Leonard J. Pfc.	Co. H 262nd Regiment	Providence [M]
Masssey, Joseph D. S. Sgt.	Co. F 262nd Regiment	Providence [M]

Lt. Col. Victor E. Phasey

Victor Emmanuel Phasey was born in New York City on October 28, 1900. He enlisted in the army in July 1919 and entered West Point with the Class of 1924. He became one of the Cadet Glee Club's foremost soloists. Lt. Phasey married Jessie Irene DeNike on October 5, 1926. While stationed in Hawaii his two daughters were born, Dorothy Jane in 1927 and Jessie DeNike in 1929. He had a succession of peacetime assignments back in the states. After Pearl Harbor he was promoted to Lt. Colonel. His wife and daughters remained in Columbia, South Carolina during the war years. Lt. Colonel Phasey was assigned to the 66th Division in October 1944. After the war Lt. Col. Phasey planned to retire from the army and devote his time to writing. His wife, Jessie, died on May 30, 1965.

South Carolina (14)

Berry, Leonard E. Sgt.	Co. B 264th Regiment	Bowman
Brown, Dessie W. Pvt.	Hdq. Co. 2nd Bat. 262nd Reg.	Kingstree
Hentz, James E. S. Sgt.	Co. H 262nd Regiment	Newberry [M]
James, John E., Jr. 2d. Lt.	Co. C 264th Regiment	Summerton
Lawrence, William I. Sgt.	Co. F 262nd Regiment	Sumter [M]
Loftis, James L. Sgt.	Co. E 264th Regiment	Greenville
Martin, Roddy A. 2d. Lt.	Co. L 262nd Regiment	Mullins
McCurley, James W. Pfc.	Co. A 264th Regiment	[M]
McCormick, Robert L. Pfc.	Co. L 262nd Regiment	Sumter
McNair, James L. Pfc.	Co. I 262nd Regiment	Calhoun Falls [M]
Moseley, James O. Sgt.	Co. F 262nd Regiment	Spartanburg [M]
Phasey, Victor E. Lt. Col.	Hdq. 3rd Bat. 264th Regiment	[F]
Reece, Walter W. Pfc.	Co. H 262nd Regiment	Pickens [M]
Richardson, Francis J. Pfc.	Co. K 262nd Regiment	Florence

South Dakota (3)

Husby, Garland O. S. Sgt.	Co. F 262nd Regiment	Yankton [M]
Pauls, Elwood G. T/5.	Med. Det. 262nd Regiment	Bryant [M]
Smith, Donald W. Pvt.	Co. E 262nd Regiment	Aberdeen [M]

Tennessee (30)

Ailey, Burl W. Pfc.	Co. E 262nd Regiment	Dandridge [M]
Black, Charles H. Pfc.	Co. I 262nd Regiment	Concord [M]
Boleyn, Floyd P. Pfc.	Co. F 262nd Regiment	Adamsville [M]
Brown, Daniel H., Jr. Pfc.	Co. L 262nd Regiment	Ooltewah [M]
Cannon, Fay Pvt.	Co. K 262nd Regiment	Greenville [M]
Chockley, Harold Y. S. Sgt.	Co. E 264th Regiment	Shelbyville
Clark, John W. Pfc.	Co. F 262nd Regiment	Medon [M]
Conner, Thomas D. Pvt.	Co. I 264th Regiment	Tiptonville
Gillespie, John O. Pfc.	Co. L 262nd Regiment	Lewisburg [M]
Gilley, Thomas W. S. Sgt.	Co. G 262nd Regiment	Morrison
Gillis, James C. Pfc.	Co. H 262nd Regiment	Cypress Inn [M]
Gregory, Charles H. Pfc.	Hdq. Co. 3rd Battalion 262nd Reg.	Red Boiling Springs[M]
Henderson, Edward L. Pfc.	Co. K 262nd Regiment	Knoxville
Henry, Glenn H. Pfc.	Co. E 262nd Regiment	Sevierville [M]
Holmes, William K. Pfc.	Co. I 262nd Regiment	St. Elino
Howard, James L. Pvt.	Co. H 262nd Regiment	Ridgely [M]
Jackson, Earl S. Pfc.	Co. H 262nd Regiment	Bloomington Springs [M]
Jarnagin, Charles E. Pfc.	Co. K 262nd Regiment	Harriman
Jones, Henry M. Pvt.	Co. H 262nd Regiment	Gainsboro [M]

Pfc. Bill Pearl

Pfc. Bill Pearl was born on October 17, 1925. He entered the army at Fort Sam Houston on April 4, 1944. His body was never found. A white memorial stone furnished by the United States government reposes near his father's grave in the Little Saline cemetery.

Lipford, Arnold A. Pfc.	Co. F 262nd Regiment	Finger [M]
McCorkle, Wallace Pvt.	Co. F 262nd Regiment	Columbia [M]
Milam, Neal Sgt.	Co. I 262nd Regiment	Cedar Grove [M]
Miller, Robert R. Pfc.	Co. F 262nd Regiment	Knoxville [M]
Mixon, Robert L. Pfc.	Co. F 262nd Regiment	Charlotte [M]
Palmer, William H. Pfc.	Co. H 262nd Regiment	Kerrville [M]
Roberts, Wardell J. Sgt.	Co. K 262nd Regiment	Hendersonville [F]
Smith, James P. Pfc.	Co. F 262nd Regiment	Lenoir City [M]
Stills, Robert Pfc.	Co. I 262nd Regiment	Johnson City [R]
Sweeney, Leonard B. T/5.	Co. L 262nd Regiment	Franklin
Williams, Heiskell M. Pfc.	Co. L 262nd Regiment	Rogersville [M]

Texas (35)

Anderson, Marvin C. Pvt.	Hdq. Co. 1st Battalion 264th Reg.	Fort Worth
Andrews, Lloyd L. Pfc.	Co. I 262nd Regiment	Center [M]
Appleby, Preston B. 1st Lt.	Co. B 264th Regiment	Houston [R]
Ayala, Modesto Pfc.	Co. E 262nd Regiment	McAllen [M]
Caviness, Billy T. Pvt.	Co. F 262nd Regiment	Clarksville [M]
Christian, Jim B. Pfc.	Co. E 262nd Regiment	Houston [M]
Contreras, Gregorio V. Pfc.	Co. I 264th Regiment	Del Rio
Edler, Tony W., Jr. T. Sgt.	Co. H 262nd Regiment	Texas City [M]
Foester, James C. Pvt.	Co. K 262nd Regiment	El Paso [M]
Ford, Arthur L. Pfc.	Co. B 264th Regiment	Wellington [M]
Garcia, Paul M. Pfc.	Co. H 262nd Regiment	San Benito [M]
Garza, Alejandro L. Pfc.	Co. K 262nd Regiment	San Antonio [M]
Gillem, Dee R. S. Sgt.	Co. L 262nd Regiment	Tell [M]
Gilmore, Lester D. Pvt.	Co. I 262nd Regiment	San Antonio
Green, Herman N. Pvt.	Co. F 262nd Regiment	Selsbee [M]
Head, Art S. Pfc.	Co. I 262nd Regiment	Houston [F]
Horne, Albert C. Pfc.	Co. I 264th Regiment	Galveston [M]
Jeter, G. C., Jr. Pfc.	Co. I 264th Regiment	Dallas [F]
Koehler, Herbert O., Jr. Pvt.	Co. E 262nd Regiment	Yoakum [M]
Noto, Sam W., Jr. Pfc.	Co. E 262nd Regiment	Bryan [M]
O'bryan, Glenn A. Pvt.	Co. I 264th Regiment	Houston [M]
Pearl, Bill M. Pfc.	Co. B 264th Regiment	[M]
Perea, Joaquin Pvt.	Co. E 262nd Regiment	El Paso [M]
Pickett, Joe D. Pfc.	Co. L 262nd Regiment	Freeport [M]
Ragle, Billie K. T. Sgt.	Co. E 262nd Regiment	Aledo [M]
Ransom, James R. S. Sgt.	Co. E 262nd Regiment	Dallas [M]
Reichle, Ernest C. Pfc.	Co. A 264th Regiment	[F]

Pfc. Willie Paul Wilson

Pfc. Willie Paul Wilson from Julian, West Virginia was born on November 11, 1925. His last letter home dated December 16, 1944 read in part, "Dearest mother, Just a few lines to say hello and how are all the family getting along. Fine I hope and as for myself I am fine . . . What is little Michael doing. (His youngest brother) I'll bet he is as mean as ever. I sure would love to see him. I will write as often as I can whether I get any mail from you or not . . . Well I can't think of any more to write so I will close for this time. Your Son, Willie Wilson. Pfc. Wilson's body was recovered and after the war returned to the United States. He was buried at Ivy Branch, West Virginia in the same cemetery where his father, mother, and sisters Opal and Kathleen were later buried.

Rice, Walter H. Pvt.	Co. K 264th Regiment	Houston [M]
Robison, Harry C. Pfc.	Co. A 264th Regiment	[F]
Rouch, Wilbur L. Pvt.	Co. K 262nd Regiment	Atlanta [F]
Simmons, Chester B., Jr Pvt.	Co. I 264th Regiment	Camp Seale [M]
Springfield, James F. Pfc.	Co. F 262nd Regiment	Gainesville [M]
Thompson, Claude C. Pvt.	Co. B 264th Regiment	Amarillo [F]
Watson, Tommie J. Pfc.	Co. K 262nd Regiment	Amarillo
Wiley, William H. T/5.	Med. Det. 262nd Regiment	Houston [M]

Utah (2)

Poulton, Glenn E. Sgt.	Co. F 262nd Regiment	[M]
Warner, Edwin R. Pfc.	Co. F 262nd Regiment	[M]

Vermont (1)

Decell, Harold J. Pfc.	Co. L 262nd Regiment	Lyndonville

Virginia (7)

Bradley, Claude P., Jr. Sgt.	Co. E 262nd Regiment	Stuarts Draft [M]
Bush, Charles L. Pfc.	Co. L 262nd Regiment	Ewing
Fox, Earl B. Pfc.	Co. K 262nd Regiment	Hornsbyville [F]
Goins, Charles E. Pvt.	Co. B 264th Regiment	Duffield [M]
Nunn, Melvin E. Sgt.	Co. F 262nd Regiment	Martinsville [M]
Roberson, William G. Pfc.	Co. K 262nd Regiment	[M]
Scott, William E. Pfc.	Co. A 264th Regiment	Roanoke [M]

Washington (8)

Bransmo, Robert S. S. Sgt.	Co. C 264th Regiment	Mt. Vernon
Lewis, Raymond R. Pfc.	Co. I 262nd Regiment	Yakima [M]
Lewis, William K. Pfc.	Co. L 262nd Regiment	Spokane
Rodal, Paul M. T. Sgt.	Co. K 264th Regiment	Seattle [F]
Rumburg, Ira C. Lt. Col.	Hdq. 1st Battalion 264th Reg.	Spokane [M]
Rust, David S. Pfc.	Co. E 262nd Regiment	Monroe [M]
Warring, Hugh N. Pfc.	Co. L 262nd Regiment	Kapowsin [M]
Wyatt, Frank E. Pfc.	Co. E 262nd Regiment	Moxee [M]

West Virginia (14)

Adkins, Amon Pfc.	Co. B 264th Regiment	Huntington
Bowyer, James M., Jr. Sgt.	Co. L 262nd Regiment	Minden
Cole, Edgle W. Pfc.	Co. H 262nd Regiment	Sophia [M]
Estep, Hobert O. Pfc.	Co. H 262nd Regiment	Ashford [M]
Hartley, Jack R. Pfc.	Co. H 262nd Regiment	Beckley [M]
Huffman, Johnnie O. Pvt.	Co. D 264th Regiment	Fowlers Knob
Killeen, John W. Pfc.	Co. F 262nd Regiment	Wheeling [M]
Pyles, George E. Pfc.	Co. E 264th Regiment	New Martinsville

Smith, Bulah Pvt.	Co. C 264th Regiment	Meadow Creek
Spaulding, Sherman A. Pfc.	Co. F 262nd Regiment	Webb [M]
Thompson, Robert L. Pfc.	Co. L 262nd Regiment	[F]
Williamson, Clyde J. Pfc.	Co. B 264th Regiment	Seebert
Wilson, Willie P. Pfc.	Co. K 262nd Regiment	[R] Julian
Wright, John D. Sgt.	Co. A 264th Regiment	Park

Wisconsin (12)

Brady, Douglas F. Pvt.	Med. Det. 262nd Regiment	[M]
Cutnaw, Kent P. Pfc.	Co. E 264th Regiment	Stevens Point
Gaudynski, Raymond W. Pfc.	Co. L 262nd Regiment	Milwaukee [M]
Grant, Irving Pvt.	Co. I 262nd Regiment	Milwaukee [M]
Hanson, Fred W. Pfc.	Co. E 264th Regiment	Iron River
Kritselis, Christ A. Pvt.	Co. F 262nd Regiment	Milwaukee [M]
Mc Hugh, Dean J. Pfc.	Hdq. Co. 3rd Battalion 262nd Reg.	Holmen
Moen, Ernest M. Pfc.	Co. A 264th Regiment	Whitehall
Peters, Howard C. Pvt.	Co. I 262nd Regiment	[M]
Pettersen, Einar T. Pfc.	Co. H 262nd Regiment	Racine [M]
Prueher, Franklin L. Pvt.	Hdq. Co. 1st Battalion 264th Reg.	Burlington
Schulz, William R. Pfc.	Co. B 264th Regiment	[M]

Washington, D.C. (1)

Mugan, Joseph P. Pvt.	Co. B 264th Regiment

Canada (1)

Mazzone, Vincent J. Cpl.	Hdq. Co. 1st Bat. 264th Reg.	Cornwall, Ontario [M]

State Unknown (5)

Baginski, Henry Pfc.	Co. A 264th Regiment
Faerber, Richard P. Pfc.	Co. A 264th Regiment
Heffernan, Joseph A. Pvt.	Co. A 264th Regiment
Tedford, Joe E. Pvt.	Co. B 264th Regiment
Vanderpool, Fred A. Pvt.	Co. E 264th Regiment

Survivors

It is possible that some 66th division soldiers were "walk ons" not included on the formal Leopoldville passenger list. In order to be as accurate as possible, this list of survivors records only those 66th division soldiers whose names appear on the official U.S. Army Leopoldville casualty lists prepared on 12/29/1944 and 01/05/1945.

*Hospitalized.

262nd Infantry

A

Pfc. Adams, William O.* .... Co. K (3rd Platoon)

Pfc. Adkinson, John W.* .... Co. K (2nd Platoon)

Pvt. Agnello, Maurg A. .... Co. I (1st Platoon)

Pfc. Alexander, John W. .... Co. H (1st Platoon)

Pfc. Allison, William T.* .... Co. K ((Weapons Platoon))

T/4 Altomare, James* .... Co. I (Hdq.)

Pfc. Ambrose, Albert J.* .... 2nd Battalion Ammo & Pioneer

Pfc. Ames, William M. .... Co. K (3rd Platoon)

Pfc. Anderson, Henry W. .... Co. E (Weapons Platoon)

Pfc. Andrew, William L.* .... 3rd Battalion Ammo & Pioneer

T. Sgt. Archer, Fred J. .... Co. L (2nd Platoon)

Pvt. Archer, Ruel P. .... Co. L (Weapons Platoon)

1st Lt. Ard, Henry N. .... 2nd Battalion Communications.

Pfc. Atwell, Donald R.* .... Co. K (1st Platoon)

2d. Lt. Austin, Leon F.* .... Co. I (1st Platoon)

B

Pvt. Bachmann, Vernon C.* .... 2nd Battalion Med. Det.

Pfc. Badger, Oliver M. .... Co. L (Weapons Platoon)

Sgt. Bailey, Harold S. .... Co. L (1st Platoon)

T. Sgt. Baker, Frederic A. .... *Co. K (1st Platoon)

Cpl. Balttel, James G.* .... 2nd Battalion Hdq. Co.

Pfc. Baltz, Delton R. .... Co. K (3rd Platoon)

Pfc. Banks, Robert K.* .... Co. I (Weapons Platoon)

Pvt. Baraldi, Henry J. .... Co. K (3rd Platoon)

S. Sgt. Barboza, John M.* .... Co. L (1st Platoon)

Pvt. Barrett, Joseph J. .... Co. K (1st Platoon)

Pfc. Barrile, James J.* .... 3rd Battalion Anti-Tank Platoon

Pvt. Barry, William R. .... Co. I (1st Platoon)

Pfc. Bartels, Bernard E. .... Co. L (1st Platoon)

Pfc. Bartlett, Alden D.* .... Co. H (2nd Platoon)

Pfc. Bartley, James, Jr.* .... Co. K (Hdq.)

Pvt. Bauer, George W.* .... 2nd Battalion Hdq. Co.

Pfc. Belanger, Leroy J.* .... Co. K (3rd Platoon)

Pvt. Bell, Charles E.* .... Co. K (3rd Platoon)

Pfc. Beran, Walter F.* .... Co. I (3rd Platoon)

Pfc. Biddle, Thomas W. .... Co. L (Weapons Platoon)

S. Sgt. Bigelow, George E.* .... Co. I (1st Platoon)

Pfc. Blair, Joe H.* .... 3rd Battalion Ammo & Pioneer

Pfc. Blake, Donald L.* .... Co. F (Weapons Platoon)

Pfc. Blanchard, Fred P. .... Co. L (3rd Platoon)

2d. Lt. Blaney, John J.* .... Co. L (Hdq.)

S. Sgt. Blanton, Theron L.* .... Co. L (Hdq.)

Pfc. Blum, Paul H.* .... Co. L (2nd Platoon)

Pfc. Blunt, Walter E.* .... Co. L (1st Platoon)

Sgt. Bobst, Merwin M. .... 2nd Battalion Ammo & Pioneer

2d. Lt. Bogan, Stanley A. .... 3rd Battalion Anti-Tank Platoon

2d. Lt. Bonner, Robert F. .... Co. F (2nd Platoon)

Pfc. Bookhout, Andy .... Co. I (2nd Platoon)

Pfc. Borlin, George L. .... Co. I (1st Platoon)

Pfc. Bostick, Howard W.* .... Co. L (Weapons Platoon)

Pvt. Botta, Marion* .... 3rd Battalion Communications.

2d. Lt. Boudwin, Rodney W.* .... Co. L (3rd Platoon)

Pfc. Boyajian, Vane .... Co. L (2nd Platoon)

Pfc. Boyer, Harold E.* .... Co. I (Weapons Platoon)

Pfc. Brassor, Henry R. .... Co. I (Weapons Platoon)

Sgt. Brewer, Robert S. .... Co. I (Weapons Platoon)

Pvt. Brooks, Melvin D. .... Co. L (Weapons Platoon)

2d. Lt. Brown, Alex S., Jr..Co. H (3rd Platoon)

2d. Lt. Brown, Gerard*...2nd Battalion Ammo & Pioneer

Pvt. Brown, Gilbert E.*...Co. F (3rd Platoon)

S. Sgt. Brown, Walter T. ....Co. F (Weapons Platoon)

S. Sgt. Bruck, Thomas N.*...Co. L (3rd Platoon)

Pfc. Bryant, William A...Co. F (2nd Platoon)

Pfc. Bryant, William L.*...Co. K (2nd Platoon)

Sgt. Budd, Winford, L...Co. L (2nd Platoon)

Pvt. Bueche, Bernard M..Co. K (Hdq.)

T/5 Buhdar, Fred* (AKA Brent) ....2nd Battalion Hdq. Co.

Pfc. Bullett, Norman C. ....Co. L (2nd Platoon)

Pfc. Bulzgis, John P.*...Co. K (Weapons Platoon)

T/5 Burke, James*.. 3rd Battalion Communications.

Pvt. Bushem, Anthony J.* ....Co. I (Hdq.)

Pfc. Byrd, William E., Jr.*..3rd Battalion Ammo & Pioneer

Pfc. Bysiorek, Benny ....3rd Battalion Ammo & Pioneer

C

Pfc. Campbell, Kenneth R.*..Co. L (Weapons Platoon)

Pfc. Capehart, Jack R.* ....Co. F (3rd Platoon)

T/5 Cardoza, Herbert ....2nd Battalion Med. Det.

2d. Lt. Carey, Paul* ....Co. I (2nd Platoon)

Pfc. Carnes, Lane* ....Co. K (3rd Platoon)

Pvt. Carrillo, Mazario R. ....Co. L (Weapons Platoon)

Pvt. Castillo, Carlos V. ....Co. L (1st Platoon)

Pfc. Chambers, Milton L., Jr. ....2nd Battalion Communications.

Pvt. Christopulos, George L.* ....Co. I (3rd Platoon)

T. Sgt. Chun Fat, George ....Co. I (1st Platoon)

Pfc. Codianni, Vincent*..Co. K (2nd Platoon)

Pvt. Coffin, Alson D. ....Co. L (Weapons Platoon)

S. Sgt. Colemen, Billy A.* ....Co. K (Weapons Platoon)

Pvt. Cooter, Raymond L...Co. L (Weapons Platoon)

Pfc. Coster, Normand*...Co. L (1st Platoon)

Pfc. Cowdery, James R.*...Co. I (Weapons Platoon)

Pvt. Cox, Roscoe W. ....Co. I (Weapons Platoon)

Sgt. Cremonini, Robert P.*...3rd Battalion Ammo & Pioneer

Pvt. Croxen, Wilbur E.* ....Co. L (Weapons Platoon)

S. Sgt. Cycon, Joseph P...Co. F (2nd Platoon)

D

Pfc. Dahlke, Arnold F.* ....Co. I (3rd Platoon)

Sgt. Daigneault, Walter E.* .... Co. L (2nd Platoon)

Pfc. Daily, Leroy* .... Co. L (2nd Platoon)

Pfc. Daniel, Neil L. .... Co. K (2nd Platoon)

Pfc. Daniel, Raymond R.* ....Co. K (3rd Platoon)

Pvt. Darle, Robert H.* .... Co. F (3rd Platoon)

Pfc. Daves, John W.* .... 3rd Battalion Ammo & Pioneer

Pfc. Dean, Othel A.* ....Co. L (Weapons Platoon)

Pfc. Deemer, Arthur W.*....................................2nd Battalion Communications.

Pfc. DeFilippo, Anthony* .... Co. K (2nd Platoon)

Pfc. Dehoyos, Antonio* ....Co. K (1st Platoon)

Pfc. Delacruz, Leo* .... Co. K (Weapons Platoon)

Pfc. Deribas, Fred P.* ....Co. L (3rd Platoon)

T. Sgt. Deslauriers, James A. ....Co. L (Weapons Platoon)

Pfc. Deutsch, William R.* .... Co. L (2nd Platoon)

Pfc. DeVors, John A.* .... Co. K (Hdq.)

Pfc. Dicesare, Robert T. .... 2nd Battalion Hdq. Co.

Capt. Dinwiddie, Clyde M.* ....2nd Battalion Hdq. Co.

Pvt. Dionne, Henry A.* ....Co. L (3rd Platoon)

Pfc. DiSalvo, Arthur* .... Co. L (2nd Platoon)

Pfc. Dixon, Thomas L.* ....Co. K (1st Platoon)

1st Sgt. Doepker, Norbert J.*...2nd Battalion Hdq. Co.

Pfc. Doran, William R.* ....Co. L (3rd Platoon)

Sgt. Dorso, Gerald J.* ....Co. I (3rd Platoon)

Lt. Col. Doyle, Ernest W. ....2nd Battalion Hdq. Co.

Pfc. Dreger, William R. .... Co. K (Weapons Platoon)

Pfc. Drew, Raymond E.* ....Co. E (3rd Platoon)

Pvt. Duncan, Everett* ....Co. K (1st Platoon)

Pfc. Dunn, John J. ....Co. I (Weapons Platoon)

Pvt. Dunn, Loyce G. .... Co. I (Hdq.)

Sgt. Durham, Robert E. .... 3rd Battalion Ammo & Pioneer

Pfc. Dyer, Robert L... Co. I (Hdq.)

E

Pfc. Eads, Carl W.* .... Co. L (2nd Platoon)

Pfc. Earle, Isadore* ....3rd Battalion Anti-Tank Platoon

Pvt. Easley, John N.* .... Co. K (Weapons Platoon)

Pfc. Edwards, Howard L.* .... Co. I (1st Platoon)

Pfc. Ellis, John L.* .... Co. I (3rd Platoon)

Pvt. Elswick, Richard* .... Co. K (2nd Platoon)

Pfc. Eppelsheimer, Melvern J. .... Co. K (2nd Platoon)

Pfc. Esparza, Alfredo B.* .... Co. I (2nd Platoon)

Pfc. Evans, Gilbert W. .... Co. L (1st Platoon)

Pfc. Evensen, Roy B. .... 3rd Battalion Ammo & Pioneer

F

Pvt. Feiman, Robert D. .... 3rd Battalion Anti-Tank Platoon

2d. Lt. Feldner, Allen L. .... Co. F (3rd Platoon)

Pfc. Fellitti, Frank A. .... Co. H (Hdq.)

Sgt. Ferguson, Paul S., Jr.* .... Co. L (1st Platoon)

T/4 Flynn, Maurice F. X.* .... 2nd Battalion Communications.

Pvt. Forman, Max* .... Co. K (3rd Platoon)

Pfc. Franks, Andrew A.* .... Co. I (1st Platoon)

Pfc. Fraser, Ralph S. .... Co. K (3rd Platoon)

Pfc. Friant, William G.* .... Co. K (Weapons Platoon)

Sgt. Frye, Ira H.* .... Co. I (Weapons Platoon)

G

Pfc. Gainey, Robert* .... Co. L (Weapons Platoon)

Pfc. Gallo, Vincent L.* .... Co. I (3rd Platoon)

Capt. Gangwere, Jack F.* .... Co. I (Hdq.)

Pfc. Garcia, Jose B.* .... Co. L (Weapons Platoon)

Pfc. Garstensen, Donald K. .... Co. I (3rd Platoon)

2d. Lt. Gee, James L.* .... 2nd Battalion Anti-Tank Platoon

S. Sgt. Gengler, Donald E.* .... Co. K (2nd Platoon)

Pfc. Gerwing, Robert W.* .... Co. K (3rd Platoon)

Pfc. Gianiodis, Constantine* .... Co. I (Weapons Platoon)

Pfc. Gilhooley, John J.* .... Co. K (2nd Platoon)

Pvt. Gillick, Hugh C.* .... 3rd Battalion Hdq. Co.

Pfc. Gittemier, Aloysius W.* .... 3rd Battalion Ammo & Pioneer

Pvt. Gittlen, Harold .... Co. I (1st Platoon)

S. Sgt. Glazier, David .... Co. I (1st Platoon)

S. Sgt. Goble, Donald W. .... Co. I (1st Platoon)

Pfc. Goldstein, Julius M.* .... Co. K (3rd Platoon)

Pvt. Goode, Charles O. .... 3rd Battalion Communications.

Pfc. Gottlieb, Donald C.* .... Co. I (Weapons Platoon)

Sgt. Graves, Barton H.* .... 3rd Battalion Hdq. Co.

Pfc. Gray, Frank R.* .... Co. K (1st Platoon)

Pfc. Gray, Freeman C.* .... 3rd Battalion Anti-Tank Platoon

Pvt. Greathouse, Dallas L.*.. Co. L (1st Platoon)

Cpl. Greeley, John M... 3rd Battalion Hdq. Co.

Pfc. Gregg, Victor*... Co. K (Weapons Platoon)

Pfc. Gregory, Joseph F.. 3rd Battalion Anti-Tank Platoon

Pvt. Groont, Bernard .... 2nd Battalion Ammo & Pioneer

T/4 Grubb, Cloyd .... 2nd Battalion Med. Det.

Pfc. Grunewald, James M.. Co. E (3rd Platoon)

H

Pfc. Haberstumpf, Harold E.*.. 2nd Battalion Med. Det.

Pfc. Hadden, George M...Co. K (3rd Platoon)

Pfc. Hahn, James E. ....Co. K (3rd Platoon)

Pfc. Hall, Clarence H.* .... Co. K (Weapons Platoon)

Pfc. Hall, Clay E.*... Co. I (2nd Platoon)

1st Lt. Hall, John F.* .... Co. I (Hdq.)

Sgt. Hamilton, Millard F.*..Co. L (3rd Platoon)

Sgt. Hand, Marvin B. .... Co. K (Weapons Platoon)

Pfc. Hardbeck, George W., Jr.*........................... 2nd Battalion Ammo & Pioneer

Pfc. Hardy, Leonidas, Jr. .... 3rd Battalion Anti-Tank Platoon

Pfc. Hardy, Richard L.*... Co. I (1st Platoon)

Pvt. Harrison, Lawrence .... Co. I (1st Platoon)

Pfc. Harwood, Ripley B., Jr.* .... Co. K (Hdq.)

1st Lt. Hausner, John W.* .... Co. H (Hdq.)

Pfc. Hazelwood, George M.* ....Co. K (1st Platoon)

Pfc. Healy, John T.*... 3rd Battalion Hdq. Co.

S. Sgt. Heckman, Thomas E. ....Co. I (Weapons Platoon)

T. Sgt. Hester, Aubrey W. .... Co. I (Hdq.)

Pfc. Higgins, James J.* ....Co. I (3rd Platoon)

Cpl. Higgins, Joseph G., Jr.*.............................. Co. H (2nd Platoon)

Pfc. Hoffman, James W.*.................................... Co. H (3rd Platoon)

Pfc. Hoffman, Raymond W.................................... Co. I (2nd Platoon)

S. Sgt. Holevar, Andrew G.*................................... Co. K (Weapons Platoon)

Pfc. Holowich, Joseph*... Co. L (2nd Platoon)

Pvt. Hook, Goodwin J.* .... 2nd Battalion Ammo & Pioneer

T. Sgt. Howard, Gerald D.*..................................... Co. K (2nd Platoon)

Pvt. Hranek, Anthony* .... Co. I (2nd Platoon)

Pfc. Hrovat, John A.* ....Co. L (Weapons Platoon)

Pvt. Hughes, Eugene W. .... Co. I (1st Platoon)

2d. Lt. Hughes, James F., Jr.* .... Co. F (1st Platoon)

J

Pvt. Jackson, James P.* .... Co. L (1st Platoon)

Pfc. Jackson, Lehman D.* .... Co. L (1st Platoon)

Pfc. Jackson, Ted F.* .... Co. L (3rd Platoon)

Pvt. Jacobs, Earl E. .... Co. I (3rd Platoon)

Pvt. Janos, Edward J.* .... Co. I (1st Platoon)

Pvt. Jennings, Frank L., Jr. .... Co. L (2nd Platoon)

Pfc. Jensen, Ole S. .... Co. E (Weapons Platoon)

Pvt. Jepson, Ronald W. .... Co. I (1st Platoon)

Sgt. Jex, John M.* .... Co. K (1st Platoon)

Pfc. Johnson, Eulus O. .... Co. L (1st Platoon)

Pfc. Johnson, Kenneth H. .... Co. L (1st Platoon)

Pvt. Jones, Edwin O., Jr.* .... 3rd Battalion Ammo & Pioneer

2d. Lt. Jones, Leonard F. .... Co. K (1st Platoon)

Pvt. Jones, Samuel E.* .... Co. K (Hdq.)

K

Pvt. Kackley, Francis M.* .... Co. K (1st Platoon)

Pvt. Kalinowski, William S.* .... Co. L (1st Platoon)

Pvt. Karas, Stephen* .... Co. K (Hdq.)

Pfc. Katus, Robert G.* .... Co. L (3rd Platoon)

Pvt. Keddy, James W.* .... Co. K (1st Platoon)

1st Lt. Keddy, Roden A.* .... Co. E (Weapons Platoon)

Pvt. Kelly, Joseph P. .... Co. F (2nd Platoon)

Pfc. Kemp, John A. .... Co. I (Hdq.)

Pvt. Kern, James R.* .... 3rd Battalion Hdq. Co.

Pvt. Kesterson, Raymond .... Co. I (1st Platoon)

Pfc. Kile, Corwin M.* .... Co. I (Weapons Platoon)

T/5 Kincaid, Newman E.* .... 2nd Battalion Communications

Pfc. King, Kenneth R. .... Co. K (Hdq.)

Pfc. Kirschenbaum, Bernard* .... Co. L (3rd Platoon)

Pvt. Kleinerman, Mack .... 2nd Battalion Anti-Tank Platoon

Pvt. Kleinsasser, Amos W. .... 2nd Battalion Ammo & Pioneer

T/5 Kline, Kenneth* .... Co. H (Hdq.)

S. Sgt. Kloster, Walter F.* .... 2nd Battalion Ammo & Pioneer

Pfc. Knepp, Delmont L.* .... Co. L (Weapons Platoon)

T/4 Knieriem, Robert D... 3rd Battalion Communications.

Pfc. Knotowicz, Frank C.*... Co. I (2nd Platoon)

Pvt. Knuth, Arno H.* ....Co. I (3rd Platoon)

Pfc. Kosminski, Peter P. ....3rd Battalion Anti-Tank Platoon

Pfc. Kowalski, Chester L.* .... 2nd Battalion Hdq. Co.

Pvt. Krushinsky, Gerald A. .... Co. F (1st Platoon)

L

Pfc. Lake, Clayton J. .... Co. L (2nd Platoon)

Pfc. Lalonde, Philip L. .... Co. I (1st Platoon)

Pfc. Lancaster, James A.* .... 2nd Battalion Ammo & Pioneer

2d. Lt. Lee, David C. .... Co. H (2nd Platoon)

S. Sgt. Legerski, Joseph W.*..................................Co. L (Weapons Platoon)

T. Sgt. LeMay, Albert A.* ....3rd Battalion Ammo & Pioneer

Pvt. Leo, Carl H., Jr. .... Co. I (1st Platoon)

Pfc. Levins, Delbert J... Co. I (1st Platoon)

Pfc. Libby, George T., Jr.* ....Co. L (3rd Platoon)

Pfc. Lierly, Richard C. .... Co. L (1st Platoon)

Cpl. Lindahl, Vernon M.*.. Co. F (Hdq.)

Pfc. Lindquist, Paul A.* .... Co. L (2nd Platoon)

Pfc. Lopez, Gonzalo M.*...Co. I (3rd Platoon)

Sgt. Lott, Robert L.* .... 3rd Battalion Ammo & Pioneer

Pfc. Loughborough, William E. ....Co. E (Weapons Platoon)

S. Sgt. Loverro, John E., Jr. ....2nd Battalion Communications

Pfc. Luhning, Joseph C., Jr. .... Co. L (2nd Platoon)

Pfc. Lundahl, Dean C.* .... Co. K (2nd Platoon)

M

Pfc. Maassen, Ronald L.*...................................3rd Battalion Ammo & Pioneer

2d. Lt. MacWilliams, Donald G.* ....Co. E (Weapons Platoon)

Pfc. Madison, George S.*...Co. K (1st Platoon)

Pvt. Maegdlin, Robert G. ....Co. L (Weapons Platoon)

Pfc. Maier, Thomas P.*...Co. K (2nd Platoon)

T/4 Mansfield, Raymond E.* ....Co. K (Hdq.)

Pvt. Marcus, Harvey W.* .... 2nd Battalion Anti-Tank Platoon

Lt. Col. Martindale, John*..3rd Battalion Hdq. Co.

1st Lt. Masters, John B.* .... 2nd Battalion Med. Det.

Pfc. Matson, Richard W. ....Co. I (3rd Platoon)

Pfc. Matthews, Edward E. .... Co. I (1st Platoon)

Sgt. Mauro, Edward A.* ....Co. K (1st Platoon)

Cpl. McAfee, Robert L. ....2nd Battalion Anti-Tank Platoon

Pfc. McArdle, George J.* .... 2nd Battalion Hdq. Co.

2d. Lt. McArthur, John D., Jr.* ....Co. F (Weapons Platoon)

Pfc. McCarty, Travis J.* ....Co. K (Hdq.)

Sgt. McCrea, Albert J.* ....Co. I (3rd Platoon)

T/5 McDonnell, John F.* .... 2nd Battalion Hdq. Co.

Pvt. McElwee, Francis E.* ....2nd Battalion Anti-Tank Platoon

Pfc. McFall, John H.* ....Co. E (Weapons Platoon)

2d. Lt. McGregor, Malcolm R.* ....Co. K (Weapons Platoon)

Pfc. McHugh, Anthony P.* .... Co. L (2nd Platoon)

Cpl. McKernan, William E. ....3rd Battalion Anti-Tank Platoon

Pfc. McKie, Robert C.* .... Co. K (Weapons Platoon)

Pvt. McMicken, Lee W.* ....3rd Battalion Anti-Tank Platoon

Pvt. McMurphy, John H.* .... Co. I (1st Platoon)

S. Sgt. Meeker, Bernard ....Co. L (Hdq.)

Pfc. Mendell, Chas H.* .... 2nd Battalion Hdq. Co.

Pfc. Middleton, Richard W.* .... 2nd Battalion Hdq. Co.

2d. Lt. Mikell, Julian P. ....Co. K (2nd Platoon)

T/5 Miles, Maurice E. ....3rd Battalion Hdq. Co.

Pfc. Miller, Don C. ....3rd Battalion Hdq. Co.

Pvt. Miller, George E. ....Co. E (Weapons Platoon)

Pfc. Miller, William F., Jr.* ....Co. K (Hdq.)

Pvt. Minnich, Allen B. ....Co. K (2nd Platoon)

2d. Lt. Mohan, John J. ....Co. L (1st Platoon)

Sgt. Montagna, Albert J. ....Co. L (Weapons Platoon)

Pfc. Mooney, William R. ....Co. E (Weapons Platoon)

T/4 Moore, Earl D.* .... Co. I (Hdq.)

Pfc. Moore, Erwin, H. ....Co. L (2nd Platoon)

Pfc. Moore, Samuel W.* ....Co. K (2nd Platoon)

S. Sgt. Moorman, Wilbur A. ....Co. L (3rd Platoon)

Pfc. Morhar, Robert ....3rd Battalion Ammo & Pioneer

Pvt. Moylan, James J. .... Co. I (Hdq.)

Pvt. Murphy, William P.* ....Co. L (Weapons Platoon)

N

Pfc. Nagy, William .... 2nd Battalion Hdq. Co.

Pvt. Napier, Clarence* ....Co. K (1st Platoon)

T/4 Naso, Thomas F. ....3rd Battalion Hdq. Co.

Pvt. Nason, Bernard F.* .... Co. L (3rd Platoon)

Sgt. Natole, Joseph J.*.. Co. K (Weapons Platoon)

Pvt. Nay, Benjamin J.*...Co. K (1st Platoon)

Pfc. Neale, James E.* .... Co. I (Hdq.)

Pvt. Needelman, Coleman*...Co. K (Hdq.)

1st Sgt. Nokes, James C.*..Co. K (Hdq.)

S. Sgt. Nolen Curtis L., Jr.* ....Co. L (Weapons Platoon)

Pfc. Noonan, Robert T.* ....Co. K (3rd Platoon)

O

S. Sgt. Olshefski, Edward B.*..Co. L (1st Platoon)

T. Sgt. O'Neill, John K. .... 2nd Battalion Hdq. Co.

Capt. Orr, Howard C.*..Co. L (Hdq.)

Pfc. Orris, Robert R. .... Co. F (2nd Platoon)

S. Sgt. Owens, Eugene F...Co. K (3rd Platoon)

P

Pfc. Pabian, Francis J.*.................................... Co. K (Weapons Platoon)

Pfc. Pacius, Anthony J.* ....3rd Battalion Anti-Tank Platoon

S. Sgt. Paczkowski, Jan J. ....Co. K (1st Platoon)

S. Sgt. Padgett, Loami B.* .... Co. K (2nd Platoon)

Pvt. Parent, Edgar J. .... Co. I (Hdq.)

Pfc. Parker, Howard A.............................. 2nd Battalion Ammo & Pioneer

Pvt. Pate, James W.* .... Co. F (Hdq.)

Pfc. Patton, Allen L.* ....Co. K (1st Platoon)

Pfc. Perdew, Dean E. ....Co. L (Weapons Platoon)

S. Sgt. Perkins, Frederick J.* .... Co. I (Hdq.)

Pvt. Perley, Kenneth H..Co. L (Weapons Platoon)

T/5 Perritt, Rayloen L.* ....3rd Battalion Hdq. Co.

Pfc. Petersen, Wallace E...Co. K (3rd Platoon)

Pfc. Peterson, Everett E.* ....Co. K (1st Platoon)

Pvt. Petteway, Alton M.*... Co. I (2nd Platoon)

Pfc. Petty, Guy O.*...Co. I (3rd Platoon)

T/3 Petty, Leslie A. ....2nd Battalion Med. Det.

Pvt. Phillips, Edwin C.* ....3rd Battalion Anti-Tank Platoon

Sgt. Pieper, Norman J. .... Co. F (1st Platoon)

2d. Lt. Pisano, Fred G.* ....Co. K (3rd Platoon)

Pfc. Plotkin, Paul A. .... Co. L (2nd Platoon)

Pvt. Pordon, John H.* .... Co. K (2nd Platoon)

Pvt. Provencio, Oscar* .... 2nd Battalion Hdq. Co.

Capt. Pursley, William E. .... 2nd Battalion Hdq. Co.

Pfc. Pusateri, John A.* .... Co. I (2nd Platoon)

Q

Pvt. Quick, John P. .... Co. K (2nd Platoon)

R

Sgt. Randles, Jack C.* .... Co. I (Weapons Platoon)

Pvt. Raymond, Gerald W.* .... 3rd Battalion Ammo & Pioneer

2d. Lt. Rehder, George S. .... Co. H (3rd Platoon)

Pfc. Reilly, Fred F., Jr.* .... Co. K (2nd Platoon)

Pfc. Reisteter, George F. .... Co. I (Hdq.)

Cpl. Reitz, John U. .... 3rd Battalion Hdq. Co.

Pfc. Reshetiloff, Cyril B.* .... 2nd Battalion Ammo & Pioneer

Pfc. Rhoads, Tom E. .... 2nd Battalion Ammo & Pioneer

S. Sgt. Rice, James R., Jr. .... Co. I (1st Platoon)

Pfc. Richards, Miles S.* .... Co. K (Hdq.)

Sgt. Richards, Raymond R.* .... Co. I (Weapons Platoon)

T/5 Richardson, Ralph J. .... Co. I (Hdq.)

Sgt. Riebe, Harvey D. .... Co. K (3rd Platoon)

Pfc. Rikerd, Emerson* .... Co. L (3rd Platoon)

S. Sgt. Rist, Paul R. .... Co. F (1st Platoon)

Pfc. Robbins, Joe B.* .... Co. I (Hdq.)

T/3 Roberts, Eugene C. .... 2nd Battalion Med. Det.

S. Sgt. Rolwes, Jack E. .... Co. K (1st Platoon)

Sgt. Rosenberg, Daniel* .... 2nd Battalion Hdq. Co.

Pfc. Rosenblum, Sidney* .... Co. L (Weapons Platoon)

Pvt. Rudolph, Oscar B. .... Co. I (2nd Platoon)

Pfc. Ruede, Junior G.* .... Co. L (3rd Platoon)

S. Sgt. Ruff, Paul N. .... Co. I (3rd Platoon)

S. Sgt. Rura, Gustie E.* .... 3rd Battalion Ammo & Pioneer

Pfc. Rush, Ernest F. .... Co. L (3rd Platoon)

S

Sgt. Salata, Albert .... Co. E (Weapons Platoon)

2d. Lt. Salmon, Maurice L.* .... Co. I (3rd Platoon)

Pvt. Salpini, Ernest C.* .... Co. I (2nd Platoon)

Pfc. Santow, Eugene O... Co. I (Hdq.)

S. Sgt. Saunders, Ross H.* .... Co. K (1st Platoon)

Pfc. Sawyer, Guy C.* .... Co. I (3rd Platoon)

Pvt. Say, Frank .... Co. L (2nd Platoon)

Pfc. Scarborough, James M.* ....Co. I (Weapons Platoon)

Pvt. Schaufele, William P. .... 2nd Battalion Ammo & Pioneer

Pvt. Schiller, Richard B.* .... Co. K (2nd Platoon)

Pfc. Schmaltz, Clemens S.*... Co. L (2nd Platoon)

Pfc. Schmidt, Warren E. .... Co. I (1st Platoon)

Pfc. Schneider, Paul H.* ....Co. K (3rd Platoon)

S. Sgt. Schultz, John R.* .... 2nd Battalion Anti-Tank Platoon

Sgt. Schulze, Paul C. .... Co. L (3rd Platoon)

Pfc. Schwartz, Kermit L.*...Co. I (Weapons Platoon)

S. Sgt. Scott, Charles A., Jr.* ....Co. K (3rd Platoon)

Pvt. Seaman, Morton N.*.. Co. I (3rd Platoon)

Pfc. Searle, Howard C.* .... 3rd Battalion Ammo & Pioneer

Pvt. Seeger, Garland L. .... Co. K (1st Platoon)

Pfc. Shaeffer, John E., Jr.*... Co. L (3rd Platoon)

Pfc. Shanaway, Robert R.* .... Co. K (Weapons Platoon)

Pfc. Shelby, John B., Jr. .... Co. F (1st Platoon)

Pvt. Shoaf, James M.*.. Co. K (2nd Platoon)

Pfc. Sibson, Carl K..3rd Battalion Ammo & Pioneer

Pfc. Sidwell, James S.*.. Co. L (3rd Platoon)

Pfc. Simons, Keith L...Co. I (Weapons Platoon)

Pfc. Skunca, Thomas P...Co. L (3rd Platoon)

Pvt. Slotnick, Jack* .... 2nd Battalion Ammo & Pioneer

Sgt. Smith, Henry W.*... Co. K (Weapons Platoon)

Pvt. Smotherman, Ray B.* .... 3rd Battalion Hdq. Co.

Sgt. Sosnicki, William*.. Co. K (Weapons Platoon)

Pfc. Spiro, Sidney B., Jr. ....3rd Battalion Hdq. Co.

Pfc. Sprague, Paul P. .... Co. I (3rd Platoon)

S. Sgt. Spriggs, Chester* .... Co. K (2nd Platoon)

Pfc. Stahr, Lloyd J. .... Co. L (2nd Platoon)

Pfc. Steinberg, Benjamin... Co. L (1st Platoon)

Pvt. Stone, Howard R. ....Co. L (Weapons Platoon)

Pfc. Stout, Eugene E.* ....Co. I (Weapons Platoon)

T. Sgt. Stratton, Wilbur C. .... Co. L (2nd Platoon)

Sgt. Stuaffer, Samuel M.. Co. L (3rd Platoon)

Pfc. Stutzman, Russell D. .... Co. L (2nd Platoon)

Sgt. Sumpter, James R.*... Co. I (2nd Platoon)

Pfc. Surfield, Robert L.*... Co. L (2nd Platoon)

Pfc. Sweren, Emanuel P. .... 2nd Battalion Anti-Tank Platoon

T

Pvt. Tanner, Clare A. .... 2nd Battalion Anti-Tank Platoon

Pfc. Teneyck, Perry, Jr.* ....Co. I (Weapons Platoon)

Pfc. Terry, George .... Co. L (1st Platoon)

Pfc. Tesinsky, Harry A.* .... Co. I (2nd Platoon)

Pfc. Thibodeaux, Henson J. ....Co. K (3rd Platoon)

Pvt. Thompson, Victor B. ....Co. K (3rd Platoon)

2d. Lt. Thompson, William F.*... Co. H (3rd Platoon)

Pfc. Thorpe, Henry D.* .... Co. K (2nd Platoon)

Capt. Thorpe, William A.* ....3rd Battalion Hdq. Co.

Pfc. Thrasher, Melvin E. .... Co. I (2nd Platoon)

Pvt. Titone, Charles A. .... Co. K (Hdq.)

Sgt. Tohey, Lawrence G., Jr.*...Co. K (3rd Platoon)

Pfc. Tokarz, Edward J.* .... Co. I (Hdq.)

Pfc. Toth, Steve*...Co. I (Weapons Platoon)

Sgt. Tripp, Charles R., Jr.* .... 2nd Battalion Ammo & Pioneer

Pfc. Troyka, David* ....Co. I (Weapons Platoon)

T. Sgt. Trzos, George E.*..3rd Battalion Anti-Tank Platoon

Pfc. Turner, Henry D. ....Co. I (Weapons Platoon)

Pfc. Twomey, Timothy J.* ....Co. L (3rd Platoon)

U

Pfc. Uppinghouse, Glen W.*.. Co. L (1st Platoon)

V

S. Sgt. Vallejo, Macario L. ....3rd Battalion Anti-Tank Platoon

Pfc. VanHoozer, Donnie R. ....Co. K (1st Platoon)

Capt. VanSickle, John C.*... Co. K (Hdq.)

T/5 Vaughan, Richard L.* .... Co. L (Hdq.)

Pfc. Vernon, Virgel H..Co. I (3rd Platoon)

T. Sgt. Vogler, Oscar P.* .... Co. K (Weapons Platoon)

W

Pfc. Wagner, Raymond G.* ....Co. K (3rd Platoon)

Pfc. Waller, Ralph* .... Co. I (2nd Platoon)

S. Sgt. Wallis, Thomas E..2nd Battalion Communications.

Sgt. Walstron, Frederick J., Jr...Co. K (1st Platoon)

Pvt. Walton, Raymond E.* .... Co. L (2nd Platoon)

1st Sgt. Ward, Irving K.* .... Co. I (Hdq.)

Pfc. Warnish, Murray .... Co. L (2nd Platoon)

Pfc. Washer, Millard S., Jr...Co. L (3rd Platoon)

Pfc. Wasser, Clarence M.* .... 2nd Battalion Ammo & Pioneer

Pvt. Way, Clifford R.* ....Co. K (Hdq.)

2d. Lt. Weber, Walter J... 2nd Battalion Med. Det.

T/5 Webster, Donald M... 3rd Battalion Communications.

Pfc. Webster, Ival W.* ....Co. I (1st Platoon)

Pfc. Welsh, Francis E.* .... 2nd Battalion Ammo & Pioneer

Pvt. Wemyss, Edwin J.* .... Co. K (2nd Platoon)

Pvt. Whalen, Charles F.* ....Co. K (1st Platoon)

Sgt. Whalen, Donald J...Co. L (Weapons Platoon)

Pfc. Whiteley, Earl G.* ....Co. L (3rd Platoon)

Pfc. Widmer, James H.* ....3rd Battalion Ammo & Pioneer

Pfc. Wiegert, Bernard W. .... Co. I (1st Platoon)

Pfc. Wiley, Alfred A.* .... Co. K (Weapons Platoon)

S. Sgt. Wiley, Frank S.*.. Co. H (3rd Platoon)

Pvt. Willadsen, Donald F..3rd Battalion Anti-Tank Platoon

Pvt. Williams, Frederick L..Co. I (3rd Platoon)

T/4 Windhold, Harry S.* .... Co. I (Hdq.)

Pfc. Winslow, Arthur J., Jr.* ....Co. L (3rd Platoon)

Pfc. Wittig, Wilbur L.* .... Co. L (1st Platoon)

Pvt. Wolf, Ferdinand A..3rd Battalion Anti-Tank Platoon

Pfc. Woods, John C. .... 2nd Battalion Anti-Tank Platoon

Pvt. Wooten, Lewis J.* .... Co. L (1st Platoon)

Pfc. Worthington, Thomas A..Co. K (Hdq.)

1st Lt. Wurdeman, Robert M................................... 3rd Battalion Communications

Pvt. Wynn, Clifford E.* .... Co. L (3rd Platoon)

Y

Pfc. Yarbrough, Jack R. ....Co. E (Weapons Platoon)

Pfc. Yasbez, Joe* .... Co. I (3rd Platoon)

Sgt. Yeager, Amos* .... Co. K (Weapons Platoon)

Z

Pfc. Ziegler, Bruce E.* ....Co. I (Weapons Platoon)

S. Sgt. Zink, Emmet E. .... Co. I (2nd Platoon)

Sgt. Zoub, Burton I.* .... Co. L (3rd Platoon)

S. Sgt. Zuba, Stanley W.* .... Co. L (3rd Platoon)

Pvt. Zuber, Millard R. .... Co. I (1st Platoon)

264th Infantry

A

Pfc. Abernathie, Charles L. ....Co. D (Hdq.)

Pfc. Ackman, Joseph W. ....Co. C (3rd Platoon)

Pvt. Adams, Frank S. ....Co. C (3rd Platoon)

Pfc. Agnew, Robert A.* .... Co. C (1st Platoon)

Pvt. Akers, Jack .... Co. B (1st Platoon)

Pfc. Aldinger, Edwin E. .... Co. K (2nd Platoon)

2d. Lt. Aldrich, Edwin M. .... Co. E (2nd Platoon)

Pvt. Allen, Harold E. .... Co. E (3rd Platoon)

S. Sgt. Alligood, Archie R. .... Co. I (1st Platoon)

Pfc. Alonzo, Ray* .... Co. B (2nd Platoon)

S. Sgt. Alsbrooks, Alvin D. .... Co. A (Weapons Platoon)

Pvt. Amato, Paul N. ....Co. C (Hdq.)

Pfc. Anderson, Carl A. .... Co. A (2nd Platoon)

Pfc. Anderson, Ray H. ....Co. C (1st Platoon)

T/5 Anderson, Robert .... Co. I (Hdq.)

S. Sgt. Andrade, John J. ....Co. D (2nd Platoon)

Pvt. Andrews, Robert L. .... Co. K (1st Platoon)

Pfc. Angelini, Dominic V.* .... Co. I (3rd Platoon)

2d. Lt. Antman, Charles H.* .... Co. C (2nd Platoon)

Pfc. Antolic, Francis E.* .... Co. B (1st Platoon)

Pfc. App, David T. ....Co. B (Weapons Platoon)

Pvt. Arnold, Charles G.R.* .... Co. B (1st Platoon)

Pfc. Arnold, John G. .... Co. K (1st Platoon)

Pvt. Arruda, Honorato* .... Co. B (Hdq.)

Pvt. Ash, Clarence J. .... Co. I (1st Platoon)

S. Sgt. Asher, Joseph A. ....Co. D (2nd Platoon)

Sgt. Atkerson, George R. ....Co. B (Weapons Platoon)

Pvt. Avery, Raymond J.* .... Co. I (1st Platoon)

Pfc. Avila, John ....Co. K (1st Platoon)

B

Pfc. Babiel, Matthew J.,Jr..Co. C (1st Platoon)

Pfc. Bada, Steve E..Co. E (1st Platoon)

Pvt. Bagley, Milton G..Co. D (Mortar Platoon)

S. Sgt. Bailey, Bernice B.* ....Co. I (1st Platoon)

Pfc. Bailey, Walter J. ....Co. C (1st Platoon)

Sgt. Bakarich, John J. ....Co. K (1st Platoon)

S. Sgt. Baker, George C., Jr.* ....Co. B (Weapons Platoon)

2d. Lt. Balboni, Henry L...Co. E (3rd Platoon)

Pvt. Baldwin, Carl F., Jr..Co. I (3rd Platoon)

S. Sgt. Bales, Dewey L. ....Co. A (2nd Platoon)

Pfc. Ball, Leonard V.* ....Co. A (3rd Platoon)

Pfc. Band, Richard E..Co. E (2nd Platoon)

Pvt. Barnes, Dudley A.*.......................................Co. E (Weapons Platoon)

T/5 Barton, Bernard P...Co. I (Hdq.)

Sgt. Barton, Leroy A..Co. B (Weapons Platoon)

Pfc. Barwick, Lawrence R., Jr......................................Co. A (3rd Platoon)

Pfc. Baumann, Francis W...Co. I (2nd Platoon)

Pfc. Bear, Jay T. ....Co. E (2nd Platoon)

S. Sgt. Becker, Herman* ....Co. I (Hdq.)

Pfc. Bedalow, John F...Co. E (2nd Platoon)

Pvt. Bedrick, Ernest*..Co. A (1st Platoon)

Pfc. Beeman, Charles W...Co. B (2nd Platoon)

S. Sgt. Bell, Garland S. ....Co. I (3rd Platoon)

Pfc. Bell, Ralph E. ....Co. E (Hdq.)

Sgt. Benn, Hurbert E. ....Co. C (1st Platoon)

Pvt. Bennett, Charles T., Jr..Co. E (1st Platoon)

Pvt. Bennett, George W. ....Co. K (1st Platoon)

Pfc. Bennett, John W...Co. K (3rd Platoon)

Pfc. Bensley, Carl..Co. E (1st Platoon)

Pfc. Berarducci, Gino A. ....Co. I (2nd Platoon)

Pfc. Berger, Clifford W...Co. C (Hdq.)

T/5 Bergerson, Harold H. ....Co. C (Hdq.)

Sgt. Bergerson, Robert B. ....Co. A (Weapons Platoon)

T/4 Berhalter, Howard R.* ....1st Battalion Hdq. Co.

S. Sgt. Bertoldo, Juan M.* ....Co. C (Weapons Platoon)

S. Sgt. Berwick, Harold E..Co. E (1st Platoon)

Pvt. Betson, Robert A.* ....Co. D (Mortar Platoon)

Pvt. Bettin, Melvin .... Co. I (1st Platoon)

Pvt. B'Hymer, Joffre M.* ....Co. E (Weapons Platoon)

Pvt. Bieleski, John R.* .... 1st Battalion Med. Sect.

Pfc. Bien, Alfred ....Co. A (3rd Platoon)

1st Sgt. Biggerstaff, Hubert* .... Co. E (Hdq.)

Pfc. Bigler, Emil D. ....Co. C (3rd Platoon)

S. Sgt. Birkenbach, Edward ....Co. D (Mortar Platoon)

Pfc. Bishop, Alfred E. ....Co. I (Weapons Platoon)

Pfc. Black, James L.* .... Co. B (1st Platoon)

Pvt. Blackwelder, Dwight M.* .... 1st Battalion Hdq. Co.

Pfc. Blanton, Sidney L. ....Co. A (3rd Platoon)

Pvt. Blinski, Max* .... Co. B (Hdq.)

Pvt. Boggs, William E. ....Co. D (Mortar Platoon)

Sgt. Bohn, Ivan K. .... Co. I (2nd Platoon)

Pvt. Bol, Frederick J.* ....Co. C (3rd Platoon)

Pfc. Bolhuis, Marvin ....Co. I (Weapons Platoon)

Pvt. Bollig, Raymond R. .... Co. K (2nd Platoon)

Cpl. Bonorand, Theodore R.* .... 1st Battalion Hdq. Co.

T. Sgt. Borchardt, Marlin F. .... Co. A (Weapons Platoon)

Pfc. Bordelon, Ernest J. .... Co. I (Hdq.)

1st Sgt. Boston, June R. .... Co. K (Hdq.)

T/5 Botches, Marshall M. .... 1st Battalion Med. Sect.

Pfc. Bouchard, Alcide ....3rd Battalion Med. Sect.

Pfc. Boucher, Raymond N.* .... Co. I (Hdq.)

Pvt. Boyd, Robert E.* .... 1st Battalion Med. Sect.

T/5 Bracy, James E.* .... Co. I (Hdq.)

Pvt. Bradshaw, Noah, H. ....Co. I (3rd Platoon)

Pvt. Brann, Curtis B. ....Co. C (1st Platoon)

Pfc. Brewer, Claude H., Jr.* ....Co. C (3rd Platoon)

Sgt. Briamonte, Vito M.* ....Co. E (Weapons Platoon)

Pvt. Brierton, Edward J. .... Co. A (1st Platoon)

Pfc. Briggs, Clifford L.* .... Co. A (Hdq.)

Pfc. Brock, Gordon W. .... Co. A (1st Platoon)

S. Sgt. Broderick, Francis M. .... Co. E (3rd Platoon)

Pfc. Brooks, William P. .... Co. A (2nd Platoon)

Pfc. Brookshire, Wallace ....Co. I (Weapons Platoon)

Pvt. Brown, Daniel A. ....Co. D (1st Platoon)

Pvt. Brown, James S. ....Co. D (Mortar Platoon)

Pfc. Bryington, Lloyd W.* .... Co. C (1st Platoon)
Pfc. Buchwald, William E. .... Co. C (Hdq.)
T. Sgt. Buckley, Edward L. .... Co. I (3rd Platoon)
Pfc. Buckley, William J.* .... Co. A (Hdq.)
T/4 Buckman, Leslie G.* .... Co. C (Hdq.)
Pvt. Buczek, Richard* .... Co. B (Weapons Platoon)
Pvt. Budzynski, Anthony .... Co. E (2nd Platoon)
Pfc. Burchfield, Charles G. .... Co. E (Hdq.)
Pvt. Burford, Thomas G. .... Co. D (Mortar Platoon)
Sgt. Burga, Billy* .... Co. E (Weapons Platoon)
T. Sgt. Burke, Cornelius P.* .... Co. E (Weapons Platoon)
Pvt. Burke, David W. .... Co. E (2nd Platoon)
S. Sgt. Burton, Hinton G. .... Co. C (3rd Platoon)
Sgt. Busby, George R., Jr. .... Co. A (Weapons Platoon)
Pfc. Bushnell, Joel V. .... Co. A (1st Platoon)
Pvt. Buzman, Julian R.* .... Co. E (Weapons Platoon)
Pfc. Bye, John A. .... Co. I (2nd Platoon)
Pfc. Byerly, Edwin R. .... Co. E (3rd Platoon)

C

Pfc. Calabrese, Stefano .... Co. E (2nd Platoon)
Pvt. Calender, Guy N. .... Co. E (3rd Platoon)
Pfc. Cardoza, Daniel A. .... Co. C (Weapons Platoon)
T/4 Caprino, Joe* .... Co. B (Hdq.)
Pvt. Carchietta, Frank F. .... Co. E (3rd Platoon)
Pfc. Carichner, Rolland G. .... 1st Battalion Hdq. Co.
Pvt. Carlson, Carl L. .... Co. E (2nd Platoon)
Pvt. Carlson, Ernest. .... Co. I (Hdq.)
Pfc. Carlson, Roy E. .... Co. C (1st Platoon)
Sgt. Carmichael, Robert C. .... Co. A (Weapons Platoon)
T/5 Carpenter, Mason W.* .... Co. B (Hdq.)
Pvt. Carr, James F.* .... Co. E (Weapons Platoon)
Pfc. Carr, Kenneth J. .... Co. A (2nd Platoon)
Sgt. Carrier, Valdor E. .... Co. A (Weapons Platoon)
S. Sgt. Carroll, Hollis C., Jr. .... Co. A (1st Platoon)
Sgt. Carroll, Richard S. .... Co. E (3rd Platoon)
Pfc. Carroll, William F.* .... Co. E (2nd Platoon)
Pvt. Carstens, Karl H.* .... Co. B (3rd Platoon)
Pvt. Carver, Russell L.* .... Co. D (Mortar Platoon)

Pfc. Cassell, William J.* .... Co. B (3rd Platoon)

Pvt. Cassidy, Edward D.* .... 1st Battalion Med. Sect.

Pvt. Casso, Jesse .... Co. B (1st Platoon)

S. Sgt. Catt, Bernard .... Co. K (Hdq.)

Pfc. Celio, James L.* .... Co. B (1st Platoon)

Pfc. Celli, Joseph B., Jr.* .... Co. I (Weapons Platoon)

2d. Lt. Chalmers, James S. .... Co. A (2nd Platoon)

T. Sgt. Chamberlain, Ted .... Co. D (Mortar Platoon)

Pfc. Chamberlain, Warren M. .... Co. E (Weapons Platoon)

Pfc. Chamberlain, William A. .... Co. K (Hdq.)

Pfc. Chance, James W.* .... Co. A (2nd Platoon)

T/4 Chandler, Gentry* .... Co. E (Hdq.)

S. Sgt. Chapman, Donald H. .... Co. A (2nd Platoon)

2d. Lt. Chapman, Joseph* .... 3rd Battalion Med. Sect.

Pvt. Chapman, Sidney S.* .... Co. B (1st Platoon)

Pfc. Chase, Romulus E. .... Co. I (Weapons Platoon)

Pvt. Cheatham, James L. .... Co. D (Mortar Platoon)

Pvt. Christman, Francis V. .... Co. K (2nd Platoon)

Pvt. Chuick, Melvin* .... 1st Battalion Med. Sect.

Pfc. Clark, Warren D. .... Co. E (1st Platoon)

Sgt. Clark, Ray M. .... Co. C (2nd Platoon)

Sgt. Clyde, Calvin G.* .... Co. I (1st Platoon)

Pvt. Coard, Howard S.* .... Co. D (Mortar Platoon)

Pfc. Cochran, Robert F. .... Co. I (2nd Platoon)

Pfc. Coffee, Carol L. .... Co. C (1st Platoon)

S. Sgt. Coffey, George W.* .... Co. C (3rd Platoon)

Pfc. Coffey, Robert P. .... Co. C (Hdq.)

Pfc. Colasurdo, Anthony V. .... Co. I (Weapons Platoon)

Pfc. Coley, Raymond B. .... Co. A (Weapons Platoon)

Pvt. Colorito, Joseph .... Co. I (Hdq.)

Pvt. Colucci, John B. .... Co. C (1st Platoon)

Pvt. Colyer, Hobart M. .... Co. D (2nd Platoon)

Pvt. Comley, James E. .... Co. A (2nd Platoon)

Pvt. Companion, Richard L. .... Co. I (3rd Platoon)

T/5 Conley, William D. .... Co. K (Hdq.)

Pvt. Connor, Robert C. .... Co. A (3rd Platoon)

Sgt. Conner, Windolyn S. .... Co. B (3rd Platoon)

Pfc. Cook, Gerald L. .... Co. B (2nd Platoon)

Pfc. Cook, Robert D. .... Co. D (2nd Platoon)

T/5 Cooper, Edward C.* .... Co. B (Hdq.)

Pvt. Cooper, George W.* .... 1st Battalion Hdq. Co.

Pvt. Copeland, Jesse E.* .... Co. B (Hdq.)

Pvt. Corban, Frank O. .... Co. D (Hdq.)

Pfc. Cord, Robert T. .... Co. B (Hdq.)

Pvt. Corti, Alfred .... Co. E (Weapons Platoon)

Pfc. Couch, Grover M. .... Co. E (3rd Platoon)

S. Sgt. Craig, Ralph W.* .... Co. C (1st Platoon)

Pvt. Cram, Robert W. .... Co. B (2nd Platoon)

S. Sgt. Crean, Gerald C.* .... Co. B (1st Platoon)

Pfc. Crenshaw, Charles S. .... Co. C (1st Platoon)

Pvt. Croke, Raymond D. .... Co. B (3rd Platoon)

Pvt. Cruce, Robert M. .... Co. E (2nd Platoon)

Pfc. Crucitti, John P. .... Co. K (2nd Platoon)

Pfc. Culligan, James A., Jr. .... Co. K (1st Platoon)

Pfc. Cumbay, Steve, Jr. .... Co. E (3rd Platoon)

2d. Lt. Curtis, John M.* .... Co. D (Mortar Platoon)

Pfc. Cutts, Crawford L. .... Co. A (3rd Platoon)

Pvt. Cyr, Edgar .... Co. I (2nd Platoon)

Pvt. Cyr, Udo .... Co. C (Hdq.)

D

Pfc. Dahl, Charles E.* .... Co. A (Weapons Platoon)

Pfc. Danton, James V., Jr. .... Co. A (2nd Platoon)

Pfc. Danvir, Walter C. .... Co. B (2nd Platoon)

Pvt. Daugherty, Clarence J. .... Co. B (3rd Platoon)

T/4 D'Aulizio, Michael .... Co. K (Hdq.)

Pfc. Davidter, Paul W.* .... Co. A (Weapons Platoon)

Sgt. Davis, William C. .... Co. A (3rd Platoon)

Pfc. Davis, William W. .... Co. K (1st Platoon)

Pfc. Dayton, Merritt W. .... Co. C (Weapons Platoon)

Sgt. Deboer, Jake H. .... Co. A (Weapons Platoon)

Pvt. Debray, Gilbert W. .... Co. I (1st Platoon)

Pfc. DeCarlo, Frank C.* .... Co. C (Hdq.)

Pfc. Delateur, William R.* .... Co. I (Weapons Platoon)

Pfc. Deluca, Frank T. .... Co. I (Hdq.)

Pvt. DeMarti, Raymond A. .... Co. B (Weapons Platoon)

T/4 Dennis, George .... Co. A (Hdq.)

S. Sgt. Dennis, Luther A.* .... Co. E (3rd Platoon)

Cpl. Dennis, Stanley W.* .... Co. E (3rd Platoon)

Pvt. Dennis, William B. .... Co. B (2nd Platoon)

2d. Lt. Denny, Hermin B. .... Co. A (Weapons Platoon)

Pvt. Denobraga, Joseph M. .... Co. K (1st Platoon)

S. Sgt. Desnoyers, Robert E. .... Co. B (1st Platoon)

Pfc. Deutsch, Kenneth P. .... Co. D (2nd Platoon)

Pfc. DeViney, Warren E. .... Co. B (Weapons Platoon)

Pfc. Deyoung, Robert J. .... Co. A (Hdq.)

Pvt. DiBischeglia, Frank .... Co. C (Hdq.)

Pfc. Dickamore, Walter A. .... Co. I (2nd Platoon)

Pvt. Didio, Joseph V. .... Co. A (2nd Platoon)

Sgt. Digristina, Philip N. .... Co. E (1st Platoon)

Pvt. Dillon, Alvie P. .... Co. D (1st Platoon)

Pfc. Dillon, Samuel V.* .... Co. C (2nd Platoon)

Pfc. Dilly, Robert L. .... Co. I (Hdq.)

Sgt. Dipietra, Gaetano J.* .... Co. A (1st Platoon)

Pfc. Dodge, Kent R.* .... Co. I (1st Platoon)

Pvt. Doellman, Donald L.* .... Co. E (Weapons Platoon)

Pfc. Doll, Joseph P.* .... Co. A (2nd Platoon)

Sgt. Donaldson, Gene S.* .... Co. A (1st Platoon)

Pvt. Doyle, Robert C. .... Co. A (2nd Platoon)

Pvt. Drew, Ralph F.* .... Co. I (3rd Platoon)

Pvt. Driggs, James G. .... Co. D (2nd Platoon)

Pvt. Driscoll, James P.* .... Co. I (1st Platoon)

Sgt. Driscoll, Paul T. .... Co. C (Weapons Platoon)

S. Sgt. Dubowski, Henry J. .... Co. A (3rd Platoon)

Capt. Dudderar, Sam K., Jr.* .... Co. C (Hdq.)

Pvt. Duke, Howard C. .... Co. D (2nd Platoon)

Pfc. Dunn, Roy E. .... Co. I (3rd Platoon)

Pvt. Dussault, Robert W.* .... Co. B (Hdq.)

Pfc. Dutka, Richard L.* .... Co. A (3rd Platoon)

Pfc. Dysart, Kenneth H.* .... Co. I (1st Platoon)

E

S. Sgt. Eastridge, Charles R. .... Co. K (1st Platoon)

Pvt. Eberhardt, Thomas J. .... Co. B (3rd Platoon)

Pfc. Echelberger, Frank L. .... Co. I (1st Platoon)

Pfc. Einert, Herman L. .... Co. I (3rd Platoon)

Pfc. Elliott, Thomas B. .... Co. A (1st Platoon)

Pfc. Ellis, Bertie H., Jr. .... Co. E (2nd Platoon)

Pfc. Ellis, Jacob R. .... Co. K (2nd Platoon)

Pvt. Embrey, Everett E... 1st Battalion Hdq. Co.

T. Sgt. Embs, George J. .... 1st Battalion Hdq. Co.

Pfc. Emerson, James H.* .... Co. K (2nd Platoon)

Pfc. Epstein, Leonard .... Co. K (Hdq.)

Pvt. Erd, Francis W. .... 1st Battalion Hdq. Co.

S. Sgt. Erker, Aloysius J. .... Co. A (1st Platoon)

Pfc. Erskine, Jack L. .... Co. A (1st Platoon)

Pfc. Erspamer, Gerald R. .... Co. B (Weapons Platoon)

Pfc. Evans, Cleburne .... Co. K (2nd Platoon)

Pfc. Evans, Jack M. .... Co. A (1st Platoon)

Pfc. Evans, James W.. Co. C (1st Platoon)

Pfc. Evans, Joseph W. .... Co. K (Hdq.)

Pfc. Evans, Remus H. .... Co. B (3rd Platoon)

2d. Lt. Everhard, Edgar P., Jr. .... Co. B (3rd Platoon)

F

Pfc. Featherston, Charles H. .... Co. C (Weapons Platoon)

T/5 Fekety, Steven J. .... 1st Battalion Med. Sect.

Pvt. Ferrare, August P... Co. A (Weapons Platoon)

Pvt. Ferrell, Donald W... Co. C (3rd Platoon)

Pfc. Fields, Everette.. Co. A (Weapons Platoon)

Sgt. Finn, Louis H. .... Co. B (2nd Platoon)

Pvt. Fisch, Samuel A.* .... Co. K (2nd Platoon)

Pfc. Flagge, Bruce D'E .... Co. E (1st Platoon)

Pvt. Flatt, Gerald C... Co. D (Mortar Platoon)

Sgt. Fletcher, Donald R... Co. I (2nd Platoon)

Pfc. Fletcher, Robert H. .... Co. I (2nd Platoon)

Pvt. Flores, Juan J. .... Co. E (Weapons Platoon)

Pvt. Flynn, L. V... Co. C (2nd Platoon)

Cpl. Fogel, Morton G.* .... Co. A (Hdq.)

Pvt. Fong, Bennett .... Co. C (3rd Platoon)

S. Sgt. Ford, James E. .... Co. A (2nd Platoon)

Pfc. Foster, Herbert C. .... Co. K (2nd Platoon)

Sgt. Foust, Ed... Co. K (1st Platoon)

Pfc. Fowler, Isaiah.. Co. A (3rd Platoon)

Pfc. Foxworth, Cecil E.* .... Co. E (2nd Platoon)

S. Sgt. Frankunas, Albert F.. Co. E (3rd Platoon)

S. Sgt. Frates, Anthony J. .... Co. E (Hdq.)

Pfc. Frear, Jacob E. .... Co. E (1st Platoon)

Pfc. French, Leon W.* .... Co. A (3rd Platoon)

Pvt. Fried, L. R.*.. Co. A (3rd Platoon)

Capt. Friedberg, Arthur A. .... Co. E (Hdq.)

Pfc. Friedman, Charles H.* .... Co. B (Hdq.)

Pvt. Frontz, Donald .... Co. D (2nd Platoon)

Pfc. Furci, William.. Co. K (2nd Platoon)

Pvt. Fusaro, Anthony*... Co. A (Hdq.)

G

S. Sgt. Gallaher, Daniel A... Co. A (3rd Platoon)

Pfc. Gallagher Edward R.*.. Co. I (2nd Platoon)

Pfc. Games, Robert H. .... Co. D (Mortar Platoon)

Pvt. Ganeos, Theodore J... 1st Battalion Med. Sect.

Pfc. Gant, George M. .... Co. E (2nd Platoon)

Cpl. Garcia, Orfelio .... Co. A (Hdq.)

Pfc. Gardner, William B... Co. C (3rd Platoon)

T/5 Gargano, Joseph, Jr. .... Co. A (Hdq.)

Pfc. Gaskin, Elbert .... Co. B (Weapons Platoon)

Pfc. Gass, Walter R. .... Co. K (3rd Platoon)

Pfc. Gautier, Charles H. .... Co. E (1st Platoon)

Pfc. Gerberich, Wayne G. .... Co. E (3rd Platoon)

Cpl. Gibney, Gerard X. .... Co. E (Hdq.)

S. Sgt. Gilbreath, Abner J. .... Co. E (2nd Platoon)

S. Sgt. Giles, George W.* .... Co. I (2nd Platoon)

Pfc. Gillispie, Marshall C.* .... Co. B (Weapons Platoon)

Pvt. Giombolini, Samuel S... Co. D (2nd Platoon)

Pvt. Gisman, Albert .... Co. I (3rd Platoon)

S. Sgt. Godsey, Holley L., Jr. .... Co. B (Weapons Platoon)

Pfc. Goldstein, Harry .... Co. A (Weapons Platoon)

Pfc. Gong, Chee L.*... Co. A (Hdq.)

Pfc. Gonzalez, Pete G... Co. C (2nd Platoon)

Pfc. Goodenough, Robert D.. Co. D (Mortar Platoon)

Pvt. Goodnow, Roger C... Co. E (2nd Platoon)

Pvt. Goodrich, Alvin F. .... Co. K (1st Platoon)

Pfc. Gorbutt, Raymond E. .... Co. C (1st Platoon)

Pfc. Gorra, Joseph N. .... Co. B (2nd Platoon)

Pfc. Gouveia, Joseph T. .... Co. C (1st Platoon)

Pvt. Grandstaff, Lee R. .... Co. K (3rd Platoon)

Pfc. Grattan, Christopher J. .... Co. E (3rd Platoon)

Pfc. Graziadio, Francesco D. .... Co. E (2nd Platoon)

Pfc. Green, Robert E. .... Co. E (Hdq.)

Cpl. Green, Robert L. .... Co. K (3rd Platoon)

Sgt. Green, William H. ....Co. I (Weapons Platoon)

S. Sgt. Gresham, Warren A. .... Co. E (3rd Platoon)

Pvt. Grimes, Francis R., Jr. .... Co. B (2nd Platoon)

Pfc. Groll, Louis J. .... Co. K (2nd Platoon)

Sgt. Groshong, Richard H. .... 1st Battalion Hdq. Co.

Pvt. Gross, Robert A. .... 1st Battalion Hdq. Co.

Pvt. Groves, Vernon W. .... Co. D (1st Platoon)

Pfc. Guerrieri, Charles A. .... Co. I (2nd Platoon)

T/5 Gulbranson, Noval O.* .... 1st Battalion Med. Sect.

Pfc. Gutierrez, Ramiro* .... Co. I (Hdq.)

H

Sgt. Hagelgans, George* .... Co. A (2nd Platoon)

Pfc. Haggerty, Myron E. .... Co. B (3rd Platoon)

Pfc. Haher, Anthony .... 1st Battalion Med. Sect.

Pfc. Hahn, Matthew ....Co. B (Weapons Platoon)

Pfc. Hale, Sidney .... Co. B (2nd Platoon)

Pfc. Hall, Arlis E. .... Co. C (1st Platoon)

Pfc. Hall, Henry .... 3rd Battalion Med. Sect.

Pvt. Hall, Leonard .... Co. E (1st Platoon)

S. Sgt. Hall, Robert L. .... 1st Battalion Hdq. Co.

T/5 Hamilton, Gerard J. ....Co. E (Weapons Platoon)

Pfc. Hamilton, Omah L. ....Co. D (Mortar Platoon)

Sgt. Hamm, John A. .... Co. C (Hdq.)

Pvt. Handy, William V. .... Co. E (2nd Platoon)

Pfc. Hanson, Everett S.* .... Co. E (3rd Platoon)

Pvt. Harrah, William T., Jr. ....Co. D (Mortar Platoon)

Pfc. Harris, Harvey H. .... Co. E (1st Platoon)

Pfc. Harris, Joe H., Jr. .... Co. C (1st Platoon)

Pfc. Hart, Frederick J. .... Co. K (2nd Platoon)

Pfc. Hartman, Leonard C., Jr.* .... Co. C (1st Platoon)

Pfc. Hartman, Raymond .... Co. C (Weapons Platoon)

Pfc. Harville, Clifford J., Jr. .... Co. E (3rd Platoon)

Pvt. Hasandras, George J.* .... Co. A (2nd Platoon)

T/5 Hasman, Raymond J.. 1st Battalion Hdq. Co.

Pfc. Haugh, Frank C. ....Co. D (2nd Platoon)

Pvt. Haycraft, Carl T. ....Co. D (1st Platoon)

Pfc. Hayden, John H. ....Co. A (1st Platoon)

Pfc. Hays, Samuel Q... Co. C (Hdq.)

Pvt. Heath, Clyde W. .... Co. E (2nd Platoon)

S. Sgt. Heckel, John W. .... Co. I (1st Platoon)

Pfc. Hedding, Albert H., Jr. .... Co. I (1st Platoon)

T. Sgt. Heffner, Harry J...Co. E (3rd Platoon)

Pfc. Heinicke, David J. .... Co. I (1st Platoon)

Pfc. Heishman, Charles M. .... Co. E (1st Platoon)

Capt. Henning, Everett E. .... Co. K (Hdq.)

Pfc. Henrikson, Bertram F..Co. C (2nd Platoon)

Pfc. Henriot, John E.* .... Co. C (Weapons Platoon)

Sgt. Hernandez, Ray F..Co. I (3rd Platoon)

T. Sgt. Hesse, Robert M. ....Co. D (1st Platoon)

Pvt. Hilderbrand, Thomas J. ....Co. B (Weapons Platoon)

Pfc. Hill, Charles W... 1st Battalion Hdq. Co.

Pvt. Hill, James W. ....Co. I (3rd Platoon)

S. Sgt. Hinkle, Russel G. ....Co. D (Mortar Platoon)

S. Sgt. Hinkle, William B.* ....Co. A (3rd Platoon)

S. Sgt. Hinton, James C.*...Co. B (3rd Platoon)

Pfc. Hizel, Victor ....Co. I (3rd Platoon)

Pfc. Hodal, Anthony J.* .... Co. A (2nd Platoon)

Pvt. Hofferbert, Charles J. .... Co. A (1st Platoon)

Pvt. Hoffman, Erwin E. .... 1st Battalion Hdq. Co.

Pvt. Hogins, Lawrence F. ....Co. I (3rd Platoon)

Pfc. Holl, Joseph P., Jr..Co. C (2nd Platoon)

Sgt. Holmstrom, Fred E... Co. C (Weapons Platoon)

Pvt. Holt, Corlis L...Co. D (2nd Platoon)

T. Sgt. Hooper, Gordon R...Co. C (2nd Platoon)

Pfc. Hoover, Harry L.* ....Co. K (2nd Platoon)

Pvt. Horton, Dwight O..Co. B (3rd Platoon)

Pvt. House, Clarence L.* ....Co. K (2nd Platoon)

Pvt. Howard, James W. ....Co. E (3rd Platoon)

Pfc. Howard, Owen S. ....Co. B (2nd Platoon)

Pvt. Howard, Wesley H..Co. B (2nd Platoon)

Pvt. Hubbard, Willard T.*.. Co. A (Weapons Platoon)

Pfc. Hudson, Harrell P...Co. I (2nd Platoon)

S. Sgt. Huff, Floyd E.* .... Co. I (2nd Platoon)
Pvt. Hughes, Lloyd E.* .... Co. I (1st Platoon)
Pfc. Hughes, Virgil L. .... Co. C (2nd Platoon)
Pfc. Hull, John E. .... Co. I (Hdq.)
Pfc. Humphrey, Robert B. .... Co. E (Weapons Platoon)
Pvt. Hunt, Lyle P. .... Co. K (1st Platoon)
S. Sgt. Hunt, Rexford C. .... Co. B (2nd Platoon)
Pvt. Hurd, Charles E. .... Co. C (Hdq.)
Pfc. Hutchens, James .... 3rd Battalion Med. Sect.
Pfc. Hutcheson, Kenneth A. .... Co. A (1st Platoon)

I

Pfc. Iannone, Joseph A. .... Co. I (1st Platoon)
Pfc. Idol, Cleat J. .... Co. I (2nd Platoon)
Pvt. Iliff, Clyde E. .... Co. D (1st Platoon)
Pfc. Inglefield, Charles F. .... Co. A (Weapons Platoon)
Capt. Irvin, William K.* .... Co. A (Hdq.)

J

Pvt. Jacobo, John G. .... Co. B (3rd Platoon)
Pfc. Jacobs, Donald L.* .... Co. C (Weapons Platoon)
Sgt. James, Charles E. .... Co. A (2nd Platoon)
Pfc. Jancher, Burnett G.* .... Co. B (1st Platoon)
Pfc. Janecek, Elmer C. .... Co. E (2nd Platoon)
Pvt. Jennings, Richard D. .... Co. B (3rd Platoon)
Pfc. Joens, Charles I. .... Co. E (Weapons Platoon)
T/5 Johns, Harold E. .... Co. A (Hdq.)
Pfc. Johnson, Chadbourne W. .... Co. D (Mortar Platoon)
Pfc. Johnson, John A.* .... Co. E (2nd Platoon)
Pvt. Johnson, Lloyd O.* .... Co. K (1st Platoon)
Pfc. Johnson, Mark J. .... Co. E (3rd Platoon)
Pvt. Johnson, Vernon A. .... Co. C (Hdq.)
Sgt. Jolly, James L., Jr.* .... Co. C (1st Platoon)
Pfc. Jones, Carl R. .... Co. B (2nd Platoon)
Pvt. Jones, Claude K. .... Co. B (Hdq.)
Pvt. Jozwiak, Arthur V. .... Co. A (1st Platoon)
Pfc. Judd, Philip D.* .... Co. A (3rd Platoon)
Pvt. Julin, Arthur R. .... Co. E (3rd Platoon)

K

Pvt. Kacoure, Peter T. .... Co. C (Hdq.)

S. Sgt. Kail, Robert L. .... Co. E (2nd Platoon)

Pvt. Kalinowski, Edward J. .... Co. A (1st Platoon)

Pfc. Kaminsky, William E., Jr. .... Co. B (1st Platoon)

Pfc. Kaspereen, Arthur L. .... Co. E (2nd Platoon)

Pfc. Katel, William C. .... Co. A (3rd Platoon)

Pfc. Keeley, Jerimiah D.* .... Co. A (Weapons Platoon)

Pfc. Kelly, Nathan C.* .... Co. C (Weapons Platoon)

Pfc. Kenney, Thomas H.* .... Co. A (Weapons Platoon)

Pfc. King, James J.* .... Co. C (2nd Platoon)

Pvt. Kinney, Elmer N. .... Co. B (Hdq.)

Pfc. Kirk, Kermit C. .... Co. E (3rd Platoon)

Pfc. Kish, Julius W.* .... 1st Battalion Med. Sect.

Pfc. Klock, Grant D. .... Co. I (2nd Platoon)

Pfc. Knapp, Justin A. .... Co. I (2nd Platoon)

S. Sgt. Knox, Merle B., Jr. .... Co. K (2nd Platoon)

Sgt. Koetje, Henry .... Co. I (Weapons Platoon)

Pvt. Kolski, Joe* .... 1st Battalion Hdq. Co.

Pvt. Kotkis, Alexander J. .... Co. K (1st Platoon)

Pvt. Kowalski, John .... Co. I (1st Platoon)

Pfc. Kretheotis, Pete .... Co. K (1st Platoon)

Pfc. Kreutzer, Herman R. .... Co. A (Hdq.)

Pvt. Kubena, Robert A. .... Co. I (2nd Platoon)

L

Pvt. Lacy, William C. .... Co. K (Hdq.)

Pfc. Laird, John S. .... Co. A (1st Platoon)

Pfc. Lalla, Michael J. .... Co. I (Hdq.)

Pfc. Landovitz, Jack B.* .... Co. C (Weapons Platoon)

Pfc. Landrum, Ernest W., Sr. .... Co. D (1st Platoon)

Pvt. Lane, William B. .... Co. D (2nd Platoon)

Pvt. Lang, Otis W. .... Co. C (Hdq.)

Pfc. Lanthorn, William R.* .... Co. I (Weapons Platoon)

Pfc. LaPlace, Robert G. .... Co. K (2nd Platoon)

Pvt. LaRosa, Russel F.* .... Co. I (1st Platoon)

S. Sgt. Larson, Donald H. .... Co. K (2nd Platoon)

T/5 LaSala, Anthony W. .... Co. C (Hdq.)

Pfc. Lass, Isidore* .... 1st Battalion Hdq. Co.

Pfc. LaVoie, Bernard H...Co. A (1st Platoon)

Pfc. Lawes, Ernest A. J.*..Co. K (Hdq.)

Pfc. Lawler, Harold B...Co. A (Hdq.)

Pfc. Laxganas, Charles A. ....Co. K (Hdq.)

Pfc. Layaou, Lawrence L..Co. D (2nd Platoon)

Pfc. Leach, Lee G.L..Co. A (1st Platoon)

Pvt. Leady, Vaine C...Co. D (2nd Platoon)

Pfc. Leaf, William E., Jr. ....Co. K (2nd Platoon)

2d. Lt. Leahy, Robert W. ....Co. I (2nd Platoon)

Pfc. Leclair, Antonio E..Co. I (Hdq.)

S. Sgt. Leduc, Philip F. ....Co. I (3rd Platoon)

Pfc. Lee, Mason M.*...Co. A (3rd Platoon)

Pfc. Leeper, Joseph H., Jr..Co. C (2nd Platoon)

Pvt. Leines, Reuben T.* ....Co. I (3rd Platoon)

Pfc. Lemon, Donald R. ....Co. A (3rd Platoon)

Pfc. Lenane, Gerald* .... Co. C (Weapons Platoon)

Pfc. Leonard, James P.* ....Co. C (2nd Platoon)

Pvt. Lerner, George E. ....Co. E (1st Platoon)

Pfc. Leven, Benjamin ....Co. I (2nd Platoon)

Pvt. Levin, Norman* ....1st Battalion Hdq. Co.

Pvt. Levy, Ben ....Co. K (Hdq.)

Pvt. Lewallen, Marion W..Co. K (2nd Platoon)

Pvt. Lewis, Felix J..Co. K (1st Platoon)

Sgt. Leyser, Conrad F.* ....Co. I (Weapons Platoon)

Pfc. Libby, Woodrow M..Co. C (1st Platoon)

Cpl. Lieberman, William ....3rd Battalion Med. Sect.

Pfc. Lind, Orbie E., Jr...Co. I (2nd Platoon)

Pvt. Linder, Hiram W., Jr..1st Battalion Hdq. Co.

Sgt. Linthwaite, John W. ....Co. K (1st Platoon)

Pvt. Lipowitz, Albert*...Co. A (3rd Platoon)

Pfc. Lippard, Harry B.*...Co. E (Hdq.)

Pfc. Liston, Edwin R.. Co. C (Weapons Platoon)

Pvt. Littleton, Kenneth P. ....Co. E (1st Platoon)

Pvt. Logan, Paul, Jr..Co. C (2nd Platoon)

Sgt. Lokis, John J. ....Co. I (3rd Platoon)

T. Sgt. Long, Ralph L..Co. I (1st Platoon)

Pfc. Lopez, Joe..Co. A (1st Platoon)

Pvt. Lott, Curtis L. ....Co. E (Hdq.)

Sgt. Love, Richard D.* ....Co. I (Weapons Platoon)

Pfc. Ludlow, Max L.* .... Co. C (2nd Platoon)

Pfc. Luna, Edgar L. .... Co. E (3rd Platoon)

Sgt. Lunz, John L.* .... Co. A (2nd Platoon)

Cpl. Lynch, Michael F.* .... Co. D (Hdq.)

Pvt. Lyon, Jack C. .... Co. D (Mortar Platoon)

M

Pvt. Maccanico, Joe .... Co. B (2nd Platoon)

Pfc. MacColl, Calcolm D. .... Co. I (2nd Platoon)

Capt. MacGregor, Allan A.* .... Co. I (Hdq.)

Pvt. Maddox, Larry H.* .... 1st Battalion Hdq. Co.

S. Sgt. Magie, Morton E. .... Co. C (1st Platoon)

Pfc. Mahoney, Lester K. .... Co. E (2nd Platoon)

Pfc. Main, Glenn R. .... Co. E (3rd Platoon)

Pfc. Majowicz, Joseph M.* .... Co. A (Weapons Platoon)

Cpl. Malone, Malachy* .... Co. B (Hdq.)

Pfc. Maloney, Jack .... Co. E (2nd Platoon)

Pfc. Marchi, George A.* .... Co. B (3rd Platoon)

T/5 Marcinail, Joseph J. .... Co. A (Hdq.)

Pfc. Marcinko, Stephen M. .... Co. I (3rd Platoon)

Pvt. Marek, Harry J.* .... Co. B (3rd Platoon)

Pfc. Margolies, Saul .... Co. C (3rd Platoon)

1st Sgt. Margulies, Bill R. .... 1st Battalion Hdq. Co.

Pvt. Markley, Raymond B. .... Co. B (Hdq.)

Pfc. Marozzi, Dominick* .... Co. A (3rd Platoon)

Pfc. Marsh, John W. .... Co. C (2nd Platoon)

T/4 Martin, Clarence B. .... Co. A (Hdq.)

Pvt. Martinez, Antonio R.* .... Co. B (1st Platoon)

Pfc. Martinez, Joe .... Co. C (2nd Platoon)

S. Sgt. Martinson, Jack N. .... Co. C (Hdq.)

Pfc. Maas, Ralph A. .... Co. B (2nd Platoon)

S. Sgt. Mathews, Paul C. .... Co. D (Mortar Platoon)

T. Sgt. Mathias, David, Jr. .... Co. A (Hdq.)

T/5 Matusiak, Joseph T.* .... Co. D (Hdq.)

Pfc. Matzkanich, William, Jr. .... Co. C (Hdq.)

Pfc. Mauro, Isadore J. .... 1st Battalion Hdq. Co.

Pvt. Maxwell, Harold .... 1st Battalion Hdq. Co.

Pfc. May, Jack A. .... Co. D (Mortar Platoon)

Pvt. McCarty, Kenneth T. .... Co. E (3rd Platoon)

Pvt. McClain, Elwin H. .... Co. E (1st Platoon)

Pvt. McClain, John P.* .... 1st Battalion Hdq. Co.

Pfc. McClellan, Robert E.* ....Co. E (Weapons Platoon)

Pfc. McClinton, Leroy C. .... Co. E (1st Platoon)

Pfc. McCormic, James A. .... Co. E (2nd Platoon)

Pfc. McCormick, Ralph L. .... Co. K (1st Platoon)

Pfc. McDermott, Richard S.* .... Co. E (Hdq.)

Pvt. McDonald, Alex P. .... Co. E (2nd Platoon)

T. Sgt. McDonald, George S. ....Co. B (3rd Platoon)

Pfc. McDonald, Gerard R. .... Co. E (Hdq.)

Pvt. McDonald, Neal R.* .... Co. I (Hdq.)

Pfc. McDonough, Francis M. .... Co. C (Weapons Platoon)

T/5 McGee, Robert G. ....Co. D (Hdq.)

Pvt. McGee, Robert J. .... 1st Battalion Med. Sect.

Pvt. McGowan, Eugene M. .... Co. I (2nd Platoon)

Pfc. McKenzie, William E. ....Co. A (3rd Platoon)

Pfc. McMillen, Ralph L. .... Co. B (2nd Platoon)

2d. Lt. McMinn, Theodore D. .... 1st Battalion Hdq. Co.

Sgt. McPherson, David B. ....Co. E (3rd Platoon)

Sgt. McPherson, Emerson T.* .... Co. I (1st Platoon)

Pvt. Meade, James W. .... Co. I (3rd Platoon)

Pvt. Meade, Sidney A. ....Co. A (3rd Platoon)

T/4 Meadows, William W. .... Co. A (Hdq.)

T/5 Meeks, Herman .... Co. A (Hdq.)

Sgt. Meigs, Daniel K. .... Co. K (1st Platoon)

Pfc. Mello, Manuel ....Co. A (3rd Platoon)

Pfc. Melson, Jesse J. .... Co. B (2nd Platoon)

Pfc. Memmer, Carlton E. ....Co. C (1st Platoon)

Pvt. Mendenhall, Carrol H. ....Co. E (3rd Platoon)

Pfc. Mercier, Romeo L.* ....Co. C (2nd Platoon)

Pvt. Merkerh, Lawrence* .... 1st Battalion Med. Sect.

Pfc. Meyer, Houston H., Jr.* .... Co. C (Weapons Platoon)

Pfc. Mickley, Albert .... Co. E (1st Platoon)

Pvt. Miller, Gayle W. ....Co. D (Mortar Platoon)

Pvt. Minyard, James W.* .... Co. B (2nd Platoon)

Pfc. Mitchell, Joseph A.* .... Co. E (2nd Platoon)

Pfc. Mitri, Romeo .... Co. I (2nd Platoon)

T/4 Mollet, Ralph A. ....Co. A (Hdq.)

Pfc. Mondot, Peter J., Jr. ....Co. I (3rd Platoon)

Sgt. Monk, Neal J. .... Co. K (2nd Platoon)

Sgt. Monteleone, Anthony .... Co. C (3rd Platoon)

Pfc. Moore, Gordan M. .... Co. E (3rd Platoon)

Pfc. Moore, James E. .... Co. E (2nd Platoon)

Pvt. Mowery, Walter S.* .... Co. I (1st Platoon)

Sgt. Moyer, Walter G. .... Co. B (3rd Platoon)

S. Sgt. Mudge, Franklin W. .... Co. I (2nd Platoon)

Pvt. Murdoch, Robert .... Co. E (1st Platoon)

S. Sgt. Murdter, George .... Co. K (2nd Platoon)

Pvt. Murning, David C. .... Co. E (2nd Platoon)

Pfc. Murphy, Floyd H. .... Co. B (Hdq.)

1st Sgt. Murphy, Leo M. .... Co. A (Hdq.)

Pvt. Murr, Edwin D.* .... Co. C (2nd Platoon)

Pfc. Myers, Gerald C. .... Co. I (3rd Platoon)

Pfc. Myers, Richard C. .... Co. I (2nd Platoon)

N

Sgt. Nabors, James M. .... Co. A (1st Platoon)

Pfc. Nadle, Walter .... Co. A (3rd Platoon)

Pfc. Nanes, George .... Co. I (Hdq.)

Pvt. Nealey, William G., Jr.* .... Co. B (3rd Platoon)

Pvt. Nealin, Donald E.* .... Co. I (3rd Platoon)

Pvt. Neate, Orley W.* .... Co. B (Weapons Platoon)

Pfc. Negrey, Stephen J., Jr. .... Co. K (1st Platoon)

T/5 Nemchick, Clair W.* .... Co. A (Hdq.)

Pfc. Nester, Lloyd B. .... Co. B (2nd Platoon)

1st Lt. Neufeld, Walter J. .... Co. E (Hdq.)

Pvt. New, Domenic V. .... 1st Battalion Med. Sect.

Pfc. Newell, Norris N. .... Co. I (1st Platoon)

Pvt. Newman, James K.* .... Co. K (Hdq.)

Pvt. Newton, Johnnie L. .... Co. E (Hdq.)

Pfc. Nichols, Harland A. .... Co. E (1st Platoon)

Pvt. Nichols, Lorenzo D. .... Co. B (2nd Platoon)

Pvt. Nicholson, Albert E. .... Co. I (Hdq.)

Pvt. Nickells, Elbert H.* .... Co. I (2nd Platoon)

Pfc. Niemisto, Toivo W. .... Co. I (Weapons Platoon)

Pfc. Nilep, Frank G.* .... Co. K (2nd Platoon)

Pfc. Nixon, Charlie, Jr. .... Co. I (1st Platoon)

Pfc. Nolan, Michael M. .... 1st Battalion Hdq. Co.

Capt. Novak, Raymond J.. Co. B (Hdq.)
Pfc. Nowak, Marion F.. Co. E (1st Platoon)
Sgt. Nungester, Carl J.* .... Co. C (Weapons Platoon)
Pvt. Nusbaum, Harold .... Co. C (Hdq.)

O

Pvt. Oakley, John L.. Co. B (2nd Platoon)
Pvt. O'Banion, Robert* ....Co. I (3rd Platoon)
S. Sgt. Oberholtzer, Robert P... Co. B (2nd Platoon)
T/4 O'Connor, Thomas J..Co. D (Hdq.)
Pvt. Odom, William F. ....Co. K (Hdq.)
Pvt. Offerman, William .... Co. I (Hdq.)
T/4 Olguin, Robert C...Co. C (Hdq.)
Pfc. Oliver, Bertram L., Jr.*............................... Co. C (Weapons Platoon)
Pfc. Olson, Carl F. ....Co. K (3rd Platoon)
Pfc. Olson, Franklin P.* .... Co. B (1st Platoon)
Pfc. Olson, Philip N. ....Co. C (2nd Platoon)
Pfc. Olthoff, Fred C. .... Co. A (Weapons Platoon)
Pfc. Orlando, Adolph C..Co. B (Weapons Platoon)
Pfc. Ostien, Harry E. .... Co. A (Weapons Platoon)
Pfc. Overlander, John L. ....Co. C (1st Platoon)
Pfc. Owen, Eibert E... Co. B (1st Platoon)

P

T/5 Pagliaro, Ribello D. .... Co. K (Hdq.)
Pfc. Palmer, Aaron, Jr...Co. C (2nd Platoon)
Pvt. Palmer, Francis D. .... Co. B (2nd Platoon)
Pfc. Palumbo, Nick .... Co. E (2nd Platoon)
S. Sgt. Panto, John N. ....Co. A (3rd Platoon)
Pfc. Papa, Charles ....Co. C (1st Platoon)
Pfc. Parker, Allen T.*..Co. C (1st Platoon)
Pvt. Parker, Franklin*..Co. C (2nd Platoon)
Pfc. Parker, John R. ....Co. C (3rd Platoon)
Pvt. Parker, Taulbee, Jr.* .... 1st Battalion Hdq. Co.
Pvt. Parker, Wayland A. ....Co. B (3rd Platoon)
Pvt. Parrey, Jessy ....Co. K (1st Platoon)
Cpl. Parrish, Robert A... Co. E (3rd Platoon)
Pvt. Parsons, Calvin* ....Co. B (3rd Platoon)
S. Sgt. Partin, Bruce ....Co. I (3rd Platoon)

Pfc. Pasbrig, Raymond C. .... Co. K (1st Platoon)

Pvt. Paskanik, Michael J.* .... Co. I (2nd Platoon)

S. Sgt. Patterson, E.W.* .... Co. E (1st Platoon)

Pvt. Paulick, Robert L.* .... Co. E (2nd Platoon)

Pvt. Pellegrini, Emelio A.* .... Co. B (1st Platoon)

S. Sgt. Penton, Virgil L. .... Co. A (1st Platoon)

Pvt. Perelman, Marshall .... Co. A (2nd Platoon)

Pfc. Peterson, Charles W. .... Co. I (1st Platoon)

Pfc. Peterson, George W. .... Co. C (2nd Platoon)

Pfc. Peterson, Robert A.* .... Co. C (Weapons Platoon)

Pfc. Petras, George J.* .... Co. E (Hdq.)

Pfc. Pfeifer, Edward J. .... Co. E (Hdq.)

S. Sgt. Phelps, Henry P. .... Co. K (1st Platoon)

Pvt. Phillips, Charles L. .... Co. D (1st Platoon)

Pfc. Phillipson, John E.* .... Co. E (Weapons Platoon)

Pfc. Phipps, Luther O., Jr. .... Co. C (Hdq.)

Pfc. Pichler, Harry M. .... Co. E (3rd Platoon)

Sgt. Pickle, Thomas E. .... Co. A (3rd Platoon)

2d. Lt. Pieper, Harry J. .... Co. E (1st Platoon)

Pfc. Pierce, David R. .... Co. E (1st Platoon)

Pvt. Pignatone, Anthony J. .... Co. E (3rd Platoon)

Pfc. Pinchok, John .... Co. A (2nd Platoon)

Pfc. Pinckney, Warren J. .... Co. B (Weapons Platoon)

Sgt. Plaga, Joseph W. .... Co. B (3rd Platoon)

S. Sgt. Plummer, Robert M. .... Co. A (Hdq.)

S. Sgt. Pogue, Ralph D. .... Co. E (2nd Platoon)

Pfc. Polk, Claudies D. .... Co. I (Weapons Platoon)

Pfc. Pometto, Albert R. .... Co. C (2nd Platoon)

Pfc. Pomprowicz, Mitchell J. .... Co. C (3rd Platoon)

Pfc. Poorman, Omer F. .... Co. E (2nd Platoon)

T/5 Pope, Donald R.* .... Co. B (Hdq.)

Pfc. Poplin, Earl A. .... Co. E (Weapons Platoon)

Pfc. Popovich, George E. .... Co. I (1st Platoon)

Pvt. Porter, James A., Jr. .... Co. I (3rd Platoon)

Pfc. Porter, Wesley A. .... Co. E (3rd Platoon)

Pvt. Portier, Clovis J., Jr.* .... Co. I (1st Platoon)

Pvt. Portwood, William D. .... Co. I (Hdq.)

Pfc. Pospisil, Jerry, Jr. .... Co. I (1st Platoon)

Pvt. Potter, Lee H. .... 1st Battalion Hdq. Co.

Pfc. Potter, Wyatt F. ....Co. I (3rd Platoon)
S. Sgt. Powell, William, Jr.* ....Co. C (2nd Platoon)
Pfc. Powers, Donald F.* ....Co. C (3rd Platoon)
Pvt. Prange, Frederick J. ....1st Battalion Hdq. Co.
Pvt. Precise, Lloyd B. ....Co. E (3rd Platoon)
Pvt. Prescott, George D. ....Co. K (2nd Platoon)
Pvt. Price, William A. ....Co. K (Hdq.)
Pfc. Prichard, Marcell ....Co. K (3rd Platoon)
Sgt. Pridemore, Floyd ....Co. K (2nd Platoon)
Pfc. Puckett, Floyd O.* ....Co. B (1st Platoon)

Q
Sgt. Quillen, Mack ....Co. C (2nd Platoon)

R
Pfc. Ranker, Leroy A.* ....Co. I (Hdq.)
Pfc. Ray, John K. ....Co. I (3rd Platoon)
Pfc. Reagan, Calvin T. ....Co. K (1st Platoon)
Pfc. Reagan, Claude J. ....Co. I (3rd Platoon)
Pvt. Reed, Parker E. ....Co. A (3rd Platoon)
Pvt. Reedy, Clifford A.* ....Co. A (3rd Platoon)
Pfc. Reeks, Henry P. ....Co. I (1st Platoon)
T. Sgt. Renner, Glenn L. ....Co. B (Weapons Platoon)
2d. Lt. Replogie, John L.* ....Co. B (Hdq.)
Pfc. Reyer, John* ....1st Battalion Med. Sect.
Pfc. Reynolds, Charles E. ....Co. D (Hdq.)
Pfc. Rhind, William J. ....Co. K (1st Platoon)
Pfc. Ribarich, Frank J. ....Co. A (1st Platoon)
Pfc. Ribblet, Clarence W. ....Co. K (2nd Platoon)
Pvt. Richman, Clifford R. ....Co. A (Hdq.)
Pvt. Ricucci, Dominick ....Co. A (Hdq.)
Pfc. Riggins, Willard F.* ....Co. B (2nd Platoon)
S. Sgt. Riley, Edward J. ....Co. D (1st Platoon)
Sgt. Robinson, Frank I., Jr. ....Co. B (1st Platoon)
Pvt. Robinson, Jesse C. ....Co. B (1st Platoon)
Sgt. Roell, Elmer H. ....Co. E (2nd Platoon)
Pvt. Rogel, John M., Jr. ....Co. E (1st Platoon)
Pvt. Rojas, Frank F.* ....Co. K (Hdq.)
Sgt. Ross, Fred A. ....Co. K (2nd Platoon)

Capt. Roth, Chrles E. .... 1st Battalion Hdq. Co.

Pfc. Rotham, Arwin W. .... Co. C (2nd Platoon)

Pfc. Rothwell, Joseph W. .... Co. C (Hdq.)

Pvt. Roux, Adolph C., Jr.* .... Co. C (1st Platoon)

Pvt. Rowe, Roscoe .... Co. C (Hdq.)

Pfc. Rowell, Warren E. .... Co. K (2nd Platoon)

Sgt. Roybal, Joe C. .... Co. I (3rd Platoon)

Pvt. Rudolph, Charles W. .... Co. I (2nd Platoon)

Pfc. Ruscito, John .... Co. A (2nd Platoon)

Pvt. Russo, Ralph F. .... Co. A (Weapons Platoon)

Pfc. Ruzowski, Thaddeus* .... Co. E (Weapons Platoon)

Sgt. Ryan, John J. .... Co. I (Hdq.)

S

Pfc. Salter, Charles E., Jr. .... Co. K (2nd Platoon)

Pvt. Sample, Frank A. N. .... Co. D (Mortar Platoon)

Pvt. Sanchez, Thomas G.* .... Co. E (Weapons Platoon)

Pfc. Sanela, William C. .... Co. B (3rd Platoon)

Pvt. Sanner, Harper L. .... Co. I (1st Platoon)

S. Sgt. Santos, August C.* .... 1st Battalion Med. Sect.

Pvt. Sauermann, Herbert L. .... Co. K (1st Platoon)

Pvt. Sawyer, Stanley .... Co. E (1st Platoon)

Pvt. Schackner, Daniel .... Co. B (2nd Platoon)

Pfc. Schaffer, Robert W.* .... 1st Battalion Med. Sect.

Pvt. Scheibeler, Joseph J. .... Co. B (1st Platoon)

Pfc. Schlanger, Charles J. .... Co. C (2nd Platoon)

Pvt. Schmelke, Richard H. .... 1st Battalion Med. Sect.

S. Sgt. Schmidt, Arthur J. .... Co. C (3rd Platoon)

Pfc. Schottelkotte, Thomas J. .... Co. E (3rd Platoon)

T/5 Schultz, Bernard A.* .... Co. E (Hdq.)

Pfc. Schuppert, Arnold N. .... Co. I (2nd Platoon)

Pfc. Schwartz, Leon H. .... Co. E (1st Platoon)

Pvt. Schwarze, Richard .... Co. K (1st Platoon)

Pvt. Scott, Bernard W. .... 1st Battalion Hdq. Co.

Pfc. Scott, Clarence F. .... Co. K (3rd Platoon)

Pfc. Scott, Donald L. .... Co. E (1st Platoon)

Pvt. Scott, Wayne P. .... Co. K (1st Platoon)

T/5 Sechnik, John F. .... Co. A (Hdq.)

Pvt. Secondi, Frank .... Co. I (3rd Platoon)

Pvt. Seidel, Louis...3rd Battalion Med. Sect.

Pfc. Shannon, John E..Co. A (2nd Platoon)

Pfc. Sharp, Clyde..Co. C (3rd Platoon)

Pfc. Shaub, Donald P. ....Co. E (3rd Platoon)

Pfc. Shaver, Russell A. ....Co. E (2nd Platoon)

Pfc. Shaw, Eugene T.. Co. I (Hdq.)

2d. Lt. Shaw, Paul*...Co. A (3rd Platoon)

Pvt. Shedron, Dickie D. ....Co. B (1st Platoon)

Pfc. Shepperd, J. C..Co. B (Weapons Platoon)

Pvt. Short, Earl B., Jr. ....Co. E (1st Platoon)

Pfc. Shortridge, Marvin W. ....Co. K (2nd Platoon)

Pfc. Shuey, Jack L.* ....Co. A (3rd Platoon)

Pfc. Sides, Lawrence ....Co. B (1st Platoon)

Pfc. Siegrist, William P. ....Co. I (Weapons Platoon)

Sgt. Sieplinga, Frank R.* ....Co. B (1st Platoon)

Pfc. Silka, William E.. Co. A (Hdq.)

Pvt. Silver, Harry N...Co. D (1st Platoon)

Pvt. Simon, John F...Co. D (Hdq.)

Sgt. Simpkins, John, Jr. ....Co. E (Weapons Platoon)

Pfc. Sizemore, Henry ....Co. I (3rd Platoon)

Pvt. Skillthorpe, Joseph R. ....Co. D (Hdq.)

Pfc. Skrebunas, Stanley A. ....Co. A (2nd Platoon)

Pfc. Slattery, Clarence J...Co. C (3rd Platoon)

Sgt. Sloane, Michael A. ....Co. B (Weapons Platoon)

Pfc. Slover, Rodney J. ....Co. B (3rd Platoon)

Pvt. Smazenka, Robert J...Co. E (Hdq.)

Pvt. Smith, Dewey E. ....Co. A (1st Platoon)

Pvt. Smith, Elbert D.* ....Co. D (1st Platoon)

Pfc. Smith, Farris D.* .... Co. I (Hdq.)

Pfc. Smith, Floyd E..Co. C (3rd Platoon)

Pfc. Smith, Harlow S., Jr...Co. E (1st Platoon)

Pfc. Smith, Hoyt E.* ....Co. C (3rd Platoon)

S. Sgt. Smith, James E. ....Co. C (1st Platoon)

Pfc. Smith, Kenneth E. ....Co. A (Weapons Platoon)

Pvt. Smith, Richard M.* ....Co. A (3rd Platoon)

Pfc. Smith, Robert C.* .... Co. I (1st Platoon)

Pfc. Smith, Scott V..Co. A (Hdq.)

Pvt. Smith, T. J. ....Co. D (Mortar Platoon)

Pfc. Smith, Walter M.. Co. I (Hdq.)

Pfc. Snyder, Hubert L.* .... Co. B (1st Platoon)

Pvt. Snyder, John C. .... Co. D (2nd Platoon)

Pfc. Southworth, Joseph L. .... Co. K (2nd Platoon)

Pvt. Sowards, Paul C.* .... 1st Battalion Hdq. Co.

Cpl. Speer, Frank D., Jr. .... Co. I (Hdq.)

Pvt. Spencer, Alvah L. .... Co. K (1st Platoon)

Pvt. Spevock, Bernard .... Co. E (2nd Platoon)

Pfc. Spontyl, Ephram N. .... Co. E (Hdq.)

Pvt. Spradlin, J. B. .... Co. E (2nd Platoon)

Pfc. Springer, Robert A. .... Co. E (1st Platoon)

Pvt. Staab, Rudolph C. .... Co. K (1st Platoon)

Pfc. Stafford, Richard H. .... Co. C (3rd Platoon)

Pvt. Stagg, Emory L., Jr. .... Co. A (2nd Platoon)

Pfc. Stam, Gerrit .... Co. D (1st Platoon)

Pfc. Stamps, Dewey .... Co. B (2nd Platoon)

Pfc. Stanfield, Robert W. .... Co. I (Hdq.)

Pfc. Stanton, Gail H. .... Co. E (3rd Platoon)

Pfc. Staples, James H.* .... Co. C (3rd Platoon)

Pfc. Steadman, Ruben E. .... Co. C (3rd Platoon)

Pfc. Stefancin, Andrew T. .... Co. C (2nd Platoon)

T/4 Steier, Melvin J. .... Co. K (Hdq.)

1st Lt. Stein, Hyman A.* .... 1st Battalion Med. Sect.

Pfc. Steinberg, Milton A.* .... Co. E (Weapons Platoon)

Pfc. Steinberg, Norman .... Co. B (1st Platoon)

2d. Lt. Stevens, Houghton T.* .... Co. C (3rd Platoon)

Pfc. Stewart, Robert H. .... Co. E (3rd Platoon)

T. Sgt. Stinson, Durrell .... Co. D (2nd Platoon)

T/4 Stoddard, Mervin* .... Co. B (Hdq.)

Pfc. Stoklosa, Edward A. .... Co. D (Hdq.)

Pvt. Stone, John L.* .... Co. E (Weapons Platoon)

Pfc. Storey, Robert L. .... Co. I (1st Platoon)

Pfc. Stout, Robert R. .... Co. E (3rd Platoon)

Sgt. Strailey, Robert L. .... Co. E (1st Platoon)

T. Sgt. Strand, Arthur K. .... Co. I (2nd Platoon)

Pfc. Stratigos, Theodore .... Co. E (Hdq.)

Pfc. Strickland, Ray D.* .... Co. A (3rd Platoon)

Pfc. Stringer, James R. .... Co. I (Weapons Platoon)

T. Sgt. Strossi, Louis E.* .... Co. A (2nd Platoon)

S. Sgt. Subera, Frank L. .... Co. B (2nd Platoon)

2d. Lt. Suhr, George F. .... Co. I (1st Platoon)

Pfc. Sullivan, Truman B. .... Co. C (Hdq.)

Pfc. Swade, Louie J.* .... Co. I (Weapons Platoon)

Pfc. Swanson, Jack L.* .... Co. C (3rd Platoon)

T/5 Swart, Henry C.* .... 1st Battalion Hdq. Co.

Pfc. Swauger, Albert, Jr. .... Co. E (1st Platoon)

Pfc. Swenson, John W.* .... Co. C (3rd Platoon)

1st Sgt. Swenson, Raymond E. .... Co. I (Hdq.)

Pvt. Swisher, Jacob H. .... Co. K (1st Platoon)

Sgt. Swore, Melvin R.* .... Co. I (Weapons Platoon)

S. Sgt. Synenki, Michael .... Co. E (1st Platoon)

Pvt. Szoke, Frank J. .... Co. B (2nd Platoon)

T

Pvt. Tackitt, Lawrence D. .... Co. K (Hdq.)

Pfc. Talty, Robert D.* .... 1st Battalion Hdq. Co.

S. Sgt. Tatro, Fred A., Jr. .... Co. B (2nd Platoon)

Sgt. Taylor, David J., Jr. .... Co. C (3rd Platoon)

Pvt. Taylor, Jim D. .... Co. B (2nd Platoon)

Cpl. Taylor, Luther L. .... Co. K (Hdq.)

Pfc. Taylor, Thomas R.* .... Co. I (3rd Platoon)

Pvt. Taylor, Vernie C. .... Co. B (2nd Platoon)

Pfc. Tenenbaum, Jerome H.* .... Co. A (Weapons Platoon)

Pvt. Thibault, Edward* .... Co. B (1st Platoon)

Pfc. Thomas, Glenn K.* .... Co. A (3rd Platoon)

Pfc. Thomas, Guy .... Co. B (2nd Platoon)

Pvt. Thompson, Guy* .... Co. K (Hdq.)

Pfc. Thompson, Harry C. .... Co. E (2nd Platoon)

Pvt. Tibbetts, Edward M. .... Co. A (3rd Platoon)

Pfc. Tillotson, James E. .... Co. K (2nd Platoon)

Pfc. Tincher, Don .... Co. A (3rd Platoon)

Pfc. Tinker, James T.* .... Co. A (3rd Platoon)

T. Sgt. Todd, Asley K. .... Co. E (2nd Platoon)

Pvt. Torrez, Tony D. .... Co. I (2nd Platoon)

Pfc. Townsend, Jackson V. .... Co. B (3rd Platoon)

2d. Lt. Traihill, Benjamin E.* .... Co. K (3rd Platoon)

Pfc. Tranter, Clifford A.* .... Co. B (Hdq.)

Pfc. Trenda, James W. .... Co. A (1st Platoon)

Pvt. Trout, Daniel J.* .... Co. B (3rd Platoon)

Pvt. Troxel, Charles P. ....Co. D (1st Platoon)

Pfc. Troyan, Clarence F. ....Co. K (Hdq.)

Pfc. Tundis, Ralph ....3rd Battalion Med. Sect.

Pfc. Turner, John M. ....Co. C (3rd Platoon)

Pvt. Turner, Joseph A.* ....Co. A (Hdq.)

Pvt. Turner, Herbert J. ....Co. E (1st Platoon)

Pvt. Turner, Martin R. ....Co. E (1st Platoon)

Pvt. Tyborowski, Stanley L. ....Co. A (1st Platoon)

U

Pvt. Uran, Irwin ....Co. K (1st Platoon)

Pvt. Urrutia, John F., Jr. ....Co. A (1st Platoon)

Pfc. Utt, Morvale F.* ....Co. D (Mortar Platoon)

V

Pvt. Via, Albert J. ....Co. K (Hdq.)

Pfc. Vail, Kenneth W. ....Co. C (3rd Platoon)

Capt. VanPelt, Franklin H. ....1st Battalion Hdq. Co.

Pfc. Vanvelsor, Frederick H. ....Co. E (3rd Platoon)

Pvt. Vassey, Edwin Y. ....Co. E (Hdq.)

Pvt. Vaughn, James L. ....Co. A (2nd Platoon)

Pfc. Vaughn, Thomas M. ....Co. A (2nd Platoon)

Pvt. Victory, Walter G. ....1st Battalion Hdq. Co.

Sgt. Vieira, Raymond J. ....Co. B (1st Platoon)

Pvt. Vieni, Nicholas ....1st Battalion Hdq. Co.

T. Sgt. Viets, Sterling H.* ....Co. A (1st Platoon)

Pfc. Vitali, John J.* ....Co. B (Weapons Platoon)

Sgt. Volk, Leon E. ....Co. E (2nd Platoon)

W

S. Sgt. Wagner, Robert E. ....Co. K (Hdq.)

T/5 Wahr, George J., Jr. ....Co. K (Hdq.)

Pfc. Walker, James W. ....Co. D (Hdq.)

Pfc. Walker, Joseph C. ....Co. I (Weapons Platoon)

Pfc. Walker, Robert E. ....Co. A (3rd Platoon)

2d. Lt. Wallace, John E. ....Co. K (Weapons Platoon)

Pfc. Waller, John S. ....Co. B (Weapons Platoon)

Pfc. Waller, William R. ....Co. I (Hdq.)

T/5 Wallers, Marvin L.* ....1st Battalion Med. Sect.

1st Lt. Walsh, Thomas R. .... Co. I (Hdq.)

S. Sgt. Walters, Willis G. ....Co. E (Weapons Platoon)

Pfc. Wargacki, Frank T.* .... Co. C (Weapons Platoon)

2d. Lt. Washko, George P.* .... Co. K (2nd Platoon)

Pfc. Wasserman, Paul* .... 1st Battalion Hdq. Co.

Pvt. Watkins, Loyd E. .... 1st Battalion Med. Sect.

1st Sgt. Watson, George H. ....Co. D (Hdq.)

Pvt. Watson, Homer A. .... Co. K (Hdq.)

Pfc. Weatherbee, Dudley .... Co. A (1st Platoon)

Pvt. Webb, Orbie J. ....Co. C (3rd Platoon)

Pvt. Webber, Walter C.* .... Co. A (Weapons Platoon)

Pvt. Weekley, Maurice A.* ....Co. B (Hdq.)

Pfc. Wehner, Jerome G. .... Co. A (Hdq.)

Pvt. Weiman, Elwood N. .... Co. E (2nd Platoon)

Pfc. Welch, Claude A. .... Co. I (3rd Platoon)

S. Sgt. Wells, James N. .... Co. K (2nd Platoon)

Pfc. Welp, Bernard* ....Co. D (Hdq.)

Pfc. Westarp, Thomas W.* ....Co. B (Weapons Platoon)

1st Lt. Westendorf, Joseph W.* .... Co. A (Hdq.)

Pfc. Westfall, Bobbie V. .... Co. C (2nd Platoon)

Pfc. Wheeler, Delbert T.* ....Co. C (1st Platoon)

T/5 Wheeler, James ....3rd Battalion Med. Sect.

Pvt. Whitaker, Lewis A. .... Co. K (2nd Platoon)

T/5 Whitcomb, Robert W. .... Co. E (Hdq.)

Pfc. White, Andrew B. .... 1st Battalion Hdq. Co.

Pfc. White, Frederick H., Jr. .... Co. E (1st Platoon)

Pfc. Whitman, Delmar F. .... Co. I (2nd Platoon)

Sgt. Whitwell, Jesse L.* .... 1st Battalion Hdq. Co.

Pfc. Wilcox, Billings R.* ....Co. A (3rd Platoon)

Pfc. Wildemuth, Kenneth L.* ....Co. C (1st Platoon)

Pvt. Williams, Walter R. ....Co. K (1st Platoon)

Pvt. Wilson, Darrell .... Co. I (1st Platoon)

Pvt. Wilson, Ray H. ....Co. K (2nd Platoon)

Pvt. Windy, Frank G. .... Co. A (Hdq.)

Pfc. Winkler, Russell E. .... Co. I (Hdq.)

Sgt. Winslow, Charlie E. .... Co. E (2nd Platoon)

Pvt. Winter, William M. .... 1st Battalion Hdq. Co.

T/4 Winters, Andrew A. .... Co. I (Hdq.)

Pvt. Wiscarver, James L. ....Co. C (3rd Platoon)

Pfc. Wise, Robert W.. 1st Battalion Med. Sect.
Pvt. Wisniewski, Joseph F.* .... 1st Battalion Med. Sect.
Sgt. Wolfe, Cornelius N. .... 1st Battalion Hdq. Co.
Pvt. Wolfson, Gerald G.. Co. C (Weapons Platoon)
Pfc. Wood, Charles S.. Co. A (2nd Platoon)
Pfc. Wood, Daniel W.* ....Co. E (Weapons Platoon)
2d. Lt. Wood, Morton, Jr.. Co. I (3rd Platoon)
1st Sgt. Woods, Cilman P. .... Co. B (Hdq.)
Pfc. Woods, Elmer L..Co. C (3rd Platoon)
Pvt. Worley, Lewis H..Co. C (3rd Platoon)
Pfc. Worth, Forrest W.. Co. B (2nd Platoon)
Pvt. Wright, Anton A.* ....Co. I (3rd Platoon)
Pfc. Wuorinen, Jorma P. ....Co. C (2nd Platoon)
Pfc. Wynkoop, William U. .... Co. A (1st Platoon)

Y

Pvt. Yarbrough, James E.. Co. E (1st Platoon)
S. Sgt. Yarmosh, Alexander ....Co. D (1st Platoon)
T. Sgt. Yates, Tom F.*...Co. I (Weapons Platoon)
S. Sgt. Yoachim, Laverle W. ....Co. K (3rd Platoon)
Pvt. Young, Merelin A. ....Co. A (1st Platoon)
Pfc. Young, Oscar B.. Co. A (2nd Platoon)

Z

Sgt. Zanetti, Joseph S.* .... Co. B (Hdq.)
Pfc. Zangrillo, Raymond J.*... 1st Battalion Med. Sect.
Pfc. Zarnosky, Leo F. ....Co. B (3rd Platoon)
Pfc. Zaugg, Theldon B...Co. E (1st Platoon)
Pfc. Zdonick, Chester E. ....Co. E (3rd Platoon)
S. Sgt. Zdrojeski, Casimir J. ....Co. C (2nd Platoon)
S. Sgt. Zimmerman, George J..Co. E (1st Platoon)
Pvt. Zoldak, John J. .... Co. C (Hdq.)

CPSIA information can be obtained
at www.ICGtesting.com
Printed in the USA
LVHW031249091218
599826LV00003B/407/P